THE GREEK HISTORIANS OF THE WEST

Philological Monographs

of the

American Philological Association

NUMBER XXXV
edited by

Timothy D. Barnes

Accepted for Publication by the Editorial Board for Monographs
of the American Philological Association

THE GREEK HISTORIANS
OF THE WEST
Timaeus and His Predecessors

by
LIONEL PEARSON

Published for

The American Philological Association

by

Scholars Press

Atlanta, Georgia

THE GREEK HISTORIANS OF THE WEST
Timaeus and His Predecessors

by
Lionel Pearson

© 1987

The American Philological Association

Library of Congress Cataloging in Publication Data

Pearson, Lionel Ignacius Cusack.
  The Greek historians of the West.

  (Philological monographs ; no. 35)
  Bibliography: p.
  Includes indexes.
  1. Magna Graecia (Italy) — Historiography.
I. Title. II. Series.
DG55.M3P32 1987   945'.755   87-4877

ISBN 1-55540-078-7 (alk. paper)
ISBN 1-55540-151-1 (pbk. : alk. paper)

DG
55
·M3
P32
1987

Printed in the United States of America
on acid-free paper

Contents

PREFACE

"Writing books about books that don't exist" sounds like a suitable occupation for Wonderland, and it deserves an explanation that would satisfy Alice. "How can you understand the books that exist," they might have told her, "unless you read the non–existent books first?" "Yes, I know," Alice might reply, "but there are so many lost Greek historians." There are indeed. In Felix Jacoby's collection, *Die Fragmente der griechischen Historiker,* Timaeus is no. 566, and there will be over a thousand when the collection is complete.

It is fifty years since I first started trying to read these lost books, and I was fortunate in receiving good advice at the start. Professor Hendrickson at Yale urged me to consult William Arthur Heidel, the distinguished authority on early Greek science, who was teaching at Wesleyan University. I went to Middletown to see him, and told him, in my youthful folly, that I proposed to make a study of Hecataeus the Milesian, relying on the evidence of the fragments in Jacoby, and he replied without hesitation, "No, that is the wrong way. What you should do is read Herodotus and ask yourself, What does this presuppose?"

I have never forgotten this advice, and it is particularly appropriate for anyone who is trying to study the work of Timaeus and his predecessors. Although nothing of Timaeus' history of the Greeks in the West has survived in any codex or even in any papyrus fragment so far discovered, his influence can be seen clearly in many later writers, Latin as well as Greek. Many of them mention him by name, referring to some particular passage in his *History* and citing the number of the book in which it occurs, or discussing some quality or characteristic of his writing, and a quick reading of the *Testimonia* and *Fragmenta* in Jacoby's collection shows that Timaeus was well known and widely read for many centuries after his death, which was probably about 250 B.C. But, as Jacoby knew better than anyone, there is much more that can be learnt about Timaeus than is revealed in these "fragments." There are quite a few authors whom one must read carefully, asking the question "What does this presuppose? How well does this author know Timaeus and how much is he borrowing from him?"

Diodorus Siculus, writing in the age of Augustus, is the first author who must be interrogated in this way. In his *Library of History* he attempted to give an account of Mediterranean history for the general reader, relying on the standard authorities. And since Timaeus was the standard authority for the history of the Greeks in Italy and Sicily, he naturally drew upon him extensively when he interrupted his narrative of events in Aegean Greece to tell of western events. Timaeus was useful to him not only in Books XI–XIV for the fifth and fourth centuries, but also for his account of early times in Books IV–V, and the fragments of his lost books VI–X tell us something of what Timaeus had to say about the sixth century.

Unfortunately, Diodorus never tells us "My main source here is Timaeus." It is always necessary to ask if he might not be using another source. He refers to Timaeus on a number of occasions, as he also does to Ephorus, whose history was his principal source for the mainstream of Greek history, and there are also occasional references to other writers who wrote about the Greek West—Philistus, Theopompus, and Duris of Samos. All of these writers dealt with some of the same areas and the same events as Timaeus, and it is hardly ever possible to say that their account of an event was unknown to Diodorus. But Diodorus is not a critical scholar, and shows little taste for comparing one source with another or explaining why he prefers one to another. In fact, it will be argued that when he does mention a difference between Timaeus and an earlier writer, it is most likely that he has found the difference recorded in the text of Timaeus.

Scholars in modern times have become accustomed to working at a table covered with books and papers, as they consult different sources, looking up various passages and comparing one with another. But if, instead of working with printed books, with indices and chapter headings, they had to use papyrus rolls, it would be almost impossible to work in this manner. A wealthy man like Pliny the Elder might have six or seven well trained slaves sitting on the floor, each with a papyrus roll in his hand, ready to answer the master's questions: "What does Timaeus say about this? Is there anything different in Duris' account?" And so on. But if Pliny had written a *Library of History* instead of his *Naturalis Historia,* using some such method as this, it would have been a very different book from what Diodorus has written. It would have reflected his way of working. Diodorus' narrative does not read like the work of a man who has compared and is trying to combine more than one source.

There are many passages in Diodorus where it is clear that Timaeus is his source, where no serious claim for another source can be made. Initial probability is established when his narrative presents features that are known from other evidence to be characteristic of Timaeus, and it is strengthened when a similar account is offered by another writer who is known to have used Timaeus. Likewise, if a passage in Diodorus illustrates or confirms something that is said about Timaeus by a critic like Polybius or Plutarch, one can suspect that Diodorus is following Timaeus. Anyone who reads widely in Diodorus learns to recognize the Timaean passages and realizes how constantly he must have paraphrased or summarized Timaeus' text. So also in reading Strabo's books on Italy and Sicily (V and VI) one learns to recognize the mythological and topographical detail that must come from Timaeus. The scholia to Lycophron and Apollonius of Rhodes leave us in no doubt of the debt that these poets owe to him.

Polybius, like Plutarch, is severely critical of Timaeus. He has no respect for his judgment or his accuracy. Indeed, most of the ancient writers who speak of Timaeus seem not to be interested in telling what he accomplished in the way of historical investigation. They tell us clearly enough, on the other hand, why he was a popular writer, that he had a taste and a talent for dramatic narrative, with portents and miracles playing their part; that he appealed to the conventional piety of readers and that he revealed what critics thought was an exaggerated Siceliot patriotism. Some of Polybius' criticisms may be unfair and exaggerated. But it is difficult to be sure about this until we have some of Timaeus' actual text on papyrus.

A brief papyrus fragment has been confidently identified by some critics as part of the work of Philistus. Attempts have also been made to identify passages in Diodorus that are based on his history rather than on Timaeus—not successfully in my opinion. The earlier writers, Hippys and Antiochus, are much more shadowy figures. We may think it likely that Thucydides borrowed from Antiochus when he wrote his short account of early Sicilian history in Book VI, just as Timaeus must have borrowed from him and from Philistus. But when we have no text of Timaeus, we cannot learn much more about any of these earlier historians than what the fragments tell us.

There is, therefore, good reason for devoting the major part of this book to Timaeus. My object is to recover as much as possible of his history, to discover what he included in it (and, so far as possible, how he arranged his material), how he described events and situations and how he characterized individuals (though, without any but brief verbatim quotations from his actual text, we must be cautious in passing judgment on his style and language), what opinions he expressed and how he differed from or agreed with contemporaries and predecessors (though this is a hard question to answer when we cannot read the work of other historians with whom he seems to have quarrelled). Some readers, however, will complain that I have not done enough, that I should offer a much more closely argued critical estimate of Timaeus' historical method, his place in the development of Greek historiography, his contribution to chronological research, and so on. Some will also say that I should have undertaken a more thorough investigation of Diodorus' method in using his sources, that I have been too hasty in deciding when he is following Timaeus and how closely he follows him.

I could answer such complaints simply by saying that, if I attempted to do all this, my book would be so long that no one would have the patience to read it to the end, even if a publisher was foolish enough to print it. I have offered brief answers in my final chapter to some of the questions that critics will raise. But the sources of Diodorus have been discussed by scholars for over a hundred years. I do not propose to repeat or describe all the work that they have done, though I have tried to take account of it and to make adequate acknowledgment of it in my footnotes and bibliography. Scholars differ in their opinions over many details, and it has to be admitted that conclusive answers are not possible to every question.

It must, in fact, be admitted that a certain amount of circular argument is inevitable in all *Quellenkritik* of this kind. One can decide that the style and manner of Timaeus is sometimes recognizable when Diodorus is writing about the Greeks in the West and that there is no sign of it in other passages. Or one may decide in advance that Diodorus, when he writes about the West, is most likely to be using Timaeus and that his chapters offer evidence for the style and manner of Timaeus. No progress can be made unless one or the other of these assumptions is made. And if the conclusions that result from relying on these assumptions are consistent in themselves and consistent with what other ancient writers have to say about Timaeus, these conclusions need not be rejected because there is a logical flaw in the argument that led to them. In a few individual instances the conclusions may be wrong. That is a risk that has to be undertaken.

I have attempted a partial answer to the problem of Diodorus' sources in two recent articles. There are other articles that ought to be written. I am not at all satisfied with existing attempts to reconstruct the chronological systems of Antiochus and Timaeus, but I have no alternative that I can offer with any confidence.

There are limits to what one can hope to learn about books that do not exist, but I have learnt much more than I expected about Timaeus' history, and I hope that I shall be able to convince readers that he deserves more attention than the few paragraphs that are commonly devoted to him in histories of Greek literature. I am sure that if any part of his text survived, it would be well worth reading; even if it did not enable us to understand the history of the Greek West much better, it would certainly help us to understand why later Greek writers write as they do.

This book has gradually taken shape in the years since I retired from teaching at Stanford in 1973. Some valuable preliminary work was done in the winter and spring of 1972, when I enjoyed sabbatical leave from Stanford and the hospitality of libraries and the company and advice of friends in Oxford and at the American Academy in Rome. Since that time the Stanford University libraries and the University of California library at Berkeley have provided most of the books that I needed to consult, and the Interlibrary Loan Service has provided the rest. To all who have helped, friends, colleagues, and librarians, I am profoundly grateful.

Los Altos Hills, California
August 1985

CHAPTER I

INTRODUCTION: THE EARLIEST WESTERN HISTORIANS

A number of Greek writers from Sicily and Southern Italy are known to us by name, men who wrote the history of the Greeks in the West.[1] Information is scanty about Hippys of Rhegium, supposedly the earliest of them, and Antiochus of Syracuse, the contemporary of Thucydides, but Philistus, in the fourth century, and Timaeus of Tauromenium, in the third, are well known both as personalities and as historians. Their work was widely read in later centuries, and Timaeus was commonly regarded as the most important historian between Ephorus and Polybius. Polybius thought him careless and uncritical and Plutarch found fault with his prejudice and his quarrelsome manner,[2] but his reputation was firmly established. His book was the source to which Cicero and the elder Pliny were likely to turn, as were Diodorus and Dionysius of Halicarnassus, if they wanted to read about the history of the Greeks in Sicily. Ever since its first appearance it had been more influential than any of its predecessors. By the time of Polybius the history of the Greek West had already acquired fairly firm outlines. It was Timaeus who had established them.

The history of the older Greek world in the Eastern Mediterranean, from Homer to Philip, had taken on a definite form much earlier, because a few historians came to be regarded as the standard authorities—Herodotus, Thucydides, Xenophon, and Ephorus, and perhaps to a lesser extent Hellanicus and Theopompus. These are the authors on whom any author was bound to rely for the mainstream of Greek history. Like modern writers of history text books, Diodorus may to some degree be dependent on intermediate or secondary sources, "standard works of reference," as we call them, but, except when he states otherwise, his ultimate source of information will generally be one of the established historians.

We have no texts of Ephorus, Hellanicus, or Theopompus, and papyri have not yet made any substantial contribution to our knowledge of their work,[3] but we can read Herodotus, Thucydides, and Xenophon, and claim

---

[1] The *Testimonia* (T) and *Fragmenta* (F) are collected in Felix Jacoby, *Die Fragmente der griechischen Historiker* (henceforth cited as *FGrH*) IIIB, nos. 554–577.

[2] Note the criticism of Polybius throughout Book XII, the complaints of Plutarch in *Nic.* 1 and *Dion* 35, and Jacoby's remarks in *FGrH* IIIb (Kommentar), pp. 526–27.

[3] No papyrus fragment of Ephorus has so far been positively identified, though a number

to know their work as well as Diodorus knew it. For the history of the Greek West the situation is entirely different. We have no text of Antiochus, Philistus, or Timaeus, or any of the other historians of the West. When Diodorus or Strabo or Dionysius of Halicarnassus refers to one of them, we cannot always be sure that his quotation is accurate or even that it is taken directly from the actual text. He may be relying on his memory or on a later author like Posidonius for his quotation, but we cannot verify his reference, because no text of Posidonius has survived, and we know his work only through references in later authors still. We have no access to the "standard works of reference" that authors of the first century of the Roman Empire could have used.

For our present purpose it is not a matter of great importance whether a later writer takes his material directly from an older historian or from an intermediary. When an author like Strabo or Diodorus or Dionysius of Halicarnassus says "as Timaeus reports," or when we have good reason to believe he has taken a certain piece of information from him without acknowledgment, our concern is to decide how much of the immediate context is taken from the same source and how accurately he is reproducing what he has found there. But we can be reasonably sure that a quotation has a better chance of being accurate if it is taken directly from the source. Error and confusion can easily result in transmission through more hands than one.

Poets and collectors of mythological curiosities found much to interest them in Timaeus, because he and his predecessors followed the tradition or convention of starting their histories at the beginning. Not only did they describe how and when cities were founded, but they provided a very substantial section on very early times, showing the part that these cities and the surrounding countryside played in the heroic age. It is easy to forget or minimize the strength of this convention. It was not observed by Herodotus, Thucydides, Xenophon, or Polybius. It was observed, however, by Hellanicus and Ephorus and numerous other writers of the fifth and fourth centuries whose works have not survived. When Herodotus refuses to undertake a long discussion of the problems of the Trojan War and announces his intention of beginning with Croesus, and when Thucydides declares his intention of confining himself to a short span of time, they may have disappointed many readers.

---

of texts have been claimed for him. One short sentence of Hellanicus is known from a papyrus text, and two fragments of Theopompus as well as an *Epitome* of his *Philippica;* see the entries under each of these authors in R. A. Pack, *The Greek and Latin Literary Texts from Greco-Roman Egypt* (2nd. ed., Ann Arbor 1965).

Despite their unwillingness to linger on τὰ πάνυ ἀρχαῖα, Herodotus and Thucydides often find occasion to recall mythological details. Mythology is a matter of very real importance for Greeks and can affect their way of thinking. Greeks were proud of a tradition which gave their city a divine or heroic founder, and they could exploit this tradition in political argument. A place could acquire dignity or even sanctity if great events of olden times were said to have occurred there or if a god was supposed to have revealed his power there.[4] Some cities established such traditions in quite early days and could maintain that a venerable tradition was more authentic than a "founding story" invented or supposedly discovered by some fifth century historian.[5] The newer cities, the colonies, were not always content with what we should call the historical dates of their foundations, and in order that they should not be at a disadvantage against the older Greek cities, historians wrote *Foundation Histories* (Κτίσεις) for them, taking their origin back into mythical times and documenting the story with relics and miracles. Titles of many such works survive,[6] and together with *Horoi* (*Annals*)[7] they recall the effort that was made to provide cities in Asia Minor and the islands with an early history, and to give colonies on the coast of the Euxine a history that went back beyond the time of their foundation, the date of which was generally known.[8]

The authors of these works had at their disposal the enormous corpus of post-Homeric epic that is lost to us, the poetry attributed to Hesiod, and all the Greek lyric poetry of archaic times that has vanished. And when poetry failed them, they were quite ready to invent a tradition, adding to the familiar adventures of a Greek or Trojan hero the details that suited

---

[4] A good example from the West is the visit of Apollo to Metapontum described by Herodotus (4.15).

[5] The poems and fragments of Hesiod and the Hesiodic circle give us the best evidence of pre–fifth century traditions of this kind. Even when there is no Hesiodic reference, we must conclude that certain legends, like that of Athena revealing the olive to the Athenians or Triptolemus the art of grain–growing, originated earlier than the fifth century. But it is unlikely that the legend of Dionysus (at Thebes) or Asclepius (at Epidaurus) or Theseus (at Athens) had made much progress before that time.

[6] E.g., by Hellanicus, Charon of Lampsacus, Ion of Chios, and others of later date like Aristides, author of a *Ktisis* of Cnidos (*FGrH* IIIB 444).

[7] E.g. by Charon of Lampsacus, Euagon of Samos (and other Samians of later date, *FGrH* IIIB 535–544), Heropythos of Colophon (*FGrH* IIIB 448), as well as later writers credited with *Horoi* of Lesbos and Siphnos (IIIB 478, 552). Jacoby is quite right to point out that there is no record of such works being written about cities in Italy or Sicily, and he maintains that this kind of local history did not develop even in Ionia until the middle of the fifth century (*FGrH* IIIa, pp. 1–2; IIIb, pp. 480–81, 487).

[8] Herodotus (6.38) shows us that even a real historical character of the late sixth century can become a heroized *ktistes* soon after his death.

their purpose. Herodotus provides us with some interesting examples of the work done by such writers. At the beginning of his discussion of Scythia he asks himself the question, "Who were the Scythians?" He first gives the version "as the Scythians tell it," that they are the youngest *ethnos* of all, descended from a certain Targitaos who, so they say, ἐμοὶ μὲν οὐ πιστὰ λέγοντες, is the son of Zeus and the daughter of the River Borysthenes (4.5). Herodotus may have learnt this story by talking with hellenized Scythians or from Greeks who claimed to know about Scythian traditions, or he may have found it in a book about Scythia written by a Greek. But when he goes on to give the version preferred by Greeks living in the Pontic colonies, whether he was told about it on his travels or had read it in a book, he is certainly reproducing a Greek fiction, not a folk–tale, not a piece of genuine mythology, but a story devised by some writer of "Pontic history."

The story is that Heracles came to Scythia on his journey to fetch the cattle of Geryones, that the island Erytheia, where Geryones lived, was somewhere "outside the Pontus," that Heracles went to sleep, wrapped up in his lion–skin to keep him warm in the intense cold, and woke up to find that the mares which pulled his chariot had mysteriously disappeared (θείη τύχῃ). He went off in search of them, and after much wandering through uninhabited country met a μιξοπάρθενος ἔχιδνα, half–woman, half–serpent, who kept him as her lover long enough to bear him three sons; since he then insisted on leaving, she gave him back the mares and let him go (4.8–10). The kings of Scythia are supposed to be descended from Scythes, the youngest of the three sons.[9]

The point of the story is that by bringing Heracles to Scythia it makes Scythia a Greek land which the colonists can claim as their own by right of descent. In similar style, Heracles was supposed to have won the land near Eryx in Sicily as the prize for his victory over the local champion Eryx, making it the rightful property of the Dorians (the Heraclidae). Dorieus, the unsuccessful rival of King Cleomenes of Sparta, was urged to found a colony there and assert his right, and he expected his claim to be taken seriously (Hdt. 5.43).

In the fragments that have survived of the poetry of the archaic period, very few mythical events are set in Italy or Sicily. Western place–names appear from time to time and there are vague references to the West, but poets seem not to have localized many events of heroic times in particular

---

[9] In similar fashion the Macedonian kings are supposed to be descended from the youngest of three brothers who came from Argos (Hdt.5.22,8.137; Thuc.2.99).

cities or areas. New papyrus discoveries may refute this statement, but the fragmentary text of Stesichorus' *Geryoneis* is disappointing in its lack of topographical precision.[10] It looks as if the historians of Western Greece, unlike the early Ionian writers, found little to help them in their literary heritage and were obliged to create their own mythological background.[11] It will be the task of a later chapter to show how they created a pre–history for Sicily and Italy, introducing into the Greek "new world" heroic figures who had not previously been associated with it.

If there was scanty material out of which to create the pre–history of the West, there was even less for the so–called dark age that followed, the four hundred years before the Greek colonists came in the eighth century. Polybius tells us that the earlier books of Timaeus were concerned with migrations, as well as with foundings of cities and genealogies,[12] and he is thinking not only of the incoming colonists at the end of the period, but of the Sicels and Sicans and other non-Greek peoples and their search for permanent settlement in earlier times.

In Aegean Greece, a standard version of the dark age migrations established itself quite early. The Dorians were thought to have invaded the Peloponnese after the Trojan War, causing great destruction and bringing the heroic age to a close, forcing many of the older population to seek new homes and found colonies on the Asian coast. And the Greeks in the time of Herodotus could point to the ruins of Mycenae, Tiryns and Pylos as proof of the catastrophe that marked the end of the older civilization.

In the West, things were quite different. There was no standard version of what happened there when the heroic age came to an end. It may be doubted if many Greeks were seriously interested in finding an answer to the question, though the historians seem to have done their best to contradict one another's theories. But whereas, in old Greece, archaeology can show that traditional belief was not entirely fiction, in the West excavation has led archaeologists to reject almost all of the theories propounded by Greek writers.[13]

On the other hand, Greeks were certainly interested in establishing the foundation date of their city and in tracing their descent from one of the founding fathers. Thucydides gives the impression that the foundation

[10] *P.Oxy.* 32.2617; see M. Robertson, "*Geryoneis:*Stesichorus and the Vase-painters," *CQ* 19 (1969) 207–21; L. Pearson, *YCS* 24 (1975) 187–89.

[11] Those who maintain that Timaeus took his material from lost poetry cannot tell us what the poems were that Timaeus knew, nor who wrote them or when.

[12] Polyb. 12.26d—T19.

[13] See F. Bernabò Brea, *Sicily before the Greeks* (2nd. ed., New York 1966); below, pp. 13, 55–56.

dates of all the major colonies were known,[14] that there was no uncertainty about them. But there were some disputes, as will be seen, and when the Delphic oracle appears as commanding the foundation of a colony at an early date, we can often be sure that we are being presented with a contrived fiction, not reliable historical record.[15]

There is no indication that anyone wrote a *History of Syracuse* or a *Chronicle of Acragas,* or that any of the western historians worked to produce the kind of local history that was apparently welcomed by cities on the Greek mainland or in Asia Minor.[16] They seem to have written either *Sicelica* or *Italica,* or a combination of the two, perhaps also including some account of the colonies in Spain and Southern France—general histories of the Greeks in the West, comparable to the general histories of Aegean Greece that were written in the fifth and fourth centuries, *Hellenica* as Thucydides calls them (1.97.2).

Since all these *Hellenica* are lost (unless one includes the *Histories* of Herodotus among them), it is impossible to say with any confidence what form they took and how their material was organized. Like Herodotus (and like Ephorus) their authors probably found it necessary to offer readers some geographical description and discussion, and we might expect the same of the authors of *Sicelica* and *Italica.* Timaeus certainly provided enough geographical and topographical material to interest geographers (as is shown by the frequent references in Strabo). But the question we have to ask is, How much more would we know about the Greeks in the West if the work of Timaeus and his predecessors had been preserved?

For pre–history and the dark age the answer is simple. We would find little there that we could trust. But if we had their books describing the early history of the colonies, their expansion and political development, or even if we had the complete text of Books VI–X of Diodorus, who drew extensively on Timaeus' history, would we learn, for example, how close a resemblance there was between the political development of the city–states in the old Greek world and the new? We know that the colonies experienced the same conflict between oligarchy and democracy as in old Greece, and that the development of democracy was interrupted by the rise of tyrants in many cities. Were the causes of this the same? And would we learn more than we know now about economic and political relations between the colonies and their mother cities? Between Syracuse and Corinth, for example?

[14] Thuc. 6.3–5.
[15] Below, pp. 96–97, 107.
[16] See above, note 7.

Here too the answer seems to be "No", though the evidence must be scrutinized before a final decision is made. So far as we can tell, unlike Herodotus and Thucydides, who wanted to know why things happened as they did, these historians seem to have been content to describe how they happened.

What Thucydides learnt about the colonial foundations in Sicily must have been taken from Antiochus or some other written source. But when Herodotus wrote about the Deinomenid tyrants and about Gelon's great victory at Himera, he was probably recording what he had been told in conversation. This, together with what he has to say about Sybaris and Croton, can be recognized as genuine oral tradition. But when Ephorus, in the next century, set out to fill in the gaps left by Herodotus and Thucydides, he had to rely on what he could learn from written accounts. We have no genuine Siceliot or Italiot oral tradition for events of the fifth century after 480 (not even for the revolt of Ducetius) until we come to the Athenian expedition against Syracuse. Philistus was a boy when the Athenians came, and he may have felt himself entitled to fill in some gaps left by Thucydides.

Timaeus, on the other hand, was too young to have spoken with men who endured the siege and witnessed the Athenian defeat (though he could have spoken with their sons or grandsons). He was not content with the Thucydidean account, and Plutarch finds fault with him for attempting to improve on it, whereas Philistus was a great admirer of Thucydides.[17] Nor was Timaeus content with the Herodotean account of the Battle of Himera. When he offers us "marvels" and rhetorical elaboration, we need not think of them as part of the tradition. We can be confident in calling them pure fiction, and some of them must be his own invention.[18] But his readers, unless they were critical readers, did not complain of his telling lies, because the "tradition" was no longer alive enough or strong enough to discredit him.

Polybius thinks Timaeus one of the worst of the Hellenistic historians. Yet, despite his faults, he became the standard authority for the history of the Greeks in the West, and he was never superseded. Though Diodorus and Plutarch, as well as Polybius, criticize him severely, they do not suggest any other author whom they prefer to him.[19] Our first task, however, must be to examine briefly the evidence about the authors who preceded him.

[17] Plut. *Nic.* 1 and 19.6.
[18] See Chapters V and VI.
[19] Plut. *Dion* 36; Diod. 21.17.

Hippys of Rhegium

Hippys of Rhegium[20] is supposed to be the oldest Greek historian from the West, but there are good reasons for doubting his real existence and adding his name to the list of imaginary writers whose works were invented in Hellenistic times in order to supply "evidence" from early literature when it was required to support some theory. Modern scholarship is exceedingly sceptical about Cadmus of Miletus, supposed to be the earliest of the Ionian historians, a predecessor of Hecataeus, and almost equally doubtful about accepting Dionysius of Miletus.[21]

The *Suda* informs us that Hippys was the first to write Sicilian history at the time of the Persian Wars, writing *Ktiseis of Italy, Sicelica* in five books, *Chronica* in five books, and *Argolica* in three; and that an *Epitome* of his work was made by someone called Myes.[22] Mention of this supposed epitomator should remind us that "Cadmus the Milesian" was "epitomized" (or invented) by Bion of Proconnesus or someone using his name, who said that Cadmus was the pioneer of Ionian historiography, though general opinion gave the credit to Hecataeus. If Hippys really was the first historian of the West, it is surprising that there is no word of him in Dionysius of Halicarnassus, Diodorus, Strabo, or Pausanias, who are familiar with the other writers from the West. Stephanus of Byzantium mentions him, but only once.[23]

Fragments attributed to Hippys show him offering new dates for events and developments of earlier times and contradicting generally accepted

---

[20] *FGrH* IIIB 554. Hippys (Ἵππυς) is generally accepted as the correct form of the name, though the manuscripts in some passages present it as Hippeus, Hippon, or Hippias.

[21] For Cadmus, see Jacoby's commentary on the fragments, *FGrH* IIIb, p.403. He thinks that this historian was invented by Bion of Proconnesus or someone else who wrote using his name. Clement of Alexandria (*Strom.* 6.26.8) says that Bion τὰ Κάδμου τοῦ παλαιοῦ μετέγραψεν κεφαλαιούμενος. A.Gitti, "Nuove discussioni su Cadmo di Mileto," *Atene e Roma,* N.S.2 (1957) 85–93, thinks that Clement is accurate in what he says and that Cadmus is a genuine early historian. Dionysius of Miletus may be an invention of the Hellenistic writer Dionysius Scytobrachion; see H. Gärtner, *Der kleine Pauly,* s.v. Dionysios (19).

[22] T 1—Suda s.v. Ἵππυς Ῥηγῖνος, ἱστορικός, γεγονὼς ἐπὶ τῶν Περσικῶν.

[23] See Jacoby, *FGrH* IIIb, pp.482–83, which supersedes his earlier discussion in *RE* VIII.1927–30. The question was first raised by Wilamowitz in a tangled article, "Hippys von Rhegion," *Hermes* 19 (1884) 442–52. For a good restatement, with some new arguments, see now L.Pareti, "L'opera e l'età di Hippys di Regio," *Riv. di cult. class. e mediev.* 1 (1959) 106–12.

The most faithful believers in the authenticity and early date of Hippys are Italian scholars: e.g., G.De Sanctis, *Ricerche sulla Storiografia Siceliota, Sikelika* I (Palermo, 1957) 1–8; A.Momigliano, *Enc.Ital.,* App. 1, s.v. *Ippi di Reggio;* E.Manni, *Kokalos* 3 (1957) 136–64; 9 (1963) 253–68. References to further literature will be found in *FGrH* IIIb, pp.285–86, note 2; W.Spoerri, *Der kleine Pauly,* s.v. *Hippys,* and R.van Compernolle, *Étude de Chronologie et d'Historiographie siciliotes* (Brussels–Rome, 1960), 441–50.

opinions in various ways. Authors of *Schwindelliteratur* catered for the pedantic taste that welcomed scraps of information or misinformation, and if their creations appeared in a so–called epitome (of a text that never existed), there were credulous readers ready to accept them. We hear about these curious items from various authors.

According to Plutarch, Hippys had discovered an early Pythagorean, Petron, who believed in the existence of a hundred and eighty-three universes (*kosmoi*),[24] though it was generally supposed that no Greek before the atomists thought it possible that there could be more than one universe. Hippys is also supposed to have said that the Arcadians were a "pre–lunar" people (thus contradicting the story of Herodotus which proved that the Phrygians were the oldest people), and to have told the tale of Jason bringing Medea to Corinth (in order to suggest that he was the source of Euripides in the *Medea*).[25] He is cited as authority for an early king of Syracuse called Pollis, an Argive, who was supposed to have given his name to a wine, and, according to Antigonus of Carystus, he described a place of mystery in Sicily where a visitor would die if he lay down, though he was in no danger if he remained on his feet; and this death trap had been constructed, so he said, "when King Epainetos was reigning in Athens, in the thirty–sixth Olympiad, when the Spartan Arytamas won the stadion." Neither of these kings is mentioned elsewhere, and it is likely that both are imaginary.[26] If Antigonus knew of this reference, it appears that the "epitomator" wrote no later than 280 B.C.—and not much earlier, since earlier historians did not date by Olympiads.

The most interesting fragment concerns a miraculous cure in the sanctuary of Asclepius. The epigraphical record of cures at Epidaurus includes the story of Aristagora of Troezen, who suffered from a tape worm and sought a cure at the sanctuary of Asclepius at Troezen.[27] "The god was

---

[24] F 5—Plut. *Mor.* 422 D–E. Plutarch has not seen a text of Hippys or Petron, αὐτοῦ μὲν ἐκείνου βιβλίδιον οὐκ ἀνέγνων οὐδ' οἶδα διασῳζόμενον, Ἵππυς δ'ὁ Ῥηγῖνος, οὗ μέμνηται Φανίας ὁ Ἐρέσιος, ἱστορεῖ δόξαν εἶναι ταύτην Πέτρωνος καὶ λόγον, ὡς ἑκατὸν καὶ ὀγδοήκοντα καὶ τρεῖς κόσμους ὄντας, ἁπτομένους δ'ἀλλήλων κατὰ στοιχεῖον. This text was taken seriously as evidence of early Pythagorean thought and language by W.Vollgraf, *Mnemosyne*, ser. 4, 2 (1949) 91–92 and W.Burkert, *Philologus* 103 (1959) 185–86. Burkert becomes more sceptical later in his *Weisheit und Wissenschaft* (Nuremberg 1962) 180: "Petron vielleicht fingiert."

[25] F 6—Schol. Ap. Rhod. 4.257–62c; F 7—Steph. Byz., s.v. Ἀρκαδία.

[26] F 4—Ath. 1.31A–B; F 3—Antig. Caryst. *Hist.Mir.* 121. For comment on Epainetos as 'king,' and Arytamas as victor (not otherwise attested) cf. T. J. Cadoux, *JHS* 68 (1948) 91.

[27] *IG*² IV.i.122; see R. Herzog, "Die Wunderheilungen von Epidauros," *Philologus*, Supp. 22.3 (1931) 16; E. J. and L. Edelstein, *Asclepius* (Baltimore 1945) I, T423B; II, pp. 102, 160.

away" when she came (he had gone to Epidaurus), but "the sons of the god" (that is, the priests, the medical assistants) decided to attempt a cure without him. She was put to sleep in the proper place, and dreamt that they cut off her head, but could not complete the cure (and next day they saw her without her head); fortunately, the god soon returned, and that night she dreamt that he replaced her head, cut open her abdomen, and removed the worm—she was cured. This, it seems, was an account intended for the faithful, reminding them that dream therapy must not be attempted without the god's assistance and consent. Only the literal–minded would ask what happened to the poor woman if she awoke "without her head." The story in this form must be at least as old as 300 or 320.[28]

The version of Hippys, as recorded by Aelian, is that a woman came to Epidaurus (not Troezen) with the same trouble, found the god away, and his assistants decided to operate on their own; they cut off her head and removed the worm ("a great brute of a thing"), but could not put her head back until the god returned next day and completed the cure.[29]

Is the version attributed to Hippys an older, simpler, and cruder version, or a grotesque parody of the pious story, with "surgery" substituted for dream therapy? Was it seriously told in this form and recorded by Hippys in the fifth century, or was it invented in the third century by some humorist who announced boldly that it was the "original" version? Believers in the early date of Hippys' work are prepared to accept it as the older form of the story. It seems to me, however, that the version attributed to Hippys must be meant as a parody on miracle cures, perhaps intended to cast ridicule on the good brothers of Epidaurus.[30] Its author, the "epitomator," in Hellenistic times, might perhaps expect his readers to think it typical of the simple faith of older times.

Not everyone will be convinced that Hippys is an imaginary author, invented by his "epitomator." Some will prefer the more difficult alternative of accepting him as a genuine writer from the fifth century. I have tried to show how difficult that alternative is.[31]

---

[28] The actual inscription is generally dated in the fourth century; the story may have an earlier origin.

[29] F 2—Aelian, *NA* 9.33.

[30] Nevertheless, Herzog (op.cit., n.27) 77–78, thinks the Hippys version is earlier, cf. O. Weinreich, "Antike Heilungswunder," *Religionsgesch. Versuche u. Vorarbeiten* 9 (Giessen 1909) 81–85. F.W. Walbank, *Kokalos* 14–15 (1968–69) 478, speaks of it as perhaps derived from a "better source." Edelstein (op.cit., n. 27), who thinks it is later, calls it rationalized. Pareti (op.cit., n. 23) puts the case well: "Pare indubbio che la redazione grossolamente deformata della 'novella', riferita da Hippys, presuppone la più fine ed umoristica tradizione epidauria, fissata nella stele iscritta" (109).

[31] A papyrus text (F 9—*P. Oxy.* II.221), which includes the words Ἱππευς ἐν τῷ, is too

Antiochus of Syracuse

With Antiochus we are on more solid ground, since Strabo and Dionysius of Halicarnassus cite his authority for a number of details, and his work was known also to Diodorus and Pausanias.[32] Diodorus (12.71.2) says that his narrative extended as far as the year 424–23 B.C., evidently supposing him to be as young as Herodotus, perhaps no older than Thucydides. Dionysius (*AR* 1.12.3) nevertheless calls him "very early." He wrote in the Ionic dialect, not in Attic or in the Doric of Syracuse, and this choice suggests that he wanted to be ranked with Ionian writers, or even to be recognized as the Herodotus of the West. His history, Diodorus tells us, was divided into nine books, perhaps because someone in the library at Alexandria thought it should be arranged in the same way as the history of Herodotus.

Like Herodotus, Antiochus probably gave no title to his work, and those who quote from it give it different names.[33] Dionysius quotes what seems to be an introductory sentence (*AR* 1.12.3—F 2):

Ἀντίοχος Ξενοφάνεος τάδε συνέγραψε περὶ Ἰταλίης ἐκ τῶν ἀρχαίων λόγων τὰ πιστότατα καὶ σαφέστατα· τὴν γῆν ταύτην, ἥτις νῦν Ἰταλίη καλεῖται, τὸ παλαιὸν εἶχον Οἴνωτροι.[34]

The sentence announces no central theme, no intention to describe a conflict, like the opening sentences of Herodotus and Thucydides, but simply to record the more trustworthy *logoi* "about Italy." He began, evidently, "at the beginning," describing the pre–Greek populations and their movements, first on the mainland ("the original inhabitants of Italy were the Oinotroi") and then in Sicily, and he wrote probably quite dogmatically in

---

fragmentary to be of any help. For F 1, on the origin of the proverb, δῶρον δ᾽ ὅ τι δῷ τις ἐπαίνει, see below p. 107.

[32] *FGrH* IIIB 555 (with commentary in IIIb, pp. 486–96). For the latest general discussion (somewhat arbitrary in places) see K.von Fritz, *Die griechische Geschichtschreibung* (Berlin 1967) 1.507–18. Among older work, it will be enough here to mention E. Wölfflin, *Antiochos von Syrakus und Coelius Antipater* (Winterthur 1872); G.M. Columba, "Antioco," *Archivio storico siciliano*, N.S.14 (1889) 84–107, and G.De Sanctis, *Ricerche sulla storiografia siceliota. Sikelika* I (Palermo 1957) 9–16. On the question whether Thucydides used Antiochus, see below pp. 15–16.

[33] ἐν τῷ περὶ τῆς Ἰταλίας συγγράμματι (F 3—Strabo 6.1.4), ἐν τῇ Σικελιώτιδι συγγραφῇ (F 1—Paus. 10.11.3), ἡ τῶν Σικελικῶν ἱστορία (T 3—Diod. 12.71.2). It seems to me unnecessary to believe that there are separate works on Sicily and Italy; cf. Jacoby's cautious remarks, *FGrH* IIIb, p. 487, in contrast with von Fritz and the earlier writers mentioned in note 32 above, who assume that there must have been two separate works.

[34] When Antiochus says "Italy" he does not mean the whole peninsula or even Magna Graecia, but a much more narrowly limited area; περὶ Ἰταλίης, therefore, cannot be taken as a title for his work (though Strabo may have thought so). It shows that he is starting his history by speaking of the Ἰταλοί, before the Sicels migrate to Sicily.

the manner of Hecataeus. who announced his intention of presenting *logoi* "in my version" (ὡς ἐμοὶ δοκεῖ).[35] When Diodorus says that he began with Kokalos, the early Sican king,[36] this means that he started with Kokalos when he went on to write about Sicily (there is no need to suppose he is speaking of two different works).

Surviving literature from the fifth and fourth centuries suggests that few readers were interested in the non-Greek peoples of Italy and Sicily. Thucydides does not think it necessary to tell us what the Sicels and Sicans were like, what stage of political or cultural development they had reached, or what kind of relationship different Greek colonies established with their non–Greek neighbours. It is the same in Latin literature. Etruscans and Samnites and some other Italic communities demanded attention, because the Romans had to fight them, but apart from the adventures of Greek and Trojan heroes on their wanderings after the fall of Troy, neither Livy nor any other writer whose work survives seems to have concerned himself with what might have happened in the South of Italy before the Greek colonists came.

It is Dionysius of Halicarnassus who tells us what less widely known writers had to say about such matters. They presented the early history of Southern Italy in a pattern of migrations and expulsions. Antiochus called the aboriginal people by the Greek name of Oinotroi, and says that they called themselves Italoi after a "good and wise" king, Italos, then Morgetes after his successor Morges. Then, in the words of Antiochus, as reported by Dionysius: "When Italos grew old, Morges became king, and during his reign a man arrived who was an exile from Rome, Sikelos by name." Sikelos split the people in two with his attempt to establish a kingdom for himself, and his adherents, called Sikeloi after him, were expelled and made their way to Sicily. It was a matter of dispute whether this took place before or after the Trojan War. It seems that Antiochus did not say when it happened.[37]

Dionysius does not tell us who the dwellers on the site of Rome at the time were supposed to be. Were they Arcadians? It is too early, in the fifth

[35] τάδε γράφω, ὥς μοι δοκεῖ ἀληθέα εἶναι· οἱ γὰρ Ἑλλήνων λόγοι πολλοί τε καὶ γελοῖοι, ὡς ἐμοὶ φαίνονται, εἰσίν (F1a).

[36] T 3—Diod. 12.71.2 Ἀντίοχος ὁ Συρακόσιος τὴν τῶν Σικελικῶν ἱστορίαν εἰς τοῦτον τὸν ἐνιαυτὸν (424–3) κατέστρεψεν, ἀρξάμενος ἀπὸ Κωκάλου τοῦ Σικανῶν βασιλέως, ἐν βιβλίοις ἐννέα.

[37] F 4, 5, 6—Dion.Hal. AR 1.22, 35, 73; cf. Aristot. Pol. 7.1329b, whose language seems to indicate that he had seen the text of Antiochus. See also G. Huxley, "Antiochos on Italos," Φιλίας χάριν, Miscellanea di studi in onore di E.Manni III (Rome 1980) 1199–1204.

century, for Romans to be concerned with establishing their Trojan origin, but it seems that Greek writers were already eager to establish a Greek claim to the site of Rome. Hellanicus of Lesbos, the contemporary of Antiochus, brought Aeneas to Rome and made him and Odysseus co–founders of the city. It would not be surprising if Antiochus brought Greeks there.[38] This pretence of early Greek settlement in Italy (it rests on no real "tradition" and deserves no better name than pretence) is the beginning of an effort to represent all Italy as "Greek territory," settled by Greeks at the time of the Trojan War or earlier. But Dionysius, in his rather naive fashion, is trying to establish "the facts," and he seems to think he is dealing with real evidence, genuine tradition recorded by conscientious writers, not with ingenious fiction.[39]

Even if Antiochus represented himself as questioning non–Greek communities about their traditions, following the method of Herodotus, one must recognize that such a method could not be practised in Italy or Sicily with the same hope of fruitful results as in Greece or the Near East. Herodotus learnt much in Egypt and Babylonia (not all of it was entirely accurate), but he seems not to have made extensive inquiries in Italy, or if he did he did not think the results worth recording. The Italic and Siculan peoples were apparently not literate until they learnt the art of writing from Greeks or Etruscans. Oral tradition can be preserved without writing, but national tradition, as distinct from family tradition, will not establish itself without vigorous political development and the growth of political centres. There is archaeological evidence of a high cultural level in the Bronze Age in Sicily and Southern Italy, but not of political development on any great scale. We cannot expect to find folk memory of mass migrations that took place five or six hundred years previously more vivid and more articulate than in Greek communities.[40] Polybius found fault with Timaeus for not

[38] *FGrH* I 4, F 31, 84—Dion.Hal. *AR* 1.45–48, 72.

[39] L.Bernabò Brea, *Sicily before the Greeks* (2nd ed, New York 1966), and "Leggenda e archeologia nella protostoria siciliana," *Kokalos* 10–11 (1964–65) 1–33, insists that we must reject the ancient notion of a Sicel migration from Italy, because excavation has revealed nothing in Eastern Sicily that is reminiscent of "the Apennine or sub–Apennine cultures of the Italian mainland, which the sources would lead us to expect were brought by the Sicels." His predecessors were not so ready to dismiss the so–called ancient tradition, which should be called a "theory" rather than a tradition.

[40] Nevertheless, C. F. Crispo, *Contributo alla storia della più antica civiltà della Magna Grecia* (Tivoli 1940) 95, believes not only in "tradizioni orali attinte sui luoghi e non prive di contenuto veridico," but also in "scrittori locali," from whom Antiochus could derive his information, and some archaeologists persist in the belief that "indigenous legends" were in some way absorbed and transformed by the early settlers (see e.g., L.Braccesi, in *La Sicilia*

making inquiries in the Herodotean manner,[41] but he must have known (as Timaeus certainly did) that such inquiries among the non–Greek population would be unlikely to elicit any information comparable to what Herodotus was able to collect in the Near East.

Antiochus evidently wanted to present the history of Southern Italy, before the Greeks came, as the history of an "Italian" kingdom, established by people whom he called Oinotroi. He was careful to establish boundaries of this kingdom, excluding the toe and heel of Italy to the south and the Opici or Ausones (Oscans, Samnites, or Campanians, as the Romans called them) to the north.[42] If he observed his own distinctions and confined himself to "Italy," as he says in his opening sentence (τάδε συνέγραψε περὶ ᾿Ιταλίης), this should mean that he was not obliged to give an account of the Etruscans[43] or Rome or even of the Greeks of Campania.

In writing about Sicily it is not clear how he made the distinction between Sicans and Sicels. The Greeks in Sicily, one must suppose, made the distinction readily enough. If their appearance was different and they had different customs, the distinction would rest on ὄψις and not on ἀκοή. Why did Antiochus decide that the Sicels came from Italy? Was he told so, or did he claim to have τεκμήρια? There is no reason to think that he knew more about the origin of the Sicels than we know about the origin of the Etruscans. Like him, we are dependent on λόγοι and τεκμήρια.

When Dionysius writes about the Sicans, he may be giving what he thinks is the *communis opinio,* and one cannot be sure how much of what he says is taken from Antiochus. He says that they were an Iberian people, who settled in Sicily not long before the Sicel invasion, coming in flight from the Ligurians, that they were not very numerous, and that much of the island remained uninhabited, but nevertheless it came to be called Sicania after them, its previous name having been Trinacria (*AR* 1.22). This change of names, with the earliest one a Greek name, seems in the manner of Antiochus, like the sequence Oinotroi, Italoi, Morgetes. Trinacria is evidently a Greek "explanation" of the Homeric Thrinacia.

No fragment has been preserved to tell us what Antiochus had to say about the period between the Sicel migration and the first Greek colonial

---

antica, ed. E. Gabba–G. Vallet [Naples 1980] I.i.53–55). For a protest against this belief and an attempt to explain how these "traditions" were created, L.Pareti, *Kokalos* 2 (1956) 5–19.

[41] Polyb. 12.27.

[42] F 3—Strabo 6.1.4; F 5—Dion.Hal. *AR* 1.35.

[43] It is Hellanicus, not one of the early historians of the West, who is cited by Dionysius for the Greek settlement of Etruria in heroic times (*AR* 1.28).

expeditions. Nor is there any fragment that gives us his date for the founding of Syracuse. But since Thucydides certainly knew the work of Antiochus and apparently followed him in what he said about the Sicels,[44] it is commonly supposed that he is indebted to him also for his account of the earliest Greek foundations—Naxos first, Syracuse in the next year, Leontini "in the fifth year" after Syracuse, and the Megarians settling at Thapsos "at about the same time." Thucydides gives no absolute date for the founding of Syracuse, dating other colonies in relation to Syracuse, which is what we might expect from a Syracusan writer. Even if in fact he is telling us what he discovered by independent inquiry in cities in Sicily, the information, accurate or otherwise, must have been available in Antiochus' history.

By combining what Thucydides says (6.4.2) with Herodotus on the date of the destruction of Megara Hyblaea (7.156–7), we arrive at the date 733 B.C. for the founding of Syracuse. Strabo, however, citing Antiochus as his authority, says that Archias, the Corinthian founder of Syracuse, and Myscellus, the founder of Croton, set out together, that Archias landed at the site of Croton on the voyage out and that he was able to assist Myscellus in establishing the colony there.[45] Dionysius (*AR* 2.59) tells us that Croton was founded in *Ol*. 17.3 (710–09 B.C.) and the chronology of Eusebius (Armenian version) gives a similar date (two years later). It is unlikely that Antiochus, presumably a patriotic Syracusan, would date his city's foundation as late as this; more probably he advanced the date of the founding of Croton, so as to have the two colonies established at about the same time.

Strabo also says, without citing any authority, that Locri was founded "not long after the founding of Croton and Syracuse," and that their settlement, after they moved from their original site on Cape Zephyrion, was

---

[44] Thucydides (6.2.4) says that the Sicels crossed "probably on rafts, as we are told," in flight from the Opici, and this corresponds with what Dionysius of Halicarnassus says of Antiochus ("Antiochus gives no date for the crossing, but says that the migrants were Sicels, forced out by Oenotrians and Opici," *AR* 1.22). When Dionysius adds that "Thucydides dates the crossing many years after the Trojan War," this is inaccurate because Thucydides (like Antiochus) gives no date at all. Perhaps he wants to represent Thucydides as disagreeing with Hellanicus who preferred a much earlier date, "in the third generation before the Trojan War." But it seems to me unnecessary to multiply the written sources of Thucydides. For further discussion, see A. W. Gomme, A. Andrewes, K. J. Dover, *Historical Commentary on Thucydides* IV (Oxford 1970) 200–01.

[45] F 10—Strabo 6.1.12. In 6.2.4, without citing any source, Strabo gives further details of the story, including the visit of Archias and Myscellus to Delphi and the oracle that directed Myscellus to Croton.

organized "with the co–operation of the Syracusans" (6.1.7). This repeated motif of "Syracusan co–operation" certainly suggests the hand of Antiochus.

Inquiries about early history in a Greek colony must have been more productive than attempts to obtain information about pre–historic times in Sicel or Sican communities. Even if there were no official records that went back very far,[46] old–established families might often be able to provide important items of family history and the kind of genealogical detail that sometimes extended as far back as one of the founding fathers. It is important to remember that the start of colonial activity in the West coincides with the date usually accepted for the introduction of the alphabet into the Greek world. It is surely no accident that the earliest dates in Greek history, apart from the conventional date for the Trojan War, are dates in the eighth century, the first "literate" century—the date of the first Olympiad and dates of colonial foundations in the West, including those of Rome and Carthage. Eighth century dates are the earliest that one could expect to be established by written record.

By whatever means these dates came to be remembered or established and recognized,[47] the simplest explanation of the figures that Thucydides gives is that he took them from Antiochus. But the simplest explanation is not always the right one. Jacoby prefers to believe that Thucydides took them from Hellanicus, whose chronological interests are well known, and that Antiochus did not concern himself much with details of chronology.[48]

The fragments tell us that Antiochus described how several cities were colonized,[49] and we should expect him to continue with an account of their subsequent history. We may suspect that Thucydides took his account of Zancle (6.4.5–6) from him, but there is no fragment to prove it. Strabo,

[46] There is no clear evidence that any such records existed; see Jacoby, *FGrH* IIIb, p. 488; K. J. Dover, "La colonizzazione della Sicilia in Tucidide," *Maia* 6 (1953) 1–20. De Sanctis (op cit. [n. 32] 13) thinks it "not impossible" that lists of eponymous magistrates were preserved as far back as the eighth century.

[47] It has been argued, e.g., by van Compernolle, op.cit. (n. 23) and M. Miller, *The Sicilian colony dates* (Albany 1970), that the dates were arrived at by generation–counting (the details of their argument cannot be considered here). It is hard to believe that Thucydides would accept dates as reasonably accurate if he knew or thought that such a rough and ready method had been used. When he writes ἐγγύς or ἐγγύτατα (6.4.4, 5.2, 5.3) this means something better than a rough approximation. Argument about actual foundation dates, supposed to be confirmed by archaeological evidence, cannot be attempted here.

[48] *FGrH* IIIb, pp. 488–89. For a useful summary of the whole question, see *Historical Commentary on Thucydides* IV. 198–210.

[49] F 1 (Lipari islands), 8 (Velia), 9 (Rhegium), 10 (Croton), 11 and 13 (Tarentum), 12 (Metapomtum),

however, refers to his account of Rhegium: "Rhegium is a foundation of the Chalcidians. The story is that some Chalcidians were dedicated to Apollo, one man out of every ten, in obedience to an oracle, after a crop–failure, and they came later, from Delphi, to settle here. But according to Antiochus it was the Zanclaeans who sent for the Chalcidians, and they appointed Antimnestus as their oecist."[50] The Rhegines would want to encourage the belief that Apollo had given his blessing to their colony, and Antiochus may be offering an alternative rationalist version of their foundation.

For Tarentum, Antiochus accepted the story that it was founded by Spartan Partheniai, and Partheniai in his version are the sons born to Spartans who avoided active service in the Messenian War. These boys, like their fathers, were denied full civic rights; they made plans for an uprising, but their secret was discovered and their ranks were infiltrated by agents of the governing class. On the day when their leader, Phalanthus, was to give the signal by putting on a cap, a herald cried out forbidding him to do so. And in a spirit of reconciliation very rare in Greek revolutions the Partheniai were then permitted to depart, with Apollo's approval, to colonize Tarentum, led by Phalanthus himself (F 13—Strabo 6.3.2).[51]

The account of the founding of Metapontum also deserves mention. Strabo (6.1.15—F 12) notes the belief that it was originally colonized by men from Nestor's Pylos on their return from Troy (this is probably what Timaeus said, who brought as many figures of the heroic age as he could to Italy), and adds: "But Antiochus says that the site was abandoned, and Achaeans settled there who had been sent for (μεταπεμφθέντας) by the Achaeans in Sybaris." This recalls how the Chalcidian settlers at Rhegium were "sent for" by the Chalcidians of Zancle. The Achaeans are said to bear a grudge against the Spartans for forcing Achaeans to leave the Peloponnese and to be alarmed for fear that the Spartans in Tarentum might anticipate them in annexing the site. Antiochus also noted that the original name of the colony was Metabos, which was changed to Metapontum. This is in keeping with his interest in changes of ethnic names. Fourth century

---

[50] Strabo 6.1.6—F 9. There is no proof that Antiochus said anything about Messenians from the Peloponnese joining the settlers. Their story cannot be traced back beyond the fourth century.

[51] There are some obscurities in the story and Strabo's text is uncertain at several critical points. He goes on to report the somewhat different account of the Partheniai given by Ephorus. For recent discussion and bibliography, see M. Philippides, "The Partheniai and the foundation of Taras," *Ancient World* 2 (1979) 79–82.

coins have been found bearing the legend METABO, and it may be that a hero Metabos was in fact recognized in local tradition.[52]

In some of his other foundation stories, Antiochus shows how, just as the founders of Croton had to abandon their first settlement on Cape Zephyrion, the Cnidians who settled in the Lipari Islands were driven out by Elymians and Phoenicians from the site they had first chosen on Cape Pachynos, and how the Phocaeans who colonized Velia had first tried to settle in Corsica.[53] And the colonies in which settlers of different origin collaborate provide a model for the fifth century colony of Siris, which he says was founded in common by Tarentines and Thurians (who would presumably be Athenians) with an exiled Spartan at their head, though the colony was commonly regarded as a Tarentine establishment—"and later it changed its name to Heraclea."[54]

It is interesting to see how characteristic motifs recur in these stories about colonial foundations, but we know very little else about Antiochus' story of colonial development. His account of later times, from the colonial beginnings to the fifth century, has disappeared completely. Except for the lexicographers, Pausanias, Strabo, and Dionysius of Halicarnassus are the only writers who actually cite passages from his history. Pausanias and Dionysius seem to have had direct access to his text, but Strabo's quotations may be taken from Timaeus, who was notorious for criticizing earlier writers. An earlier generation of scholars concluded that Strabo was dependent mainly on Polybius and the *Geographoumena* of Artemidorus for his geographical information about Italy, and that it was Artemidorus who supplied him with quotations from Timaeus[55]—quotations which might often contain allusions to and criticism of Antiochus. Strabo does not seem to have a wide-ranging acquaintance with Greek literature, and it is much easier to believe that he learnt about the opinions of Antiochus in this way than that he had access to the actual text of a little–known early historian.

[52] S. P. Noe, *The Coinage of Metapontum* (revised ed., New York 1984) II.65–66, cf. Lasserre's note on Strabo 6.1.15.

[53] F 1—Paus. 10.11.3; F 8—Strabo 6.1.1. For the full story of the Phocaeans' adventures, Hdt. 1.165–168.

[54] F 11—Strabo 6.1.14. Since this fragment refers to events of 433 B.C., we may believe Diodorus when he says that the history went down to 424.

[55] See F. Lasserre, *Strabon* III (Budé ed. 1967) 9–25, who gives bibliographical detail. Among the earlier literature the following works deserve particular mention: G. Hunrath, *Die Quellen Strabos im sechsten Buch* (Cassel 1879), F. Sollima, *Le fonti di Strabone nella geografia della Sicilia* (Messina 1897), K. J. Beloch, "Le fonti di Strabone nella descrizione della Campania," *Atti accad. dei Lincei,* ser. 3.10 (1882) 429–48, and, above all, J. Geffcken, *Timaios' Geographie des Westens (Philologische Untersuchungen* 13, Berlin 1892).

CHAPTER II

PHILISTUS AND SOME OTHERS

i. Philistus

Philistus belongs to another generation, a much more clearly defined character, prominent in political life and familiar to a wider circle of readers than Antiochus. As a Syracusan politician and military leader, who served both Dionysius I and Dionysius II, he appears frequently in Diodorus' account of Sicilian affairs and in Plutarch's *Dion.* We are told that he was not only a supporter of these tyrants but was φιλοτύραννος in principle, a believer in tyranny as a political system.[1] Writers who held this unpopular view are not easy to find in Greek literature; it would be particularly interesting to have the whole text of an historian who approved of tyrants and tyranny.

Plutarch says that he feared Plato's influence on the younger Dionysius and was largely responsible for Plato's second departure from Syracuse; and, although his name does not occur in the letters attributed to Plato, there is a reference in the Third Letter to the hostility of "Philistides and others."[2] Plutarch also mentions Philistus in his *Nicias,* cites his account of the fighting at Syracuse in 414 B.C., and speaks of him as an eyewitness of the events there.[3] But his first known political appearance is in 406, when Dionysius comes forward for the first time, after Acragas has fallen to the Carthaginians, and causes so much offence by his denunciation of the generals that he is fined. Philistus, who is a wealthy man, pays his fine, and offers to continue paying any fines he may incur, "all day long if necessary."[4] Two years later, when the Syracusans make a determined

---

[1] For fragments and testimonia see *FGrH* IIIB 556, with addenda in *FGrH* IIIb (Noten), pp. 401–02.

Plutarch, *Dion* 36 (T 23a), finds fault with Ephorus for praising him, though he cannot conceal the fact that he is φιλοτυραννότατος ἀνθρώπων and μάλιστα πάντων ἀεὶ ζηλώσας καὶ θαυμάσας τρυφὴν καὶ δύναμιν καὶ πλούτους καὶ γάμους τοὺς τῶν τυράννων. Dionysius of Halicarnassus complains of his character as κολακικὸν καὶ φιλοτύραννον καὶ ταπεινόν (*Ad Pomp.* 5—T 16b). Cf. T 5d—Nepos, *Dion* 3: Philistum historicum . . . hominem amicum non magis tyranno quam tyrannidi.

[2] T 5c, 6a—Plut. *Dion* 11, 13–14; T 6b—Plato, *Ep.* 3.315d–e.

[3] F 56—Plut. *Nic.* 19: τῶν πραγμάτων ὁρατὴς γενόμενος, cf. F 54, 55—Plut. *Nic.* 1, 28.

[4] T 3—Diod. 13.91.

19

effort to oust Dionysius from the tyranny and he seems to be in a desperate situation, shut up in the fortifications of the Island, Philistus is shown refusing to let him consider any thought of giving up or deserting to the Carthaginians; he urges him to hold on to the tyranny "until he is dragged away by the leg."[5] It is likely that there were many autobiographical touches in his history. It may be supposed that he was in his mid–twenties when he first came forward in defence of Dionysius, about fifteen years old perhaps during the Athenian attack on Syracuse, hence born about 430—as Jacoby says, "a contemporary of Plato, at least twenty years younger than Thucydides."[6]

Philistus' name does not appear again in extant accounts of Syracusan affairs until 386 B.C. This was the year, according to Diodorus, when Dionysius took to writing poetry and developed a paranoid attitude towards anyone who criticized his efforts, sending Philoxenus off to the quarries when he refused to praise them and then regretting his severity and recalling him. Among the other victims of his mania, when he suspected everyone, were Philistus and his brother Leptines.[7] According to Diodorus they were both quickly recalled and restored to favour, as was Philoxenus, Leptines actually marrying the tyrant's daughter.[8] Plutarch, however, is quite definite that Philistus was not recalled during the lifetime of the elder Dionysius, not until twenty years later, when the opponents of Dion persuaded Dionysius II to recall him, hoping that he would minimize the influence of Plato.[9] Plutarch goes on to explain that he took advantage of the leisure that his life in exile provided to write history, thus putting him in the select company of men who profited by their exile and used it to good purpose.[10]

---

[5] T 4—Diod. 14.8.5: προσήκειν ἔφησεν οὐκ ἐφ' ἵππου θέοντος ἐκπηδᾶν ἐκ τῆς τυραννίδος, ἀλλὰ τοῦ σκέλους ἑλκόμενον ἐκπίπτειν. It seems that Philistus did not himself take credit for making this remark. Elsewhere Diodorus attributes it to a relative of the tyrant (20.78), cf. F 59—Plut. *Dion* 35.

[6] *FGrH* IIIb, p.497. It has been argued that some incidents at Syracuse described by Plutarch, but not mentioned by Thucydides, are taken from Philistus' account, reminiscence perhaps romanticized or exaggerated of his boyhood; see G. Busolt, "Plutarchs *Nikias* und Philistos," *Hermes* 34 (1898) 280–97.

[7] This is after his lyrics have not been well received at the Olympic festival (Diod. 15.7.2–3). The Olympic year would be 384, not 386 as in Diodorus. This was noted by Grote, *History of Greece*, 2nd ed., XI.31, note 1.

[8] Two seats in the theatre of Dionysus bear the name Βασιλίσσης Φιλιστίδος, Βασιλέος Ἱέρωνος (T 10—*IG* XIV.3). Philistis must be their great–granddaughter. Polybius (1.9.3) tells us that Hiero in 272 B.C. married the daughter of a man called Leptines.

[9] This may be the reason that would appeal to Plutarch. The real reason may be that Dionysius wants support against Dion; see W. Koerber, *De Philisto* (Breslau 1874) 10.

[10] T 5a—Plut. *De Exil.* 605C, T 17b—Cic. *De Orat.* 2.57. For speculation about Philistus' activities during his exile, L. Braccesi, *Grecità adriatica* (Bologna 1971) 93–94.

Each of these two versions serves its own rhetorical purpose. One shows Philistus taking advantage of his exile to write history, like Thucydides, the other shows the fickleness of tyrannical paranoia. Jacoby prefers the "short exile" version, and thinks that the supposed exile may really be an appointment to a naval command in the Adriatic, from which he is eventually recalled by Dionysius II.[11] On the other hand the "long exile" may seem more likely, because there is no indication in our sources that Philistus exercised any influence in the later years of the elder Dionysius and no surviving fragment shows any special knowledge of these years.

Whatever the truth may be, it is only after the death of the elder Dionysius, when Plato is back in Syracuse (on his second visit), that Philistus is shown again asserting his influence. The story of Dion's downfall, as told by Plutarch (*Dion* 14), although undoubtedly based on Timaeus' account, may contain details that are taken from autobiographical passages in Philistus' history. He is said to be infuriated at Plato's efforts to persuade the younger Dionysius that a tyrant is an "unfortunate" man. He argues that Dion is plotting to gain the power for himself and his nephews (the children of Dionysius I and Aristomache), that he is using Plato to persuade the tyrant to abdicate and seek τὸ σιωπώμενον ἀγαθόν in the philosophy of the Academy, so that the more solid happiness of wealth and power will pass into the hands of Dion.[12] Here is the true φιλοτύραννος speaking, full of scorn for Plato and his philosophic ideals. Finally, Dionysius obtains a copy of a letter written by Dion, which appears to prove that he is guilty of treason and in league with the Carthaginians. After showing it to Philistus, he takes Dion on a walk, pretending that he wants to put an end to their quarrel; but when he reaches the harbour, he accuses him bluntly of treason and has him put on board a ship that takes him to Italy.

When Dion returns from exile at the head of an expedition, determined to free Syracuse from the tyrant, Philistus makes his final appearance as an admiral of Dionysius; he is an elderly man now. There are minor differences between the accounts of Plutarch and Diodorus,[13] but the outline is clear enough. Philistus failed to intercept Dion's ships off the coast of Italy, was summoned back to Sicily by Dionysius, tried without success to sub-

---

[11] *FGrH* IIIb, pp. 497–98. He also argues that the tyrant's quick change of mind is "psychologically more probable;" cf. E. Manni, *Kokalos* 3 (1957) 139. For argument in favour of the longer exile, see A. Gitti, "Ricerche sulla vita di Filisto," *Mem. Acc. dei Lincei*, Classe di scienze morali, ser. 8.4 (1952) 225–72, at 228–39; K.F. Stroheker, *Dionysios* I (Wiesbaden 1958) 227, n. 116.

[12] T 6a—Plut. *Dion* 13.

[13] T 9a, b, c—Plut. *Dion* 25; Diod. 16.11 and 16. In Book XVI Diodorus is no longer following Timaeus.

due a rebellious movement at Leontini, and was given command of the fleet in the final battle with Dion. When it became clear that Dion had won the victory, Ephorus says that he committed suicide; but according to Timaeus and Timonides, who represented the Academy as one of Dion's officers, he was captured and tortured savagely before being put to death. Timaeus says he was dragged through the city by his lame leg, in revenge for the advice he gave the elder Dionysius, when he told him not to give up until he was dragged away by the leg. Philistus had denied making this remark, but Timaeus sees the opportunity of a rhetorical effect which he cannot resist.

Not much is known yet about a building in Taormina which is thought to be a library, probably of late hellenistic date, except that it had inscriptions (*dipinti*) on the walls listing names of historians including Callisthenes, Fabius Pictor, and Philistus, with a few remarks about their significance.[14] Nothing is said of Philistus' history in what survives on the stone, but "they say he was the pupil of the elegiac poet Evenus" (this confirms what is said in the *Suda*, T 1a, b), "and that he established an ἄστυ in its present prosperity, the first to do so, and divided the people." The meaning of this activity is completely obscure. Can it perhaps refer to one of the foundations of Dionysius I? Or does it refer to Syracuse or Tauromenion? It is equally impossible to know what is meant by saying that "he previously set out *diagrammata* about the tyrants." But the text is far from certain here.[15] Whatever these activities were, we are forced to the conclusion that Philistus showed considerable initiative in politics either on his own or as minister of Dionysius I, in ways of which nothing is said in our literary sources. One may reasonably suppose that the library was established in Taormina as a tribute to its notable citizen Timaeus, and it is interesting to see that Philistus is also given some recognition.

We are told that Philistus' history was divided into two nearly equal parts, a general history of Sicily (Περὶ Σικελίας) in seven books, from the earliest times down to the year 406, and a more specialized account of the time of Dionysius I (Περὶ Διονυσίου) in four books down to 367, followed by two books devoted to the next five years, the beginning of an

---

[14] G. Manganaro, "Una biblioteca storica nel ginnasio di Tauromenium," *Parola del Passato* 29 (1974) 389–409, with photographs.

[15] The text as restored by Manganaro reads: Φίλιστος Συρακόσ [ιος˙]/ τοῦτον Εὐήνου Π[..]/ φασὶ γενέσθαι μαθη-/ τὴν τοῦ τὰς ἐλεγείας/ γράψαντος· πρῶτον ἄσ- /τυ στήσασθαι τὸν νῦν / εὐημεροῦντα τρόπον/ μερίσασθαί τε τὸν δῆ-/ μον ὅμως πρότε-/ [ρον (?) ἐχθ] ἔσθαι [τὰ δια] γράμ-/ [ματα περὶ τῶν τυράν-]/ νων (?), ἔπειτα δὲ . . .

The text is reproduced without comment in *SEG* 26 (1976–77) 1123; J. and L. Robert, *REG* 89 (1976) 593–94, add some appropriate question marks.

account of the younger Dionysius,[16] which Athanis of Syracuse completed.[17]

Philistus began, like Antiochus, with the Sican king Kokalos and the arrival of Daedalus in Sicily during his reign, so that Kokalos is dated in what we should call late Minoan times, "several centuries before the Trojan War."[18] He regarded the Sicans as immigrants from Spain, "taking their name from the Iberian river Sicanos." The account of very early times that Diodorus gives at the beginning of his fifth book may contain some elements that Timaeus took over from Philistus, but all that we know for certain is that, like Hellanicus, Philistus brought the Sicels over from Italy, led by Sicelos, eighty years before the Trojan War, and that he regarded them as a Ligurian people, "driven out of Italy by Umbrians and Pelasgians."[19] According to him, the Sicans had by this time abandoned most of Eastern Sicily, because eruptions of Etna had devastated the countryside and (as in Antiochus' version) there was plenty of vacant land on which the Sicels could settle. A reference in Eusebius' *Chronicle* under the year of Abraham 802 (1215 B.C.) tells us that Philistus recorded the foundation of Carthage "at about this time" by the Tyrians Azorus and Carchedon.[20] He evidently supported the Carthaginians in their claim to have settled in the West long before the first Greek colonists came.

Stephanus of Byzantium cites a number of Sicilian place–names from the history, some of them unknown from other sources, and quite often gives the number of the book in which they occurred. From his note on the city of Dyme (F 2), we learn that Philistus recorded the Olympic victory of Oebotas of Dyme in the stadion; this was in the sixth Olympiad according to Pausanias (7.17.6). Mactorion (F 3) is known from Herodotus (7.153.2). It was inland from Gela, and Philistus mentioned its foundation, presumably from Gela, which cannot be earlier than the seventh century.[21]

---

[16] T 11 a, b—Diod. 13.103,15.89; T 12—Dion. Hal.*Ad Pomp.* 12; cf. T 17a—Cic. *Ad Q.fr.* 2.11.4, and the confused statements in Suda s.v. Φίλιστος and Φίλισκος (T 1).

[17] *FGrH* IIIB 562 T 2—Diod. 15.94.4.

[18] *FGrH* 556 F 1—Theon, *Progymn.* 2, p. 66 Spengel. The arrival of Daedalus was described by Ephorus in his seventh book, by Philistus in his first.

[19] F 46 — *Dion.Hal. AR* 1.22.3: ὡς μὲν Ἑλλάνικος ὁ Λέσβιός φησι τρίτη γενεᾷ πρότερον τῶν Τρωικῶν . . . ὡς δὲ Φίλιστος ὁ Συρακούσιος ἔγραψε, χρόνος μὲν τῆς διαβάσεως ἦν ἔτος ὀγδοηκοστὸν πρὸ τοῦ Τρωικοῦ πολέμου.

[20] F 47—Euseb. *Chron.*, Anno 802, cf. Appian 8.1.1, who says Carthage was founded fifty years before the fall of Troy. The names of the founders are clearly Greek inventions, Azoros taken from the old name of Tyre; see O. Eissfeldt, *RE* VIIA.1876, s.v.Tyros.

[21] P. Orlandini, *Kokalos* 7 (1961) 148–49, thinks the site may be Monte Bubbonio. Ὕκκαρον, φρούριον Σικελίας, must be the Sican town mentioned by Thucydides (6.62). Nothing is known of its history at this early stage.

Book II seems to begin with events of the sixth century. Dionysius of Halicarnassus quotes a sentence from the beginning of the book: Συρα-κόσιοι δὲ παραλαβόντες Μεγαρεῖς καὶ Ἐνναίους, Καμαριναῖοι δὲ Σικελοὺς καὶ τοὺς ἄλλους συμμάχους πλὴν Γελῴων ἀθροίσαντες· Γελῷοι δὲ Συρακοσίοις οὐκ ἔφασαν πολεμήσειν· Συρακόσιοι δὲ πυνθανόμενοι Καμαριναίους τὸν Ὕσμινον διαβάντας. . . . Dionysius does not complete the sentence, but breaks off to complain that the style is "displeasing." He thinks that Philistus' style is generally dull and monotonous.[22] His criticism of this sentence is of very little value without some indication of its context. This might be a summarizing sentence or a formal outline of a narrative that is to follow, not at all a typical specimen of the author's narrative style. It is evidently part of the description of the first stage of the conflict between Syracuse and Camarina. As Thucydides tells the story (6.5.3), the people of Camarina attempt to break away from Syracuse, but are unable to obtain any support from the people of Gela. The Syracusans destroy the town, but it is refounded by Hippocrates, the tyrant of Gela, as his dependency. Later developments, its second destruction and second refounding by Hippocrates, were described by Philistus in Book III.[23]

   Dionysius is clearly prejudiced against Philistus because of his political attitude: he thinks his writing reveals his "tyrant–loving character." Philistus admired Thucydides, but Dionysius says he succeeded only in avoiding some of the awkwardness of Thucydidean language and failed completely to match any of his real excellence, showing no gift for pathos and no talent for argument, while his descriptions of military operations were feeble, and the speeches merely bombastic and quite unworthy of the characters to whom they were attributed; nor did he succeed in explaining the different qualities and the political aims and policies of individuals. Dionysius finishes his discussion of Philistus by saying that he showed some intelligence in his exposition and was perhaps more useful than Thucydides πρὸς τοὺς ἀληθινοὺς ἀγῶνας.[24] This seems to mean that practising orators might find him a more useful model to study and imitate than Thucydides.[25] We

[22] *Ad Pomp*. 5.5—F 5.

[23] F 15—Schol. Pind. *Ol*.5.19: Φίλιστος ἐν γ' φησὶν ὅτι Γέλων Καμάριναν κατέσ-καψεν. Ἱπποκράτης δὲ πολεμήσας Συρακοσίοις καὶ πολλοὺς αἰχμαλώτους λαβών, ὑπὲρ τοῦ τούτους ἀποδοῦναι ἔλαβε τὴν Καμάριναν καὶ συνῴκισεν αὐτήν.

[24] *Ad Pomp*.5.6—T 16b, cf. the similar language in the Epitome of *De Imitatione* 3.2— T 16a. There are some minor textual problems in both passages.

[25] Cf. W. Rhys Roberts, *Dionysius of Halicarnassus, The three literary letters* (Cambridge 1901) 121. R. Lauritano, *Kokalos* 3 (1957) 101–02, thinks that the meaning is he was "molto più utile per le vere battaglie." This cannot be right. The "contests" must be lawsuits. When Dionysius (*De Imitatione* 3.1) says that Philistus and other historians are "worthy of imitation," he means "useful for the orator."

have too little of the actual text of Philistus to evaluate this criticism, but other ancient critics have greater respect for Philistus. Quintilian calls him "imitator Thucydidis et, ut multo infirmior, ita aliquatenus lucidior" (10.1.74). Cicero gives him higher praise; he respects his political under-standing and the value of his close association with a tyrant, ranks him with Thucydides as a writer of "concisae sententiae" which are not always easy to follow, and calls him "capitalis, creber, acutus, brevis, paene pusillus Thucydides." [26] This foreshadows Quintilian's more famous appreciation of Thucydides as "densus et brevis et semper instans sibi" (10.1.73). The rhetorical critics have less to say. Demetrius found his style obscure and he receives only faint praise in *On the Sublime,* but Theon found good ex-amples of narrative in various parts of his history, mentioning his descrip-tion of the meeting of Kokalos and Daedalus in Book I and the myth or fable of "the horse" in Book II, perhaps one of the tales told about the tyrant Phalaris, to which Aristotle alludes (*Rhet.* 2.1393b). [27]

Book II might have much of interest to tell us about the earliest Sicilian tyrants, if Philistus' sympathies as *philotyrannos* extended to them, but the fragments are not helpful. Stephanus of Byzantium cites Book II for six towns or smaller centres in Sicily and one in Italy, but no event from this early period is known to be connected with any of them. [28] Of the cities and χωρία said to have been mentioned in Books III and IV, two cannot be identified, [29] but one can see how all the other places might be mentioned if one turns to the narrative of Sicilian events in Herodotus (7.154–67). Xouthia, the area of which Leontini is the centre, was mentioned in Book III, [30] and Philistus must have described the siege of Leontini, where Gelon came to the notice of Hippocrates. He also described the surrender of Ca-marina to Hippocrates and its destruction by Gelon. [31] Hippocrates died at Megara Hyblaea fighting the Sicels (Hdt. 7.155), and this gives the occa-sion for the city to be mentioned in Book IV. [32]

---

[26] *Ad Q.fr.* 2.11.4, *De Orat.*2.57, Brut. 66— T 17a, b, 21. For discussion of this criti-cism, see R. Zoepffel, *Untersuchungen zum Geschichtswerk des Philistos* (Freiburg 1965) 25–61.

[27] Demetrius, *De Eloc.* 198—T 19; *De Sublim.*40–T 18; Theon, *Progymn.* 2.66.9—F 6.

[28] F 8–14. Pollux 10.116—F 7 cites a phrase used in Book II, τὰς νύκτας ἐπαίρεσθαι λαμπτῆρας ἀντιπεφραγμένους, which recalls the "stratagem" of Himilco described by Po-lyaenus (*Strat.* 5.10.2) when he sailed to Sicily in 397 or 396 with his ships' lanterns "blacked out" to avoid detection. An allusion to this event in so early a book seems inappropriate. The book number may be wrong.

[29] Therma and Lichandos (F 16, 17).

[30] F 18—Steph. Byz. s.v. Ξουθία.

[31] F 15—Schol. Pind. *Ol.* 5.19c (quoted in note 23 above).

[32] F 20—Steph. Byz. s.v. "Υβλαι (not a very helpful fragment, because the text is un-certain).

An Oxyrhynchus papyrus gives a list of what appear to be fifth century events in Sicily, which looks like a summary or outline taken from some historian of Sicily.[33] It may list part of the contents of Philistus' fourth book: "Attack on Gela by the *xenoi* in Omphake[34] and Kakyros. Syracusans come to the help of Gela. *Xenoi* march to meet Syracusans. Battle with Syracusans in Owls' Plain ([ἐν τῷ] Γλαυκῶν πε[δίῳ])." Then after a gap of about ten lines: "Acragantines attack Crastos.[35] Battle near Crastos, Acragantines against Himeraeans and Geloans. How the *xenoi* living in Minoa were picked (ἠρέθησαν) by Acragantines and Syracusans."[36]

These are events of which there is no record elsewhere. The *xenoi* must be the mercenaries formerly employed by tyrants, who found refuge in non-Greek cities, or they may be mercenaries settled in these cities by the tyrants themselves. In either case, the fighting between them and the citizen forces of Greek cities must take place soon after the downfall of the tyrants.

An account of the Sicel uprising led by Ducetius should have been given in Book IV or V, but there are no helpful fragments. A note that Elba was mentioned in Book V[37] seems to tell us that something was said about the Syracusan efforts to control Etruscan piracy and their attack on Elba led by Phayllus, as described by Diodorus under the year 453–2.

Another longer papyrus text can be recognized as a fragment from some historian of events in the West, and Philistus has been claimed as its author.[38] Two columns with short lines are partially preserved. The first seventeen lines of column I are well preserved. The writer is evidently describing the progress of the Athenian expedition sent to Sicily in 427 B.C., twenty ships under Laches and Charoeades. Thucydides gives only a bare outline of the story in Book III, and it is summarized in Diodorus (12.54.4–7). It is explained that the ships were sent out to help Leontini in its war against Syracuse, that Camarina, the Chalcidian colonies, and Rhe-

---

[33] *P. Oxy.* IV. 665—*FGrH* IIIB 577 F 1. See also G. De Sanctis, *RFIC* 33 (1905) 66—73; F. Bilabel, *Die kleineren Historikerfragmente auf Papyrus (Kleine Texte* 149) 11–13; F. H. Heichelheim, *Symbolae Osloenses* 31 (1955) 88–95.

[34] Cf. F 19—Steph. Byz. s.v. Ὀμφάκη and Paus. 8.46.2. Omphake was a Sican town and Kakyros must be near by.

[35] Cf. F 44—Steph. Byz. s.v. Κραστός (another Sican town).

[36] These mercenary garrisons must have been put there as outposts in case of a Carthaginian attack.

[37] F 21—Steph. Byz. s.v. Αἰθάλη.

[38] *PSI* XII.1283—*FGrH* IIIB 577 F 2, first published by G. Coppola and A. Momigliano, *RFIC* 58 (1930) 449–70; cf. G. Perrotta, *SIFC* 8 (1930) 311–15; S. Mazzarino, *Bollettino storico Catanese* 4 (1939) 5–72; G. Bartoletti, *SIFC* 24 (1950) 159–60; L. Pearson, *BASP* 20 (1983) 151–58, where some new restorations of the text are offered.

gium were supporting Leontini, while Locri and the Dorian colonies (except Camarina) were on the Syracusan side. All that Thucydides has to say of their first summer's campaign is that they landed at Rhegium and τὸν πόλεμον ἐποιοῦντο μετὰ τῶν συμμάχων. καὶ τὸ θέρος ἐτελεύτα (3.86). In the winter that follows they make an attack on the Lipari islands that produces no results ("the people did not come over to them") and return to Rhegium (3.88). Before starting on an account of the next summer, he announces that he will describe only the events that are "particularly worthy of mention." Before he begins his story of Laches' attack on Mylae he reports that Charoeades is dead, "killed fighting the Syracusans," but he does not say when or where the fighting has taken place (3.90.2). The battle must have been during the previous summer.

This battle, apparently off the coast near Megara Hyblaea, was evidently described by the author of the papyrus text, but the description is finished by the time that Column I begins. There we learn that the Syracusans "recovered the ships and the men" (it is not clear whether they had been captured or put out of action in some way),[39] that Charoeades was wounded and died of his wounds, "within the next six months" if the text has been correctly restored,[40] that one of Laches' ships was captured, and that he made arrangements for the attack on the Lipari islands. The loss of a ship is not noticed by Thucydides. He says that Laches had thirty ships in his raid on the Lipari Islands, but since, according to the papyrus, there were only ten Rhegine ships, he can only have had twenty-nine.[41]

Any restoration of the second column is highly speculative, but it seems to describe one of the raids that the Athenians made on Locrian territory during the next summer and winter, perhaps the raid described by Diodorus (12.54.4), rather than one of those described by Thucydides (in 3.99 or 103). Thanks to the surviving letters σας. . . . . εσρ . . . πειρα. . . .Λοκρω. . . .and καικιν, we may reasonably suppose that the text described a landing in Locrian territory near the River Caecinus, and when we read αναχω . . . . περιτυγχαν . . . . τοναλυκ . . . . ηρεσιλοκρισι, it looks like a description of what happened when they withdrew,

---

[39] The column begins: πρέσβεις κομίζων ἐς / ʽΡήγιον· καὶ τὰς ναῦς / καὶ τοὺς ἄνδρας ἀνέ / λαβον οἱ Συρακόσιοι. It may be that these ambassadors were from Camarina, because Thucydides tells us (6.75.3) that an alliance with Camarina was made ἐπὶ Λάχητος. The text continues: Χα / ριάδης δὲ τραυματι / σθεὶς ἐκ τῶν τραυμα / μάτων ἀποθνήσκει/ τοῦ [ἑξαμή] νου τούτου / καὶ τῶν μετὰ Λάχη / τος τριήρων ἥλω μία /κατὰ Μεγαρέας.

[40] Χαριάδης is the reading of the text, as in Diodorus 12.54, corrected from Χειριάδης.

[41] ἀναλαβὼν / τὰς οἰκείας ναῦς καὶ / παρὰ ʽΡ[ηγίνων] δέκα. For details of the restored text and the restoration previously proposed by Bartoletti (op.cit., n. 38), see BASP 20 (1983) 155–57.

how they met some Locrian triremes at the mouth of the Alyx and captured five of them (Diodorus 12.54.4).

Since Philistus was probably a boy in his 'teens during the subsequent Athenian invasion of Sicily, it is particularly disappointing that so little is known of his narrative of these years. Diodorus' narrative (13.1–19) is certainly based on Ephorus, and when it differs from the Thucydidean account, the reason may be that Ephorus has borrowed from Philistus.[42] We are told, however, that Philistus, like Thucydides, gave full credit to Gylippus for the final victory (which Timaeus denied him),[43] and that, like Thucydides, he said Nicias and Demosthenes were killed by the Syracusans, not allowed to die by their own hand, as Timaeus maintained.[44]

Philistus apparently reported also that Demosthenes refused to consider himself included in the surrender that he arranged for his men, and attempted to save his honour as a soldier by committing suicide before he was captured, but was prevented by his captors, when they apprehended him; and that Nicias was thought to have disgraced himself by surrendering without any attempt to avoid capture, so that his name was omitted from the inscription in Athens that recorded the names of all who died in Sicily. When Pausanias mentions this inscription he says "I record only what Philistus writes."[45]

The Athenian attack on Syracuse was described in Book VI.[46] There is much that Philistus might have added to the Thucydidean account, what he could have learnt from talking with his elders and what he must have observed himself as a boy. He might have told us some of the reasons why the Athenians came so near to succeeding in an operation that must have seemed ill–judged to most Sicilian Greeks. He will also have known whether the Syracusans were seriously afraid that non–Dorian cities in Sicily and Italy would support the Athenians effectively. Thucydides seems reluctant to answer these questions, and it would be useful to know what Philistus and his contemporaries had to say about them.

Book VII must have described the war with Carthage up to the rise of Dionysius. Books VIII–XI (the second σύνταξις as Diodorus calls it) dealt with the rule of Dionysius I,[47] and the two final books were concerned

---

[42] Direct use of Philistus by Diodorus or Plutarch is less likely; see Jacoby, *FGrH* IIIb, p.304, n.149.

[43] F 56—Plut. *Nic*. 19.5–6.

[44] F 55—Plut. *Nic*. 28.5.

[45] F 53—Paus. 1.29.12; cf. Dover's note on Thuc. 7.86.5 and D.W. Bradeen's discussion of the inscriptions identified as "casualty lists", *CQ* 19 (1969) 156–59.

[46] F 24—Steph.Byz. s.v. Δάσκων.

[47] F 28—Theon, *Progymn*. 2.68.17; T 11a—Diod. 13.103.3.

with Dionysius II.[48] We have hardly any significant information about these books apart from the autobiographical passages that they must have contained, discussed earlier in this chapter. Philistus is of course severely criticized by ancient writers for his friendship with Dionysius I and his favourable account of him.[49] It is taken for granted by them that he deliberately concealed the darker side of the tyrant's behaviour and that he did so for personal reasons, so as to keep on good terms with him.

Philistus' account of Dionysius included the usual features that are expected, in later writers at least, in the description of a man's rise to power. Before Dionysius was born, his mother dreamt that she gave birth to a little satyr, and the Galeotae, the recognized interpreters of dreams in Sicily, gave it as their professional opinion that this was a good omen: her son would be a great man.[50] A surer prediction of greatness presented itself shortly before he actually seized power. He thought he had lost his horse when crossing a river; he managed to reach the bank himself and was walking away greatly distressed when "he heard a whinny behind him and was delighted to see his horse approaching him with a swarm of bees in its mane."[51] This is the kind of compliment to a ruler that becomes conventional in later times.

Stephanus has a long list of place–names from the later books (F 29–44), Sicilian, Italian, and Libyan, such as would be mentioned in accounts of the campaigns of Dionysius in Italy and Africa. And a reference to Ἐρεβίδαι· μέρος Λωτοφάγων (F 31) suggests that he allowed himself an occasional mythological digression, in the Thucydidean manner perhaps.[52] The lexicographers cite him for a number of unusual words (F 69–76), and one has to wonder how far the Greeks of the West had developed a vocabulary of their own.

The admirers of Philistus who thought his style was Thucydidean quote no examples to illustrate what they meant, except for Clement of Alexandria who shows him borrowing a *gnome* from Thucydides.[53] The severe criticism of Dionysius of Halicarnassus[54] is offset by Theon, who mentions two notable descriptive passages, his account of the military preparations

---

[48] T 11 b, c—Diod. 15.89.3, 94.4.

[49] T 13 a, b, c—Paus. 1.13.9; Plut. *De mal. Her.* 855C; Marcellinus, *Vita Thuc.* 27; T 23a—Plut. *Dion* 36.

[50] F 57 a, b—Cic. *De Div.* 1.39; Paus. 5.23.6.

[51] F 58—Cic. *De Div.* 1.73. There is also supposed to be a swarm of bees that predicts the tyranny of Agathocles (Diod. 19.2.9).

[52] Cf., e.g., Thuc. 2.68.3, 102.5.

[53] F 67—Clem.Alex. *Strom.* 6.8.9, cf. Thuc. 3.39.4.

[54] *Ad Pomp.* 5.5.

of Dionysius I against the Carthaginians and his description of the tyrant's funeral (which Plutarch thought too elaborate).[55] When fragments offer us so little of the actual text of Philistus we must be content to notice that the critics disagreed with one another. His work was certainly overshadowed and superseded by the history of Timaeus. But we may suspect that Timaeus borrowed extensively from him, though he often disagreed with him.

ii. From Philistus to Timaeus.

There were quite a number of historians of the West who wrote in the fourth or early third centuries, but not much is heard about them in later times. Most of them are known to us only from passing references in later writers, who may in fact have borrowed their references from Timaeus' history or some other book that they were reading. The *Suda* credits Dionysius the Elder with some historical works,[56] but no one else says anything about them. Little more is known about the work of Hermias of Methymna and Polycritus of Mende, perhaps the first writers about the Greek West who were not Siceliots or Italiots.[57]

Diodorus says that Hermias wrote a full–scale history of Sicily ending with the year 376–5 B.C.[58] But he never mentions him again. In his account of the year 404–3 (14.10.2–4), which is certainly based on Timaeus,[59] he describes how the Spartans sent Aristus to Sicily with instructions to stir up opposition against Dionysius, but to make sure that the movement failed, so as to strengthen the tyrant's position. He killed the leader of the popular movement, the Corinthian Nicoteles, and when Athenaeus comments "Hermias of Methymna says that Nicoteles was a heavy drinker,"[60] we must suspect that he owes the information to Timaeus.

Polycritus of Mende is mentioned by Diogenes Laertius, who says that he wrote a book about Dionysius the Younger and described how the Socratic philosopher Aeschines spent some time at his court, remaining there

---

[55] F 28—Theon, *Progymn.* 2.68.17(Sp.); F 40—Plut. *Pelop.* 34.

[56] Suda s.v. Διονύσιος Σικελίας τύραννος· ἔγραψε τραγῳδίας καὶ κωμῳδίας καὶ ἱστορικά (*FGrH* IIIB 557 T 1). For all writers considered in this section see the brief discussion in Brown, *Timaeus* 18–20.

[57] For *Testimonia* and *Fragmenta*, see *FGrH* IIIB 558, 559.

[58] T 1—Diod. 15.37.3.

[59] See pp. 172–173 below.

[60] F 1—Ath. 10.438C. With less than his usual caution Jacoby takes this fragment as evidence that Hermias may have been in the service of Dionysius the Elder.

until the return of Dion in 356.[61] He is also cited in the pseudo–Aristotelian *Thaumasia Akousmata* as an author of *Sikelika* in epic verse, and as authority for the existence of a remarkable lake in the interior of Sicily, which conveniently enlarged itself as more people entered it to bathe; when the number of persons reached fifty, it blew them out on to dry land.[62] Timaeus is one of the principal sources of the *Thaumasia Akousmata,* and this reference to Polycritus is probably taken from him. Diodorus may possibly be referring to the same man when he cites the history of a man called Πολύκλειτος in his account of the wealth and hospitable tradition of Acragas—an account which, as he tells us himself, he has taken from Timaeus.[63] But there are numerous references to authors called Polycritus and Polyclitus, and the identification cannot be pressed.

Whatever the sympathies of Polycritus may have been, Timonides of Leucas, the next author to be considered, was a vigorous supporter of Dion. He was a member of the Academy who took an active part in organizing the campaign for Dion's return, served as one of Dion's officers on the expedition, and is supposed to have sent a personal report in the form of a letter or letters to Speusippus, the head of the Academy. His report, if a genuine copy of it survived, would be of enormous interest, but it is known to us only through Diogenes Laertius and Plutarch, who cites it several times in his *Dion,* noting how it differs from the accounts of Ephorus and Timaeus.[64] It may be that he owes his information about it to Timaeus and never saw the actual text, but he seems to have no doubt that it was a genuine report and deserved to be treated with respect.[65]

Another contemporary source for the closing years of Dionysius II is the history of the Syracusan Athanis, whom Theopompus mentioned as a supporter of Heraclides against Dion after Dion's capture of Syracuse. Athanis is said to have taken up the story where Philistus' account broke

[61] *FGrH* IIIB 559 F 1—Diog.Laert. 2.63.

[62] F 2—*Mir.Ausc.* 112.

[63] Diod. 13.83.3—F 3. Jacoby accepts the emendation Πολύκριτος and thinks it not unlikely that Timaeus used this author's history.

[64] *FGrH* IIIB 561—Diog. Laert. 4.5; Plut. *Dion* 22, 30, 31, 35.

[65] There has been much controversy about the sources used by Plutarch and Diodorus in their accounts of Dion. J. Harward, *The Platonic Epistles* (Cambridge 1932) 53–59, argues that a genuine report by Timonides was seen by Plutarch, and H. Berve, "Dion," *Abh. d.Akad.Mainz,* Geistes– u.Sozialwiss. Kl., 1956. 10, 748–50, thinks of the report as something that was probably published. Some earlier critics were more inclined to believe that fictitious letters attributed to Timonides were published in the form of a *Briefroman,* and that Timonides is really a *Schwindelautor;* see F. Susemihl, *Geschichte der griechischen Literatur in der Alexandrinerzeit* II (Leipzig 1892) 589, E. Howald, *Die Briefe Platons* (Zurich 1923) 155.

off (though his sympathies will have been very different from those of Philistus).[66] Plutarch mentions him only in his *Timoleon*. According to his account Timoleon brought sixty thousand new settlers to Sicily and arranged for their settlement and housing, raising money by the sale of confiscated properties. He also described how Timoleon's eyesight began to fail during his fight against the Sicilian tyrants.[67]

The tyranny of Agathocles produced two historians, Callias and Antander, the brothers of Agathocles. They are mentioned by Diodorus, Athenaeus, Dionysius of Halicarnassus, and Aelian,[68] but not by Plutarch. Timaeus knew of Callias, but had a low opinion of him, and when Diodorus says he was "taken up by Agathocles and, in return for substantial gifts, sold History, the Mouthpiece of Truth, to him, never ceasing to offer his benefactor unworthy praise," this sounds like the language of Timaeus.[69]

Callias' history, commonly given the title Τὰ περὶ τὸν Ἀγαθοκλέα, is said to have been in twenty-two books, but there is no fragment referring to any event in the life of Agathocles or indeed to any event of historical times. Like some of his predecessors he shows an interest in early cities and their supposed founders, in the mythological associations of volcanic areas, and various topographical oddities. He has Rome founded in the generation after Aeneas, by Romulus and Remus and a third brother, who are supposed to be the children of Latinus and Roma, a Trojan woman who came with the first Trojan party, unrelated to Aeneas.[70] He noted the extensive orchards in the neighbourhood of Palermo (F 2), had something to say about the Lipari Islands and the tradition that Hephaestus' forge was there (F 4), and spoke of the ancient city of Eryce, ninety stades from Gela, with volcanic craters near it which had some association with the Palici (F 1), those mythical characters who continue to appear in writers about Sicily.[71] His remarks about the Psylli and their method of treating snake–bite may perhaps come from a description of the African expedition of Agathocles.[72]

[66] *FGrH* IIIB 562 T 1—Steph. Byz. s.v. Δύμη, quoting Theopompus, T 2—Diod. 15.94.4. There may have been some digressions about earlier times; see F 1—Ath. 3.98D.

[67] F 2, 3—Plut. *Timol.* 23, 37. Plutarch may not have seen a text of Athanis. He might have found the references in Timaeus or in a later biography based on Timaeus, which many critics believe to have been his main source for Timoleon; cf. Westlake, *CQ* 32 (1938) 70 n.8.

[68] *FGrH* IIIB 564, 565.

[69] T 3, 4—Diod. 12.17.4; Josephus, *C.Ap.* 1.17.

[70] F 5a—Dion.Hal. *AR* 1.72.5. The name of the third brother is lost in the manuscripts. Syncellus, p. 363 Dindorf, gives it as Telegonus.

[71] Diod. 11.88.6. Macrobius quotes the actual words of Callias (5.19.25—F 1).

[72] F 3—Aelian, *NA* 16.28, cf. Diod. 20.42.2, who describes the sufferings of men from

Antander is mentioned several times by Diodorus, who tells us that he was an historian like Callias.[73] Nothing is known of what he wrote.

Similar interests to those of Callias are revealed by the fragments of Alcimus.[74] He said that Rome was founded by Romus, son of Romulus, who was the son of Aeneas and Tyrrhenia (F 4). The introduction of Tyrrhenia might indicate an Etruscophile tendency, but we know only that, like so many others, he recorded tales of Etruscan luxury and decadence (F 3). Perhaps it was to point a contrast with Etruscan decadence that he recorded an *aition* which explained why Italian women did not drink wine. When Heracles was on his way through Italy he went to a house to ask for a drink. The mistress of the house had been tippling secretly, and not wanting her husband to know that she had broached the wine cask, she asked him to bring Heracles a drink of water. But Heracles, wanting wine, sent him back into the house to look at the cask which had turned to stone. Henceforth women were ashamed to drink wine.[75]

The fragments of these various writers suggest a certain similarity in tastes and interests, and similar characteristics appear very clearly in the much more abundant fragments of Timaeus. We may, therefore be inclined to think that he followed a well–established tradition of historical writing, which reached its full development in himself. But this is where some caution is necessary. It must be suspected that in many instances later authors who refer to a little-known writer like Alcimus or Hermias have never seen his text, but are taking the "fragment" out of the text of Timaeus, with which they are probably familiar. If that is the case, the fragments reveal not so much the tendencies of these earlier writers as the taste of Timaeus himself, who cites only what happens to interest him. It is always dangerous to assume that a few fragments quoted from an earlier author are representative of the character of his work,[76] and the danger seems particularly serious here. We have good evidence that Timaeus shared certain interests with his predecessors, but we should not conclude that they had no other interests; and we know too little to characterize them as individual writers,

---

poisonous snakes. Discussion of the Lipari islands in Book X (F 4b) might have been occasioned by the plundering expedition of Agathocles, cf. Diod. 20.101.

[73] *FGrH* IIIB 565, cf. T 5—Diod. 21.16.5.

[74] *FGrH* IIIB 560. He is said to have written *Sicelica,* with a book specially devoted to Italy. Jacoby dates him tentatively in the mid–fourth century.

[75] F 2—Ath. 10.440E–441B. Alcimus also linked Etna with Greek mythology, perhaps following Simonides (F 5—Schol. Theoc. 1.65–66), and noted the birthplaces of some literary figures (F 1).

[76] This danger has been very properly emphasized by Peter Brunt, "On Historical Fragments and Epitomes," *CQ* 30 (1980) 477–94.

except for Philistus, whose reputation endured longer and who still commanded respect from Roman critics.

If we count the three major historians among the predecessors of Timaeus, we must admit that he could not have learnt much about the history of the West from them. Xenophon shows no interest in it; he mentions the tyrants of Syracuse and the Carthaginians only in isolated sentences.[77] Thucydides of course offered the classic account of the Athenian expedition to Sicily, and Herodotus ended his life as a Western Greek, when he settled at Thurii. But apart from occasional remarks about geography and topography and brief references to isolated events, the only contribution of Herodotus is his description of the political development of Sicily at the time of the Persian Wars.[78] Every historian of Sicily must have studied this part of his work and borrowed from it, but so far as the earlier history of the island was concerned, he left the field clear for Antiochus, who perhaps aspired to be hailed as the Herodotus of the West.

The first historian from the older Greek world who wrote extensively about the West was Ephorus, who allotted a due proportion of his comprehensive history to Italy and Sicily, dealing with geography and mythological traditions as well as political history.[79] He is without doubt one of the main sources from which our knowledge about the Greek West is ultimately derived, second in importance only to Timaeus, if not actually equal to him.

Diodorus used Ephorus extensively in various parts of his work, and in his chapters devoted to events of the West when he seems not to be following Timaeus, there is always a good chance that Ephorus is his source, although when he contrasts their accounts, comparing, for example, the numbers of the Carthaginian invading army given by them both, it is generally likely that he is reporting Timaeus' criticism without checking his reference in the actual text of Ephorus.[80] Ephorus was a standard authority. There must in fact have been large areas where Timaeus adopted his account with little change or comment. His emphasis and his judgment of individuals may have been different, but when Timaeus was looking for

---

[77] There is a longer passage describing the fortunes of the Syracusan ships sent to the Aegean to help the Spartans (*Hell.* 1.1.18–31), but three or four lines are considered enough for the Carthaginian invasion of 409 (1.1.37) and the rise of Dionysius (2.2.24), and some critics think that even these few lines are spurious.

[78] 7.153–67. The following passages deserve special mention: 1.94 (the Etruscans), 1.166–67 (Phocaean emigration to the West), 5.43–48 (Sybaris), 6.126–29 (the wooers of Agariste), 7.170 (the story of Daedalus).

[79] *FGrH* IIA 70, with Jacoby's discussion in *FGrH* IIC, pp. 26–30.

[80] Diod. 13.54,60,80 and 14.54, cf. p. 152 below.

factual information, it is likely that he consulted Ephorus more often than Antiochus or Philistus or any of the minor writers. The wars with Carthage in the late fifth century and the rise of Dionysius I were described in Ephorus' sixteenth book, the story of Dionysius II and Dion in Books XXVIII and XXIX.[81] It is likely that Timaeus found many details here that interested him, but there is no direct evidence of borrowing.

No trace has survived of what Ephorus had to say about the pre-Greek inhabitants of Italy and Sicily and hardly anything of his account of Greek colonization of the West. But he devoted two books to a geographical introduction to his history, and like Western historians he was interested in the mythological associations of different places. For example, he maintained that there was an entry to the underworld at Lake Avernus and he placed the Cimmerians there, living in caves so that they never saw the light of day.[82] He may indeed have provided Timaeus with a precedent for combining mythological fantasy with a show of rationalistic scepticism. Strabo says that he seems not to have kept the promise he made in his earlier books, when he found fault with "lovers of myth" and insisted on the claims of "truth," a criticism that might equally well be applied to Timaeus.[83]

There are two other writers who deserve a brief mention here, Theopompus and Duris of Samos. Theopompus never attempted a general history of the West, so far as we know, but Diodorus says that he devoted Books XLI–XLIII of his *Philippica* to the period when the Dionysii were in power in Syracuse.[84] The *Philippica* was a work on an enormous scale, in seventy–two books according to the *Suda*,[85] so that lengthy digressions, taking the reader far away from the scene of Philip's activities, need not surprise us. Since Diodorus knew of this digression, he may have consulted it in writing about the Dionysii, but attempts to isolate passages dependent on Theopompus have not been convincing.[86]

Duris, who was tyrant of Samos, probably in the early years of the third century, and is commonly regarded as one of the pioneers in the so–called

---

[81] F 68,69, 89–92, 201–204, 218–221.

[82] F 134a, b–Strabo 5.4.5; Ps.–Scymnus 236.

[83] F 31b–Strabo 9.3.11.

[84] *FGrH* IIB 115 F 184—Diod. 16.71.3. Books XXXIX and XL are also cited for events and places in the West (F 185–196).

[85] T 1—Suda s.v. Θεόπομπος.

[86] N.G.L. Hammond, *CQ* 32 (1938) 137–51, believed that Diodorus followed the digression of Theopompus quite consistently. For discussion and further bibliography see H.D. Westlake, "The Sicilian books of Theopompus' *Philippica*," *Historia* 2 (1954) 288–307, reprinted in his *Essays on the Greek historians and Greek history* (Manchester–New York 1969) 226–50.

'tragic' style of historiography,[87] wrote a book about Agathocles, Τὰ περὶ Ἀγαθοκλέα, in addition to his other work. Unluckily, the few citations from it[88] tell us very little about its content and show only that he seems to have been interested in the same kind of detail as Timaeus—anecdotes about little-known but unusual characters, mythological associations of places in Italy, heterodox and even bizarre versions of myths. Thus Timaeus might have found his work congenial (though we could hardly have felt kindly towards a writer who had been tyrant), but there is no positive evidence that he knew it or paid any attention to it.

Timaeus, like Polybius, was constantly critical of his predecessors, and if we could read his actual text we should probably learn much about earlier historiography.

---

[87] *FGrH* IIA 76 T 1–3. For recent discussion of Duris and full bibliography, see R. B. Kebric, *In the shadow of Macedon: Duris of Samos* (*Historia Einzelschriften* 29, Wiesbaden 1977).

[88] F 16–20, 56–59.

CHAPTER III

TIMAEUS OF TAUROMENIUM: PRELIMINARY SURVEY

In the year 345 B.C., Timoleon's expedition reached Sicily and was given a warm welcome at Tauromenium by Timaeus' father Andromachus. Andromachus had founded Tauromenium as a city of refuge for the dispossessed people of Naxos when Dionysius destroyed their city, and he continued as their "dynast" for many years, "governing them in a just and constitutional manner," so Plutarch says, "firmly and bitterly opposed to tyrants."[1] We may suspect that Andromachus owes some of this good reputation to his son's account of him in his history, but we are told only that Timaeus was grateful to Timoleon for letting his father continue in power as "dynast" and praised him exuberantly.[2] Subsequently, Timaeus was forced by Agathocles to leave Sicily. He went to Athens and spent fifty years there, in the course of which he wrote his history, carrying it down as far as the one hundred and twenty–ninth Olympiad (264 B.C.). It was in this year that the Romans first crossed the sea to set foot on Greek soil.[3] This is Polybius' formal reason for starting his history in this year, and we can hardly doubt his word when he says that Timaeus came down as far as this.

It is natural to suppose that Timaeus was living, even though only a small boy, in 345 when Timoleon appeared at Tauromenium, and it is no surprise that the author of *Long-lived Men* makes him live to the age of ninety–six.[4] We cannot determine the date of his birth, but it is possible that he did not die until about 250. The date of his exile is not recorded (though it is likely to be later than 317, rather than earlier) and we do not know how he supported himself in Athens, whether he became a professional rhetorician, engaged in some business or industry, or lived on

[1] *FGrH* IIIB 566 T 3a, b—Diod. 16.7.1; Plut. *Timol.* 10.6–8.

[2] T 13—Marcellinus, *Vita Thuc.* 27: Τίμαιος δ'ὁ Ταυρομενίτης Τιμολέοντα ὑπερεπήνεσε τοῦ μετρίου, καθότι ᾿Ανδρόμαχον τὸν αὐτοῦ πατέρα οὐ κατέλυσε τῆς μοναρχίας, cf. F 119a, b, c—Polyb. 12.23.4; Plut. *Timol.* 36; Cic. *Ad Fam.* 5.12.7.

[3] T 4 a,b,c,d, e—Diod. 21.17.1; Polyb. 12.25d.1, 25h.1, 28.6; Plut. *De Exil.* 605C; T 6a, b—Polyb. 1.5.1, 39.8.4. Attempts have been made, without success, to establish the year when Agathocles forced him to leave Sicily; see Laqueur, *RE* VI A. 1077–78 s.v. Timaios (3); K.Meister, *Kokalos* 16 (1970) 53–59.

[4] T 5—[Lucian], *Macrob.* 22. A statement by this author is valueless as evidence when it is merely an inference from sources that we can trace.

income from family estates in Sicily. He may have returned to Sicily towards the end of his life, since obstacles were presumably removed at the death of Agathocles in 289, but no one says that he did so. We must be content with the information that he spent fifty years in Athens and wrote most, if not all, of his history there.[5]

Whatever the exact span of these fifty years, whether from 320 to 270 or ten or twenty years later, they were eventful and critical years in Athenian history. Timaeus may have thought of himself as a second Herodotus, settled in Athens after being driven into exile by a tyrant, and observing in Athens a political struggle on a greater scale than what he had witnessed in Sicily, as Athens faced Cassander, Demetrius of Phalerum, Demetrius Poliorcetes, and finally Antigonus Gonatas, after looking in vain for help from Egypt. This was not a contest between liberty and tyranny, as in Sicily, but a struggle between different kinds of autocrats, with the people of Athens trying to avoid being crushed between them. Timaeus may have felt that his opportunities of observation in Athens set him apart from his Sicilian predecessors and gave him a chance to take his place beside Herodotus and Thucydides. An attitude of this kind would explain his contempt for his predecessors.

Polybius and Plutarch will not let us believe that these opportunities made a real historian out of him. They complain that he was intolerant and arrogant, unreasonable and excessive in finding fault with his predecessors, often showing poor judgment, and that his criticism was sometimes purely malicious.[6] Since he completed his work at a time when Alexandrian literature was insisting on originality, and writers loved to display their learning, it should not surprise us if he disagreed with other historians and strove after novelty. A critical, even a quarrelsome style of scholarship would be in keeping with the literary spirit of the age.

There is no indication that he ever went to Alexandria, but this was a time when relations between Athens and the Ptolemies were close, and sympathy with the artistic tendencies of Alexandria is not unexpected in

---

[5] Timaeus announces in his thirty–fourth book that he has been there fifty years (F 34—Polyb. 12.25h). There are still more books to come; he may have returned to Sicily before writing them. The various attempts to reconstruct his biography are summarized by Brown, *Timaeus* 1–7. L. Pareti, *Sicilia antica* (Palermo 1959) 319–22, says that he studied in Syracuse in his youth and travelled extensively all over the Mediterranean; that he left Athens in 263–62 and returned to Sicily, where he was welcomed in Syracuse and made a citizen; that he published his history in instalments, eight books at a time, and revised some of the instalments after his return to Sicily, continuing to write until he was eighty. Some of this might be true, but none of it is properly attested.

[6] Plut. *Nic.*1; Polyb. 12 *passim*—T 18,19.

someone who writes in Athens. His work was appreciated, and indeed exploited by Lycophron and Apollonius of Rhodes, as will be shown. On the other hand, he offended Polybius and Plutarch, because, so far as literary taste is concerned, they belong to a different world. They cling to the ideals and fashions of the classical age and take little account of Alexandrian poetry. Despite the wide range of his literary interests and his numerous quotations, Plutarch never mentions Apollonius or Lycophron and has only a few references to Callimachus or Theocritus.[7] Polybius shows no particular interest in any poet except Homer, and he certainly did not approve of prose literature that seemed to ape the poets.[8] He can be just as intolerant as the authors whom he criticizes, and so can Plutarch when his sensibilities are offended. But Plutarch is rarely, if ever, malicious, and it is easier to sympathize with him than with Polybius. We may find some of his judgments of character and some of his accounts of events preferable to what Timaeus offers.

For a writer of history to achieve popularity in the early third century it was not enough merely to disagree with his predecessors. He could best attract attention by making his story more "tragic," using some of the devices that earned Euripides his reputation as the "most tragic" of the dramatists. This meant telling a story that would hold the attention of readers, arouse their pity and fear by describing what was marvellous, terrible, or pitiful, with omens, portents, and dreams introduced at appropriate moments, and oracles and soothsayers giving warning of inevitable disaster. He might also appeal to the *deisidaimonia* of his readers and remind them, whenever possible, that the gods punished sacrilegious men who had no respect for sacred things or divine precepts. Polybius, highly irritated that Timaeus should adopt this pietistic approach to history (which was of course an old-fashioned convention), accused him of "debased superstition and unmanly miracle-mongering,"[9] but he seems not to be equally offended by Timaeus' conventional rhetoric when he insists on "paradoxical happenings," "great prosperity pulled down," "high hopes disappointed," or comments on the misery of helpless captives who bewail their lot when a city falls into the hands of the enemy and is mercilessly looted.[10] There are many other similar *topoi*. One can only ask if Timaeus' readers accepted

[7] For references, see W.C. Helmbold and E. O'Neil, *Plutarch's Quotations* (APA Philological Monographs 19, 1959).

[8] F.W. Walbank, *Polybius* (Berkeley 1972) 32–39.

[9] T 19—Polyb. 12.24.5: ἐν δὲ ταῖς ἰδίαις ἀποφάσεσιν ἐνυπνίων καὶ τεράτων καὶ μύθων ἀπιθάνων καὶ συλλήβδην δεισιδαιμονίας ἀγεννοῦς καὶ τερατείας γυναικώδους ἐστὶ πλήρης.

[10] For good examples see Diod. 13 *passim*.

this kind of rhetorical pathos without demur as readily as readers of Charles Dickens must have accepted it in his novels when they first appeared.

It is no surprise that Timaeus gave speeches to many of his characters and described many debates in which different proposals were made by opposing speakers. Thucydides had set the tradition that later writers followed. But whereas Thucydides must have heard some of the original speeches and reports of others, so that he could claim to reproduce the general sense of what had been said or at least work out "what they must have said,"[11] Timaeus' speeches must be almost pure fiction, and those of Ephorus can hardly be different. Polybius complains not only that Timaeus' speeches are fictitious, but that they are unrealistic, ill–suited to the speaker and the occasion. He thinks they indicate now little Timaeus knew of the realities of public life, that he simply did not know what kind of argument can be used in political debate. He complains that in at least one instance he gave the speaker nothing to say except trite commonplaces.[12]

Politicians in Greek cities, except when under tyrannical rule, seem to have been quite uninhibited in their abusive remarks about one another, if the speeches of the Attic orators are a trustworthy guide. Polybius thought that historians should be restrained and circumspect in their language, and consider "what it was fitting for them to say."[13] He was deeply offended at the way in which Timaeus gave vent to his feelings in writing about men, especially tyrants, whom he disliked. It seems to have been Theopompus who started the fashion of merciless characterization, and Plutarch found such a way of writing malicious and offensive.[14]

Whatever some critics may have thought, the general reading public seems to have welcomed the "tragic" or rhetorical style of writing, which made history more popular reading. This style is well illustrated by the history of Alexander's expedition that Clitarchus wrote, which was certainly in circulation before Timaeus finished his history.[15] Clitarchus portrayed Alexander as a man of many weaknesses, a man who could be corrupted by power and luxury, adopting Oriental customs that were repellent

[11] Thuc. 1.22.

[12] Polyb. 12.25k—F 22.

[13] Polyb. 12. 14.3–4, cf. Diod. 11.92.3. Polybius is evidently adapting Timaeus' own expression.

[14] Plut. De mal. Her. 855A: the κακοήθεια of Herodotus is perhaps λειοτέρα καὶ μαλακωτέρα τῆς Θεοπόμπου.

[15] My own preference is for a late date of publication, about 280 B.C.; see The Lost Histories of Alexander (APA Philological Monographs 20, 1960) 152–54, 226–42. Others think that Clitarchus wrote about 300; see J.R. Hamilton, Plutarch, Alexander, A Commentary (Oxford 1969) liv–lv; P. Goukowsky, Diodore de Sicile, Livre XVII (Budé ed., 1976) xx–xxii; N.G.L. Hammond, Three Historians of Alexander (Cambridge 1983) 83–85.

to Greek taste, proving himself to be more Macedonian than Greek by heavy drinking and acts of ruthless cruelty, afraid of rivals even if he was fearless in battle, distrustful of generals who revealed too much talent and having them murdered if he thought they threatened his position. Clitarchus was probably not primarily interested in characterization, nor was he trying to provide moral examples such as Plutarch sought. His object was to tell a dramatic and plausible story that would attract readers.

Timaeus became famous for his severe criticism of his predecessors, and Polybius says that he criticized others for faults of which he was equally guilty himself, that he found no excuse for Callisthenes, who encouraged Alexander to believe that he had supernatural powers, though his own praise of Timoleon was so excessive that it amounted to deification.[16] Polybius thinks him totally arbitrary in his distribution of praise and blame. He took a piece of scandalous gossip about Demochares seriously, but was full of admiration for Demosthenes and his determined resistance to Philip, ignoring all accusations against him.[17] In his hatred of tyrants he abused Agathocles furiously, and he was full of scorn for Aristotle,[18] thinking evidently that a philosopher should have known better than to support and flatter an enemy of freedom like Alexander. But he was prepared to accept Gelon of Syracuse as a true national hero. While he was unwilling to give much credit to other tyrants, like Dionysius I or Agathocles, for any success they had in fighting the Carthaginians, he wanted Gelon's victory at Himera to be recognized as matching the victories of Salamis and Plataea.

Polybius, indeed, thinks that Timaeus' patriotic zeal as a Sicilian Greek is excessive, that he goes to absurd lengths trying to represent Sicily as more populous than all the rest of Greece put together and in praising its achievements, as also in praising the genius and intelligence of its political leaders and its men of learning, especially those from Syracuse.[19]

Polybius seems to be correct in his understanding of Timaeus' intention to exalt Gelon's achievements, but his criticism may not always be fair and must always be treated with caution. One might be tempted to conclude from his remarks that Timaeus gave a full and perhaps rather misleading account of the development of philosophy and science in Sicily and Magna Graecia, and of Sicily's early contributions to the study of rhetoric and the eminence of its poets. But there is no evidence that Timaeus did anything of the kind. He had much to say about the political and social influence of

[16] F 119a—Polyb. 12.23.4.
[17] F 35b—Polyb. 12.13; F 155—Polyb. 12.12b.3.
[18] F 124a, b—Polyb. 8.10.12, 12.15.1–2; F 156—12.8.1–4.
[19] F 94—Polyb. 12.26b.

Pythagoras and his followers in Croton, and he offered a biography of Pythagoras that cleared up some problems of chronology; he also had some interesting detail to report about the political importance of Empedocles in Acragas.[20] But there is no indication that he had any interest in or understanding of philosophy or mathematics or the technical details of rhetoric.[21] And it is extremely doubtful if there were other Syracusan politicians besides Gelon and Hermocrates whose efforts and talents he praised excessively.

It is not easy to find solid justification of Polybius' criticism. On the contrary, one might wish that Timaeus had offered a fuller account of intellectual and artistic achievements in the West. It is to be regretted that his description of Syracuse has not survived, and one must welcome his few remarks about architectural detail in Acragas.[22]

If Timaeus was determined to show that the achievements of the Western Greeks in 480 were equal to or greater than those of the Athenians or Spartans, it might be expected that he would make a similar effort for events of earlier centuries. The record of earlier wars against Carthaginians and Etruscans was scanty, and little is known of what Timaeus had to say about them. But when we read in Dionysius of Halicarnassus that Aristodemus, tyrant of Cyme in the late sixth century, defeated an Etruscan invasion force of half a million men, it can hardly be denied that the story was in Timaeus.[23]

Wars on this great scale were not to be expected in early times, but Greek cities could boast of their greatness in other ways besides pointing to victories against heavy odds. Every city was proud of its early origin, and those that claimed to have been founded before the Trojan War would generally claim a god or at least some heroic figure as their founder. Colonial cities unfortunately could not pretend that they had been founded until the eighth or the seventh century, but they could claim that some Greek hero had been on the site of their city on his return journey from Troy, when he was blown out of his course to Italy or Sicily, and that he had claimed the land as Greek territory, perhaps even starting a settlement there of which it could be said that traces were still visible; even earlier than that, it could be argued that Heracles or Jason and Medea had been there.

---

[20] See below, pp. 160–62.

[21] He described the sensation caused in Athens by Gorgias' speech (F 137—Dion.Hal. *Lysias* 3), but this does not mean that he explained his rhetorical technique.

[22] Diod. 13.82—F 26.

[23] Dion.Hal. *AR* 7.3; cf. M. Frederiksen, ed. N. Purcell, *Campania* (British School at Rome, 1984) 96–97, where further bibliography will be found.

Identification of places mentioned in the Odyssey or elsewhere in early Greek poetry was of course the first step. "Proof" of Greek presence in pre–historic times could be provided either by some curious survival in custom or religious ritual, by remains of supposedly ancient buildings, or by Greek etymologies of place–names, however absurd by modern standards. It was extremely important for Greek cities to have mythological associations, and the colonists may have "discovered" them for themselves at quite an early date. But whether Timaeus found the stories and the "proofs" ready made for him or invented them himself, he was certainly the first to introduce many of them into literature. The Alexandrian poets, eager for novelty and *aitia,* were delighted with these new pieces of mythology, and Latin poets could accept it as natural that events of heroic times should have a setting in Italy or Sicily, that the site of the rape of Persephone, for example, should be at Enna in Sicily. References in literature, or in the scholia to Lycophron and Apollonius, name Timaeus as the source of many items, and other details can be claimed for him when they are found in authors who are known to have borrowed from him. As the next chapter will show, it is possible to recover much material from the five books that Timaeus devoted to pre–history. The history of the native peoples, Sicels and Sicans, Oenotrians and Ausones and others, also claimed his attention, and he was not deterred by the lack of a trustworthy record. Pre–history for Timaeus was something to be recovered by pure ingenuity, by appealing to "what was likely to have happened" (τὸ εἰκός).

Timaeus' treatment of the early historical period, from the first colonial foundations to the end of the sixth century, cannot be so easily described. Thanks to some fragments we know something of what he had to say about the Italian colonies, especially Locri, Croton, and Sybaris, but hardly anything survives of his account of the development of the Sicilian settlements. We cannot determine to what extent he agreed or disagreed with Ephorus and other predecessors, how much new information or misinformation he had to offer (our knowledge, as things are, is very scanty, and we should welcome any addition to it). Polybius tells us, however, that he used or at least claimed to use official records quite extensively, and that he made an effort to achieve chronological accuracy. It is the one virtue that he is prepared to admire in Timaeus: "I think we all recognize," he says, "the special characteristic of Timaeus in which he excels and which has won him recognition. I mean his great emphasis on accuracy in the matter of dates, his use of official records, and his attention to this side of his work."[24] After such a statement one might expect some examples of Ti-

---

[24] F 12—Polyb. 12.10.4: καίτοι διότι τοῦτ᾽ ἴδιόν ἐστι Τιμαίου καὶ ταύτῃ παρημίλ-

maeus' accuracy and attention to detail to be given. But with typical perversity Polybius disappoints us; he is always ready to document his complaints, but not his rare compliments.

In fact the apparent compliment here is really part of a long complaint. In the course of an argument about the origin of the colony of Locri in South Italy,[25] Polybius takes Timaeus to task for being evasive about his manner of making inquiries and in particular for speaking of a document without revealing where and how he found it. He comes close to accusing him of presenting an imaginary document in evidence—a kind of scholarly fraud of which he was probably quite capable—and he finds this vagueness particularly shocking in a man who was accustomed to investigating documents: "After all, this is the man who offers us a comparison of the Spartan ephor list (from olden times) with the Spartan king list, who compares the archon list in Athens and the list of priestesses in Argos with the list of Olympic victors, and reveals the errors that cities have made in their records, with a discrepancy amounting to three months. It was Timaeus who discovered the inscribed columns in the inner chambers of temples and the proxeny decrees inscribed in their doorways. If a document of this kind really existed, it is incredible that he did not know the details about it or that he would fail to say how he discovered it. And there is no excuse for him if he made a statement that was inexact."[26]

This kind of complaint may be valid criticism, but what we really want to know is how carefully and conscientiously Timaeus carried out his research into temple records and civic archives, and what kind of contribution he made towards establishing a trustworthy basis for dating historical events. His contemporaries were doing their best to establish an accurate chronology for Athenian history. Philochorus in his *Atthis* was careful to order events from the fifth and fourth century under each archon year, and

λῆται τοὺς ἄλλους οὑγγραφέας καὶ καθόλου τῇδέ πη ⟨τέτευχε⟩ τῆς ἀποδοχῆς (λέγω δὲ κατὰ τὴν ἐν τοῖς χρόνοις καὶ ταῖς ἀναγραφαῖς ἐπίφασιν τῆς ἀκριβείας καὶ τὴν περὶ τοῦτο τὸ μέρος ἐπιμέλειαν), δοκῶ, πάντες γιγνώσκομεν. This is the text of Pédech (Budé ed.). τέτευχε or some similar supplement is evidently needed.

[25] According to one version (which Aristotle had accepted), the colony was founded by the illegitimate sons of Locrian women, born during the Messenian War when the women formed unions with slaves during the absence of their husbands,who were fighting on the Spartan side (a parallel story to the tradition of the foundation of Tarentum). Timaeus argued against this version, and Polybius defends Aristotle.

[26] Polyb. 12.11.1—T.10: ὁ γὰρ τὰς συγκρίσεις ποιούμενος ἀνέκαθεν τῶν ἐφόρων πρὸς τοὺς βασιλεῖς τοὺς ἐν Λακεδαίμονι καὶ τοὺς ἄρχοντας τοὺς Ἀθήνησι, καὶ τὰς ἱερείας τὰς ἐν Ἄργει παραβάλλων πρὸς τοὺς Ὀλυμπιονίκας καὶ τὰς ἁμαρτίας τῶν πόλεων περὶ τὰς ἀναγραφὰς τὰς τούτων ἐξελέγχων, παρὰ τρίμηνον ἐχούσας τὸ διαφέρον, οὗτός ἐστι. καὶ μὴν ὁ τὰς ὀπισθοδόμους στήλας καὶ τὰς ἐν ταῖς φλιαῖς τῶν νεῶν προξενίας ἐξευρηκὼς Τίμαιός ἐστιν.

the Ἀρχόντων ἀναγραφή drawn up by Demetrius of Phalerum will have been available to anyone. Thucydides had preferred to date events by counting years from the start of the war and noting the different seasons of the year, but he dated the opening incident of the Peloponnesian War, the Theban attack on Plataea, by reference to the various lists: "In the fifteenth year (after the fall of Euboea and the making of the Thirty Years' Peace), when Chrysis was two years short of completing her fiftieth year as priestess in Argos, when Aenesias was ephor in Sparta, and Pythodorus still had two months to run as archon in Athens, in the sixth month after the battle of Potidaea, in early spring . . ." (2.1).

Hellanicus dated events by archon years in his *Atthis* (which Thucydides said was not accurate in its chronology [1.97]), and in his *Priestesses of Hera at Argos* he sought a basis for chronology in the Argive list. But no one tells us how much ingenuity or how much guesswork was involved in assigning actual events to the years of each archon or ephor or priestess. We have no definite evidence that anything was entered on these lists except the names of the officeholders and the length of time for which they held office; yet we cannot actually deny that some further details were added. An archon list from the Athenian agora[27] seems to have given the sequence of archons from the latter half of the sixth century, perhaps even since the time of Solon, but it is a mere list of names, and there is no clear indication that anything else was ever recorded there.[28]

In Athens, the epigraphical record of treaties with other cities and decisions made by the *ecclesia* and *boule* was available for anyone to consult. It may not have been easy to find the inscription that one was looking for, but perhaps there grew up a specialized class of archivists who could help a searcher on the Acropolis and in the various temples. Comparison of some of these inscriptions with the archon list would make it possible to establish a number of dates. We may suppose that the various historians of the fifth and fourth century, beginning with Thucydides and Hellanicus, examined inscriptions with varying degrees of industry and perseverance, even if Timaeus was the first to boast of the great pains that he took and his success in finding texts that had eluded others. He also pointed out some discrepancies of several months between one list (or calendar) and another, discrepancies which may have resulted from the practice of inserting intercalary months.[29]

[27] R. Meiggs and D. Lewis, *Greek Historical Inscriptions* (Oxford 1969) no. 6 (with full bibliography).

[28] F. Jacoby, *Atthis* (Oxford 1949) 174–76.

[29] Polyb. 12.11.1 (quoted in note 26 above).

Timaeus' Athenian contemporary Philochorus published a volume or volumes of Ἐπιγράμματα Ἀττικά. This must have been a collection of epigraphical texts, a documentary source book that could save future historians the trouble of looking out the original stelae.[30] The Συναγωγὴ τῶν ψηφισμάτων (in nine or more books) by Craterus must have appeared at about the same time, and, as the fragments show, it contained commentary as well as the actual texts. It must have been an extremely valuable source book.[31]

The Atthidographers arranged events under archon years, as numerous fragments show,[32] but Ephorus needed more information than they could give if he was to set up a chronological framework for a general Hellenic history. Diodorus, from Book XI on, if not earlier, orders the events of each year by reference to Athenian archons, even in books where he cannot be following Ephorus, but he never tells us where he found the information or how much progress Ephorus made in setting up a Panhellenic chronology such as Timaeus might have used.

Polybius says that Timaeus compared the Athenian archon list with the Spartan king list, the list of Argive priestesses, and the list of Olympic victors.[33] This might mean only that he compared the dates given in different lists for a few isolated events, or it might mean that he compiled a comprehensive chronological table.[34] And it is not clear what exactly is meant by the statement in the *Suda* that he published a list of Olympic victors, "also known as *Chronica*."[35] It seems that lists of Olympic and Pythian victors were compiled and made available to the public in the course of the fourth century. Aristotle and Callisthenes compiled a list of Pythian victors,[36] and there must have been enough epigraphical evidence

[30] *FGrH* IIIB 328 T 1.

[31] For the fragments of Craterus see *FGrH* IIIB 342, with Jacoby's good discussion (*FGrH* IIIb, pp.94–96). He thinks it possible that Philochorus' *Epigrammata* may have been the predecessor of Craterus' *Psephismata* (IIIb, Supp. i.228).

[32] E.g., Hellanicus, *FGrH* IIIB 323a F 26; Androtion, *FGrH* 324 F 40, 44, 52; Philochorus, *FGrH* 328 F 49, 54, 56, etc.

[33] Polyb. 12.11.1 (quoted in note 26 above).

[34] A. Momigliano believes that he published a comparative table of this kind, "un trattato complessivo di cronologia greca in una forma apparentemente nuova di tavole comparative" (*Riv. stor. ital.* 71 (1959) 545). See also Jacoby *FGrH* IIIb, p.538; IIIb Supp. i 382, and Brown, *Timaeus* 13, who is ready to hail the work as "a brilliant scholarly monograph."

[35] T 1—Suda s.v. Τίμαιος . . . Ὀλυμπιονίκας ἤτοι Χρονικὰ Πραξιδικά. A goddess Praxidica, "Exacter of Penalties," is known to have been recognized at Delphi, but her name is known only from later sources. It is not clear whether the title has anything to do with her. Cf. Frazer's note on Paus. 9.33.3.

[36] *FGrH* IIB 124 T 23—*SIG³* 275; M.N. Tod, *Greek Historical Inscriptions* II (Oxford 1948) no. 187. For Olympic lists (of uncertain date), see *FGrH* 257a, 415.

at Olympia, as at Delphi, to encourage anyone who wanted to make a list. It would certainly have been possible for Timaeus to compile one, whether by doing his own research at Olympia or by collating existing lists. Diodorus (5.1.3) notes Timaeus' attention to chronological detail in the same sentence in which he rebukes him for his attitude to other historians. Praise given reluctantly is good evidence. Timaeus deserves credit for some degree of independent research.

Unfortunately, the few dates that the fragments provide do not look like the result of serious investigation. Some are Olympic dates. He put the Trojan War 417 years before the first Olympiad (i.e., in 1193 B.C.), evidently reckoning from the start of the war, while Eratosthenes, who counted 407 years, must have counted from the fall of Troy.[37] He dated the return of the Heraclidae 820 years before Alexander's crossing to Asia, i.e., in 1155 B.C., about a generation after the fall of Troy, in agreement with Clitarchus, whose book he may have read. This was earlier than the date that Eratosthenes gave, but Duris counted a thousand years before the crossing. Perhaps Timaeus was happy to disagree with him.[38] His date for the foundation of Rome is unusual, 38 years before the first Olympiad (i.e., in 814 B.C.).[39] His predecessors, so far as we know them, did not allow more than two generations after Aeneas' arrival in Italy, but 814 is still two generations earlier than the date that the Romans subsequently adopted (754 B.C.). Dionysius of Halicarnassus was puzzled by Timaeus' date, and it is not clear why he chose it unless he wanted to make the foundation dates of Rome and Carthage approximately the same.[40]

These dates of events in pre-history tell us nothing of any serious chronological research. Only very few dates from later centuries are recorded in the fragments. Diodorus gives only one date in the sixth century. In describing the settlement of Lipara, where he must be following Timaeus, he says that the Cnidians and Rhodians who settled there "deter-

[37] F 125—Censorinus, *De die natal.* 21.2, with Jacoby's note.
[38] F 126—Clem. Alex. *Strom.* 1.139.4. Clement gives the various proposed dates for the Return of the Heraclidae, in years before Alexander's crossing to Asia in 335–4 B.C.: according to Phanias 715, Ephorus 735, Timaeus and Clitarchus 820, Eratosthenes 774; but according to Duris the crossing was 1000 years after the fall of Troy. Since Clement cites Timaeus elsewhere, but not Duris, his reference to Duris may be taken from Timaeus (who would welcome the chance to improve on the chronology of his contemporary).
[39] F 60—Dion.Hal. *AR* 1.74.1.
[40] *AR* 1.74.1: οὐκ οἶδ ὅτῳ κάνονι χρησάμενος, ἅμα Καρχηδόνι κτιζομένῃ γενέσθαι φησίν, ὀγδόῳ καὶ τριακοοτῷ πρότερον ἔτει τῆς πρώτης 'Ολυμπιάδος. Timaeus' figures seem not to have been reached by generation–counting, and there is no evidence that he had any faith in this method of establishing dates, though it may have been used by earlier historians of Sicily.

mined to settle in the West" in the fiftieth Olympiad (580 B.C.).[41] This may be a date taken from local tradition, not the result of calculation, and the same can be said of the date that Timaeus gives for the colony of Massalia, a hundred and twenty years before Salamis (600 B.C.).[42] He is reported to have said that the colony of Corcyra was not founded until six hundred years after the Trojan War, i.e., not until 593 B.C.,[43] which is surprising, because the more usual account regarded the settlement as part of the enterprise that led to the founding of Syracuse at least a hundred years earlier.

There was less likelihood of controversy over dates for events in the fifth and fourth centuries. Diodorus describes the refounding of Camarina by the Geloans under the year 461 (Ol. 79.4), and the scholiast on Pindar must be wrong or the text corrupt in giving Timaeus' date for this event as the forty–second Olympiad.[44] Whatever Timaeus may in fact have learnt from comparing Olympic lists with other epigraphic records, no real traces of this investigation have survived. Even if Diodorus was right to respect his concern for exact chronology, we have no substantial evidence of his work in establishing dates before the fifth century. For the fifth and fourth centuries we may suspect that he was content to rely on his Siceliot and Italiot predecessors. But how accurate their work was we cannot know, nor indeed do we know how much detailed chronological information Timaeus actually provided.

It is possible that there was far greater emphasis on chronology in his history than appears from the fragments. Fragments will not always tell us what we want to know. If Timaeus examined Athenian archon lists, and boasted about his careful investigation, he may also have had something to say about records that he examined or might have examined in Syracuse and elsewhere. Neither Polybius nor Diodorus tells us what he actually did.

We must not regard the fragments as a trustworthy guide to the whole character and content of Timaeus' work. It is only when we can look to Diodorus and Plutarch, and when we are confident that we are following him, that we acquire a better understanding of his manner and the tendency of his work. Jacoby includes a long extract from Diodorus Book V as a fragment (F 164), because there are many details here that correspond with what we are told in attested fragments, and in every chapter we find

[41] Diod. 5.9.2—F 164.

[42] F 71—Ps–Scymnus, *Perieg.* 209.

[43] F 80—Schol. Ap. Rhod. 4.1216. If the figure of 600 is not corrupt, it might be taken from Duris, who dated the Trojan War early.

[44] F 19—Schol. Pind. *Ol.* 5.19b, cf. Diod. 11.76.5.

evidence of the interests, the prejudices and the way of thinking that fragments have warned us to expect. Jacoby refrains from offering fuller commentary on this passage of Diodorus only because it would take up too much space.[45] There must have been parts of Books VI–X that would have been equally helpful. Some of the surviving fragments from these books show a clear dependence on Timaeus.

When Diodorus appears to abandon Timaeus for another source, we can turn to Plutarch's *Dion* and *Timoleon*. In Plutarch's time, as earlier, Timaeus was still the standard authority on the tyrants of Syracuse and their wars with the Carthaginians, and Plutarch was prepared to use him, even if he sometimes had to disagree with him. He was much more widely read in Greek literature than Diodorus, but even when he had the opportunity of turning to another writer for his information, Ephorus perhaps or Duris, he did not think it necessary to apologize for using Timaeus.

The history was a long work. Polybius cites a thirty–fourth book and the *Suda* a thirty–eighth (F 34, 35), and there may have been extensive digressions, some of them planned and published separately, but we know of only one, on "The Wars of Pyrrhus." Cicero speaks of this in his letter to Lucceius, suggesting that it provides a precedent for a monograph on the conspiracy of Catiline, and Dionysius of Halicarnassus says distinctly that it was a separate work.[46]

The history itself may have contained some account of Pyrrhus' wars in Italy and Sicily. Polybius tells us that it went down as far as 264 B.C. (Ol.129), and that he will begin his own history from that year.[47] He is following established precedent in starting where a predecessor left off, just as Xenophon and Theopompus began their *Hellenica* where the history of Thucydides broke off, and Callisthenes took up the narrative a few years after Theopompus' *Hellenica* ended.[48] Polybius had a good reason for beginning in 264, since the Roman landing in Sicily marked the first step in Rome's progress in becoming a great power. But he does not tell us why Timaeus stopped in that year.

We know very little about the closing sections of Timaeus' history. We

[45] *FGrH* IIIb, pp. 593–94.

[46] T 9a, b—Cic. *Ad Fam.* 5.12.2: Ut multi Graeci fecerunt, Callisthenes Phocicum bellum, Timaeus Pyrrhi, Polybius Numantinum, qui omnes a perpetuis suis historiis ea quae dixi bella separaverunt; Dion.Hal. *AR* 1.6.1: Τιμαίου τοῦ Σικελιώτου τὰ μὲν ἀρχαῖα τῶν ἱστοριῶν ἐν ταῖς κοιναῖς ἱστορίαις ἀφηγησαμένου, τοὺς δὲ πρὸς Πύρρον τὸν Ἠπειρώτην πολέμους εἰς ἰδίαν καταχωρίσαντος πραγματείαν. Polybius cites a passage ἐν τοῖς περὶ Πύρρου (12.4b—F 36), but there is no other reference to any such monograph.

[47] T 6a—Polyb. 1.5.1.

[48] *FGrH* IIB 124 T 27.

cannot estimate on what scale the later books were designed or what sort
of events they described. There are no fragments referring to any event
later than Pyrrhus' wars, and we are not entitled to say that Timaeus fore-
saw Rome's greatness or that he lived to experience Roman control of
Sicily, since we do not know how long he lived after 264. We are told only
in general terms that he gave some account of Roman history.[49] Polybius
has neither praise nor blame for his account of events in the half–century
before the outbreak of the First Punic War, but an account by a Greek from
the West would be of great interest, giving important information about the
Greek cities in Italy and balancing the rather anti–Greek version that Livy
chose to present. It is impossible to determine whether Livy had read Timaeus' account or was content to dismiss him as an unreliable witness,
sharing Polybius' prejudice against him.

Timaeus must have described how the gradual extension of Roman
power in Southern Italy affected the Greek cities there during the fifty years
from 320 to 270, not only why some of them joined Pyrrhus in fighting
against Rome, but their position as a third party during Rome's long
struggle with the Samnites. Since the later books of Diodorus have been
lost, one looks to Plutarch's *Pyrrhus* for traces of Timaeus' account. But
though Plutarch must have read it, his main source in this *Life* seems to
have been Hieronymus of Cardia.[50] It is perhaps understandable that there
are few references to this part of Timaeus' history. Not many readers in
Aegean Greece will have taken much interest in the Greeks of the West
after their cities lost their political independence and seemed to have passed
from the Greek world into the Roman.

Any Greek student of history would know that in writing about his own
times he would have to seek information from contemporaries and attempt
to reconcile their different accounts and explanations. But for earlier times
it would be enough to read the older historians, criticize them, fill in the
gaps by appeals to τὸ εἰκός, finding an occasional piece of documentary
evidence if he were lucky, that clarified this detail or that. And in dealing
with pre–historic times he would be free to exercise his imagination and
develop new theories of his own. This was how Timaeus dealt with earlier
times, with remarkable and sometimes perverse ingenuity. But for the important half–century before 264 no one tells us whether in fact he followed
the procedure that Herodotus and Thucydides recommended.

Did he return to the West before his history was completed, travel

---

[49] F 42a—Aulus Gellius, *NA* 11.1.1: Timaeus in historiis quas oratione Graeca de rebus
populi Romani composuit. Timaeus is cited for his etymology of Italia.

[50] See below, pp. 256–57.

through Sicily and Southern Italy and question persons who had played a part in public events? Or, if he never left Athens, did he talk with many visitors from the West, who could bring him information? Or did his standards fall short of those that Thucydides set himself, was he content to accept the accounts that passed from one man to another ἀβασανίστως, with merely ἀταλαίπωρος ζήτησις τῆς ἀληθείας? We may be sure that he knew these famous chapters of Thucydides (1.20–22), but we cannot answer these questions. We can only give him the benefit of the doubt, remembering that there were not yet any written accounts of these events with which he might want to quarrel and that he might have recognized the great opportunity he had of explaining to Greek readers what the extension of Roman power portended. Polybius, a hundred years later, recognized the opportunity and the obligation, and claimed to be the first to do so. His claim may be justified, but we are not bound to believe him, since he is capable of φϑόνος and ἐπιτίμησις just as well as Timaeus.

It is indeed possible to argue that Timaeus understood the rise of Rome as well as Polybius, that his hatred for tyranny made him sympathetic towards the Roman Republic, that he studied the consequences of the conflict with Pyrrhus and recognized that Rome by her victory over him was ready to take the place of the Greeks as the principal enemy of Carthage.[51] But there is no direct evidence that Timaeus favoured Rome over Pyrrhus or that he welcomed Rome's victory. And if there were Roman readers who were pleased with his account and his attitude towards Rome, no trace of their opinion has survived.

[51] A. Momigliano, "Athens in the third century B.C. and the discovery of Rome in the histories of Timaeus," *Essays in Ancient and Modern Historiography* (Oxford–Middletown, Ct. 1977) 37–66 (the original Italian version, *Riv. stor. ital* 71 [1959] 530–556 is reprinted in his *Terzo Contributo alla storia degli studi classici* [Rome 1966] 23–53); K. Hanell, *Histoire et Historiens dans l'Antiquité* (*Entretiens Hardt* 4, 1956) 150–52.

CHAPTER IV

THE PRE-GREEK INHABITANTS AND THE HEROIC AGE

No title more precise than *Historiai* is attested for Timaeus' major work, and he appears not to have made any formal division between Sicilian and Italian history, with separate books devoted to each.[1] Polybius tells us, however, that his early books were concerned with "migrations, foundings of cities, and genealogies."[2] He also tells us that there were some remarks about historiography and how it differed from oratory in the introduction to Book VI. It seems that Timaeus was provoked by something that Ephorus had said about the difficulty of writing history, and he attempted a comparison between history and oratory, arguing that history was a superior and more exacting form of literary art.[3] An argument of this kind would come naturally at this point, if this was where he began his "history" in the narrower sense, his treatment of historical times. It can be argued, therefore, that the first five books constituted a long introduction, what Jacoby, using a Polybian term, calls a προπαρασκευή.[4]

Whatever arrangement was adopted of the material in the first five books,[5] Timaeus would have to describe the migrations of the Sicans and Sicels and the various Italic peoples. Other newcomers would be the immigrants from the Aegean, the Cretans before the Trojan War (Minoans as we should call them), then the Achaean and Trojan heroes on their wanderings after the fall of Troy, and finally the Greek colonists of the eighth century. And if continuity with the heroic age was to be established, some attention to genealogy would be necessary.

We can recover many details of Timaeus' *Proparaskeue*, and we are not dependent solely on the attested fragments. We can identify extensive borrowings from him that are not specifically acknowledged anywhere.

[1] Antiochus seems to have used the titles *Sicelica* and *Italica* for different sections of his work. But when the *Suda* says that Timaeus wrote *Italica* and *Sicelica*, *Hellenica* and *Sicelica*, this probably refers to his subject matter, not to works with separate titles.

[2] T 7—Polyb. 12.26d.

[3] F 7—Polyb. 12.28.8—28a3. Polybius probably regarded any form of literary criticism as a complete waste of time, and he thought Timaeus' argument was fatuous (ἀτοπώτατον). His ill-tempered outburst is not a trustworthy guide, and does not help us to recover what Timaeus actually said.

[4] *FGrH* IIIb p.533: "Es ist der beste Name für die ersten Bücher."

[5] Little can be learnt from the references to individual books in F 1–6. The conclusions of Laqueur about the contents of particular books (*RE* VIA. 1078–79) seem to me quite unreliable, and the same must be said of Kothe, *De Timaei vita et scriptis* (Breslau 1874) 2–21.

It is not simply a matter of convincing ourselves that we can recognize the hand of Timaeus when we see it. We can count as potential borrowers from Timaeus a number of authors whose names do not appear in the text of Jacoby's *Fragmente,* though they find frequent mention in his commentary. Among them we must include some Latin poets, Virgil, Ovid, and their sources. In some instances these poets may have read the actual text of Timaeus themselves, but they will also have found many items borrowed from him in antiquarians like Varro and Cato.[6] A very important addition to the list of borrowers is the author of the pseudo–Aristotelian *Thaumasia Akousmata,* who had certainly read Timaeus.[7] Johannes Geffcken, who exploits all these sources skilfully and thoroughly, announces an excellent rule for identifying Timaean material.[8] If it is material that seems appropriate to Timaeus, revealing some characteristic that is attested elsewhere, and if it appears in two or more authors who are known to have read Timaeus, it can be identified as coming from him—if it appears, for example, in Strabo and the *Thaumasia Akousmata,* in Diodorus and Virgil, in Lycophron or Apollonius and Antigonus of Carystus. It is not necessary that the story appear in identical form in both authors, since some writers, especially poets, will have adapted it for their own purpose. Geffcken's judgment in identifying new fragments is very sound, and it will not often be necessary to disagree with him.

The special importance of Timaeus' *Proparaskeue* is that it succeeded in creating a distinct Western Greek mythology, which provided new material for poets. It is difficult to prove direct influence of Timaeus on early Roman historians, but his influence on poets is unmistakeable, first on the Greek poets of Alexandria, Lycophron, Callimachus, and Apollonius, then on the Roman poets who wanted to link the Roman past with heroic legend.[9]

Timaeus, who lived in Athens for most of his life, certainly knew as well as any Athenian the pattern of pre–history that Athenians had come to

[6] L. Moretti, "Le origines di Catone, Timeo ed Eratostene," *RFIC,* N.S.30 (1952) 289–302.

[7] Karl Müllenhoff, *Deutsche Altertumskunde* I (Berlin 1870) 426–42, was the first to recognize that this work contains many borrowings from Timaeus. See also Paul Guenther, *De ea quae inter Timaeum et Lycophronem intercedit ratione* (Leipzig 1889).

[8] *Timaios' Geographie des Westens (Philologische Untersuchungen* 13, 1892) 3: "Stimmen zwei Zeugen genau überein, so stammen beide aus Timaios, und dieser liegt uns dann vollständig vor, hat einer oder der andere etwas mehr, so spricht dies nicht gegen Timäische Quelle, sondern zeugt nur für die mehr oder minder genaue Arbeit der Excerptoren."

[9] P.M. Fraser, *Ptolemaic Alexandria* (Oxford 1972) 763–67, 772–77, notes the various places where these poets seem to be indebted to Timaeus, but since Timaeus is not himself an Alexandrian, he does not try to recover details of his narrative.

accept as "traditional." As a student of history he must have read Thucydides' *archaeologia* with special care, and he would know how evidence for events of the remote past could be found or devised by interpreting the old poets and by pointing to relics of old buildings and to topographical landmarks, mountains, and streams and hot springs and natural wonders of any sort, if they could be associated with heroic characters and their exploits. Thucydides was prepared to talk about the pre–Greek inhabitants of Attica, the Pelasgians, and the migrations of early times, insisting that the Athenians were autochthonous and giving reasons for thinking so. Though he said he was not really concerned with τὸ μυϑῶδες, he thought he knew what Attica was like in Theseus' time (2.15). And modern scholarship has followed him in supposing that the kind of traditional belief that he respected has some, if only limited, historical value.

In the West, the situation was entirely different. Greek belief about what happened before the first colonists arrived was not dependent on any kind of older tradition. If a Greek ever attempted to question Sicels or Sicans about their oral traditions, it is very doubtful if they could have told him anything about their history or even understood the meaning of his question. It is indeed probable that the colonists, with their contempt for barbarians as an inferior race, thought it pure folly even to question them. The alternative for anyone who wanted to provide Sicily with a pre–history was to seek the solution ἀπὸ τοῦ εἰκότος. And this is exactly what the early historians did, each writer giving his own version of what was "likely" or "reasonable."

Antiochus worked out an elaborate story, with Kokalos as king of the Sicans, and the Sicels as a group that broke away from the Oenotrian kingdom in Italy and migrated to Sicily. Philistus also began his history with Kokalos ruling over a Sican kingdom and Daedalus coming from Crete during his reign.[10] This had the advantage of making Sicilian history begin at about the same time as the first kings of Athens. And he maintained that the Sicans came from Spain, claiming to prove his point by saying that they took their name from a Spanish river Sicanos. Timaeus differed from him, insisting that they were autochthonous and that he could prove it. Diodorus says: "He offered quite a number of arguments to prove the antiquity of these inhabitants, but we do not think it necessary to repeat them."[11] It would be interesting to know what sort of arguments they were. What follows in Diodorus is certainly taken from Timaeus: "In early times

---

[10] See above, pp. 11–13, 23.

[11] F 38—Diod. 5.6.1. According to Thucydides (6.2.2), the Sicans considered them-

the Sicans lived in villages (κωμηδὸν ᾤκουν), establishing their cities on the hill–tops that were most secure against attack (because of the robbers); they were not organized under the rule of a king, but there was an individual who held monarchic power in each village" (5.6.2).[12]

Thus Timaeus disagreed with Philistus' story of King Kokalos. Archaeologists would agree with him that these so–called cities were merely hill–top villages and that political development was still in a primitive stage. But he is only arguing ἀπὸ τοῦ εἰκότος, remembering perhaps how Thucydides had described conditions in Attica before the synoecism (2.15).

Diodorus continues: "Originally they occupied the entire island, and sustained themselves by farming the land. But later on, after Etna erupted and started fires in several places and large quantities of lava were deposited in the fields, the result was a widespread devastation of the land; and as the fire continued to spread over a large area for a good many years, they took fright and abandoned the eastern part of Sicily, moving into the area towards the West. Then finally, many generations later, the Sicel people came from Italy, crossing the straits in a mass migration to Sicily, and settled on the land which had been abandoned by the Sicans."

In this account of the Sicel invasion, Timaeus seems to be following his predecessors. But the disastrous eruption of Etna, which drives the Sicans to the West, may have been his own idea, a rational explanation of their being only in that part of the island. Diodorus continues: "The Sicels constantly moved forward as they sought more land, plundering the border areas, and there were a number of wars between them and the Sicans, until finally they drew up agreements and settled their territorial boundaries. Then the Greeks arrived . . ." (5. 6.4–5).

It is a well–designed story, but there is no reason to think it has any value as history. All the Greek sources are agreed that the Sicels came from Italy, but the excavated relics of their civilization give no support to this view.[13] Nor is there any reason to describe the belief in Italian origins as traditional, unless it can be shown that Sicans and Sicels were likely to cherish or respect that kind of "old tradition."

---

selves autochthonous, but he is convinced (ὡς δὲ ἡ ἀλήθεια εὑρίσκεται) that they came from the River Sicanos in Spain. Timaeus is contradicting Thucydides as well as Philistus.

For Diodorus' borrowings from Timaeus in 5.2–6, see K. Meister, *Die sizilische Geschichte bei Diodor* (Munich 1967) 31–32.

[12] If they lived κωμηδόν, it makes no sense to say that they had πόλεις. Timaeus must have explained that their so–called cities were not really worthy of the name. And he must have noted the lack of any central organization to control the brigands who roamed the countryside.

[13] F. Bernabò Brea, *Sicily before the Greeks* 141–43, 164.

Dionysius of Halicarnassus tells us of the previous history of the Sicels before they left Italy, as told by Antiochus—how they were driven out by the "aboriginal" Oenotrians, and took their name as a people in turn from their kings Italos, Morges and Sikelos.[14] Dionysius was familiar with Timaeus' history and cites it more than once in his *Roman Antiquities;* if Timaeus found fault with the account of Antiochus, we might expect to hear about it. But Dionysius says nothing and other sources are equally silent. Diodorus has nothing to say about Italy in Book V, which he calls his "Island Book," but his opening chapters offer a good indication of the theme that Timaeus must have chosen for his *Proparaskeue.*

The island, Diodorus says, was originally called Trinacria, because of its shape, then Sicania after the Sican inhabitants, and finally was given the name Sicelia after the Sicels (5.2.1.). The Homeric name was Thrinacia (*Od.*12.127), but it seems Timaeus was content, like Thucydides, to interpret this as Trinacria, ὅτι τρεῖς ἄκρας ἔχει.[15] Timaeus does not hesitate to offer Greek etymologies for words used by non–Greeks, as numerous examples will show.[16] Diodorus goes on to say that the Greeks of Sicily inherited from their ancestors the belief that the island was sacred to Demeter and Kore. He adds that "the most respected of Greek historians" (though he uses the plural, he must really mean Timaeus) consider the Sicans autochthonous, and according to these writers Demeter and Kore were first seen in Sicily, and it was the first place where grain grew, because of the excellence of the soil. As evidence, he tells us, they quoted Homer's famous lines about the land of the Cyclopes,

"unsown, unploughed, they all grew here,
wheat, barley, vines,"

and they noted that some kinds of wheat were still to be found growing wild near Leontini and elsewhere.

It was near Enna, Diodorus says, in a meadow, still a beautiful place in his time, with sweet–scented wild flowers, that Pluto found Kore and carried her off to the underworld. The Roman poets have accustomed us to think of the meadow as being near Enna, but the Homeric hymn to Demeter

---

[14] *FGrH* IIIB 555 F 2—Dion. Hal. *AR* 1.12.3.

[15] F 37—Schol. Ap. Rhod. 4.965, cf. Thuc. 6.2.2; Strabo 6.2.1; Justin 4.2.1, whose geographical introduction to Sicilian history (4.1) seems to be borrowed from Timaeus, since it corresponds closely to *Mir. Ausc.* 130; see A. Enmann, *Untersuchungen über die Quellen des Pompeius Trogus* (Dorpat 1880) 128–33.

[16] Timaeus seems to suppose that Homer's Greek place–names, often for imaginary places, were actually used "in olden times" by a non–Greek population. Ephorus apparently said that the Iberians (i.e.Sicans) called Sicily Trinacria (FGrH 70 F 137b—Ps.Scymnus 264).

does not name the place or even mention Sicily, and it is not until the Hellenistic poets that the rape of Kore is associated with Enna.[17] Nor is there any reason to believe that Timaeus' predecessors mentioned the place. Indeed we can be sure that he deserves the credit for bringing Enna into the story when we find that all the details mentioned in Diodorus occur in the *Thaumasia Akousmata*. The author of this work draws extensively on Timaeus (this is the most recent author whom he appears to know), and when he is in agreement with Diodorus we can be sure that they are both following Timaeus.[18]

Sicily had been considered specially dedicated to Demeter and Kore since earlier times, but when Cicero in the *Verrines* (2.4.106) decides to emphasize the special sanctity of the island that Verres had desecrated, it is probably not because he remembers passages from Pindar,[19] but because he had been reading Timaeus, as a way of making himself familiar with Sicilian history in preparation for his term of duty in Sicily.

Apart from pious tradition, Timaeus had other reasons for pointing to the special favour that Demeter had shown the Sicilians. As a foreign resident in Athens he must have grown weary of hearing the Athenians

---

[17] Callimachus, *Hy.* 6. 29–30, fr. 228.43 (Pfeiffer); Lycophron 152, who gives Demeter the name Ἐνναία. The fourth century tragedian Carcinus says that Sicily groaned as Demeter searched for her daughter (Snell, *TGF* I 70 F 5—Diod. 5.5.1), but there is no fragment mentioning Enna.

[18] The entire passage is worth quoting, to show the correspondence with Diodorus: Ἐν τῇ Σικελίᾳ περὶ τὴν καλουμένην Ἔνναν σπήλαιόν τι λέγεται εἶναι περὶ ὃ κύκλῳ πεφυκέναι φασὶ τῶν τε ἄλλων ἀνθέων πλῆθος ἀνὰ πᾶσαν ὥραν, πολὺ δὲ μάλιστα τῶν ἴων ἀπέραντόν τινα τόπον συμπεπληρῶσθαι, ἃ τὴν σύνεγγυς χώραν εὐωδίας πληροῖ, ὥστε τοὺς κυνηγοῦντας, τῶν κυνῶν κρατουμένων ὑπὸ τῆς ὀδμῆς, ἐξαδυνατεῖν τοὺς λαγὼς ἰχνεύειν. διὰ δὲ τούτου τοῦ χάσματος ἀσυμφανής ἐστιν ὑπόνομος, καθ᾽ ὅν φασι τὴν ἁρπαγὴν ποιήσασθαι τὸν Πλοῦτον τῆς Κόρης. εὑρίσκεσθαι δέ φασιν ἐν τούτῳ τῷ τόπῳ πυροὺς οὔτε τοῖς ἐγχωρίοις ὁμοίους οἷς χρῶνται οὔτε ἄλλοις ἐπεισάκτοις, ἀλλ᾽ ἰδιότητά τινα μεγάλην ἔχοντας. καὶ τούτῳ σημειοῦνται τὸ πρώτως παρ᾽ αὐτοῖς φανῆναι πύρινον καρπόν. ὅθεν καὶ τῆς Δήμητρος ἀντιποιοῦνται, φάμενοι παρ᾽ αὐτοῖς τὴν θεὸν γεγονέναι (82). Compare especially Diod. 5.3.3: σπήλαιον εὐμέγεθες, ἔχον χάσμα κατάγειον πρὸς τὴν ἄρκτον νενευκός, δι᾽ οὗ μυθολογοῦσι τὸν Πλούτωνα μεθ᾽ ἅρματος ἐπελθόντα ποιήσασθαι τὴν ἁρπαγὴν τῆς Κόρης, τὰ δὲ ἴα καὶ τῶν ἄλλων ἀνθῶν τὰ παρεχόμενα τὴν εὐωδίαν παραδόξως δι᾽ ὅλου τοῦ ἐνιαυτοῦ παραμένειν θάλλοντα.

[19] E.g., *Py.* 12.1–2, *Nem.* 1.14. Also Bacchylides 3.1–2:

Ἀριστοκάρπου Σικελίας κρέουσαν
Δάματρα ἰοστέφανόν τε κούραν ὕμνει.

Coins of Sicily show that the cult of the goddesses was established there in the fifth century, but the chariot of Hades does not appear on coins of Enna until the third century; see G.F. Hill, *Coins of ancient Sicily* (London 1903) 178, 214–15. The evidence of the reliefs from Locri which portray the rape of Kore is more difficult to interpret, but it can hardly be argued that they point to Enna; see H. Prückner, *Die lokrischen Tonreliefs* (Mainz 1968); P. Zancani–Montuoro, "Il rapitore di Kore nel mito locrese," *Rend. accad. arch. Napoli* 29 (1955) 3–10.

boast of the gifts they had received from the goddesses: not only had Athena given them the gift of the olive, but (as Isocrates explained in the *Panegyricus*) Demeter came to Athens in her search for her daughter and gave them the gift of agriculture and her mystic secret.[20] Diodorus shows us how Timaeus allowed the Athenians only second place in the goddess' favour: they were the first people after the Sicilians to receive the gift of wheat (5.4.4).

Jacoby includes a long extract from Diodorus' fifth book in his collection as a supplementary fragment of Timaeus (F 164), and as we look further into Timaeus' treatment of the heroic age we can see that his argument about Demeter and Kore is part of a larger scheme. Demeter's gift of wheat establishes Sicily as the cradle of agriculture and civilized life, challenging the claim of Athens to that title. He also wants to show that Sicily and Italy were Greek lands long before the first Greek colonists arrived, that their land had been just as Greek as Attica from the earliest times, because Greek heroes had been there and had established claims to possession in many places. No ancient author tells us specifically that this was Timaeus' intention, but the indications are very clear.[21]

Mythological argument was taken seriously by Greek orators and historians, and presumably by members of the public also, when it affected the dignity of their city and countryside. Historians of Alexander's expedition took care to point out how Heracles and Dionysus had preceded Alexander on his route to India, preparing the way for him to take possession and for Greeks to settle there.[22] Heracles and Dionysus (like Demeter) were champions of Hellenism and civilization. Heracles' mission was to destroy monsters, eliminate barbarism and disorder, and further the progress of Greek customs. His labours took him to the ends of the earth, and in two of his original twelve labours he went to the far West, in search of the golden apples and the oxen of Geryon.

The legend of Heracles first took shape when the West was still a land of mystery to the Greeks, and there is no geographical precision in early versions. One might expect more topographical detail from the *Geryoneis* of Stesichorus. The fragments of his poem have not yet provided it,[23] but

[20] Isoc. *Paneg.* 28. On black–figure vases, Triptolemus is shown with the ear of grain in his hand, evidently to claim that this is a special gift to Athens (J.D. Beazley, *Attic Black–figure Vase–painters* [Oxford 1956] 309, no. 83).

[21] In what follows, there is little that I can add to my earlier discussion in *YCS* 24 (1975) 171–195, but I have tried to organize the argument differently.

[22] At Tyre (Plut. *Alex.* 24, Arr. *Anab.* 2.18.1), the oasis of Ammon (Callisthenes *FGrH* 124 F 14a—Strabo 17.1.43), and Aornus (Arr. *Anab.* 4.28).

[23] *P.Oxy.* XXIII. 2617, cf. M. Robertson, "*Geryoneis:* Stesichorus and the vase-painters," *CQ* 19 (1969) 207–21. See also J. de la Genière, "La famille d'Arès en Italie," in

Hecataeus and Hellanicus described how Heracles came down the length of Italy with the oxen he had brought from Spain, and they devised incidents for him on the way. Hecataeus brought him to Sicily and said the city of Motya was named after a woman who helped him track down thieves who had stolen part of his herd, and Aeschylus brought him to Himera, where he refreshed himself in the hot springs.[24] No account has survived explaining how he got the oxen all the way to Greece (some rationalized the story, saying he never went to Spain at all, that Geryon was a king in Epirus),[25] but Timaeus described his crossing of the strait from Italy to Sicily, when he grasped a bull by the horns and swam with him.[26] Scylla would have been a difficulty, and Lycophron is probably borrowing from Timaeus when he makes Heracles kill her (she is of course brought back to life by her father, so as to be there when Odysseus comes along).[27] It would be a proper task for Heracles to kill Scylla.

Lycophron also shows Heracles killing some of the Laestrygonians,[28] anticipating an exploit of Odysseus, and this too might be part of Timaeus' story. But an even better story for Timaeus' purpose was already current in the fifth century. According to Herodotus (5.43), the Spartan Dorieus had the support of an oracle when he claimed Eryx as Dorian territory, because Heracles had won the land for his Dorian descendants by defeating Eryx, the son of Aphrodite, in fair fight. Diodorus tells the story (4.23.2) in the chapter following his account of Heracles' crossing to Sicily, where he cited Timaeus. Eryx challenges Heracles to a wrestling match,[29] putting up his land as a stake, and Heracles in return stakes his herd, telling Eryx, who objects that it is too small a stake, that if he loses it he will lose his chance for immortality. After his victory he entrusts the land to the local people, who are to reap its fruits and hold it in trust until some descendant of his comes to claim it. Then he goes through the interior of the island with his cattle, fighting several battles with armies of the Sicans, and some

---

ʾΑΠΑΡΧΑΙ, *Nuove ricerche e studi in onore di P.E.Arias* I (Pisa 1982) 137–45, who tries to establish the influence of Stesichorus on contemporary vase–painting in Italy.

[24] Hellanicus, *FGrH* 4 F 111; Hecataeus *FGrH* 1 F 76,77; Aeschylus, fr. 64 (Mette).

[25] Hecataeus *FGrH* 1 F 26—Arrian, *Anab.* 2.16.5.

[26] *FGrH* 566, F 90—Diod. 4.22.6. Hot springs appeared to mark the line of his march to Eryx (4.23.1), cf. Schol. Pind. *Ol.* 12.27.

[27] Lyc. 44–49, 650–52.

[28] Lyc. 662–63. The scholiast's explanation may be taken straight out of Timaeus: τοὺς Λαιστρυγόνας λέγει· τούτους γὰρ ὁ Ἡρακλῆς κατετόξευσεν ἡνίκα ἤλαυνε τὰς βοῦς τοῦ Γηρυόνος, ὅτε ἐπεχείρησαν κατ᾽ αὐτοῦ πόλεμον . . . φασὶ δὲ τοὺς νῦν ἐν Σικελίᾳ Λεοντίνους οἰκεῖν τὴν Λαιστρυγονίαν ἣν Ὅμηρος λέγει.

[29] The story is best known from Virgil, *Aen.* 5.391–420 (where Eryx is a boxer, not a wrestler), but note also Apoll. *Bib.* 2.5.10; Paus. 3.16.4,4.36.4.

of their commanders whom he kills "enjoy heroic honours to this day, according to the account of certain writers" (4.23.5).

Jacoby is unwilling to believe that Diodorus' story of Heracles, which occupies a good part of the fourth book, is all taken from Timaeus,[30] but Diodorus must surely be following him here. In an earlier chapter (21.7) he wrote τοιαῦτα μυθολογοῦσί τινες, οἷς Τίμαιος ὁ συγγραφεὺς ἠκολούθησεν, and when he now says μυθολογοῦσί τινες he is probably still quoting Timaeus (appealing to "several sources" when he means only one).[31] Another sign of Timaean authorship is the use of Greek names for Sicans.[32] One of the Sican commanders is called Leucaspis. This name is found on a fourth century coin of Syracuse, which depicts a naked warrior with shield and spear,[33] and it is likely that Timaeus took the name from a coin or painting, knowing that Leucaspis was a local hero. His use (or misuse) of what we should call artistic or archaeological evidence will be discussed more fully later.[34]

On his journey through Italy, Heracles is supposed to pass through the volcanic area near Naples, and Diodorus cites Timaeus (F 89—4.21) for the hero's battle with the giants of the Phlegraean fields. Strabo says that one of the giants fled from the battle, but died and sank into the ground on the East coast between Bari and Brindisi, and that the spot was marked by a spring of foul–smelling water; the place was called Leuternia, after the name given to the giants, Leidernioi. This detail is certainly from Timaeus. It is in the *Thaumasia Akousmata* (97) and the name Leuternia occurs in Lycophron (978). Diodorus cites no source for the account that follows (22.1–2) of Heracles' earth–moving operations, when he blocks off Avernus from the sea and builds a causeway along the coast for his cattle, but since Lycophron and Strabo both mention the causeway,[35] we may be sure that these feats were in Timaeus.

---

[30] *FGrH* IIIb, pp. 577–78; cf. M.A. Levi, *Raccolta Lumbroso* (Milan 1925) 154–64.

[31] Cf. 5.2.4 (above, p. 57).

[32] Just as he maintained that the Sicans called Sicily Trinacria (F 37). Virgil may reflect the language of Timaeus when he says that Eryx was known *per omnem Trinacriam* (*Aen.* 5.392–93).

[33] G.F. Hill, *Coins of ancient Sicily* 109.

[34] Below, pp. 67–68. It has been argued that Timaeus found these exploits of Heracles in Stesichorus' *Geryoneis;* that these heroes are old Sican heroes whose names have been hellenized; and that Heracles' victory over them is represented in a black–figure vase from Gela; see G. Capovilla, *Raccolta Lumbroso,* 196–99, L. Pareti, *Sicilia antica,* 378–79. I cannot accept the interpretation of the Syracusan coins offered by E.J.P. Raven, "The Leucaspis type at Syracuse," *Actes du Congrès international de numismatique* (Paris 1953) 77–81, or by L. Lacroix, "Monnaies et colonisation dans l'Occident grec," *Mém. de l'Acad. roy. de Belgique,* Classe des lettres 58.2 (1965) 50–56.

[35] Lyc. 697; Strabo 5.4.6; *Mir. Ausc.* 85.

Antigonus of Carystus tells us specifically that Timaeus rejected the belief (spread by the inhabitants) that Avernus was a "birdless" (ἄοϱνος) lake.[36] This was one etymology that he refused to accept,[37] and he seems not to have added anything to the legend that the Greeks of the area had built up about Avernus as an entrance to the underworld. It was Ephorus, not Timaeus, who identified this volcanic area as the abode of Homer's Cimmerians who "never saw the sun." He argued that they were cave-dwellers and miners, who never emerged into the light of day, coming out only at night.[38]

Timaeus' Heracles is characterized quite distinctly. On his journey through Italy he fought with monsters and others that stood in the way of civilized life—Scylla, the giants, the Laestrygonians, the brutish Eryx, the barbarian Sicans. He left behind him a clear record of his achievements, a causeway, a spring still polluted by the blood of one giant, a memorial on a coin of a Sican fighter whom he had killed. And he acquired land for his Greek descendants and other Greeks to claim as their own. Here was a story that flattered the pride of the Greek colonists.

A similar pattern can be seen in Timaeus' treatment of the Argonauts. He seems to have added some new details to the strange geography of their homeward voyage. Apollonius brought them into the Mediterranean by a branch of the Danube, as Hecataeus had done,[39] but Diodorus has a different version, and (with a slight variation of his customary formula) leaves us to decide for ourselves how much of it he took from Timaeus: "Quite a number of the old historians, as well as some more recent writers, including Timaeus, say that the Argonauts carried out a most remarkable and extraordinary plan, after they had seized the golden fleece and heard that the exit from the Pontus was blocked by Aietes' ships. They sailed up the Tanais to its source, and at a certain place hauled their ships overland into another river which flowed into the ocean. Then, from these northern parts they sailed towards the West, keeping the land on their left, until they came

---

[36] F 57— Antig. Caryst. 152: ὁ δὲ Τίμαιος τοῦτο μὲν ψεῦδος ἡγεῖται εἶναι· τὰ πλεῖστα γὰϱ κατατυχεῖν τῶν εἰθισμένων παϱ' αὐτῇ διαιτᾶσθαι. ἐκεῖνο μέντοι λέγει, διότι συνδένδϱων τόπων ἐπικειμένων αὐτῇ, καὶ πολλῶν κλάδων καὶ φύλλων διὰ τὰ πνεύματα τῶν μὲν κατακλωμένων, τῶν δὲ ἀποσειομένων οὐδέν ἐστιν ἰδεῖν ἐπ' αὐτῇ ἐφεστηκός, ἀλλὰ διαμένειν καθαϱάν. If this is an accurate quotation, Timaeus must have visited Avernus himself. See also *Mir.Ausc.* 102: ὅτι δὲ οὐδὲν διίπταται ὄϱνεον αὐτὴν ψεῦδος. οἱ γὰϱ παϱαγενόμενοι λέγουσι πλῆθός τι κύκνων ἐν αὐτῇ γίνεσθαι. Already in Strabo's time the dense evergreen forest that made Avernus seem like a lake of darkness had been cut down to be used in building at Baiae (Strabo 5.4.5).

[37] But he evidently accepted Cyme ἀπὸ τῶν κυμάτων (Strabo 5.4.4; Lyc. 696).

[38] *FGrH* 70 F 134—Strabo 5.4.5.

[39] For the various older versions, see Schol. Ap.Rhod. 4.257–62, 282–91.

near Gades and so made their entrance into our sea. And they give proofs of this story . . ." (4.56—F 85).

It is probable that all this story comes from Timaeus, and that the reference to "old" and "more recent" authors is simply taken from his text by Diodorus (the "sources" to whom he refers may be totally imaginary). The "proofs" are in his best style.[40] The Celts living by the ocean are said to be specially devoted to the Dioscuri, thanks to their visit on this occasion, and many names are said to commemorate the coming of the Argonauts. The description of the voyage may have been quite lengthy, but the digression[41] would be justified when it brought the Argonauts to Elba—"they sailed into port in the island called Aethaleia, and named its harbour, the finest harbour in that area, Port Argo after their ship" (56.5).

Apollonius brought them to Elba, where they thought they would find Circe, and says that the proof of their visit is still to be seen, that the lumps of oil and mud that they scraped from their bodies after exercise (their στλεγγίσματα) can be recognized in the gleaming pebbles on the beach. The same story is told in the *Thaumasia Akousmata* and Strabo, and clearly goes back to Timaeus.[42]

He may have brought the Argonauts to Sicily,[43] and he evidently brought them past the Planctae, since the scholiast on Apollonius quotes

---

[40] Since he mentioned the Haemus (F 76) and the wedding of Jason and Medea in Corcyra (F 87), he must have said something about a voyage up the Danube and down its supposed Adriatic branch, if only to reject it, unless he brought them up the Adriatic as well as up the West coast of Italy. Geffcken, *Timaios' Geographie* 94, notes that Apollonius transfers Timaeus' "proofs" to the Celts of the Mediterranean, so that he can make use of them on his itinerary.

[41] He probably told also how the Colchians reached Istria in their pursuit of Jason and Medea (coming down the Adriatic branch of the Danube), and founded Pola and Corcyra, thinking it better not to return to Colchis and admit failure, see Strabo 5.1.9; Callimachus, *Aetia* fr. 11–12 (Pfeiffer); Ap. Rhod. 4.507–21; Lyc. 1021–36; Pliny, *NH* 2.129; Justin 32.3.13–15. Since the story appears in all these sources, everything points to Timaeus; cf. Lasserre's note on Strabo 5.1.9; P.M. Fraser, *Ptolemaic Alexandria*, 626–27.

[42] Ap. Rhod. 4.654–58, with the supplement suggested by Fränkel in his OCT edition:

ἐς Αἰθαλίην ἐπέρησαν
νῆσον, ἵνα ψηφῖσιν ἀπωμόρξαντο καμόντες
ἱδρῶ ἅλις· χροιῇ δὲ κατ' αἰγιαλοῖο κέχυνται
⟨εἴκελοι εἰσέτι νῦν γε λίθοι στλεγγίσμασι φωτῶν
ποικίλῃ⟩, ἐν δὲ σόλοι καὶ τρύχεα θέῳκελα κείνων
ἔνθα λιμὴν Ἀργαος ἐπωνυμίην πεφάτισται.

Cf. *Mir. Ausc.* 105; Strabo 5.2.6.

[43] Lycophron 874–76 has these oily pebbles, Μινύων εὐλιπῆ στλεγγίσματα, on a beach in Western Sicily, though there is no record elsewhere of an Argonaut landing there. Geffcken, *Timaios' Geographie* 24–25, insists that we are meant to think of Elba, despite the Sicilian context, but this can hardly be right.

his authority.[44] Strabo says that the sanctuary of Hera at the mouth of the Sele near Paestum was established by Jason, and this must be taken from Timaeus.[45] There is no parallel statement elsewhere, but in his next sentence Strabo notes that the island of Leucosia further to the south was named after the Siren who threw herself into the sea there. This story is also in Lycophron (722–4), and they are evidently both following the same source. If Jason lands near Paestum, the colonists can claim him as their heroic founder, just as the settlers on the Bay of Naples can claim Heracles.[46]

Other supposed Argonaut landings in Italy are beyond the area of Greek colonization—Elba, Formiae, Gaieta, Circeum. The identification of Circeum as Circe's island was made quite early. It was known to Theophrastus,[47] and there are already lines in the *Theogony* (perhaps not "genuine Hesiod") that speak of Odysseus' three sons by Circe, Agrios, Latinos, and Telegonos, "ruling over the Etruscans in a remote place, far from the Sacred Islands" (1011–16). Circeum was in Etruscan hands for a long time after the Greek settlers came to Cumae, and if it looked like an island from the sea, it was a likely place for them to choose as Circe's island, when they were looking for places where Odysseus had preceded them. Strabo (5.3.6) tells us that in his time the inhabitants were happy to show visitors "proofs" that this was Circe's island, a supposed sanctuary of Circe, an altar of Athena, and a cup left by Odysseus. In his day the little town would be proud to claim that it had its place in the *Odyssey,* but it might not have absorbed so much Greek *paideia* in Timaeus' time, and he may not ever have visited the place.

His only "proofs" of Argonaut landings at Formiae and Gaieta are foolish etymologies. In Diodorus' account the Argonauts are credited with giving the Etruscan harbour of Telamon its name, which at least sounds Greek, and giving the name Aieta (after Aietes) to Gaieta (4.56.6).[48] Strabo, however (5.3.6), announces boldly that Formiae was founded by Spartans (Λακωνικὸν κτίσμα ἐστίν), who called it Ὁρμίαι ("anchor-

---

[44] F 86—Schol. Ap.Rhod. 4.786–87.

[45] Strabo 6.1.1, ʼΙάσονος ἵδρυμα, cf. Pliny, *NH* 3.70; Solinus 2.5–7; Lasserre's note on Strabo 6.1.1.

[46] The Italian excavators of the Heraeum take this story of Jason with strange seriousness, as though it were evidence of an early (eighth century) settlement by Thessalians coming from the sea; see P. Zancani–Montuoro–U. Zanotti Bianco, *Heraion alla Foce del Sele* I (Rome 1951) 9–14.

[47] *Hist.Plant.* 5.8.3; Pliny, *NH* 3 .57.

[48] Cf. Lyc. 1274: ʼΑργοῦς τε κλεινὸν ὅρμον Αἰήτην μέγαν, and the explanations in paraphrase and scholia.

age") and gave Gaieta its name after a Laconian word for "bay" (καιάτας).⁴⁹ There is no mention of these etymologies elsewhere, and Timaeus is the likeliest source. He must be offering these supposedly Greek names and the fictitious Spartan settlement as "proof" that this country, which Greek colonists never reached, was Greek before it was Etruscan or Latin.

Strabo offers no protest except against the story that Spartans collaborated with Samnites in the settlement of their country: he thinks this must be a Tarentine fiction, "intended to flatter and win the friendship of a powerful neighbour" (5.4.12), as though the Samnites would think it an honour to be associated with Sparta. This story looks like another of Timaeus' inventions. Strabo says some of the population called themselves Pitanatae, and this is not a fiction, because coins with the legend ΠΙ [ΤΑ] ΝΑΤΑΝ ΠΕΡΙΠΟΛΟΝ have been found in Samnium, and are explained as the issue of a Tarentine outpost in Samnite territory in the late fourth century.⁵⁰ Timaeus might perhaps have seen coins like this and developed his idea of Spartans in Samnium, remembering what Herodotus had said about a Spartan Πιτανάτης λόχος, and how Thucydides had insisted there was no such a λόχος.⁵¹

Besides bringing Greek settlers at an early date into areas of Italy that must have been closed to them, Timaeus also brought them to the Lipari Islands. Diodorus' account of these islands (5.7–11) has many indications that point to Timaeus as his source. King Auson has a son Liparos, who is driven out of Italy by his brother and settles on an island which is called Lipara after him. He founds a city and starts farming on the islands. Subsequently, Aeolus, son of Hippotas, arrives and marries Liparos' daughter Cyane (it will be noted that all the names are Greek). Then when Liparos grows old and wants to return to Italy, Aeolus takes over his kingdom and organizes a little realm for him at Sorrento, where he dies and receives heroic honors. "This," says Diodorus, "is the Aeolus whom Odysseus is said to have visited, a very pious and just man and kind to visitors. He is said to have taught seafaring men the use of sails and learnt by careful observation to foretell the winds in the area from signs in the volcanic

⁴⁹ The derivation from Aeneas' nurse Caieta is known only from Virgil, *Aen.* 7.1–4. R. Munz, *Quellenkritische Untersuchungen zu Strabo's Geographie* (Diss. Basel 1918) wants to make Posidonius responsible for many of the etymologies in Strabo's Italian books. But most of them have no point except when they are offered in support of the theory that these places are Greek foundations.

⁵⁰ *BMC, Italy* 398, B.V. Head, *Historia Numorum* (2nd. ed., London 1911) 27; E.T. Salmon, *Samnium and the Samnites* (Cambridge 1967) 30, 71 n.6.

⁵¹ Hdt. 9.53; Thuc. 1.20.3.

fires. This is why the myth gives him the title 'Steward of the Winds'"
(5.7.5–7).

Aeolus receives due mention in other authors who drew upon Timaeus.
In the *Argonautica* of Apollonius, Jason and Medea are ordered to visit
him after their visit to Circe (4.760–65), and they find him on these volcanic islands, where Virgil has taught us to look for him (*Aen.* 1.52,
8.416). Strabo also makes his contribution. He says these islands are called
"Isles of Aeolus," and explains how changes in the winds can be foretold
by observing the volcanic phenomena; he accepts this rationalistic account
of Aeolus' title "Steward of the Winds" (6.2.10). He adds that Lipara was
formerly called Meligunis. According to Callimachus (*Hymn.* 3.47–49),
this was its name when the Cyclopes were there, another detail that must
have been in Timaeus.

Diodorus says that Aeolus had six sons (5.8.1), just as in Homer, and
he names them all; they become kings in different parts of Sicily, thus providing these areas with a suitable Greek pre–history. In time the dynasties
die out, and Sicels and Sicans take over the government with less satisfactory results. Then about the fiftieth Olympiad (the Olympic date is a further reminder of Timaean authorship) Cnidians and Rhodians come to the
islands and find no one living there. Their leader Pentathlos (whose name
was already given by Antiochus)[52] is said to trace his ancestry to Hippotas,
the descendant of Heracles. This may or may not be intended as a different
Hippotas from the son–in–law of Aeolus.

Timaeus provided other islands with early Greek settlers in similar
style. We are told specifically that he spoke of Boeotians settling in the
Balearic Islands,[53] and he must have also told how Sardinia was settled by
sons of Heracles, led by Iolaus.[54] The tale appears in the *Thaumasia Akousmata* (100) as well as in Strabo and Diodorus, and can therefore be attributed to him with complete confidence. Strabo (5.2.7) is quite brief, saying
that the mountain dwellers called Diagesbeis were formerly known as
Iolaeis, after Iolaus, and that Iolaus brought some of Heracles' sons to join
the Etruscans, who were already there, in developing the island. Diodorus
(4.29–30, 5.15) tells the story at greater length.[55] He explains that Iolaus

[52] F 1—Paus. 10.11.3. Pausanias may have found this reference in Timaeus. He does not
cite Antiochus elsewhere.

[53] F 66—Schol. Lyc. 633. Comparison of Lycophron's lines with Diod. 5.17–18 makes
it certain that Timaeus described the strange customs of these islands, including the training
of small boys in sling–shooting.

[54] Geffcken, *Timaios' Geographie* 55–58.

[55] Jacoby thinks that Diod. 5.15 is based on Timaeus (he includes it in F 164), but that
the account in 4.29–30 is not similar enough to come from the same source (note on F 63–

came at the express command of Heracles, with forty–one of the fifty sons borne to Heracles by the daughters of Thespius, together with a number of volunteer settlers. He says that the best land on the island is still called "Iolaean" and that Iolaus still receives heroic honours there.[56] Also, he says, Iolaus sent for Daedalus from Sicily and was helped by him in setting up the large buildings "that still survive," and that the buildings include gymnasia and law–courts. These would be the symbols of Greek *paideia* and free government, the "proof" that Greek settlers had really been there in early times, though the population had become barbarized before the Carthaginians came, as Diodorus points out.[57] The "proof" was in the archaeological remains, the *nuraghi,* which a Greek would readily identify as pre–historic and even a modern observer might think were Mycenaean, if he were not warned against such a rash conclusion.[58]

The introduction of Daedalus into the story is particularly interesting, because Philistus said that Daedalus came to Sicily in the time of the early king Kokalos.[59] We learn, from the tale told by Diodorus, that in Timaeus' version Iolaus also visited Sicily, that some of his group remained there, τοῖς Σικανοῖς καταμιγέντες (4.30.3), and that the descendants of the Thespiadae, when finally forced out of Sardinia, settled in the Cumae area (5.15.6). Elsewhere (4.77) Diodorus tells how Daedalus came to Sicily and was the architect for some of Kokalos' buildings at Camici near Acragas, and how Minos came in pursuit of him, was killed by Kokalos, and buried in a tomb with a temple built over it. The story of Daedalus' flight to Sicily and Minos' pursuit was known to Herodotus and Sophocles,[60] and one may suppose that Timaeus had seen the remains of a building which

---

64). It seems to me that Geffcken is right in his willingness to overlook the discrepancies. It cannot be expected that a source will always be reproduced accurately.

[56] Strabo 5.2.7 more cautiously says it was previously called Iolaean. Artemidorus, presumably his source here, will have tried to bring Timaeus up to date. The heroic honours for Iolaus are of course a complete fiction. Timaeus would not expect his readers to visit Sardinia and he could allow his imagination free rein. Pausanias says there were Athenians among the colonists led by Iolaus (1.29.5, 7.2.2, 9.23.1, 10.17.5).

[57] Diod. 4.30.5. Diodorus and Strabo would be aware that this story would please the Romans and seem to justify them in taking over Sardinia as part of their design to defend Greek lands against the Carthaginians.

[58] M. Guido, *Sardinia* (New York 1964) 32–33, 138; C. Zervos, *Civilisation de la Sardaigne* (Paris 1954) 43–104, who is not quite as firm as he should be in dismissing the "tradition" of Iolaus.

[59] F 1—Theon, *Progymn.* 2, p. 66 Spengel.

[60] Hdt. 7.169–70; Soph. *Kamikoi* fr. 324 (Pearson, Radt); cf. G. Pugliese–Carratelli, "Minos e Cocalos," *Kokalos* 2 (1956) 89–103, who thinks that the death of Minos in his bath, not the "boiling" of Pelias by Medea, may be represented in one of the archaic metopes from the temple in the Foce del Sele.

he thought was a pre–historic temple–tomb, and that he offered this building as "proof" of his story.[61] By making Heracles, Daedalus, and Kokalos contemporaries he established a good chronological landmark, since Heracles belonged to the generation before the Trojan War.

Some details about Sardinia are added in the *Thaumasia Akousmata* (100), that it was apparently once called Ichnussa, because its shape resembled a human footprint (ἴχνος), an etymology that might be Timaean, though he is said to have preferred the alternative name Sandaliotis ("sandal–shaped");[62] and it is supposed to have been fruitful in very early times, because Aristaeus had been king there, though before him it had been dominated by huge birds. This was a way of representing Sardinia as another cradle of civilization, the land of Aristaeus, just as Sicily was the land of Demeter.[63] Elsewhere Timaeus is recorded as explaining what "sardonic laughter" originally meant, that it had been a Sardinian custom for sons to strike their fathers dead when they thought that they had lived long enough, and that the old men were happy to die and often "met their death with laughter and cheerfulness."[64]

Timaeus appears to be ranging all over the Mediterranean in these early books, noting details of supposed pre-history, mythological associations,

---

[61] A building at Cnossos which may be a temple–tomb has long been known: for the latest description and a cautious verdict, see S. Hood, *The Minoans* (London–New York 1971) 144, Pl. 24. It is scarcely profitable to discuss what building Timaeus may actually have seen in Sicily, but there are tholos tombs (if not actually Minoan) at Sant' Angelo Muxaro near Acragas, possibly the site of Camici, and Timaeus could certainly have seen them; see L. Bernabò Brea, *Sicily before the Greeks,* 173–74; M. Guido, *Sicily, an archaeological guide* (London 1967) 102–03, 129–30; G. Becatti, "La leggenda di Dedalo," *Röm. Mitt.* 60–61 (1953–54) 30–32.

[62] F 63—Pliny, *NH* 3.85: Sardiniam ipsam Timaeus Sandaliotim appellavit ab effigie soleae, Myrsilus Ichnusam a similitudine vestigii; cf. Solinus 4.1—Sallust *Hist.* 2, fr.4 (Maurenbrecher): Sardinia quoque, quam apud Timaeum Sandaliotim legimus, Ichnusam apud Crispum. Timaeus may have given both names, perhaps also adding that the name Sardo was derived from Sardus, a son of Heracles.

[63] See Diod. 4.82.4 for Aristaeus' introduction of agriculture into Sardinia and his subsequent visit to Sicily, where he is said to be honoured as a god. Jacoby, *FGrH* IIIb, p. 567 will not accept Geffcken's attribution of the Aristaeus story to Timaeus, but here too his scepticism seems excessive.

Pausanians, like Solinus 4.1, tries to put the whole story of Sardinian pre–history together (10.17), in a version that looks like a later elaboration of Timaeus (cf. Geffcken, *Timaios' Geographie* 59). First come Libyans led by Sardus (who gives the island its name), then many years later Aristaeus and his group, then Iberians led by Norax, who founded Nora and gave it his name, then finally Iolaus, with a group that included Athenians and Thespians, who founded Olbia. "Some people," says Pausanias, "maintain that Daedalus took part in Aristaeus' settlement," but he rejects this as chronologically absurd. For an attempt to extract actual history out of this paragraph see Frazer's commentary on Paus. 10.17.

[64] F 64—Schol. Plato, *Resp.* 1.377a; Tzetz. ad Lyc. 796, etc.

etymologies of local names, curious customs, real or imaginary, and their origins. Diodorus in his Island Book turns his attention to the Baliaric Islands after his discussion of Sardinia. He describes their strange customs and says they were called Gymnesiae by the Greeks, because the inhabitants went without any clothes in summer, and Baleares because they were excellent slingers, ἀπὸ βάλλειν ταῖς σφενδόναις λίθους μεγάλους (5.17.1). This etymology is what one might expect from Timaeus, and the Epitome of Livy, Book LX, supplies another important detail: "Baliares a teli missu appellati sunt aut a Balio Herculis comite, ibi relicto cum Hercules ad Geryonem navigaret."[65]

Here, then, is the formal reason why Timaeus should mention the islands: Heracles had been there when seeking the oxen of Geryon.[66] Gades, where he finally found the oxen, also earns a description. Pliny tells us that the smaller island, on which the old Phoenician city stood, was called Erythea by Ephorus, Aphrodisias by Timaeus, and that Timaeus called the larger island Cotinussa ("Wild-olive island").[67] The etymology of Erythea must also come from Timaeus, "quoniam Tyri aborigines earum orti ab Erythro mari ferebantur."

Gades was considered the western extremity of the world, and Heracles by reaching it claimed authority over all the West.[68] He must be supposed to claim the Baleares on his outward journey, sending Iolaus to claim Sardinia on his homeward journey overland, or else after his arrival in Greece. Why else, one must ask, would Timaeus take the trouble to describe even in outline Heracles' journey to the Far West or the Argonauts' visit to the shores of Italy, except to claim an ancient Greek right to this territory as established by these heroes?

It would be in the final stage of Heracles' journey that his son Hyllus was sent to colonize the Illyrians and give the people his name. Pseudo-Scymnus, citing Timaeus and Eratosthenes, shows the usual pattern of Timaeus. The barbarized Hylli of the Hyllic Chersonese are said to be originally a Greek people, settled there by Hyllus:

ἑξῆς δὲ μεγάλη χερρόνησος Ὑλλική,
πρὸς τὴν Πελοπόννησόν τι ἐξισουμένη.
πόλεις δ' ἐν αὐτῇ φασὶ πέντε καὶ δέκα

---

[65] Like Virgil, Livy can hardly avoid including details that must come ultimately from Timaeus, though it would be hard to find evidence that he actually read Timaeus' history.

[66] *Mir. Ausc.* 88.

[67] F 67— Pliny, *NH* 4.120.

[68] Cf. *Mir. Ausc.* 100, where Heracles is represented as πάσης τῆς πρὸς ἑσπέραν κύριος.

Ὕλλους κατοικεῖν ὄντας Ἕλληνας γένει·
τὸν Ἡρακλέους γὰρ Ὕλλον οἰκιστὴν λαβεῖν,
ἐκβαρβαρωθῆναι δὲ τούτους τῷ χρόνῳ
τοῖς ἔθνεσιν ἱστοροῦσι τοῖς τῶν πλησίον,
ὥς φασι Τίμαιός τε καὶ Ἐρατοσθένης (405–12—F 77).

Various references show that Timaeus had something to say about places far more distant than Gades, places not only beyond the limits of Greek settlement, but beyond the limits of the known world. Why should he want to mention the rivers flowing to the Atlantic through Gaul and the tides of the ocean,[69] except in describing the return voyage of the Argonauts? Why mention Thule and other mysterious islands of the far North, the *mare concretum* and the amber which could be used instead of wood for fuel, and all the fantastic story that Pytheas had told, except to illustrate the hardships of the Argonauts' voyage? Pliny tells us that Timaeus believed Pytheas' story.[70] But there is no reason to suppose that he attempted any systematic description of this distant land of the far North. We may be sure that Polybius would have been severe in his criticism if he had.

Perhaps the old controversy about amber and the Eridanus, which aroused Herodotus to express himself quite forcibly (3.115), tempted Timaeus into a digression. Diodorus, who owes much to Timaeus in the early chapters of Book V, speaks of the island of Basileia as the only source of amber (5.23.1), and goes on to tell at some length the tale of Phaethon, his fall near the mouth of the Po, and the transformation of his sisters into poplar trees who "weep tears at the same time every year, which harden and finally become a type of amber that is brighter than other varieties and is used in ceremonial mourning for the death of young people in memory of the tragedy." He says the inventors of the story are far wide of the truth, because amber is produced only on the island of Basileia. Since Strabo (5.1.9) also objects to the story of the "poplarized" Heliades by the Eridanus ("a river which does not exist, though it is said to be near the Po"), it can be concluded that Timaeus told the story and rejected it. Polybius complains that "such material fit only for tragedy" should not be introduced into a history (F 68—Polyb. 2.16.13).

Diodorus' chapters on Britain are certainly not derived from Timaeus, whose description he would have discarded as hopelessly out of date.[71] A

---

[69] F 73—Aetius, *Plac.* 3.17.6.

[70] *NH* 4.94, 37.35—F 75 a, b.

[71] He may be thinking of Timaeus when he says that neither Heracles nor Dionysus nor any other heroes ever went to Britain (5.21.2). But he is very scornful of the incredible "myths" told by ancient writers about amber (5.23.1).

description of the Western Mediterranean would not have gone out of date so quickly, but there is no adequate evidence that Timaeus' introductory books contained such a description, comparable to the geographical introduction of Ephorus.[72] If he had written a description of this kind, he would have been in rivalry and conflict with Ephorus at every turn, and we should certainly have heard about it from Polybius.[73] It is true that Polybius complains about the inaccuracy of his geography and ethnography, but the complaints must be examined individually before any general conclusion is drawn from them.

For example, Polybius is very scornful of Timaeus' description of Corsica (12.3.7—F 3), in which he said that the population lived by hunting, as there was plenty of game, while cattle and sheep and goats ran wild over the island. Complete nonsense, says Polybius, and so it might be, if taken as a description of Corsica in Timaeus' own time. But was Timaeus attempting to describe the island as it was in 250 B.C., or as he imagined it to be in heroic times? He would hardly have left it as the one major island in the Western Mediterranean that was not visited by Heracles or his sons; even if he did, we might expect him to tell us what it was like before the Greek and Punic settlers arrived. Diodorus' paragraph about the island (5.13.3—14.3) offers us exactly the description that fits heroic times, an idyllic picture ("sentimental," as Geffcken calls it)[74] of noble savages, who live on meat, milk, and honey, which are in plentiful supply, practise the couvade, and "are honourable and upright in their relations with each other to a degree unknown elsewhere among barbarians." The emphasis on innocence rather than wildness is different from what we find in Polybius' report, but there is no real contradiction, if Polybius has mistaken a description of "Corsica in olden times" for a description of contemporary conditions.[75]

In the preceding paragraph, Polybius is equally severe on Timaeus' remarks about Libya, complaining that he says nothing about Libya's magnificent wild animals (elephants, lions, leopards) or the success of its inhabitants in breeding horses, cattle, and sheep: "And one might say that Timaeus was not only ill–informed about conditions in Libya, but totally thoughtless and childish, completely dependent on the out–dated reports

---

[72] Geffcken, *Timaios' Geographie,* follows Müllenhoff, who thought that Timaeus' history included a *Periegesis* of the Western Mediterranean (*Deutsche Altertumskunde* I.454).

[73] M.A. Levi, *Raccolta Lumbroso* 152–54.

[74] *Timaios' Geographie* 65–66.

[75] Strabo 5.2.7 is quite uncompromising in his description of the "savage" Corsicans, "wilder than the wild beasts."

that we have that represent Libya as a sandy, dry, and barren country" (F 81). He concludes that Timaeus must have set out quite deliberately to report the reverse of what was true. It looks like the same story again, that Timaeus was trying to describe what Libya was like before Greek or Punic settlers came, and that Polybius is finding fault because he did not offer an up-to-date description. If this is right, it means that Timaeus never attempted any such description. And if he failed to describe the Western Mediterranean as it was known in his day, one reason may be that he had not travelled extensively.

A regular geographical introduction should include the story of Greek colonization in Spain and its decline when the Carthaginians moved in. And it would have been relevant for Timaeus to describe Carthaginian expansion in Spain and in Africa. But there is no suggestion, either in Polybius or elsewhere, that he dealt with these subjects in depth. It is indeed probable that he never set foot in Carthaginian territory, and hence lacked the ability and the inclination to write about the geography of these areas or their economic and political development.[76]

On the other hand there is plentiful evidence that he took trouble to show the mythological associations of places outside the area of Greek colonization, telling what heroes had visited these places and claimed them for the Greek people. But no hero except Heracles is shown as having visited Spain. Many were driven by storms to Italy and Sicily during their *nostoi*, but Timaeus seems not to have taken any of them further afield, to Spain or Africa. Apart from Heracles' visit to the Baliares and Gades, Spain makes no appearance in the fragments or in Diodorus or Lycophron, and there is no sign of any borrowing from Timaeus in Strabo's book dealing with Spain.

Timaeus may have had more to say about Southern France, but there is no trace of any proper description, only Strabo's remark that Polybius found fault with him for saying that the Rhone had five mouths.[77] A few etymologies from Gaul are recorded. He derived the Greek name of Gaul,

---

[76] Polybius (12.28–29a—T 19, F 7) clearly thinks Timaeus should have done work in the field, instead of sitting in Athens "collecting and studying documentary material" and complaining of the labour that this involved. He goes on (28a): αὐτὸς γοῦν τηλικαύτην ὑπομεμένηκε δαπάνην καὶ κακοπάθειαν τοῦ συναγαγεῖν τὰ παρὰ Τυρίων ὑπομνήματα καὶ πολυπραγμονῆσαι τὰ Λιγύων ἔθη καὶ Κελτῶν, ἅμα δὲ τούτοις Ἰβήρων, ὥστε μηδ' ἂν αὐτὸς ἐλπίσαι μήτ' ἂν ἑτέροις ἐξηγούμενος πιστευθῆναι περὶ τούτων. This is the text adopted by Jacoby. Various emendations have been suggested, but without knowing what Timaeus actually said it is difficult to have much confidence in any of them. For discussion, see Walbank's commentary on Polyb. 12.28; Jacoby, *FGrH* IIIb, pp. 532, 543.

[77] F 70—Strabo 4.1.8, quoting Polyb. 34.10.5. But cf. Diod. 4.21.1 Ἡρακλῆς δὲ διελθὼν τήν τε τῶν Λιγύων καὶ τὴν τῶν Τυρρηνῶν χώραν.

Galatia, from Galatas, a son of the Cyclops and Galatea, and the name of Massalia from μᾱσαι ἁλιεῦ, "make fast, fisherman," the supposed command of the Phocaean steersman, using an otherwise unknown Aeolic verb, to a fisherman as the colonist's ship approached shore.[78] And we learn from Pseudo–Scymnus that he dated the foundation of Massalia a hundred and twenty years before the Battle of Salamis.[79] But Timaeus seems not to have placed any mythological incidents in Gaul, not even in the part colonized by Greeks.

Italy on the other hand, the North as well as the South, supplied the scene for many incidents. The story of Diomede claims our attention first. His adventures in Italy appear for the first time in Lycophron, and a reference to Timaeus in the scholia makes it certain that he was Lycophron's source. Earlier poets, perhaps even a poet of the epic cycle,[80] told how Aphrodite took vengeance on Diomede for wounding her on the battlefield, turning his wife Aegialeia against him, so that he had to leave Argos. Ibycus brought him into the Adriatic, "where there is an island called Diomedeia, on which he is honoured as a god," but it is Timaeus (according to the scholia on Lycophron) who brings him to Corcyra, "where he found the serpent from Scythia (the Colchian dragon) ravaging the land and killed it, using the golden shield of Glaucus, which the serpent mistook for the golden fleece. He was honoured greatly for his good deed, and set up a statue which was fashioned from the stones that he brought from Troy. The story is told by Timaeus and by Lycus in his third book."[81]

This episode is clear enough, but when one tries to piece together the whole story of Diomede's wanderings, as told by Lycophron (592–632), the sequence of events is far from clear, and two different versions of the tale seem to be confused in the explanations offered by the scholiasts. In one version, it appears, Diomede has to leave Corcyra (though no explanation is given, nothing is said of any quarrel), goes to Italy, and eventually dies there, killed by Daunus (no reason given, no word of a quarrel). His companions, grief–stricken at his death, are transformed into birds,[82] who build an unusual bird–community on the island Diomedeia; they recognize

---

[78] F 69—*Et.Magnum*, s.v. Γαλατία; F 72—Steph.Byz. s.v. Μασσαλία.

[79] Ps.–Scymn. 209— F 71.

[80] Mimnermus, fr. 22 West—Schol. Lyc. 610–14, cf. Eust. in Dion. Perieget. 483; Ibycus fr. 13 Page—Schol. Pind. *Nem.* 10.12.

[81] F 53—Schol. Lyc. 615 (Lycos, *FGrH* 570 F 3). Lycos, supposed to be Lycophron's father or adoptive father, presumably repeated what Timaeus had said. On the Diomede story, cf. Geffcken, *Timaios' Geographie* 5–9.

[82] Schol. Lyc. 592: ὕστερον δὲ ὁ Διομήδης πρὸς Δαύνου ἀνηρέθη, οἱ δὲ φίλοι αὐτοῦ κλαίοντες τὸν ἥρωα μετεβλήθησαν εἰς ὄρνεα κτλ.

the difference between Greek and barbarian, showing affection only to Greeks and allowing them to feed them with scraps from the table. In the other version, which conforms better to Lycophron's text, Diomede goes directly to Italy from Argos, as it seems, is cheated out of King Daunus' land by his half-brother Alaenus, and sees his companions transformed into birds,

πικρὰν ἑταίρων ἐπτερωμένην ἰδὼν
οἰωνόμικτον μοῖραν (594–95),

after which he retires apparently to Corcyra, where he slays the dragon and receives divine honours after his death, as described by Lycophron in the closing verses of his narrative (630–32).

For Timaeus, as the historian of Greek Italy, the heart of the story is what happens in Apulia and makes it into a Greek land. When Diomede arrives his men are horror–stricken at the sight of the Daunian women, dressed like avenging goddesses in dark clothing, carrying wands in their hands and with red paint on their faces. Timaeus must have offered some explanation, some *aition* for this strange costume, but his account of "ancient Daunian customs" seems to be lost beyond recovery.[83] Diomede helps Daunus defeat his enemies and founds the city which comes to be known as Arpi or Argyrippa, giving it the name Argos Hippion. This Greek etymology of the name of the city is what one expects of Timaeus, and the name fits Diomede, the tamer of horses.

As a reward for his services he is offered the choice of all the land or all the spoils of war, the alternative of land or λεία, like the stakes in Heracles' contest with Eryx.[84] But his half–brother Alaenus wants to marry the king's daughter Euippe (Timaeus naturally gives her a Greek name) and wants the land too. He sets himself up as arbitrator and decides against Diomede receiving any land. Diomede in his anger lays a curse on the soil, saying it shall never bear fruit unless tilled by his own descendants, and swearing that the stones, taken from the walls of Troy, that he had set up

---

[83] F 55— Schol. Lyc. 1137 ὁ δὲ Τίμαιός φησιν ὅτι Ἕλληνες ἐπειδὰν ἀπαντήσωσι ταῖς Δαυνίαις ὑπεσταλμέναις μὲν ἐσθῆτα φαιάν, ἐζωσμέναις δὲ ταινίαις πλατείαις, ὑποδεδεμέναις δὲ τὰ κοῖλα τῶν ὑποδημάτων, ἐχούσαις δὲ ἐν ταῖς χερσὶ ῥάβδον, ὑπαληλιμμέναις δὲ τὸ πρόσωπον κάθαπερ πυρρῷ τῷ χρώματι, τῶν Ποινῶν ἔννοιαν λαμβάνουσι τῶν τραγικῶν. Timaeus also described their coiffure, called "the Hector Style" (F 54—Pollux 2.29). Lycophron made much of their grim appearance, connecting it with their supposed cult of Cassandra, but it does not follow that he took this from Timaeus. An entirely different explanation is given in *Mir. Ausc.* 109.

[84] Above, p. 60. For Diomede as founder of Arpi, see Pliny, *NH* 3.104: Arpi, aliquando Argos Hippium Diomede condente, mox Argyripa dictum.

as boundary marks, must not be removed; when they are removed and thrown into the sea, they come flying back; no doubt they were "shown" in Timaeus' time, as proof that the tale was true.[85]

The transformation of Diomede's men into birds is described in Ovid's *Metamorphoses* and in a number of other places, including the *Thaumasia Akousmata*.[86] Ovid lets Diomede tell part of the story. In his version, as in Virgil's, Diomede sees the men changed into birds by Aphrodite, when they complain of her persistence in punishing him. But with their transformation her vengeance is complete. He lives on, married to the king's daughter:

> Ille quidem sub Iapyge maxima Dauno
> moenia condiderat dotaliaque arva tenebat (14.458–59),

and the situation is similar in the *Aeneid*.[87] This variation of the tale lets Diomede end his life peacefully in Italy.[88]

Of all the heroes whose wanderings took them to Italy, Odysseus was of course the most famous, and, like Heracles, he could supply sons and grandsons as founders of cities. Timaeus cannot have neglected him, but his version is cited only when it offers remarkable new details. For example, Lycophron took from him the etymology of Baiae. Baios, a steersman of Odysseus, was said to be buried there, giving his name to the place, as Misenus did to Misenum.[89] If Timaeus followed Ephorus in making Avernus the abode of the Cimmerians,[90] Baios' grave would be "proof" of the identification, because Avernus was the right distance from Circeum, a day's voyage from Circe's island, as Homer's account demanded (*Od.* 11.11–16).

---

[85] Schol. Lyc. 592, Lyc. 619–29. The provision that the descendant must be Aetolian (623) may be a later addition, like the tale told later in Lycophron (1056–66) that the Aetolians were stoned to death when they tried to claim the land.

There is no reason why Lycophron should not alter or add to Timaeus' story. None the less these apparent differences are used by E. Manni, *Kokalos* 7 [1961] 3–14, as part of his argument that Lycophron did not borrow from Timaeus anywhere. He believes that he wrote before him, not later than 279, using the work of Lycus of Rhegium, his adoptive father. It is difficult to accept so early a date, but the real weakness of his argument is that it takes no account of other indications of dependence on Timaeus apart from statements in the scholia.

[86] Ovid, *Met.* 14.457–511; *Mir. Ausc.* 79; Antig. Caryst. 172; Varro fr. 17 Peter; Pliny, *NH* 10. 126–27; Solinus 2.45–50. The story also appears, much changed, in Antoninus Liberalis, *Met.* 37.

[87] Virg. *Aen.* 8.9, 10.28–29, 11.226, 243–50.

[88] For another Apulian metamorphosis, Ovid, *Met.* 14.517–26; Ant. Lib. *Met.* 31.

[89] Lyc. 694; Strabo 5.4.6, cf. E.D. Phillips, "Odysseus in Italy," *JHS* 73 (1953) 53–67. For Misenus, see below, pp. 86–87.

[90] Above, p. 62.

Strabo says nothing of Odysseus' visit to the Pithecussae islands, which Lycophron describes (688–93), where Typho was supposed to be buried, on the volcanic "Island of the Giants." But he cites Timaeus as saying that "many strange tales were told about the Pithecussae by men of former times" (5.4.9—F 58). In his previous paragraph, Strabo mentioned the colony on the island of Ischia established by Hiero I, which had to be abandoned because of the volcanic disturbances, and he is presumably quoting from Timaeus' account of this colonial venture in one of his later books, where there would be no occasion to mention Odysseus, though a digression on the character of the island would be appropriate.[91]

Further south, near the Sybarite colony of Laus, Strabo notes a heroon of Dracon, a companion of Odysseus (6.1.1), and at Tempsa a heroon commemorating Polites, another companion (6.1.5), who was "treacherously slain by the barbarians." Dracon does not appear in Homer, but Polites is "one of the bravest and best" (*Od.* 10.224–28).

Some of Odysseus' sons by Circe were naturally expected to leave traces in Latium, and several towns within reach of Circeum claimed Telegonus as founder. The story of Praeneste told in the pseudo-Plutarchan *Parallela Minora* is very much in the manner of Timaeus. When Telegonus sets out from Circeum to find his father, he is told that when he meets farmers wearing wreaths and dancing, he should found a city there. He meets some countrymen dancing, wreathed with oak branches (πρινίνοις κλάδοις), and accordingly establishes a city there, calling it Priniston, "which the Romans calls Praeneste. The story is in Aristocles in Book III of his *Italica*" (316a).[92] Tusculum too claimed Telegonus as founder, as many Latin poets remind us.[93] Tibur did not claim a son of Odysseus as founder, but it was *Argeo positum colono* according to Horace (*Carm.* 2.6.5) and Artemidorus,[94] and Strabo calls it a Greek city as well as

---

[91] F. Sbordone, "Timeo, Strabone, e il Golfo di Napoli," *Studi classici in onore di Q.Cataudella* II (Catania 1972) 409–16.

[92] This reference may be ignored, since the authors cited in this work are probably imaginary; see K. Ziegler, *Plutarchos von Chaironeia* (Stuttgart 1949), 231–32; F. Jacoby, "Die Ueberlieferung von Ps. Plutarchs *Parallela Minora* und die Schwindelautoren," *Mnemosyne*, Ser. 3.8 (1940) 73–144.

[93] Hor. *Carm.* 3.29.8: Telegoni iuga parricidae, with Orelli's note.

[94] Steph. Byz. s.v. Τίβυρις. Cato, fr. 56 Peter—Solinus 2.8, adds the unexpected detail that it was founded by a son of Amphiaraus, to whom he gives the Latin name Catillus, who was serving as an officer in Evander's fleet. Other authors, not Timaeus, must be held responsible for other eponymi of these cities of Latium, like Catillus' son Tiburtus, who also appears in Cato's story, and Praenestos, mentioned by Stephanus s.v. Πραίνεστος, as a son of Latinus, grandson of Odysseus. Dionysius of Halicarnassus, *AR* 1.72.5, quotes the Hellenistic historian Xenagoras as saying that Rome, Antium, and Ardea were founded by three sons of

Praeneste (5.3.11). It is likely that Timaeus claimed a Greek origin for all three cities.

Homer did not bring Menelaus to Italy, but Lycophron's story of his wanderings certainly points to Timaeus:

ἥξει δ'ἀλήτης εἰς Ἰαπύγων στρατὸν
καὶ δῶρ' ἀνάψει παρθένῳ Σκυλλητίᾳ
Ταμάσσιον κρατῆρα καὶ βοάγριον
καὶ τὰς δάμαρτος ἀσκέρας εὐμάριδας.
ἥξει δὲ Σῖριν καὶ Λακινίου μυχούς,
ἐν οἷσι πόρτις ὄρχατον τεύξει θεᾷ
Ὁπλοσμίᾳ φυτοῖσιν ἐξησκημένον (852–58).

As the scholia explain, this means that Menelaus will visit Temesa (Tempsa) on the west coast of Bruttium, across the peninsula from Croton. It was a Greek city in the fifth century, apparently subject to Croton, but had been abandoned to the Bruttians in Timaeus' time.[95] Its claim to be an early Greek foundation is doubtful, and even more doubtful its identity with the Temese of the *Odyssey* (1.184), where Athena said she had gone in search of bronze.[96] His offerings there to Athena Scylletia (a crater, a shield of ox–hide, and some shoes belonging to Helen) must be supposed to survive there, "proof" that Menelaus had been a visitor, and claimed as identification of the place. Menelaus will also come to the Lacinian promontory, to Croton, where the *portis* (Thetis) will establish a garden for Hoplosmia, that is, the temple of Hera of which only one column now survives, giving its name to the Capo di Colonna.[97]

Other survivors from Troy are also supposed to visit Tempsa and Croton. Lycophron writes of the Phocians, "descendants of Naubolus," who will come to Tempsa:

Odysseus, Romus, Antias, and Ardias (*FGrH* 240 F 29). Pliny, *NH* 3.56 says Ardea was founded by Danae, but Strabo is content to call it a Rutulian foundation (5.3.5).

[95] Strabo 6.1.5, cf. J. Bérard, *La colonisation grecque de l'Italie méridionale et de la Sicile dans l'antiquité* (Paris 1957) 147–48. For the fifth century coins, see B.V. Head, *Historia Numorum* (2nd. ed. London 1911) 112. For the site, see S. Lagona, "Problemi archeologici e topografici della Calabria settentrionale," in *ΑΠΑΡΧΑΙ. Nuove ricerche e studi in onore di P.E. Arias* I (Pisa 1982) 161–62.

[96] The scholia ad Lyc. 854 never doubt the identification, though Strabo is sceptical. He says, however, that some abandoned copper mines are "shown" there, no doubt part of the "proof" of identification offered by Timaeus. Needless to say, there is no trace now that copper was ever mined or worked in this area.

[97] Hoplosmia is one of Lycophron's names for Hera and the scholia identify the πόρτις as Thetis.

τῶν Ναυβολείων δ᾽ εἰς Τέμεσσαν ἐγγόνων
ναῦται καταβλώξουσι (1067–68).

These are the Phocians listed in the Homeric catalogue (*Il*.2.517—18),

αὐτὰρ Φωκήων Σχεδίος καὶ ᾽Επίστροφος ἦρχον,
υἶες ᾽Ιφίτου μεγαθύμου Ναυβολίδαο,

whose leaders, Schedius and Epistrophus, were killed in battle (*Il*. 2.692, 17.306). Strabo (6.1.5) does not bring these Phocians to Italy; according to his source the settlers at Tempsa were Aetolians with Thoas, another group from the Homeric catalogue (2.638). He also mentions Polites, one of Odysseus' men, who was killed there.[98] Some of these details must certainly have been in Timaeus.

Croton was an Achaean colony, and it was appropriate that its heroic founders should be Achaeans returning from Troy. Their claim, as described by Strabo (6.1.12), is based on a typically Timaean etymology. The name of the river Neaethus is supposed to mean "ship–burning." A shipload of Achaeans from Troy landed there, and the Trojan women whom they had on board, when they were left unguarded, set fire to the ships so that the party was compelled to remain there. They found that the land was good, other Achaeans joined them, and the settlements took Trojan names. Thus there is good "proof" of the story and a good *aition* to explain the name of the river.[99] Strabo goes on to cite Antiochus for the story of the foundation in historical times. One may conclude that his source (Artemidorus) was following Timaeus, and that Timaeus referred to Antiochus.[100]

At least two other heroes are said to have visited the Achaean area of Italy on their return from Troy. According to Strabo (6.1.3) Petelia and

---

[98] Above, p. 76. Thoas' wanderings, as described by Lycophron, take him first to Libya, then to Epirus, εἰς ᾽Αργυρίνους καὶ Κεραυνίων νάπας (1017). Cf. Steph. Byz. s.v. ᾽Αργυρῖνοι· ἔθνος ᾽Ηπειρωτικόν, ὡς Τίμαιος καὶ Θέων καὶ Λυκόφρων (F 78). Timaeus may have digressed to describe Thoas' wanderings, perhaps disagreeing with writers who brought him to Italy.

[99] The story is not told in Lycophron, but in another context (921) he mentions the river called Nauaithos, and the scholia explain the etymology, giving names of the Trojan women, sisters of Priam; cf. Apoll. *Bib*. Epit. 6.15c.

[100] Strabo cites Antiochus most commonly in passages where he wants to compare his version with one that appears to come from Timaeus. And it is usually easiest to assume that the comparison was made by Timaeus himself.
Lycophron (1075–82) notes a quite different version of the ship–burning story. According to this story Setaea, one of the Trojan captives, was chained to a cliff, "like Prometheus," for vultures to devour, because she persuaded her companions to burn the ships, and the cliff is named after her. It is unlikely that this tale comes from Timaeus. It lacks the point that one looks for in his versions.

Crimissa were founded by Philoctetes, and Lycophron (913) confirms that "Crimissa shall receive the slayer of the firebrand" (Philoctetes, who killed the "firebrand" Paris with his bow). In the *Thaumasia Akousmata* (107) the tale is told that, when he settled at Macalla in Crotoniat territory, he dedicated his bow and arrows in the temple of Apollo there, but they were removed by the Crotoniats to their sanctuary of Apollo (where no doubt they were "shown"). It is added that he helped the Rhodian settlers who came with Tlepolemus in fighting against the barbarians and was buried by the River Sybaris.[101] The hand of Timaeus is easily discernible here, with each of the three sources contributing different detail.[102] Lycophron tells us that Philoctetes' tomb was claimed at two different sites, near the River Crathis and at Macalla,[103] and doubt over the site of a hero's tomb is characteristic of Timaeus.[104]

The story of Epeius, the builder of the Trojan horse, is in the same three sources. Strabo (6.1.14) describes Lagaria, between Thurii and Metapontum, as "a foundation of Epeius and the Phocians." It is probably a mere mistake that the place is called Gargaria in the *Thaumasia Akousmata* (108). Lycophron's account begins:

ὁ δ' ἱπποτέκτων Λαγαρίας ἐν ἀγκάλαις (930).

Like Philoctetes, Epeius needed a sanctuary where he could deposit the instruments that destroyed Troy (his tools). It was Athena who claimed them from him, and he dedicated them in the temple of Athena Hellenia or Eilenia. The name is supposed to be derived from the verb εἰλεῖσθαι, because he delayed in obeying the goddess' command and was "shut in" there as punishment—an etymology of the familiar type.[105]

There may have been many more of such stories following the same pattern. Some of them may have been attached to descriptions of colonies

---

[101] Cf. Strabo 6.1.14: "Some say that the Siritis and Sybaris on the Traeis were settled by Rhodians." He goes on to cite Antiochus (*FGrH* 555 F 11), and in 14.2.10 he notes that these Rhodian settlements are supposed to have been established many years before the first Olympiad (cf. Apoll. *Bib.*, *Epit.* 6.15b).

[102] Geffcken, *Timaios' Geographie* 18; Lasserre's note on Strabo 6.1.3. The tale of Philoctetes in Italy was evidently older than Timaeus, and there was presumably more than one version of it; see Justin 20.1.16; Cato fr. 70 Peter; L. Lacroix, "La légende de Philoctète en Italie méridionale, *Rev. belge de phil. et d'hist.* 43 (1965) 5–21.

[103] The etymology of Macalla, ἀπὸ τοῦ μαλακισθῆναι ἐν αὐτῇ Φιλοκτήτην (Schol. Lyc. 927; Steph. Byz. s.v. Μάκαλλα) is what one might expect from Timaeus.

[104] Cf. above, pp. 73–75: the two versions of Diomede's death.

[105] *Mir. Ausc.* 108. The scholia to Lycophron (947) say it was Philoctetes who established the temple and was "shut in" there. Other sources (Velleius 1.1.1; Justin 20.2.1) bring Epeius to Metapontum, instead of Lagaria "near Metapontum."

as they existed in later times, or to a discussion of the customs and traditions of a community. In particular, since Timaeus had much to say about
Sybaris, Croton, and Siris,[106] discussion of these cities could provide a
setting for such stories. It is likely enough that very often a mythical episode, some tale of heroic times, was introduced in a later book as an *aition*
in explanation of some custom, or that a curious custom of later times was
described in an earlier book as a consequence of the mythical episode.
Without a text of Timaeus, we cannot decide which alternative he may have
preferred in any particular situation.

Before he abandoned the age of mythology, Timaeus had other migra-
tions to describe besides the Greek movements of the heroic age and the
Sican and Sicel settlements in Sicily. There were various non–Greek
peoples in Italy claiming his attention. He had to decide or speculate where
they came from and when, how, and why they came to Italy. As for the
Etruscans, he followed Herodotus in accepting their Lydian origin.
Tertullian tells us plainly: "Lydos ex Asia transvenas in Etruria consedisse
Timaeus refert, duce Tyrrheno, qui fratri suo cesserat regni contentione;
exstant auctores multi."[107] Strabo (5.2.2) tells us that the Greeks called
them Tyrrheni because of this Tyrrhenus, that he was a son of Atys and a
descendant of Heracles and Omphale, and that the reason for the emigration was a famine in Lydia; that he and his brother drew lots to decide
which of them should stay behind as king and which should depart taking
the greater part of the people with him; and that after reaching Italy he
established twelve cities, declaring Tarcon (Tarquin) as their founder, the
city of Tarquinii taking its name from him. Tarquin, a precociously clever
child, was said to have been born with grey hair.

Lycophron seems to be following a similar account, but he does not
give names to the two brothers:

αὖθις δὲ κίρκοι Τμῶλον ἐκλελοιπότες (1351).[108]

Herodotus calls the two brothers Tyrsenus and Lydus,[109] but in his account
it is the second Lydian dynasty, from Agron to Candaules, that is de-

---

[106] F 44–52, cf. Chapter V.

[107] F 62—Tertull. *De Spectac.* 5. For comment, see the edition of E. Castorina (Florence
1961).

[108] Appropriate details are added in the scholia. Strabo's source must be Artemidorus,
who will be following Timaeus. The apparent difference from Tertullian's version, κλήρῳ as
compared with *regni contentione*, is of no importance. Timaeus may have left the matter in
doubt. Both versions are found in the scholia to Lycophron, the lot in one recension, "his
father's decision" in the other.

[109] Hdt. 1.7 and 94. Herodotus' contemporary Xanthus the Lydian knew Lydus and
Torrhebus (not Tyrrhenus) as sons of Atys (*FGrH* 765 F 16—Dion.Hal *AR* 1.28.2).

scended from Heracles, not the first, to which Atys belongs. If Timaeus wanted Etruria to be as Greek as southern Italy,[110] it would be important for him to make the change and insist that the Tyrrhenus who came to Italy was a descendant of Heracles.

In another passage Lycophron has a different version, in which the two leaders are Tarquin and Tyrsenus, of Mysian origin, but descendants of Heracles, sons of Telephus (1245–49). Timaeus may have offered more than one version, or the Mysian Tarquin may come from a different source altogether.[111]

For some Etruscan cities, the claim of Greek origin was made on other grounds, and Timaeus may have been the first in the field with some of these claims. Inevitably, Pisa was supposed to have been founded by Peloponnesians from Pisa in Elis. This was maintained not only by Virgil (*Aen.* 10.179) and Pliny (*NH* 3.50), but by Strabo,[112] who says (5.2.5): "Pisa is a city founded by people from Pisa in the Peloponnese, men who went to Troy with Nestor and on their return voyage were driven out of their course, some to the area of Metapontum, others to the country near Pisa."[113] Without support from Lycophron, this statement of Strabo hardly entitles us to say that Timaeus brought Nestor to Pisa, but in his discussion of Metapontum Strabo tells us (6.1.15) that, according to Antiochus, there had been an earlier settlement there before the Achaean colonists came, called Metabon, after a hero Metabos,[114] the name being later changed to Metapontum. If the story of Metapontus and Melanippe, as told by Hyginus (186), is taken from the *Melanippe Desmotis* of Euripides,[115] Metabos had been recognized as the eponymous hero of Metapontum long before the time of Timaeus.[116]

It is possible that Timaeus made Nestor the founder of Pisa, but it can-

---

[110] If Timaeus knew that the Etruscan alphabet was derived from the Greek, he might have argued that this proved them to be Greeks.

[111] No discussion of the "Etruscan question" can be attempted here.

[112] Also Justin 20.1.11. Lycophron (1359) recognizes Pisa as a pre–Etruscan settlement, but does not identify it as Greek. The scholia likewise do not commit themselves. Dion.Hal. *AR* 1.20.5 regards it as Pelasgian; Servius on *Aen.* 10.179 gives other versions; cf. Bérard, *La colonisation grecque* 326–27. Some modern scholars seem to treat these statements about early settlements with undue seriousness; see *Der kleine Pauly*, s.v. Pisae.

[113] Cf. 6.1.15 on Metapontum: Πυλίων δὲ λέγεται κτίσμα τῶν ἐξ Ἰλίου πλευσάντων μετὰ Νέοτορος.

[114] Note also the mention by Hecataeus, *FGrH* 1 F 84; cf. L. Lacroix, op.cit. (n. 34) 79–89.

[115] For this play, see T. B. L. Webster, the *Tragedies of Euripides* (London 1967) 150–55, listing earlier discussions.

[116] Strabo (6.1.15) writes: ἐνταῦθα δὲ καὶ τὸν Μετάποντον μυθεύουσι καὶ τὴν Μελανίππην τὴν δεσμῶτιν καὶ τὸν ἐξ αὐτῆς Βοιωτόν. Lasserre thinks this is a reference to

not be proved; and when Strabo (5.2.3) says that Caere, formerly known as Agylla, was thought to have been founded by Pelasgians from Thessaly, this is no proof that Timaeus brought Pelasgians and Greeks to Etruria (as Hellanicus did).[117] But Strabo goes on to tell how Caere acquired its name. When the Etruscans came to attack the town (a Greek colony!), they sent someone to inquire what its name was; and when someone from the wall cried out χαῖρε, they accepted the omen and after capturing the city called it Caere. Here was proof that the earlier city was Greek! If Timaeus told this story, it may take pride of place as the worst of all his etymologies.[118]

There is no indication that he brought heroic settlers into Liguria, and apart from Heracles' overland journey from Spain[119] he seems not to have brought them into Provence. In the north–east of Italy, on the other hand, Trojans as well as Greeks are supposed to have left their traces. Justin's account of *vestigia Graeci moris* in Italy counts Perusia, Spina, and Adria as "Greek cities," in addition to those noted in other sources, and among the Greek immigrants he counts not only the Etruscans, "who came from Lydia," but the Veneti, "who came from Troy after its capture, led by Antenor" (20.1.6–12). Antenor's story does not appear in extant Greek poetry, but Virgil knew it:

> Antenor potuit mediis elapsus Achivis
> Illyricos penetrare sinus atque intima tutus
> regna Liburnorum et fontem superare Timavi (*Aen*. 1.242–44).

Livy's opening statement seems to take it for granted that the story is familiar: "Iam primum omnium satis constat . . . Antenorem cum multitudine Enetum . . . venisse in intimum maris Hadriatici sinum" (1.1.1–2), and Pliny cites Cato's authority: "Venetos Troiana stirpe ortos auctor est Cato" (*NH* 3.130). Strabo (5.1.4) knew that opinion was divided about the

---

Timaeus, but it may equally well be to Euripides. The version of the story in Diod. 4.67.2–7 is not necessarily taken from Timaeus.

[117] *FGrH* 4 F 4. Lycophron brings Pisa and Agylla into his story, but gives no detail beyond καὶ Πῖσ' Ἀγύλλης θ' αἱ πολύρρηνοι νάπαι (1241). Cato, fr. 45, Peter, has *Teutanes quidam Graece loquentes* in the area of Pisa. Strabo (5.2.8) notices a sanctuary of Eilythyia, "a Pelasgian foundation," at Pyrgi, which was looted by Dionysius I on his way to Corsica, and further south on the coast at Regisvilla the palace of a Pelasgian ruler, who moved to Athens with the Pelasgian population. These items might be taken from Timaeus. He must also have expressed some opinion about the Falisci, an ἴδιον ἔθνος according to some authorities (Strabo 5.2.9), possibly from Chalcis (Justin 20.1.13); cf. Lasserre's notes on Strabo 5.2.8–9.

[118] Latin *caput* as the etymology of Etruscan Capua (Strabo 5.4.3) is almost as bad, and (as Lasserre says) "on peut se risquer à l'atttribuer à Timée."

[119] Above pp. 72–73.

Veneti, some thinking that they were Celts, "but others say that after the Trojan War some Eneti from Paphlagonia joined Antenor and made their way there. As evidence of this they note the concern for horse–breeding, which is no longer practised there, but used to be a respected occupation . . . and it was from this area that Dionysius, the Sicilian tyrant, imported his race–horse stud." The "proof" and the mention of Dionysius suggest Timaeus as Strabo's ultimate source here.[120] And this seems almost certain when we find that Polybius (2.17.5–6) prefers to think the Veneti are Celts (or very like Celts in their customs), and rejects contemptuously the sensational stories told about them in the τραγῳδιογράφοι (which in this context must mean "worthless historians").[121]

Justin seems to consider Lydians, Pelasgians, and Trojans as Greeks. If he is echoing the argument of Timaeus, his entire list of Greek cities probably goes back to him. Atria and Spina in particular deserve consideration, and Ravenna must be added to the list. "It is said to be a foundation of the Thessalians," is Strabo's comment (5.1.7), and he adds: "Unable to tolerate the *hybris* practised by the Etruscans, they made no objection to admitting Umbrian settlers, and it is Umbrians who are in possession now." Thus there are three distinct groups of settlers, as so often in Timaeus' accounts, with no trace of the Thessalians left.

If Dionysius established a colony or naval station at Atria, there would be a special reason to claim that this was Greek territory from ancient times.[122] Timaeus certainly pointed to heroic settlement in Istria and Dalmatia, as we can see from the reference in Pseudo–Scymnus' description of the "Hyllic Chersonese." He writes that "as Timaeus and Eratosthenes say," Hyllus, Heracles' son, established a settlement there, which became barbarized in the course of time.[123] Atria was only a πολισμάτιον in Strabo's day, but he comments: "They say that it was once a noble city" (5.1.8). A description of the city and of the Syracusan development of the Adriatic would come in a later book of Timaeus. When Strabo adds that

[120] See Lasserre's note on Strabo 5.1.4.
[121] See Walbank's note on Polyb. 2.17.6.
[122] Historians seem to be satisfied that Dionysius did establish a settlement at Atria, though the only direct evidence is *Etym.Mag.* s.v. Ἀδρίας, τὸ πέλαγος. Διονύσιος, Σικελίας τύραννος, ὃς πρότερον ἐπὶ τῇ (?) Ὀλυμπιάδι πόλιν ἔκτισεν Ἀδρίαν ἐν τῷ Ἰονίῳ κόλπῳ, ἀφ᾽ ἧς καὶ τὸ πέλαγος καλεῖται. The Olympic date (the figure is lost) may be due to Timaeus. Steph.Byz. s.v. Ἀτρία says the city was founded by Diomede and called Aithria. Some remarks in the *Thaumasia Akousmata* (80) about the fertility of the area may be traced back to Timaeus. They are repeated by Stephanus, s.v. Ἀδρία, as though it were a different city.
[123] F 77—Ps–Scymnus 407–12.

the Adriatic took its name from Atria, Timaeus may be credited with this derivation.

Spina was another place that declined in importance. It was cut off from the sea by silt, and Strabo calls it a mere village (5.1.7), as it may have been already in Timaeus' time. But he says it had once been "a noteworthy Greek city. A treasury of the people of Spina is pointed out at Delphi, and stories represent it as a sea power (ὡς θαλασσοκρατούντων)." Pliny also calls it "praevalens, ut Delphicis creditum est thesauris, condita a Diomede" (*NH* 3.120).[124] Archaeologists are sure that there was a city there before Etruscans took it over,[125] but the references to treasuries at Delphi[126] are not valid evidence. Visitors may have been shown "this is where there used to be a treasury of Spina," and this is no proof that it ever was there (there is no mention of it in Pausanias).[127] Delphic guides could give false information, and Timaeus was fully capable of inventing heroic pre–history for a city.

Polybius complains that Timaeus displays deplorable ignorance of the course of the Po,[128] and this may mean that he found his description of the changes in the water level in the delta quite unsatisfactory. He certainly disapproved of bringing in the story of Phaethon and the weeping willows by the river,[129] because this was τραγικὴ ὕλη, but his more serious complaint is that Timaeus was ignorant of the topography. Unluckily Polybius' topographical discussion, if it was ever written, has not survived in the fragments of Book XII.[130]

Finally there is Rome. Virgil and Livy (1.7) have made us familiar with the Greeks from Arcadia whom the Trojans found there and with Heracles' visit, when he killed the "bad man" Cacus, who was given a Greek name in the usual fashion. The attempt to provide Rome with a *ktisis* in heroic

[124] Cf. Ps–Scylax 17. Strabo evidently has his information from Artemidorus, cf. Steph. Byz. s.v. Σπῖνα· πόλις Ἰταλίας, ὡς Εὔδοξος καὶ Ἀρτεμίδωρος.

[125] They are still looking for the earliest city; see S. Ferri, "Spina I, Spina II, Spina III," *Atti del I Convegno di Studi Etruschi, Studi Etruschi* 25 Supp. (1959) 60–63; M. Baratta, "Il sito di Spina," *Athenaeum*, N.S. 10 (1932) 217–46; N. Alfieri–P.E. Arias, *Spina, die neuentdeckte Etruskerstadt* (Munich 1958); *Spina, Guida al museo archeologico in Ferrara* (Florence 1961); L. Braccesi, *Grecità adriatica*, 11–13.

[126] Strabo 5.2.3: "the so-called treasury of the Agyllaeans."

[127] It is, therefore, not quite accurate to say that Agylla and Spina are "connues pour avoir eu à Delphes leurs trésors," as P. de la Coste Messalière, *Au Musée de Delphes* (*BEFAR* 138, 1936) 476.

[128] 2.16.13–15—F 68.

[129] This passage of Polybius proves that the version of the Phaethon story in Diod. 5.23 is taken from Timaeus.

[130] Cf. Walbank's note on 2.16.15.

times had started in the fifth century, with Hellanicus and Antiochus,[131] and Timaeus may have reported what his predecessors had said, not necessarily agreeing with them. He seems to have picked out for himself the year when the descendants of Aeneas founded Rome, an Olympic date, thirty eight years before the first Olympiad (814 B.C.), "whatever his reasons may have been," says Dionysius of Halicarnassus,[132] sixty years (two generations?) earlier than the year that came to be accepted at Rome and earlier also than the foundation of Cumae or Syracuse, as generally recognized. If he was writing after the outbreak of the First Punic War, he may have thought it suitable to have Rome and Carthage founded at approximately the same time, but neither he nor his predecessors had any reason to flatter Roman pride. His concern with Rome must be part of his design to provide all of Italy with a suitable pre–history.

Once Circeum was identified as Circe's island, it was reasonable to argue that Rome was founded by a descendant of Odysseus and Circe. But there is no indication that Timaeus favoured this version, and it is in fact impossible to name the authors who did so.[133] Lycophron knows the Romulus and Remus story (1232–33), but he shows no interest in Evander or any other Greek settlers by the Tiber. In several places he shows familiarity with what Timaeus had to say about Rome, but he is probably drawing on passages from a later book, not from the account of the heroic period. The famous prophecy about Rome's future greatness (1226–30), whether written by Lycophron or by some other poet, can hardly be inspired by Timaeus.[134] And Strabo's brief discussion of the city (5.3.1–3) contains nothing that can be traced back to him, except for the reference to Evander and Heracles.

Since Timaeus brought so many heroes to Italy, it seems inevitable that he should bring Aeneas to the site of Rome. But the story was told with varying detail by so many authors both before and after him, that one can-

---

[131] Above, pp. 12–13.

[132] F 60—Dion.Hal. *AR* 1.74.1.

[133] Cf. Hygin.127: Circe et Telemacho natus est Latinus (cf. Hesiod, *Theog.* 1013), qui ex suo nomine Latinae linguae nomen imposuit; ex Penelope et Telegono natus est Italus, qui Italiam ex suo nomine denominavit (cf. Schol. Ap.Rhod. 4.552, where the eponymous Italic ruler Auson is called a son of Odysseus and Calypso). Also Plut. *Rom.* 2: ἄλλοι δὲ Ῥώμην, Ἰταλοῦ θυγατέρα καὶ Λευκαρίας (οἱ δὲ Τηλέφου τοῦ Ἡρακλέους), Αἰνείᾳ γαμηθεῖσαν (οἱ δ' Ἀσκανίῳ τῷ Αἰνείου), λέγουσι τοὔνομα θέσθαι τῇ πόλει· οἱ δὲ Ῥωμανόν, Ὀδυσσέως παῖδα καὶ Κίρκης, οἰκίσαι τὴν πόλιν.

[134] Cf. S. West, "Lycophron 'italicized'," *JHS* 104 (1984)127–52 for the most recent discussion of the "Roman" verses of the *Alexandra*. Timaeus cannot be the source for the strange story told in Diod. 4.21.1–4, of how Heracles was hospitably entertained at the site of Rome by Cacius and Pinarius.

not pick out a version for him with any certainty. The story of Rome, certainly, provided the elements that should have appealed to him, especially the three stages of settlement, Arcadians under Evander, Trojans under Aeneas, and finally Romans, a mixture of Greek and Trojan, so far as they are not mixed with Italian blood. But whatever he may have said about Romulus and Remus, his account has been completely overshadowed by later writers and cannot be recovered.

A few details can be seen of Timaeus' attempt to show the traces of Trojan settlement in Latium. He claimed to have information about Trojan relics preserved in temples at Lanuvium.[135] And Strabo's remarks about the area of Ardea can probably be identified as coming from him through Artemidorus: "The area was devastated by Samnites, and there are traces left of older cities which owe their fame to the visit of Aeneas and the sacred rituals which are said to have survived there from those days" (5.3.5). According to Pliny (NH 3.56), there was a city of Ardea before Aeneas' time, founded by Danae, and this sounds like something that would have interested Timaeus.

As the Romans became more anxious to establish their Trojan origin, further traces of Trojan presence in Italy were inevitably produced. Instead of the siren Leucosia, Leucasia, a niece of Aeneas, was discovered as giving her name to the island Leucosia.[136] Instead of a member of Odysseus' company called Baios, Boia, a nurse of Aeneas' companion Euximos, is made to give her name to Baiae, and Misenus, who in earlier literature is one of Odysseus' men, becomes Aeneas' trumpeter.[137]

The original identity of Misenus in early poetry is not so easy to establish. In the Tabula Iliaca, which claims to represent Ἰλίου Πέρσις κατὰ Στησίχορον, the final scene, when Aeneas, Anchises, and Ascanius board their ship, includes a man clearly identified as ΜΙΣΗΝΟΣ, who is carrying an object that might or might not be a trumpet (without Virgil to prompt us, we might not have thought of a musical instrument).[138] Does this mean

---

[135] F 59—Dion.Hal. AR 1.67.4.

[136] Dion.Hal. AR 1.53. For the siren, cf. Strabo 6.1.1; Lyc. 722–24.

[137] Likewise Caieta, Aeneas' nurse, is supposed to give her name to Gaieta (Virg. Aen. 7.1.1–4), while Strabo (5.3.6) prefers the older explanations, which can be traced to Timaeus (above, p. 64–65). See also Dion.Hal. AR 1.53 (Misenus, Caieta); Virg. Aen. 6.149–235 (Misenus); and Timaeus' version in Strabo 1.2.18, 5.4.6; Lyc. 735–37. For Baios, the companion of Odysseus, see above, p. 75; and for Boia, nurse of Euximus, Postumius Albinus. fr. 3 Peter—Servius, on Aen. 9.710. Cf. also J. Perret, Les origines de la légende troyenne à Rome (Paris 1942) 109, 117–18.

[138] The Tabula is in the Museo Capitolino in Rome. For illustration, see U. Mancuso, "La tabula Iliaca," Mem. acc. dei Lincei, classe di scienze morali, Ser. 5.14 (1911) 666–731. The artist has represented Misenus stepping down on to the beach, and if he is playing a wind

that Misenus was a Trojan as early as Stesichorus?[139] Not necessarily. The artist of the Tabula may not be representing Stesichorus' story with complete accuracy, and he may have introduced a Virgilian detail.

It can also be argued that Palinurus, familiar from Virgil (*Aen.* 5.833–71) as Aeneas' steersman who falls asleep and is lost overboard, was in earlier literature (and in Timaeus) one of Odysseus' men.[140]

There is no evidence that Timaeus brought Aeneas to Sicily; this part of Virgil's story cannot be traced to him. Heracles seems to be the only hero whom he brought to the western part of Sicily,[141] unless Lycophron is following Timaeus when he brings Menelaus to Eryx and Drepana, where he is to find (in a spot that cannot be identified by Lycophron's clues) a temple of Heracles built by the Argonauts and *stlengismata* on the beach commemorating their athletic exercise (869–76). But Timaeus may have brought Trojans there before the Trojan War. To counter Carthaginian claims to Western Sicily an early Trojan settlement at Eryx would be as valid as the presence of Greek heroes, and Lycophron's tale of the daughters of Phoenodamas (951–64) may be derived from him.

Phoenodamas had forced Laomedon to give up his daughter to be sacrificed to the sea–monster, and Laomedon had his revenge by making him surrender his three daughters, who were taken by sea to the far West and abandoned there. One of the girls was approached by the River Crimissus in the form of a dog, and she bore him a son Aegestes, who founded Egesta, Eryx, and a third city, probably Atalla or Entella. Aegestes then brought Elymus, a bastard son of Aeneas, to Sicily (965–67); the Elymi are supposed to be descended from him. Virgil is familiar with the story, and Elymus and Aegestes appear in the *Aeneid* as Helymus and Acestes.[142]

Coins of the fifth century from Egesta bear the image of a girl with a dog on the reverse, and other coins show a man with a dog. These coins have been explained as depicting the story of the River Crimissus, as proof

---

instrument, its position is more appropriate to an aulos, pointing downwards (Solinus 2.13 calls him a *tibicen*, not a trumpeter).

[139] As is maintained by J. Schmidt, *RE*, s.v. *Misenos*, and G. Radke, *Der kleine Pauly*, s.v. *Misenum*. There has been extensive and unprofitable discussion. See now A. Sadurska, *Les tables iliaques* (Warsaw 1964) 32–35; G.K. Galinsky, *Aeneas, Sicily, and Rome* (Princeton 1969) 106–13, where further bibliography will be found; N. Horsfall, *JHS* 99 (1979) 39–40.

[140] See E. Norden, P *Vergilius Maro Aeneis Buch VI* (4th ed., Darmstadt, 1957), 228–31; Perret, op.cit. (n. 137) 118–19.

[141] Above, p. 60

[142] *Aen.* 1.549–50, 5.30, 35–39. The story appears in rationalized form in Dion. Hal. *AR* 1.52. The metamorphosis of the Crimissus into a dog does not appear in Ovid's *Metamorphoses*.

that Lycophron's story is as old as the fifth century.[143] The argument loses its force when it is noticed that a similar dog appears on coins of Eryx, Palermo, and Motya, where a reference to the Crimissus would have no point.[144] Egesta, nevertheless, was claiming to be a Trojan foundation in the fifth century. Thucydides (6.2.3) says it was founded by Trojans who escaped from Troy after the Trojan War. Timaeus, indeed, according to Plutarch, explained the Athenian disaster in Sicily by saying that Heracles naturally favoured the Syracusans because of Persephone, who let him take Cerberus, and was angry with the Athenians for trying to help the Egestaeans; they were descendants of the Trojans, and he was bitterly hostile to them because of Laomedon, who had cheated him of his due reward for building the walls of Troy (F 102b—Plut. *Nic.* 1). Timaeus may have thought it worth while to explain how it happened that the Egestaeans were Trojan by descent.

The search for fragments of Timaeus' *Proparaskeue* could continue almost indefinitely, and there is always the possibility that a papyrus text will add something new or confirm some identification that has been claimed in the preceding discussion. But there is hardly need of further evidence to illustrate how great an effort he made to show that Greek heroes and their men had been in Italy and Sicily in early days, leaving traces of their presence in many places. Unlike modern archaeologists, Timaeus probably recognized no distinction between "traces of Greek presence" and "evidence of contact with Aegean Greece." If he had known how to identify fragments of pottery as Mycenaean, he would perhaps have taken them as evidence of "Greek presence," and they must have been much easier to find in Italy in his time than they are today. But they are of course evidence only of trade relations—and it is not even certain that the merchandise was carried in Greek ships.

Individual heroes have been treated separately in this chapter (Heracles, Jason, Diomede, Odysseus, Menelaus, Philoctetes), and likewise the different groups of Hellenic or supposedly Hellenic stock (Trojans, Pelasgians, and Etruscans), as well as recognized Greek *ethne*. It is not suggested that this arrangement corresponds to any order of argument adopted by Timaeus. Any attempt to recover his economy and arrangement offers only very doubtful answers.

Another difficult question concerns the author's originality and initiative. How and where did Timaeus find all these stories? We are told

---

[143] G.F. Hill, *Coins of ancient Sicily,* 86–87, Pl. VI 7 and 9; Geffcken, *Timaios' Geographie* 27; L. Pareti–L. von Matt, *Das antike Sizilien* (Würzburg n.d.) 172, Pl. 176.

[144] Cf. Lacroix, op.cit. (n. 34) 61–62, who is content to regard the dog simply as "le symbole de la chasse."

that he wrote his history during his long years of exile in Athens, and it cannot be argued that he travelled in Italy and Sicily industriously collecting local traditions. In fact Polybius finds fault with him for not doing so (12.27–28). He seems to have been a bookish writer, like the Hellenistic poets, not a man who worked in the field making inquiries or consulting others who did so. It may be presumed that the history of Antiochus was available to him, as well as that of Philistus, and other Sicilian writers also. From such sources he will have learnt much, but it cannot be proved that these writers travelled any more extensively than he did or that they collected "traditions." Even if, like them or like Herodotus, he claims to be reporting "what people say," it does not follow that τὰ λεγόμενα represent old traditions. A very large proportion of the tales that we find in Strabo or Diodorus or Lycophron cannot be traced back beyond the third century. The chances are that they were invented by some contemporary of Timaeus, if not by Timaeus himself.

It certainly does not follow that all the tales about Odysseus in Italy deserve to be called "traditional." Just because Timaeus or an earlier writer has much to say about Odysseus' presence there does not entitle us to say: "No other part of the world was so thickly scattered with Odyssean memories; Odysseus must from of old have been alive in the consciousness of Italians." Greeks will have read Homer, but few if any Latins or Samnites or Italians will have read him before the second century. It does not follow that there is "a mixed Graeco–Italian world of myth and legend" in which "the Italians made the Greek material their own." And when Timaeus seems to tell us of Odysseus' sons founding cities in Latium, this is not evidence that "it was mainly the Etruscans who, in Etruria as in Latium, during their dominance accepted Odysseus as a hero."[145]

It might be thought that the evidence of art would contradict the evidence of literature, that there would be vase–paintings or reliefs from the fifth or sixth centuries commemorating mythological incidents of which there is no literary record earlier than the third. It may be rash to state categorically that this is not so, but if there are such instances in the art of Magna Graecia, they are certainly very hard to find. If they do exist, they cannot be numerous; and any claim to have found one must be examined with particular care. A single example from Veii of a terracotta group showing Aeneas and Anchises, "dating from the early fifth century," cannot be said to prove anything.[146] Indeed, works of art from Etruscan sites, whether of Greek workmanship or based on Greek originals, cannot be

[145] E.D. Phillips, "Odysseus in Italy," *JHS* 73 (1953) 66–67.
[146] Phillips, op.cit. 58.

treated as evidence of local belief. Etruscan art seems to have been content with Greek mythological themes that had no connection with Italy. There is no indication of any Etruscan effort to give Greek mythological incidents an Italian setting.[147]

The evidence of Athenian vase–painting suggests that in Athens themes were as a rule taken from poetry, not that themes were exploited in painting before they appeared in literature. Without positive evidence, it can hardly be argued that the reverse was true in the Greek West. There is no trace of any part of the Diomede legend in the art of Apulia; and though the cult of Demeter and Kore was certainly established at an early date in Sicily, there is nothing in the Greek art of Sicily before the third century that associates the rape of Kore with Enna, or indeed with any part of Sicily.[148]

When one of these so–called "traditions" appears for the first time in an author of the third century or later, who is known to have borrowed from Timaeus, the most likely explanation is that it was invented or "discovered" by Timaeus himself or by some equally inventive predecessor. Ancient critics were quick to blame historians when they met the demands of a public which thought it fit that their city should have a creditable early history. Josephus tells us: "Later writers show Timaeus to be a liar, and everyone calls Herodotus a liar."[149] Timaeus certainly told "lies" about early times, giving pleasure no doubt to many readers who knew and appreciated what he was doing, and who knew (as Thucydides knew very well) that it was impossible to discover much about what happened in early times before the Greek colonists came to the West.

[147] See *YCS* 24 (1975) 181.

[148] A.D. Trendall, *The red–figured vases of Lucania, Campania and Sicily* I (Oxford 1967), reports no examples of the rape of Persephone or of any Heracles episode connected with Italy or of any of the adventures of Diomede or Menelaus or Philoctetes in Italy. For Medea and Jason he has only the scenes in Corinth, for Odysseus the blinding of Polyphemus and the consultation with the shade of Tiresias, without any indication of locality.

There is a coin from Enna (Hill, *Coins of ancient Sicily* 91) which shows Demeter in a four-horse chariot with a torch in her hand, and G. Zuntz, *Persephone* (Oxford 1971), takes this as meaning that she is searching for her daughter. But a torch in a speeding chariot is not necessarily a symbol of search.

[149] T 17—Josephus, *Contra Apionem* 1.16.

CHAPTER V

From the Eighth Century to the Sixth

We know remarkably little about what went on in Italy and Sicily during the eighth, seventh and sixth centuries. We might think that Timaeus' history, if it survived, would tell us not only when the various colonies were established, but why particular groups of colonists chose particular sites, whether they were looking for good land and good fishing grounds or for forests and metals, whether they were farmers or traders in search of new markets and merchandise. We might also hope to learn how the different colonies developed, what kind of relationship they worked out with the native population, how they exploited them, how well they succeeded in teaching them Greek handicrafts and Greek methods of farming. We would certainly look for a good account of the political development of each colony and some information about the kind of society that emerged, to what extent each colony retained the characteristics of its metropolis and how far its manners and customs were modified by intermarriage with other Greeks and non–Greeks. It would be particularly welcome if Timaeus could give us the kind of detail that Herodotus denies us for Aegean Greece.

The attested fragments do not encourage us in these hopes. Polybius warns us not to expect too much from Timaeus, but we must look beyond the fragments to find out how well his criticism is justified. He says that Timaeus was heterodox and quarrelsome in his accounts of colonial settlements; that he strove sometimes to offer proofs in support of mistaken versions; that he discussed local customs without any real knowledge of them, because he had not travelled extensively enough; and that his accounts of war and politics were unsatisfactory, because he had no experience or understanding of public life (12.26d–28d).

Polybius does not complain of the choice of subject matter. Timaeus certainly described how and when colonies were founded, often differing from his predecessors. He liked topographical description and had much to say about local customs, as has been shown in the preceding chapter. And he tried, with or without success, to discuss and describe war and politics. We may also assume that he often had something to say about subjects on which other sources have given us some information.

Timaeus' account of the development of the Sicilian colonies is com-

91

pletely lost. But the foundation dates for them had evidently been established by the time of Thucydides, probably by Antiochus,[1] and if he had
disputed these dates we should have heard about it.

About Italy, however, Timaeus was ready to argue with his predecessors. Strabo (5.4.4) tells us that Cumae (or Cyme, to give it its Greek name)
was founded by men from Chalcis and Cyme. He does not say whether this
was Euboean Cyme or Aeolian Cyme, but if (as seems almost certain) he
is following Ephorus, he must mean the Aeolian city.[2] He says that an
agreement was made between the leaders from the two cities, Hippocles
from Cyme and Megasthenes from Chalcis, that it would be considered a
Chalcidian foundation, but would bear the name of Cyme. He adds that
"some say it was called Cyme ἀπὸ τῶν κυμάτων," and this looks like
Timaeus quarrelling with Ephorus in his usual manner, and denying
Aeolian Cyme (the birthplace of Ephorus) any share in the foundation.
Indeed, we can go further, and suspect that Timaeus denied Cyme's claim
to be the earliest colony. Strabo, in a later passage (5.4.9), says that Ischia,
the largest of the Pithecussae Islands, was colonized by Chalcidians and
Eretrians; he says nothing of the date, but Livy (8.22) says that Ischia is
the older foundation. If this is Timaeus' version, archaeology appears to
have proved him right. The excavations on Ischia in recent years have produced convincing and abundant evidence that the island was settled, or at
least used as a trading station, as early as the eighth century,[3] and Timaeus
seems to be right if he argued that Greeks went there before they went to
Cyme (even though his own reason for saying so may be pure contentious-
ness).

Strabo explains that the settlers on Ischia prospered at first, thanks to
the good soil and the gold mines,[4] but later they suffered from *stasis*, and

---

[1] Above, pp. 14–16.

[2] Pseudo–Scymnus, who regularly follows Ephorus (cf. Jacoby, *FGrH* IIC, pp.32–33),
writes:

Κύμη, πρότερον ἦν Χαλκιδεῖς ἀπῴκισαν,
εἶτ' Αἰολεῖς.

Elsewhere it is only Chalcidians (or Chalcidians and Eretrians) that are mentioned. Cf. Dion.
Hal. *AR* 7.3.1; Pliny, *NH* 3.61; Steph. Byz. s.v. Χαλκίς. But Ephorus made constant attempts to bring fame to his native city of Aeolian Cyme. For recent discussion of Strabo's
sources here see A. Mele, "Eoli a Cuma in Opicia," Φιλίας χάριν, *Miscellanea in onore di
E.Manni* V (Rome 1980) 1519–30.

[3] See, e.g., G. Buchner, "Recent work at Pithecoussai (Ischia)," *Archaeological Reports
for 1970–71*, 63–67; D. Ridgway, "The first Western Greeks," *Greeks, Celts, and Romans*,
ed. C. and S. Hawkes (Totowa, New Jersey 1973) 1–36. For more recent reports see M.
Frederiksen, *Campania*, 63–64, and the literature cited there.

[4] δι' εὐκαρπίαν καὶ διὰ τὰ χρυσεῖα. Timaeus may have invented the gold mines, like

the settlement was eventually abandoned because of earthquakes and volcanic eruptions. This leads him on to discuss the tale that Typhon was buried there, and he cites Timaeus as mentioning the various *paradoxa* recorded by early writers (F 58). He continues: "And shortly before his time,
he says, the hill in the centre of the island called Epomeus was shaken by
earthquakes and burst into a fiery eruption. It pushed the land between
it and the water's edge out into the sea, and the area that was reduced to
ash was lifted up in the air and then crashed down typhoon–like
(τυφωνοειδῶς) on the island; the sea withdrew three stades and came
back in a wave that inundated the island and extinguished the fire. The
noise was enough to make people on the mainland run back from the sea
into the interior of Campania."

Here we have a sample of Timaeus' graphic style, describing a *paradoxon* from his own time to match the strange events of earlier days. Strabo
(5.4.5) reminds us that Ephorus was interested in the volcanic character of
the area, in Avernus, the Phlegraean fields, and the caves (which he identified as the dwellings of Homer's Cimmerians); but some topographical
and historical details noted by Strabo may be regarded as coming from
Timaeus, through Artemidorus.

Strabo describes Campania as the most fertile plain in all Italy (5.4.3),
and adds: "Antiochus says that the country was inhabited by Opici, who
are also called Ausones, but Polybius insists that in his opinion these are
two separate peoples." The reference to Antiochus is most probably taken
from Timaeus by Artemidorus,[5] and Polybius (34.11.7) will be criticizing
Timaeus for accepting the word of Antiochus. Strabo continues: "Others
say that in olden times Opici and Ausones occupied this territory, but then
it was taken over by the Sidicini, an Oscan people; they were dispossessed
by the Cymaeans, who in their turn were driven out by the Etruscans (the
plain was much sought after on account of its fertility). And the Etruscans
established twelve cities there, calling the principal one Capua, the 'head'
as it were." Who else but Timaeus, one might ask, would offer a Latin

---

the "extinct" and probably imaginary copper mines at Tempsa (Strabo 6.1.3, cf. p. 77 above,
n. 96). There is no need to emend the text or to suppose that goldsmiths' work, not mining,
is meant, as argued by P. Muriddu, *Parola del Passato* 27 (1972) 407–09. Timaeus may also
be credited with inventing the monkeys on Ischia (Strabo 13.4.6; Lycophron 691). Lasserre
(note on Strabo 5.4.9) inclines to the view that Timaeus drew upon a "Chronicle of Cyme,"
but it is very doubtful if such a chronicle existed.

[5] Some readers may think that this is an arbitrary and unnecessary assumption. But the
alternative is very difficult to accept, viz. that Strabo had access to a text of Antiochus (quite
an obscure author in his day), and that he actually compared *four* different accounts while
writing these pages—the accounts of Antiochus, Timaeus, Artemidorus, and Polybius (cf. p.
18 above).

etymology for an Etruscan city?[6] Strabo goes on: "The Etruscans degen-
erated because of their τρυφή, and just as they were driven out of the Po
valley, here they had to give way to the Samnites; and they in their turn
were driven out by the Romans." This concern with the succession of populations is also typical of Timaeus.

Any Greek writer would regard the Samnite invasion of Campania as a
disaster, resulting in barbarization, and though Timaeus may not be the
first to complain of Samnite *hybris,* he can hardly have failed to do so.
Strabo seems to reflect his language as he writes (5.4.4): "Subsequently
the Campanians became masters of the city (i.e., Cyme) and committed
many acts of *hybris* against the population. Indeed, they established unions
with the wives of the men. Nevertheless, many traces of the Greek way of
life are still preserved, both in religious practices and in their law. Some
say that Cyme is called "after the waves" (ἀπὸ τῶν κυμάτων), because
the coast in this area is rocky and exposed. There are also excellent tuna
fishing grounds here (κητεῖαι). At the base of the gulf there is a sort of
forest of shrubs that extends for many stades along the coast, waterless and
sandy, which they call the Gallinaria Forest."

The "traces of the Greek way of life" still surviving would certainly
have interested Timaeus, and the "waterless and sandy" forest is exactly
the kind of expression with which Polybius found fault (12.3.2) in his description of Libya. The description of Misenum, Baiae, and Avernus,
which follows in Strabo, has already been discussed.[7] If the etymology of
Puteoli "from the wells" (ἀπὸ τῶν φρεάτων, 5.4.6) is due to Timaeus,
one can say that this time he is right. And when Strabo connects the hot
springs and the smoke with the lightning strokes that killed the giants, he
is certainly following Timaeus (Diodorus actually cites Timaeus for this).[8]

From Puteoli Strabo moves on to Naples (5.4.7). After describing how
it was founded, he mentions the games held in honour of the Siren
Parthenope in obedience to an oracle, and he says that her tomb was
"shown" there.[9] Lycophron describes how her body will be washed ashore
at the site of the city, and how a monument will be set up and an annual
festival established in her honour (719–21), and a few lines later comes the
prediction that an Athenian admiral,

---

[6] Cf. p. 82 above, 118. For the Timaean origin of Strabo 5.4.3, see Lasserre's note.

[7] Above, pp. 61–62, 75.

[8] F 89—Diod. 4.21.6–7.

[9] When Strabo uses this expression, he is repeating what he has read, not describing what
he has seen; compare his remarks about the treasury of Spina which was "shown" at Delphi
(5.1.7), and his report of the statue with closed eyes at Siris (6.1.14).

κραίνων ἁπάσης Μόψοπος ναυαρχίας,

will establish a torch–race for the sailors "in obedience to an oracle" (732–37). The explanation is in the scholia. According to Timaeus, this Athenian *nauarchos* was called Diotimos; he came to Naples and founded the annual festival.[10] Timaeus may not have thought it necessary to say why or when he came, but a Diotimos, son of Strombichos, was one of the *strategoi* who went to Corcyra with the ten ships in 433 (Thuc. 1.45), and he could have been in Italy earlier or later, perhaps on a diplomatic mission.[11]

Timaeus may also be the source of the Roman historian Lutatius Daphnis (second–first century B.C.), who tells us that there had been an older city on the site of Neapolis, founded by the Cumaeans and called Parthenope after the siren, whose body was buried there; that the Cumaeans destroyed it when it became inconveniently prosperous, and subsequently, in response to an oracle, restored it; and that the restored city was of course named Neapolis,[12] the New City. The story is certainly in Timaeus' manner, whatever its value as history. Greek sources represent Neapolis as a comparatively late foundation, a New City without any Old City, but archaeologists have found traces of cemeteries which show that there was some kind of early settlement there.[13]

If Timaeus described the earliest settlements on the Bay of Naples, paying some attention to the topographical features of the area, it may be assumed that he paid similar attention to the earliest Sicilian colonies, Naxos, Megara Hyblaea, Syracuse, Leontini, and Catana, but his account cannot be recovered. Strabo never mentions Timaeus in his treatment of Sicily,[14] and his description contains none of the tell–tale phrases that recall Timaeus' manner. He cites Antiochus for the tale that Archias, the founder of Syracuse, and Myscellus, the founder of Croton, set out from Greece together,[15] but he does not record Timaeus' version.

Thanks to Cicero, we know that Timaeus praised the beauty of Syracuse,[16] and his description of Arethusa is recorded in three separate

---

[10] F 98—Schol. Lyc. 732.

[11] See Gomme's note on Thuc. 1.45 and below, p. 149. Tzetzes, with shaky geography and history, says that Diotimos was "fighting the Sicels."

[12] Fr. 2 Peter. Strabo's statement in 14.2.10 that Parthenope was a city founded 'before the first Olympiad' by Rhodians must be taken from some other source; cf. Steph.Byz. s.v. Παρθενόπη.

[13] Cf. G. Pugliese Carratelli, "Napoli antica," *Parola del Passato* 7 (1952) 243–68; M. Napoli, "Realtà storica di Partenope," ibid. 269–85; Frederiksen, *Campania* 85–87.

[14] He has only three references to Ephorus (F.135,136,137).

[15] F 10—Strabo 6.1.12, cf. also 6.2.4.

[16] F 40—Cic. *De Rep.* 3.31.43: Urbs illa praeclara, quam ait Timaeus Graecarum max-

places—by Strabo, Polybius, and Antigonus of Carystus (who cites Callimachus for the description and adds "Timaeus has the same tale").[17] Timaeus evidently stated, as though it were sober fact, that the fountain of Arethusa was the water of the River Alpheus, and that it had come beneath the sea from Olympia. The tradition was at least as old as Pindar,[18] but perhaps Timaeus is responsible for the "proof" of the story—on rainy days or on festival days at Olympia, when the bellies of the sacrificed oxen were washed in the river, the fountain ran cloudy and dirty, and on one occasion it actually cast up a golden cup, which was recognized as having been used at the festival.

When Polybius and Strabo object vigorously that this story "simply cannot be true," a modern reader may be surprised at what appears to be a display of literal–mindedness. Like the tale of the poplars by the River Po weeping tears of amber at Phaethon's death,[19] the story of Arethusa seems to have offended Polybius and Strabo as "tragic material" that had no place in serious history.[20]

Timaeus' history of Sicily during these centuries is entirely lost, but a number of fragments refer to the colonies of Bruttium, Lucania, and Calabria, and some of them provide interesting details. It will be simplest to take the cities one at a time, beginning with Rhegium.

Rhegium was called a Chalcidian colony by Thucydides, and also evidently by Ephorus,[21] but Antiochus provided a fuller story, which is quoted in part by Strabo (6.1.6). According to Antiochus, Rhegium was settled partly by Chalcidians, at the request of the colonists of Zancle across the strait, who were themselves Chalcidians, partly by Messenians from the Peloponnese, who came when they were warned by the Delphic oracle that

umam, omnium autem esse pulcherrimam (cf. also *Verr.* 2.4.117–119). One might expect Timaeus to mention the proposed etymologies, from Syraco (name of Archias' wife or of a lake) or from Syra and Cossa, Archias' daughters (Schol. Callim. fr. 43.28).

[17] F 41a,b,c—Antig.Caryst.*Hist.Mir.* 139–40 (Callimachus fr. 407, Pfeiffer); Polyb. 12.4d; Strabo 6.2.4. Other authors also may have borrowed Timaeus' description, e.g. Pliny, *NH.*2.225; Seneca, *NQ* 3.26.5; *Mir. Ausc.* 172 (cf. Jacoby's note on F 41).

[18] *Nem.* 1.1, cf. Strabo 6.2.4.

[19] 2.16.13—F 68.

[20] I cannot accept Jacoby's opinion that Timaeus' digression about Arethusa was lengthy. It does not follow that he spoke of the sacred fish in Arethusa and the fate that befell anyone who was foolish enough to eat them (Diod. 5.3.6). Though Diodorus is borrowing freely from Timaeus in these chapters, he does not repeat what Timaeus is actually known to have said about Arethusa, and he must have known many stories that were current in his own day. The story of the sacred fish seems to me too crude for Timaeus; it lacks the point and the charm of the other tales.

[21] Thuc. 3.86.2, 6.44.3,79.2; Ps.–Scymnus 311–12; Diod. 14.40.

this colony offered the only way to escape perishing with their country, which was going to fall into the hands of the Spartans.[22]

Another version, recorded by Strabo before he cites Antiochus, and by Diodorus, Dionysius of Halicarnassus, and Heraclides Lembos, has the Chalcidians also guided to Rhegium by the Delphic oracle, an improvement on Antiochus' story, because it gives greater distinction to the colony. During a famine at Chalcis, a tenth of the population was dedicated to Apollo, and when they asked the oracle where they should go, they were told "to found a city where the sacred river Apsias flows into the sea, and where the female woos the male:"

Ἀψία ᾗ ποταμὸς ἱερώτατος εἰς ἅλα πίπτει,
ἔνθ᾽ εἴσω βάλλοντι τὸν ἄρσενα θῆλυς ὀπυίει,
ἔνθα πόλιν οἴκιζε, διδοῖ δέ σοι Αὔσονα χώραν.

When they found a vine entwined about a wild fig tree by the Apsias, they knew this was the place.[23] In the version of Dionysius of Halicarnassus, the discovery is made "after sailing round the Pallantion of Italy," presumably a promontory which (according to his source) had been dedicated to Athena by earlier Greek heroes. Heraclides Lembos says they settled first "by the tomb of Jocastus, one of the sons of Aeolus" (wherever that was). These details suggest the manner of Timaeus; and the instruction to found a city "where they see something happen" recalls the tale of the founding of Praeneste, when Telegonus is told to found a city "where he sees countrymen wearing wreaths and dancing."[24] And Timaeus can hardly have failed to discuss the etymology of the name Rhegium, whether from the verb ῥήγνυμι or from a man called Regios.[25] In any case, he certainly maintained the Delphic origin of the colony.

[22] This is the only indication of date. It is commonly supposed that the First Messenian War is meant (whatever date one may wish to assign to that war). Pausanias (4.23.5–10) has an elaborate variation of Antiochus' story: he puts the Messenian migration to Italy at the end of the Second Messenian War, and it is an invitation from Anaxilaus, not a command from Delphi, that brings the Messenians to Rhegium. These stories are hardly reliable evidence for the foundation date. For discussion see J. Bérard, *La colonisation grecque*, 99–107; T.J. Dunbabin, *The Western Greeks* (Oxford 1948) 12–13; G. Vallet, *Rhégion et Zancle* (Paris 1958); J. Ducat, "Les thèmes des récits de la fondation de Rhégion," *Mélanges helléniques offerts à Georges Daux* (Paris 1974) 93–114; E. Manni, "L'oracolo delfico e la fondazione di Regio," *Perennitas, Studi in onore di Angelo Brelich* (Rome 1980) 311–20.

[23] Diod. 8.23; Dion.Hal. *AR* 19.2; Heraclid. Lemb. *Excerpta Politiarum* 25 (ed Dilts, Durham, N.C., 1971). The River Apsias has not been identified, and if the name has some hidden meaning, it has not been discovered.

[24] Above p. 76. Cf. also J. Fontenrose, *The Delphic oracle* (Berkeley 1978) 70–72.

[25] Dionysius gives both versions, Heraclides only the second. See also Diod. 4.85.3.

According to Strabo and Antigonus of Carystus, Timaeus recorded the tradition that the crickets on the Locrian side of the River Halex were vocal whereas those on the Rhegine side were silent—a nice local *paradoxon* for which Antigonus offers an explanation: Heracles was disturbed by crickets when trying to sleep there and laid a curse of silence on them.[26] A statue was shown at Locri (so Strabo says) of the citharode Eunomus with a cricket perched on his cithara, and the explanation, according to Timaeus, was the following story: Eunomus of Locri and Ariston of Rhegium were competing at the Pythian games and fell into an argument over which of them should perform first.[27] Ariston claimed that this privilege was due to him at Delphi "because his ancestors had been dedicated to Apollo and the colony had been sent out by the oracle," but Eunomus told him that he really had no right even to compete for a prize in singing, coming as he did from a country where even the crickets had no voice. And in the end Eunomus won the prize, after one of his strings broke during his performance and a cricket flew on to his instrument and supplied the missing note. The story is a fine example of a Timaean *aition,* but nothing more serious survives of his account of Rhegium during these centuries.

The colony of Locri occupied Timaeus' attention in his ninth book, as we learn from a reference in Athenaeus.[28] Its early history is full of uncertainties and there are so many points to be argued that he may have written at some length about it. Thanks to Polybius, who criticized his account very severely,[29] we know his opinions on various matters, but on two fundamental points we have no direct information, and we must be content to suppose that the version in Strabo goes back to him. There was disagreement over the date of the foundation. As with Rhegium and Taras, there was a tendency to connect it with the First Messenian War. Eusebius puts it in the 670's,[30] but Strabo puts it half a century earlier, soon after Syracuse (6.1.7), and this is likely to be what Timaeus said. He also had to make up his mind whether the founders came from Opuntian (Eastern) or Ozolian (Western) Locris. Ephorus (wrongly, says Strabo) decided in favour of the Opuntians. One might expect Timaeus to disagree and prefer the other version, but there is no proof of this, and he may in fact have followed

---

[26] F 43 a, b—Antig. Caryst. 1–2; Strabo 6.1.9; cf. also Conon, *FGrH* 26 F 1, §5; Paus. 6.6.4; *Anth.Pal.* 9.584. The crickets at Acanthus were also said to have no voice. Hence the proverb Ἀκάνθιος τέττιξ.

[27] περὶ τοῦ κλήρου. Evidently competitors drew lots to decide who should play first.

[28] F 11a—Athen. 6.264C–D.

[29] F 12—Polyb. 12.5.

[30] 678 according to Jerome, 673 in the Armenian version. Pausanias 3.3.1 has the mistaken notion that Croton and Locri were Spartan colonies.

Ephorus on this point.[31] On the other hand he disagreed fundamentally with Aristotle's account (in his *Constitution of the Locrians* presumably), and this is where Polybius takes issue with him (12.5).

Polybius had earned the gratitude of the Locrians by using his influence to have them excused from military service on Roman expeditions, and he has to apologize for defending Aristotle's account, which could be thought discreditable to their ancestors. Aristotle accepted a so–called tradition current at Locri that their founders were the illegitimate sons of Locrian women, who formed unions with slaves when their husbands were away fighting in the First Messenian War (just as Tarentum was supposed to be founded by the sons of Spartan women and helots). Timaeus objected that the account was absurd, because the Locrians in old Greece did not use "bought" slaves as their servants in early times.[32] It might indeed be regarded as offering a deadly insult to the Locrians of Italy, if it implied that they were not pure–blooded Greeks, but sons of non–Greek fathers. One would expect Timaeus to be insistent that the colonists were true Greeks, even if base–born.

Polybius says that the Locrians themselves accepted Aristotle's account, and he says it was their practice to reckon descent on the mother's side—"so that, for example, the sons of women who belong to the hundred families are always considered to be well–born."[33] He does not make his point very clearly, but his meaning must be that the Locrians are not

---

[31] See Bérard, *La colonisation grecque* 199–204.

[32] F 11a—Ath. 6.264C–D. Athenaeus quotes Timaeus' actual words: "It was not usual," he says, "in olden times to have slaves, whom they had bought, for their servants; and the Locrians accused Aristotle of not understanding Locrian customs, telling him it was not lawful for Locrians or Phocians to possess slaves as house servants, female or male, until quite recent times. In fact, they said, it was the wife of Philomelus, the man who seized possession of Delphi, who was the first to have two female slaves attend on her, and Aristotle's friend Mnason, who owned a thousand slaves, was greatly disliked by the Phocians because he deprived so many of their citizens of the employment that they needed, since it had been the custom for younger people to attend upon their elders in the tasks of the household."
It is not clear why Athenaeus thought Timaeus inconsistent and why Aristotle found fault with these remarks: Τίμαιος δ' ὁ Ταυρομενίτης ἐκλαθόμενος αὑτοῦ (ἐλέγχει δ'αὐτὸν εἰς τοῦτο Πολύβιος ὁ Μεγαλοπολίτης) οὐκ εἶναί ἔφη σύνηθες τοῖς Ἕλλησι δούλους κτᾶσθαι (Ath. 6.272A–B—F 11b).

[33] σύνοιδα γὰρ τοῖς ἀνθρώποις ὁμολογοῦσιν ὅτι παραδόσιμος αὐτοῖς ἐστιν αὕτη περὶ τῆς ἀποικίας ἡ φήμη παρὰ πατέρων, ἣν Ἀριστοτέλης εἴρηκεν, οὐ Τίμαιος. καὶ τούτων γε τοιαύτας ἔφερον ἀποδείξεις. πρῶτον μὲν ὅτι πάντα τὰ διὰ προγόνων ἔνδοξα παρ' αὐτοῖς ἀπὸ τῶν γυναικῶν, οὐκ ἀπὸ τῶν ἀνδρῶν ἐστιν, οἷον εὐθέως εὐγενεῖς παρὰ σφίσι νομίζεσθαι τοὺς ἀπὸ τῶν ἑκατὸν οἰκιῶν λεγομένους· ταύτας δ' εἶναι τὰς ἑκατὸν οἰκίας τὰς προκριθείσας ὑπὸ τῶν Λοκρῶν πρὶν ἢ τὴν ἀποικίαν ἐλθεῖν . . . τούτων δή τινας τῶν γυναικῶν συνεξᾶραι μετὰ τῆς ἀποικίας, ὧν τοὺς ἀπογόνους ἔτι νῦν εὐγενεῖς νομίζεσθαι καὶ καλεῖσθαι τοὺς ἀπὸ τῶν ἑκατὸν οἰκιῶν (Polyb. 12.5.5–8—F 12); cf. Walbank's note; Brown, *Timaeus* 45.

offended by Aristotle's account, because their tradition does not oblige them to regard sons born out of wedlock as "base–born" if their mothers are of high birth, no matter who the fathers may be. One may suppose that Timaeus was unwilling to believe that the Locrians spoke or thought like this, but his full argument has not been preserved. Aristotle may well be right in supposing that matriarchy was or had been part of Locrian tradition, but attempts in modern times to prove that he was right (or wrong) are quite unconvincing.[34]

It is clear, however, that Timaeus was deeply offended by Aristotle's remarks about the Locrians, and he responded with an angry attack on him, complaining that his account represented Locri as "a colony of runaway slaves, house–servants, seducers, and kidnappers." He thought the account was slanderous, and that Aristotle was guilty not only of carelessness, but of shameless arrogance in spreading it, behaving "as though he had been one of Alexander's generals, who fought the Persians at the Cilician Gates, instead of a half–educated sophist, just out of his father's surgery, a glutton always on the look–out for a good dinner, who poked his nose into every monarch's court and every general's tent."[35]

Polybius seems not to understand why Timaeus is so angry, but he cannot forgive this kind of language, and he retaliates by accusing him of fabricating his own account of Locri and manufacturing some kind of documentary evidence to prove it. He does tell us, however (12.10.7), that Timaeus relied on a certain Echecrates for his information about the Locrians, and that (in his usual name–dropping style, so he implies) he tried to show how important a person Echecrates was by saying that his father had been employed on a diplomatic mission by Dionysius (presumably Dionysius II).[36]

It has been suggested that this Echecrates is Echecrates of Phlius, the Pythagorean philosopher who appears in Plato's *Phaedo* and persuades Phaedo to describe to him how Socrates died.[37] Pythagoreans are expected to come from Magna Graecia, and Cicero (*De Finibus* 5.87) supposes that Echecrates came from Locri, asking why Plato went to Tarentum to meet Archytas and "Cur ad reliquos Pythagoreos, Echecratem, Timaeum, Ari-

---

[34] For a survey of opinion since 1815 see R.Van Compernolle, *Annali d. Scuola normale di Pisa,* Classe di Lettere, Ser. 3.6 (1976) 353–67.

[35] F 156—Polyb. 12.8.1–4. A. Momigliano, *Riv.storica italiana* 71 (1959) 540–41 (English version in his *Essays in Ancient and Modern historiography* [London 1977] 46–47) thinks that Timaeus' dislike for Aristotle is part of his anti–Macedonian feeling.

[36] F 12—Polyb. 12.10.8.

[37] E.g., Brown, *Timaeus* 48–51.

onem Locros?"[38] This Timaeus is of course Plato's Timaeus, who did indeed come from Locri, and we have to decide whether the Echecrates who is said to have known the philosopher Timaeus is the same as the Echecrates who knew the historian Timaeus, or a different person altogether. William Oldfather, in his Pauly–Wissowa article on *Lokroi*, is prepared to say not only that he is the same man, but that he was an aristocratic Locrian forced to leave the city when Dionysius II took it over (though his father had been in the tyrant's service); that he came to Greece and settled in Phlius, which would give him the chance of meeting the historian Timaeus in Athens; and that, as member of a leading Locrian family, he would object strongly to Aristotle's account of the colony's origin, since it would cast doubt on the purity of his lineage.[39] His conclusion may seem to explain everything, but it is reached by a series of conjectures, and must be regarded as purely speculative.

When Polybius speaks of "the hundred families" to which some of the women belonged who were among the original settlers of Locri, he says that these were the families from which the Locrians of old Greece, in obedience to an oracle, were expected to select by lot the girls who were to be sent to Athena's temple at Ilium (12.5.7). He does not describe this custom, apparently taking for granted that his readers will be familiar with it (unless there was further detail in his text which the excerptor has omitted). The Locrians in Greece considered themselves bound to obey an oracle which they believed had been given them when they were suffering from disease and barrenness soon after the Trojan War. The oracle told them (so they believed) that they were being punished for the sacrilegious assault of their countryman Ajax on Cassandra, and that they must appease Athena of Ilium by sending her two girls each year to be her servants, and must continue to do so for a thousand years. The story is in Lycophron, and thanks to the scholia (where we learn that it was told by Timaeus) and a remark in Apollodorus' *Bibliotheca* (in the *Epitome*) and a fragment of Aelian,[40] we can reconstruct something of what was supposed to have happened in historical times.

---

[38] Cicero's words are echoed by Valerius Maximus 8.7.3.

[39] *RE* XIII.1311–20. Oldfather also thinks that after the colony's experience with Dionysius popular or liberal elements may have devised the slave story to malign the best families. Without any support from Aristotle or Timaeus or Polybius this view can hardly be maintained. But see A.J. Graham, *Colony and Mother–City in Ancient Greece* (Manchester–New York 1964) 115–16.

[40] Lyc. 1141–71 with the scholia (F 146a, b), where it is said that Callimachus also mentioned the custom (fr. 35 Pfeiffer); Apoll. *Bib. Epit.* 6.20–22; Aelian fr. 67 Hercher; cf. also Strabo 13.1.40; Plut. *Mor.* 557D.

It was a severe ordeal for the girls. In theory, if not in practice, they could be killed by the people of Ilium if they were caught before they reached the shelter of Athena's sanctuary.[41] And once they reached it, they worked all day at keeping the place clean, going barefoot, μονοχίτωνες (without any heavier garment to keep themselves warm), and with their hair shorn, leaving the sanctuary and returning to the city only at night. The famous inscription of the "Locrian maidens," first published in 1911,[42] shows that the burden on the Locrians was a real one, and that girls were still being sent in the latter half of the third century (if the inscription is correctly dated to some point in the reign of Antigonus Gonatas). Apollodorus tells us that they were sent continuously until the Phocian War (the so–called Sacred War, when the Phocians occupied Delphi from 355 until 346), and that then the Locrians ceased sending them, arguing that the thousand years had now passed (though some of their contemporaries, who thought they knew the date of the Trojan War, might have thought that they had at least a century still to go). At some time after 346, as we learn from the fragment of Aelian, the oracle insisted that girls must still be sent and "King Antigonus" was asked to decide which city of the Locrians was to be responsible for this tribute (δασμός).[43]

The inscription shows that the burden was imposed on the city of Narykeion, which was supposed to be the birthplace of Ajax, and strict conditions were laid down protecting the "Ajax families" (οἱ Αἰάντειοι)

[41] Perhaps there was a ritual pursuit of the girls, as they approached the sanctuary, in which they always escaped capture. This seems to me more likely than the "fundamentalist" interpretation of G.L. Huxley, "Troy VIII and the Lokrian maidens," *Ancient Society and Institutions. Studies presented to V.Ehrenberg* (London 1967) 147–64. One cannot take everything that is written about archaic times by later authors, whether by Timaeus or Tzetzes, as though it is real "evidence," above all not the description of the pursuit and the bloodthirsty Ilians "with stone or sword in hand" by Lycophron (1167–71). Lycophron would not pretend that he is describing "what actually happened."

[42] A. Wilhelm, "Die lokrische Mädcheninschrift," *Jahreshefte d. oest. arch. Inst.* 26 (1911) 163–256. Nikitski made some improvements in the text which he published, with Russian commentary, in *Journ. Ministr. Inst. Pub.* 45 (1913) 1–100, and his text has been followed, for the most part, by later editors; see E. Schwyzer, *Dialectorum Graecarum Exempla Epigraphica potiora* (3rd ed. Leipzig 1923) no. 366; G. Klaffenbach, *IG* IX² i.3.706; H. Schmitt, *Staatsverträge des Altertums* III (Munich 1969) 472, with full bibliography.

[43] According to Aelian (fr. 47), portentous birth–defects started to occur among Locrian women, when replacements were not sent to relieve the last two girls who had been sent, and αἵ γε πεμφθεῖσαι κατεγήρασαν ἐν τῇ Τροίᾳ, τῶν διαδόχων μὴ ἀφικνουμένων. Then, when Delphi refused to receive their delegation, they recognized what the trouble was, and ἐπ' Ἀντιγόνῳ τίθενται τὴν κρίσιν ὑπὲρ τοῦ τίνα χρὴ Λοκρικὴν πόλιν πέμπειν δασμόν. E. Manni, *Miscellanea di studi in memoria di A. Rostagni* (Turin 1963) 166–79, believes that the "Phocian War" means not the Sacred War of 355–46 B.C., but the Gallic invasion of 278—so that there is no long delay before Antigonus Gonatas is consulted.

from discrimination, in case they were thought still to be tainted by the guilt of Ajax, and providing some financial help for the families from which the girls were taken. If in fact the girls ceased to be sent about 346, and if "King Antigonus" means Antigonus Gonatas (278–239), not Monophthalmos or Doson, and if the inscription describes the terms laid down by him during his reign, it seems to follow that Lycophron and Timaeus are both writing during the years when the practice had lapsed during the first half of the third century. If Timaeus had described the resumption of the practice, some mention of this in the scholia to Lycophron or elsewhere might be expected.[44] It was of course the early practice that interested Lycophron.

Very probably it was Aristotle's mention of "the hundred families" that prompted Timaeus' digression about the "Locrian maidens" in his ninth book. If we had his actual text we might know the answers to some of the puzzling questions about the earlier practice; we might even learn where the oracle came from (from Delphi or elsewhere) and at what date. The tale of an oracle "shortly after the Trojan War" can be rejected as fictitious. But it does not strain credulity too far to suppose that the Locrians obeyed an oracular injunction given them in the seventh or eighth century, perhaps as result of some dispute between the Locrians and Athena's temple at Ilium, and that popular belief supposed it had been given them in heroic times. Timaeus should also be able to tell us when and why the practice was interrupted in the fourth century. There is no suggestion anywhere that the Locrians of Italy were affected by this burden, or that girls were ever chosen from families in the colony.

Timaeus was anxious to show that the colony of Locri was a legitimate colony, regarded with approval by its mother–city, and in his criticism of Aristotle, as described by Polybius, he pointed to a document which showed that old Locris gave its blessing to the colony, "as parents to their children." Polybius was understandably suspicious of a document that Timaeus produced to support his thesis,[45] and we cannot tell whether it was

---

[44] For further discussion, see A. Momigliano, *CQ* 39 (1945) 49–53, who lists earlier bibliography, and G.L. Huxley, op.cit. (n. 40). J. Fontenrose, *The Delphic oracle*, 131–37, will not accept the inscription or the literary sources as valid evidence that any such "tribute" had been paid to Athena before the time of Antigonus Gonatas. He believes that some ritual form of "sending the maidens" was then instituted, and that "the foundation was represented as a restoration after a lapse. So the whole story of the thousand–year tribute . . . is the aetiological myth of the dramatic ritual instituted round 270." Such scepticism seems to me excessive.

[45] F 12—Polyb. 12.9.2–10.6. For Timaeus' appeals to documentary sources and Polybius' criticism, see above, pp. 43–47.

genuine or not. But the expression "as parents to their children" should probably be accepted as genuine, describing the official attitude of a mother–city.

Timaeus seems to have insisted that not only was Locri a normal Greek colony, it was also a normal Greek city, with customs and institutions that befitted men who had been born free.[46] When Polybius argues that the Locrian settlers, as former slaves "having no real customs of their own," borrowed from the customs of the neighbouring Sicels, he is clearly attacking Timaeus, trying to exploit Aristotle's authority as far as he can. He also tells of a trick that they played on the Sicels, swearing a deceitful oath that enabled them to drive them out without admitting that they had committed perjury.[47] It is most unlikely that Timaeus believed or recorded any of this, or admitted anything "un–Hellenic" about the Locrian way of life.

It has been argued, on rather slender evidence, that temple prostitution was practised in Locri, as part of their cult of Demeter and Kore.[48] If this was the case, Timaeus would certainly have known of it, and it would have been useless for him to deny it. He knew about Aphrodite's prostitutes in Corinth and the epigram of Simonides, which recorded how they joined in prayers for the safety of Hellas at the time of the Persian invasion.[49] It may well be that he spoke of Corinthian customs when describing the foundation of Syracuse, and that he took advantage of opportunities to point out differences and similarities between Syracuse and its metropolis. On one

---

[46] Polyb. 12.9.5: μεταβὰς δὲ πάλιν ἐπὶ τοὺς ἐν Ἰταλίᾳ Λοκροὺς εὑρίσκειν ἀκολούθους καὶ τοὺς νόμους φησὶ τοὺς παρ᾽ αὐτοῖς καὶ τοὺς ἐθισμοὺς οὐ τῇ τῶν οἰκετῶν ῥαδιουργίᾳ, τῇ δὲ τῶν ἐλευθέρων ἀποικίᾳ.

[47] Polyb. 12.6.2–6. This story cannot be taken as "evidence" that the Sicels of Sicily came from Italy.

[48] Cf. Clearchus fr. 43a Wehrli—Ath. 12.515f–516a, who says that the women of Epizephyrian Locri, like Lydian women, were ἄφετοι τοῖς ἐπιτυγχάνουσιν. Justin 21.3 tells the story (probably taken from Timaeus) that in the time of Dionysius I, when they were hard pressed in a war against Rhegium, the Locrians "voverant, si victores forent, ut die festo Veneris virgines suas prostituerent;" and that, when they failed to keep their promise, the younger Dionysius demanded that they should do so for the benefit of himself and his soldiers; cf. Strabo 6.1.8; Aelian, VH 9.8.

These texts are hardly valid evidence that sacred prostitution was practised in Locri, cf. R. Van Compernolle, op.cit. (n. 34) 367–81. The ἱαρὰν μίστωμα mentioned in the bronze tablets from Locri (A. de Franciscis, Stato e Società in Locri Epizefiri [Naples 1972] 31.9) is more convincingly identified as rent earned by sacred lands than as payment by ἱαραὶ γυναῖκες, hierodules of Aphrodite; cf., e.g., M. Gigante, "Le Tavole di Locri," Parola del Passato 31 (1976) 417–32; Le Tavole di Locri, Atti del Colloquio (Napoli, 26–27 Aprile 1977) (Rome 1979) 37—59, where further literature is listed.

[49] F 10—Ath. 13.573 C–D. This is from Book VII—too early a book for events of 480, but a likely book for early Syracusan history.

occasion, certainly, he described the wealth and luxury of Corinthian life, as shown by their owning sixty thousand slaves.[50]

It would be an important part of Timaeus' work, perhaps one might consider it one of his principal obligations, to explain and discuss the attitude adopted by cities of old Greece towards their colonies. Polybius tells us that Timaeus visited the Locrians of old Greece (omitting to say whether he meant Eastern or Western Locris), where he was shown the document that illustrated the parental attitude of Locris towards its colony, as well as the text of other resolutions which established *sympoliteia* with the colony (δόγματα καθ᾽ ἃ πολιτείαν ὑπάρχειν ἑκατέροις παρ᾽ ἑκατέροις, 12.9.4); and that on a subsequent visit to the colony he found their customs corresponding well with those of old Locris. These are at least two examples of his travel for purposes of inquiry, but, as Jacoby points out, evidence of this kind of travel in the West is not easy to find.[51]

We know very little about the relations, friendly or otherwise, between Achaean or Locrian cities and their Italian colonies, and it is possible that Timaeus' history would add to our knowledge. He may also have had something to say about Corinth's relations with Syracuse that would help us to decide whether Corinth exercised any significant influence on the economic and political policy of Syracuse[52]—and of Corcyra.

Timaeus showed considerable interest in Corcyra. Apollonius of Rhodes adopted his tale that the Colchians reached Corcyra in their pursuit of the Argonauts, and then decided not to return home.[53] According to his account the Corinthian colony on the island was founded by Chersicrates, one of the Bacchiadae, six hundred years after the Trojan War (a rough traditional date), when Chersicrates was "being deprived of his privileges" by the Corinthians.[54] There is no mention of Chersicrates in Herodotus or

[50] F 5—Ath. 6.272B.

[51] *FGrH* IIIb, pp. 532—33.

[52] For this vexed question, see, e.g., Dunbabin, *The Western Greeks* 226–27; A.J. Graham, *Colony and mother–city* 142–49.

[53] Above, p. 63, n. 41.

[54] F 80—Schol. Ap.Rhod. 4.1216, recension L (Wendel's text): Τίμαιος δέ φησι μετὰ ἔτη ἑξακόσια τῶν Τρωικῶν Χερσικράτη ἀπόγονον τῶν Βακχιαδῶν κατῳκηκέναι τὴν νῆσον· Κόλχοι δὲ διαβάντες εἰς τὴν πλησίον νῆσον καὶ μετὰ ταῦτα εἰς τὰ Κεραύνια ὄρη ὁρμήσαντες, εἴς τε τοὺς Ἄβαντας καὶ Νεσταίους καὶ Ὤρικον ἀπῳκίσθησαν· ἔστι δὲ τὴν ἀποικίαν ἀγαγὼν τῶν Βακχιαδῶν Χερσικράτης, ἀποστερούμενος τῶν τιμῶν ὑπὸ Κορινθίων. The version in P calls Chersicrates ἕνα τῶν Βακχιαδῶν, εἴτε ἐκπεσόντα τῆς Κορίνθου εἴτε ἑκόντα ἀπελθόντα διὰ τὸ ἠτιμῶσθαι. For the full text see H. Fränkel, *Noten zu den Argonautika* (Munich 1968) 578.

In Apollonius' version the Colchians remain in possession on Corcyra until Chersicrates

Thucydides, but Strabo seems to be giving Timaeus' version when he says that Archias, on his way to Sicily to found Syracuse, left Chersicrates and some others on Corcyra to found a colony (6.2.4).[55]

Apollonius (4.982–92) says Corcyra was called Drepane because the sickle that Zeus used against Kronos was buried there, or (as some say) after the sickle that Demeter used to teach the Titans farming. The scholia note that this second version was to be found in Aristotle's *Constitution of the Corcyraeans.* According to his account Demeter buried the sickle on the seaward side of the island, and subsequent encroachment by the sea gave the island the shape of a sickle; but according to Timaeus it was Zeus' sickle that was buried there.[56] This looks like another instance of Timaeus' disagreement with Aristotle.

He seems also to have differed from Aristotle in his account of Zaleucus, the only famous man in the early history of Locri. Zaleucus is listed among the early law–givers in Aristotle's *Politics* and elsewhere, but (like Lycurgus) he is a semi–legendary figure of uncertain date, supposed to have been a shepherd who claimed that Athena revealed to him in a dream the laws that should be enacted.[57] Authors refer to his legislation only in vague general terms,[58] but Timaeus seems to have rejected the tradition entirely, finding fault with Theophrastus for accepting it. We owe this information to Cicero, but he is not as explicit as we should like: "Quis Zaleucum leges scripsisse non dicit? Num igitur iacet Theophrastus, si id a Timaeo, tuo familiari, reprehensum est?" (*Ad. Att.* 6.1.18—F 130b). Or again: "Quid, quod Zaleucum istum negat ullum fuisse Timaeus?" (*De Legibus* 2.15—F 130a).

Cicero probably means, not that Timaeus denied the man's existence, but that he refused to recognize his importance. If, as Aristotle maintained, the colonists of Locri were half–hellenized former slaves, it would be reasonable to credit the subsequent development of the colony to a Lycurgus–like reformer and legislator, but if, as Timaeus seems to have maintained,

---

arrives, but in Strabo's account (6.2.4) it is Liburnians whom he finds there, and this is probably Timaeus' version. It would be like him to have three stages of settlement, Colchians, Liburnians, Corinthians (cf. Brown, *Timaeus* 58 n.52). He probably told the story twice over, first in the *Proparaskeue,* then in his account of the founding of Syracuse.

[55] Plutarch, *Mor.* 293A–B, is evidently following a different source with his story of Charicrates (alias Chersicrates?) fighting the Eretrians who are in possession and forcing them to leave.

[56] F 79—Schol. Ap. Rhod. 4.982–92g.

[57] Aristot. *Pol.* 3.1274a; fr. 548 Rose—Schol. Pind. *Ol.10.17.*

[58] Cf. Ephorus, *FGrH* 70 F 139—Strabo 6.1.8.

the founders were free men who had been brought up in solid aristocratic traditions, no reformer would be needed to set them on the right path.[59] This is one way of explaining why Timaeus may have belittled Zaleucus' importance.[60] We must always wonder how much anyone really knew about the early history of Locri.[61] Diodorus (12.20.1), possibly following Timaeus, represents Zaleucus as a Pythagorean, and this is what Seneca believes.[62]

Caulonia and some of the smaller settlements on the coast to the north of Locri must have received some notice in Timaeus' history, but the next major colony is Croton. Strabo (6.1.12) reports the story that Antiochus told of its foundation, at about the same time as Syracuse: Myscellus sailed for Italy when the oracle commanded the Achaeans to settle at Croton; when he attempted to disobey by landing at Sybaris, he was firmly rebuked by a second oracular response and sent on to Croton; and he was helped in starting the colony by Archias, who happened to land there on his way to found Syracuse. Since Strabo reports no other version, and elsewhere (6.1.7), without citing any authority, says that Locri was founded "shortly after Croton and Syracuse," it is likely that Timaeus accepted Antiochus' version.

Diodorus, in a fragment from Book VIII, where he is certainly following Timaeus (8.17), gives the oracular responses in full: Myscellus goes to Delphi to ask if his wife can have children, and is told that he must found the colony of Croton; he asks where Croton is, and is given instructions on how to find it; and so he goes off to Italy; when he starts establishing a settlement at Sybaris, instead of Croton, a new oracle tells him "to be content with the gift that the god offers": ἐξέπεσε χρησμὸς αὐτῷ οὗτος,

Μύσκελλε βραχύνωτε, παρὲκ θεοῦ ἄλλα ματεύων,
κλαύματα μαστεύεις· δῶρον δ' ὃ διδῷ θεὸς αἴνει.[63]

---

[59] See Jacoby's note on F 130.

[60] Here too W. Oldfather, *RE* XIII. 1311—20, would explain Timaeus' attitude by the political prejudice of his informant Echecrates, the supposed nobleman who would not admit that his ancestors could stand in need of a radical reformer.

[61] The evidence that survives about Zaleucus is not altogether convincing, but M. Mühl, "Die Gesetze des Zaleukos und Charondas," *Klio* 22 (1929) 105–24, 432–63, is prepared to accept a fair share of it.

[62] *Ep.* 90.6–7: Zaleuci leges Charondaeque laudantur. Hi non in foro nec in consultorum atrio, sed in Pythagorae tacito illo sanctoque secessu didicerunt iura quae florenti tunc Siciliae et per Italiam Graeciae ponerent.

[63] Myscellus cannot have gone back to Delphi to ask advice, and the language suggests a mysterious "voice from the forest." Fontenrose, *The Delphic oracle* 138–40, regards these responses as no better than "quasi–historical."

We are not told what evidence was offered to support the early foundation date.[64]

The varied fortunes of Croton in the sixth century certainly claimed Timaeus' attention. From the sources that survive we can put together an outline of the story.[65] Croton combined with Sybaris and Metapontum to crush Siris; a conflict between Croton and Locri followed, leading to a disastrous defeat of the Crotoniats at the River Sagra;[66] they soon recovered from this defeat, thanks to the influence of Pythagorean teaching, according to some authorities, and inflicted the decisive defeat on Sybaris, which destroyed that city.[67] Then they began to suffer from political disorders. A movement against the Pythagoreans, started by a demagogue called Cylon, culminated, many years later, in an act of terrorism. The Pythagoreans who were gathered at the house of Milo, the famous athlete, all perished when it was set on fire, except for Lysis and Archippus, who escaped.[68] Lysis went to Greece, where he spread Pythagorean doctrine; he numbered Epaminondas among his pupils, so that the fire may be dated somewhere between 450 and 430.[69] A full account of these years' events, so far as the information was obtainable, must have been in Timaeus' history. If Diodorus' eighth book had not been lost, we should know more of what he actually said, perhaps even how he arranged the chronology.[70] Unfortunately, the fragments that survive in quotations by Athenaeus give us only anecdotes about the decadent luxury of the Sybarites (and the Crotoniats after the fall of Sybaris), while a few isolated details about Pythagoras are all that other fragments have to offer.

Timaeus told the story of the man from Sybaris who said he suffered a rupture after watching men digging in the fields (one of the workers who overheard his remark said he had a pain in the side from listening to him). He noted the Sybarite habit of keeping dwarfs and miniature dogs as pets, as a sign of their decadence, and eating cabbage before they drank wine, so that they could drink as much as they liked, because cabbages (which were grown in the vineyards) were thought to prevent intoxication. He also

[64] Other versions, which gave a later date, were also current; see above, p. 15–16.

[65] Cf. e.g. G. Glotz–R. Cohen, *Histoire grecque* I (Paris 1926) 191–94; Dunbabin, *The Western Greeks* 356–64; A. J. Graham, *CAH* (2nd. ed.) III 3, 193–94.

[66] Justin 20.2–3; Strabo 6.1.10; Diod. 8.32; Pausanias 3.19.11–13; Conon, *FGrH* 26 F 1, *Narr.* 18.

[67] Hdt. 5.44, 6.21; Phylarchus, *FGrH* 81 F 45; Strabo 6.1.13; Diod. 11.90.3, 12.9–10.

[68] Diod. 10.11; Iamblichus, *Vit.Pyth.* 249–55; Porphyry, *Vit. Pyth.* 54–57.

[69] Dunbabin, *The Western Greeks* 366; K. von Fritz, *Pythagorean politics in Southern Italy* (New York 1940) 86–91.

[70] The downfall of Sybaris can be dated in or about 510 (Diod. 11.90), but earlier dates are very uncertain.

noted their admiration for Etruscans and Ionians, peoples notorious for their luxury; and that they kept on good terms with Miletus so that they could import Milesian wool for their clothing; that their "knights" wore saffron–coloured cloaks over their breastplates; that they took three days for a journey through the country that other people would complete in a day, and had shaded roads leading into the farmland; that they had caves where they could relax in shelter from the heat; that they gave golden crowns to people who were generous and lavish in their hospitality and to cooks who were especially skilful and inventive; that their vineyards were near the sea, and had specially constructed channels through which the wine could flow into the city or down to the harbour to be loaded on to ships; and they were so happy to stay in their own country, "growing old on the bridges that spanned their rivers," that they jeered at anyone from another city who left his native place to settle elsewhere.[71] All this is from Athenaeus, and he has more in the same vein. He notes that Timaeus picked up from Herodotus (6.127) the story of the Sybarite suitor for the hand of Agariste, daughter of Cleisthenes, tyrant of Sicyon, who put on an extravagant display of luxury, adding the new detail that he had a thousand cooks and bird–catchers in his train.[72]

Athenaeus also reports that, according to Timaeus, the Crotoniats "ran aground on the shoal of luxury" (ἐξώκειλαν εἰς τρυφήν) after their defeat of Sybaris, so that, for example, their archon went about the city in purple robes and white boots and with a golden crown on his head; and that they tried to set up an Olympic festival of their own in competition with Olympia (others said it was the Sybarites who made this attempt).[73] And in the few surviving fragments of Diodorus' eighth book that are concerned with the West and can be traced to Timaeus the same sort of detail is reported (8.18–20, from the *Excerpta de virtutibus et vitiis*).

Another fragment of this book (8.32, from the *Excerpta Vaticana*) describes how the Locrians, before undertaking the war against Croton and her allies that led to the Battle of the Sagra, sent to Sparta asking for help. The Spartans "offered them the Dioscuri as allies," and the Locrian envoys accordingly made suitable sacrifice and prepared a bed for the Dioscuri on the ship that took them back to Italy.[74] This story must certainly come from Timaeus, but his account of the campaign that followed has not survived.

---

[71] F 47–50—Ath. 1.34C, 12.518D–520C. Timaeus considered the people of Siris equally extravagant in their ways, F 51—Ath.12.523C.

[72] F 9—Ath. 12.541B–C, cf. Diod. 8.19.

[73] F 44, 45—Ath.12.522A–C.

[74] Cf. Justin 20.2–3.

Strabo, however, in his few remarks about the River Sagra (6.1.10), notes that there are altars of the Dioscuri there, and that "this is where ten thousand Locrians and Rhegines fought against a hundred and thirty thousand Crotoniats and won the day," thus giving rise to the proverb "Truer than the victory of the Sagra," used in replying to anyone who doubts one's word. He also says that "some authorities add the remarkable tale" that the news of the battle reached Olympia, where the festival was in progress, on the same day. The paroemiographers say it was at Sparta that the miraculous report was announced,[75] more appropriately since the Dioscuri came from Sparta, but Strabo's version must certainly come from Timaeus.

The Locrians also maintained that the Locrian Ajax fought on their side, that they left a space for him in their ranks, and that when one of the Crotoniat generals tried to rush through this space, he was wounded and did not recover from his wound until, as bidden by the Delphic oracle, he went to Achilles' isle, Leuce, at the mouth of the Danube, where both the Ajaxes appeared to him and he was cured. This tale may well have been told by Timaeus. It is not recorded by Strabo or in any fragment of Diodorus' eighth book, but it is in Justin's twentieth book, which records a number of items that are attested for Timaeus.[76]

No further account of this war between Croton and its neighbours to the South has been preserved; nothing is recorded anywhere apart from these "strange marvels" and tales of divine interference. And it is the same with the earlier war, when Croton joined Metapontum and Sybaris in the attack on Siris. They are said to have incurred the wrath of Athena, when they desecrated her temple by killing fifty young men who took refuge there, including her priest who was dressed in woman's clothing. Athena's statue closed its eyes, showing the goddess' anger, and a plague descended on the cities, until they took proper measures to placate her, as commanded by an oracle.[77]

It seems clear enough that the story must have been in Timaeus, since we find that Lycophron speaks of Athena punishing the murder of Ionians by Achaeans and says that her statue "shall close its eyes unweeping" (984–92). But there was evidently more than one explanation of the statue's "closed eyes," and Timaeus may have offered several versions. Ac-

---

[75] Zenobius 2.17; Macarius 1.84; Apostolius 2.12: ἀληθέστερα τῶν ἐπὶ Σάγρᾳ.

[76] Paus. 3.19.11–13; Justin 20.3.4–8; Conon, *FGrH* 26 F 1, *Narr.*18. For attempts to explain how these beliefs originated and developed, see R. Van Compernolle, *Hommages à Marcel Renard* (Brussels 1969)733–66; M. Sordi in *Contributo dell' Istituto di Storia antica, Univ.Cattolica*, Milan 1 (1972) 47–70.

[77] Justin 20.2.3–8; Schol. Lyc. 984.

cording to the scholia on Lycophron, the event took place in heroic times, when the Trojans arrived after the fall of Troy to find Athenians settled at Siris; they joined Achaeans from Croton in an attack on them (this cannot be an accurate account of what Timaeus said, since he would not bring Achaeans to Croton so early).

Herodotus, however, makes Themistocles say that "Siris in Italy belongs to us from of old" (8.62). This shows that the tale of an early settlement at Siris was at least as old as Antiochus,[78] and Timaeus seems to have called Siris a Trojan city (F 51). So does Strabo (6.1.14) and he writes: "As proof of the Trojan settlement they point to the statue of Athena of Ilium there, which is supposed to have closed its eyes when the suppliants were dragged away by Ionians who captured the city; and these Ionians had come to settle there to escape from Lydian rule; they took the city by force (it had been a city of the Chones) and called it Polieion. And they say that even now the statue with its eyes shut is shown there." Here is a totally different version of the tale. There is no reason why Timaeus should not have recorded these various versions, and perhaps given it as his opinion that Siris was a Trojan foundation in the first place.

One is compelled to ask if Timaeus restricted himself to mythical and marvellous details of this kind. And if he did, was this because he preferred to give the same prominence to myth and τὸ μυϑῶδες in writing about the sixth century as in his treatment of early times, or was he unable to obtain the kind of information about the sixth century that could be made the basis for a proper historian's account?

When Herodotus emigrated to Thurii, he had the opportunity of talking to people whose fathers or grandfathers had fought in the war between Croton and Sybaris and witnessed the destruction of Sybaris. He tells the story of Dorieus, who came to the West in exile from Sparta, looking for genuinely "Heraclid" country where he could settle. He says that Dorieus came to Italy, "so the Sybarites say, at the time when they and their King Telys were making preparations to go to war with Croton; and the Crotoniats, in their state of alarm, asked Dorieus to come to their assistance; he did so, fought with them and took part in the destruction of Sybaris. This is what the Sybarites say he did, he and the men with him, but the Crotoniats insist that no foreigner gave them any help in the war against Sybaris except the Iamid soothsayer Callias of Elis, and that he escaped from Telys, the tyrant of the Sybarites, and sought refuge with them after he failed

to obtain favourable omens for an attack on Croton when he offered sacrifice (ἐπείτε τὰ ἱρὰ οὐ προεχώρεε χρηστὰ θυομένῳ ἐπὶ Κρότωνα).
And each side produces evidence in support of its statement. The Sybarites
point to a sanctuary and temple of Athena of the Crathis beside the dry bed
of the River Crathis, which they say was established by Dorieus after taking part in the destruction of their city, and they point to Dorieus' death as
a strong confirmation of what they say. They say he perished because he
disobeyed the oracle's command. If he had not acted contrary to that command, he would have done what he set out to do: he would have taken the
territory of Eryx and remained in possession of it; he and his army would
not have been destroyed. The Crotoniats, on the other hand, point to many
pieces of land in their territory that were set aside for Callias of Elis, farms
still cultivated in my time by descendants of Callias, whereas nothing was
given to Dorieus or his descendants, though if Dorieus had helped them in
their war with Sybaris, he would have received many times as much in
reward as was given to Callias."

Herodotus invites readers to adopt whichever version they choose
(5.44–45). This seems exactly the kind of controversy that would have
delighted Timaeus. It is also perhaps a good example of the kind of information that might be offered to an inquirer on the spot less than a century
after the event.

There is no trace of these Herodotean stories in any of the fragments of
Timaeus or in Diodorus or Strabo. But Diodorus (12.9) records another
tale of Telys—not called king or tyrant this time, but simply demagogue—
telling how he provoked the Crotoniats to war. He describes how the Sybarites increased in numbers to an extraordinary extent, until they numbered 300,000 citizens: "But a demagogue arose called Tylis, and by making accusations against leading personages, he persuaded the people of
Sybaris to drive the wealthiest of their citizens into exile, five hundred of
them, and confiscate their property. Then, when these exiles went to Croton and sought refuge there at the altars in the agora, Tylis sent a delegation
which was instructed to demand the surrender of these exiles; otherwise
they could expect war. The Assembly met, and was asked to decide between surrendering these suppliants to the Sybarites or facing war against
a people stronger than themselves. The Council and the people were in
grave difficulty, and at first opinion inclined towards surrender of the suppliants, because of the threat of war, but when the philosopher Pythagoras
said they should protect the suppliants, they changed their minds." And so
the war follows, the battle of 10,000 Crotoniats against 300,000 Sybarites;
the hero of the victory is not Dorieus or Callias, but the famous athlete,
Milo of Croton.

Diodorus gives this account of how the war started as part of a digression on the history of Sybaris before describing the settlement at Thurii, and one can hardly doubt that he has the story from Timaeus. Many of these details, moreover, almost certainly from the same ultimate source, are found also in Strabo. Though Strabo has nothing about Tylis, he is concerned to show that Croton is famous not only for its good health and the number of its Olympic victors, but also as the home of Pythagorean philosophy.[79]

The story of Pythagoras refusing to permit the surrender of the refugees is also in Iamblichus, *De Vita Pythagorica* (177). Iamblichus' principal sources are Nicomachus and Apollonius of Tyana (who is responsible for additional detail and rhetorical embellishment), and they in their turn are mainly dependent on Aristoxenus.[80] Both Iamblichus and Porphyry, however, include in their discussion of Pythagoras some details that are familiar from fragments of Timaeus, and Porphyry actually cites Timaeus on one occasion.[81] It seems to follow, therefore, that their immediate sources knew of Timaeus' account and preserved some traces of it in their narrative, though they may have altered it or distorted it or added to it on their own initiative.

Timaeus seems not to have concerned himself particularly with intellectual history in any part of his work, but he had a number of things to say about Pythagoras and the Pythagoreans. There are seven attested fragments referring to them, cited from the ninth and tenth books, enough to indicate what Jacoby calls "an excursus on the life, teaching, and influence of Pythagoras." According to Timaeus, Pythagoras expected his followers to take the proverb κοινὰ τὰ τῶν φίλων literally. Diogenes Laertius is explicit about this: "Pythagoras was the first, so Timaeus says, to say that friends have all things in common and that friendship is equality. His pupils gave up their possessions, contributing them to a common stock, and they

---

[79] Strabo (6.1.12) explains the 300,000 men by pointing out that Sybaris had four ἔθνη and twenty-five πόλεις under its control. He also says that the war was over in seventy days, and that later the Sybarite survivors established a settlement on the site (συνελθόντες ἐπῴκουν ὀλίγοι) which was destroyed when Athenians and others came to settle there. Diodorus (11.90) puts this temporary resettlement as late as 453, only a few years before Thurii was established there, and this is probably what Timaeus said. According to Timaeus the Crathis turned the hair of anyone who bathed in it blond or white (F 46—Antig.Caryst. 134), and Strabo also recorded this *paradoxon*.

[80] See E. Rohde, "Die Quellen des Iamblichos in seiner Biographie des Pythagoras," *Rh.Mus.* 26 (1871) 554–76, 27 (1873) 23–61, reprinted in his *Kleine Schriften* II (Tübingen–Leipzig 1901) 102–72. In this instance, he thinks the source is "certainly not Timaeus," though others think Timaeus is the source, e.g., K. J. Beloch, *Jbb. für class. Phil.* 1891, 699; A. Rostagni, *Atti acc. di Torino,* Classe di scienze morali 49 (1913–14) 373–95.

[81] *Vit.Pyth.* 4—F 131.

maintained silence for a five–year period, only listening to the discussions and not actually seeing Pythagoras until they had passed the test; then they became members of his household and shared the privilege of seeing him."[82] They did not "see" Pythagoras because he lectured in the dark; his evening lectures were apparently open to the public.[83]

This account is confirmed by a Platonic scholiast, who quotes Timaeus' actual words: "When young men came to visit him and wished to share his way of life and study (συνδιατρίβειν), he did not admit them immediately, but said that all who shared his company must also share their property, holding it in common (ἔφη δεῖν καὶ τὰς οὐσίας κοινὰς εἶναι τῶν ἐντυγχανόντων) . . . And it was because of these men that the saying 'Friends have all things in common' came to be used in Italy."[84] It was considered a great privilege actually to see Pythagoras, or in later years to be accepted as a member of some inner Pythagorean circle.[85] The esoteric doctrine was supposed to be guarded carefully, and Timaeus says that Empedocles was excluded from all lectures and discussions because he was believed guilty of "stealing their thoughts" (καταγνωσθεὶς ἐπὶ λογοκλοπίᾳ),[86] even though he is supposed only to have heard Pythagoras, not to have seen him.

If Empedocles actually heard Pythagoras lecture, it can hardly have been before 470, if his conventional birth date of 484 is correct. And if Timaeus thought that Pythagoras lived until 470, we can see how he must have worked out the chronology of his life. It was conventional to believe that he lived to be nearly a hundred, and it was also widely believed that he left Samos to go to Italy in order to escape the tyranny of Polycrates "when its power was growing."[87] This would be some time soon after 535, and Cicero, who had read Timaeus' account of Pythagoras, dates this move in the sixty–second Olympiad (532–29).[88] Aristoxenus says that Pythagoras was forty years old at the time, and later writers seem to agree, since they take this event as marking his *floruit*.[89] If he is to live until 470, he cannot be older than forty at this time, and this must be what Timaeus

---

[82] F 13b—Diog.Laert. 8.10. The more detailed account in Iambl. *Vit.Pyth.* 68–74 should not be taken as evidence of Timaeus' version.

[83] Diog.Laert. 8.15.

[84] F 13a—Schol. T Plat.*Phaedr.* 279c.

[85] Timaeus tells an anecdote of his contemporary Diodorus of Aspendos, who prided himself on his "access to Pythagoras' thinking" (F 16—Ath. 4.163E–F).

[86] F 14—Diog.Laert. 8.54.

[87] Iambl. *Vit. Pyth.* 88, 265; Porph. *Vit.Pyth.*16; Strabo 14.1.16; Diog. Laert. 8.3.

[88] Cic. *De Rep.* 2.28, cf. *Tusc.* 1.38: Superbo regnante.

[89] Porph. *Vit.Pyth.* 9; Clem.Alex. *Strom.* 1.65.

thought. Authors who allot more years to his travels in Egypt and Babylonia in earlier years and suppose him to have been fifty–six when he left
for Italy about 532,[90] cannot believe that he lived until 470.

It was widely accepted that Pythagoras spent twenty years in Croton,[91]
that is, until the destruction of Sybaris in 510–09, but not long after that.
And if he left Croton at about this time to spend the rest of his life at
Metapontum, where his house was shown to Cicero,[92] it would naturally
be supposed that his departure was the result of his waning influence and
popularity, and that Pythagoreans in Croton met with increasing opposition
and periodical outbreaks of hostility until the final catastrophe about 450
or later. The tyranny of Cleinias, known only from Dionysius of Halicarnassus (*Ant.Rom.* 20.7.1), is very probably to be dated some time during
these years,[93] and the anti–Pythagorean movement was not confined to
Croton, as we learn from Polybius (2.39). These developments, we must
suppose, were described in a later book of Timaeus.

Aristoxenus (like Dicaearchus, who also had something to say about
Pythagoras) was an elder contemporary of Timaeus, so that one may have
borrowed from the other or they may have written independently. Pythagoras had already become a legendary figure by the time of Aristotle, and
there is no clear indication that Timaeus altered the legend or added much
to it. Iamblichus and Porphyry mention various details that seem to have
been in Timaeus' history (details that they probably found in Nicomachus,
or possibly in Apollonius of Tyana): that Pythagoras divided the life of
women into four stages, calling them at these different stages Korai, Nym-
phai, Meteres, Maiai;[94] that he gave an address to the young men of Croton, urging them to study and respect their parents, and to the women,
telling them to be faithful to their husbands and obedient to them; and that
he persuaded the women to give up wearing their fine clothes, with the
result that thousands of dresses were deposited in the temple of Hera as
offerings to the goddess.[95] These sermons and the great movement to abandon luxury are mentioned in a chapter of Justin (20.4), which includes
other details that are certainly from Timaeus. The account of the sermons
is conventional enough, and has no particular Timaean quality, but it could
have been included in the history as part of the current tradition.

[90] Iambl. *Vit.Pyth.* 19.
[91] Justin 20.4.17.
[92] Justin 20.4.18; Iambl. *Vit.Pyth.* 248; Cic. *De Fin.* 5.4.
[93] Cf. e.g. Glotz–Cohen, *Histoire grecque* I. 194; Dunbabin, *The Western Greeks* 367;
H. Berve, *Die Tyrannis bei den Griechen* I (Munich 1967) 158–59.
[94] Iambl. *Vit.Pyth.* 56, cf. F 17—Diog.Laert. 8.11.
[95] Iambl. *Vit. Pyth.* 37, 42, 54, 56, cf. Diog.Laert. 8.22.

It is likely that Timaeus and Aristoxenus both described Pythagoras' visit to Delos before he set out for Italy, how he made a great impression there and showed special respect for the altar of Apollo Genetor, where only bloodless sacrifice was offered. Timaeus described this altar,[96] and Cicero may be following either Timaeus or Aristoxenus when he writes (*De Nat.Deorum* 3.88): "Quamquam Pythagoras cum in geometria quiddam novi invenisset, Musis bovem immolasse dicitur; sed id quidem non credo, quoniam ille ne Apollini quidem Delio hostiam immolare voluit, ne aram sanguine aspergeret."[97]

Porphyry cites Timaeus as saying that Pythagoras' daughter was "chief among maidens in Croton and as a woman chief among women," and that the people of Croton made her house into a temple of Demeter and called the street in which she lived a shrine of the Muses.[98] Iamblichus, however, says it was the people of Metapontum who honoured his daughter in this way, and Justin says it was the philosopher's house in Metapontum (which Cicero duly visited) that was regarded as a temple.[99] There is no need to see confusion here if one supposes that Justin (i.e., Trogus) and Cicero knew Timaeus' account, and that Iamblichus is following Aristoxenus. Iamblichus and Porphyry agree that Empedocles was referring to Pythagoras in his famous lines:

ἦν δέ τις ἐν κείνοισιν ἀνὴρ περιώσια εἰδώς,
ὃς δὴ μήκιστον πραπίδων ἐκτήσατο πλοῦτον,

as Timaeus had maintained; others thought that the lines referred to Parmenides.[100]

These various details from Timaeus' account of Pythagoras still leave us uncertain how he evaluated the philosopher or described his influence on the politics and society of Croton. There is no trace of anything he may have said about Pythagoras as philosopher or mathematician or even about his doctrine of metempsychosis. And there is only one fragment that indicates respect for him: he defended him against those who accused him of inventing κοπίδες (sophistic arguments).[101]

We would certainly know more if the books of Diodorus dealing with the sixth century survived. As things are, the fragments of the eighth book

---

[96] F 147—Censorinus, *De die nat.* 2.3: Denique Deli ad Apollinis aram, ut Timaeus auctor est, nemo hostiam caedit.

[97] Cf. Iambl. *Vit.Pyth.* 25.

[98] Porph. *Vit.Pyth.* 4—F 131.

[99] Iambl. *Vit.Pyth.* 170; Justin 20.4.17–18; Cic. *De Fin.* 5.4.

[100] F 14—Diog. Laert. 8.54, cf. Iambl. *Vit.Pyth.* 67; Porph. *Vit.Pyth.* 30.

[101] F 132—Schol. Eur. *Hec.* 131.

which can be traced to Timaeus include only the story of Croton's foundation, some tales of Sybarite luxury, and the story of the Spartans sending the Dioscuri to help Locri in its war against Croton (8.17–20,32). There is nothing in the ninth book, but in Book X, which extends as far as the year 481, the *floruit* of Pythagoras is given as in the sixty–first Olympiad (536–32 B.C.), and there follows a paragraph in his praise, which seems to be Diodorus' own composition (10.3). Next comes the statement that Pythagoras sailed from Italy to take care of his former teacher Pherecydes of Syros, who was failing in health; that he stayed with him until he died, arranged for his funeral, and then returned to Italy. This may be taken from Timaeus. At least, it fits in with Timaeus' Pythagorean chronology, since Pherecydes must be supposed to die between 530 and 510.

This excerpt from Diodorus (preserved in the *Excerpta de Virtutibus et Vitiis*) is meant to illustrate the *pietas* of Pythagoras. A series of stories follows to show the generosity and loyalty of Pythagoreans to one another. There is a remark about their custom of coming to the aid of a fellow Pythagorean if he happened to lose all his money, dividing up their possessions as among brothers, and the tale is then told of Cleinias, a Tarentine, who learnt that a man in Cyrene called Prorus had been deprived of his property in a political upheaval. Though Cleinias had never set eyes on Prorus, when he learnt that he was a Pythagorean, he set off for Cyrene taking enough money with him to set the man on his feet again (Diod.10.4.1).

Next comes a remarkable tale to illustrate how loyal they could be to each other, the tale of Phintias and Damon in the time of Dionysius II of Syracuse. Phintias had been detected in a plot against the tyrant, and on being condemned to death asked to be given some time to set his affairs in order, saying that a friend would go bail for him, pledging his life and taking his place in prison. And to everyone's astonishment when he asked his friend Damon, a Pythagorean, to do this favour for him, Damon agreed without hesitation. Time passed, and it looked as though Phintias would not be back before the appointed hour to redeem his friend, but he arrived back in the nick of time, running in just as Damon was being led away to die. Dionysius was so completely amazed at this display of friendship, that he set Phintias free and asked if they would accept him as their friend to make a trio of friendship.

The story is also recorded by Porphyry and Iamblichus, but with an important difference. Phintias is not guilty or suspected of any plot, but Dionysius arranges a test to satisfy some men who are arguing about the strength of friendship among Pythagoreans, some insisting that it would not stand up to a serious test, εἴ τις περιστήσειεν εἰς φόβον ἀξιόχρεων. Dionysius sends for Phintias, tells him that he has been accused of plotting against him, that the evidence is convincing, and he must die. Phintias then asks for time, saying Damon will go bail for him, and the rest of the story is the same.[102] Porphyry and Iamblichus say that they have the story from Aristoxenus, as told by Nicomachus, and that Dionysius used to tell it himself, when he lived in Corinth after he had lost his tyranny. This may be the older and better form of the story,[103] but Diodorus evidently found his version in Timaeus, because Cicero, who knew Timaeus' account of the Pythagoreans, tells it in Diodorus' form.[104]

The tale of Cleinias and Prorus appears in the same form in Iamblichus as in Diodorus,[105] and they both have the story of the Pythagorean who returned home after a long absence to find that his estate had been grossly mismanaged by his servants, but, because he failed to control his temper, as Pythagoreans were taught to do, he would not punish them, and told them that they were lucky, because they would not have escaped so easily if he had kept his temper under control.[106]

Diodorus may have found these stories in Timaeus, but it cannot be proved, because many of them undoubtedly continued to be told in later times, accumulating variations as time went on. Diodorus, for example, cites some lines from Callimachus, that neither Timaeus nor Aristoxenus can have known.[107] We can never be sure of the exact form in which Timaeus told a tale nor how large his collection was, but it is worth knowing that he told at least some of these Pythagorean anecdotes.

If a papyrus text were to be found containing some part of Timeaeus' account of the sixth century, one of the first questions to be asked would

---

[102] Porph. *Vit.Pyth.* 59–60, Iambl. *Vit.Pyth.* 234–36. The story also appears in Valerius Maximus 4.7, Ext. 1, in the same form as in Diodorus.

[103] This version identifies the tyrant as Dionysius II, though others who record the story seem not so sure whether it is Dionysius I or II. In Cic. *Tusc.Disp.* 5.63, cf. 57, it is Dionysius I, though in *De Fin.* 2.79 and *De Off.* 3.45 he is simply *Siculus tyrannus* or *Dionysius tyrannus*.

Each version of the story has its flaw. The tyrant would hardly ask to be a friend of the man who had plotted against his life, but if the accusation was feigned, how could anyone know that Phintias would ask a friend to go bail for him? See Von Fritz, *Pythagorean Politics in Southern Italy* 24.

[104] See C.G. Cobet, *Collectanea Critica* (Leyden 1878) 430–33, who says "Timaei (non nominati) locum Latine vertit Cicero;" W. Berteman, *De Iamblichi Vitae Pythagorae fontibus* (Diss. Koenigsberg 1913); H.A. Holden's note on 3.45 in his commentary, *De Officiis libri tres* (new ed., Cambridge 1899, repr. Amsterdam 1966).

[105] Diod. 10.4.1; Iambl. *Vit.Pyth.* 239, cf. 127.

[106] Diod. 10.7.4; Iambl. *Vit.Pyth.* 197–98.

[107] Diod. 10.6.4—Callimachus fr. 191. 59–63 Pfeiffer.

be: "What does he have to say about the early tyrants?" Our knowledge of these tyrants is extremely scanty, and except for a few remarks in Aristotle all our information comes from later sources. Phalaris was the only tyrant whose name was known to everyone.[108] Greeks of later times looked upon him as a semi–legendary figure, notorious for his cruelty, especially for his instrument of torture, the brazen bull with a fire burning inside. Timaeus liked to describe the so–called historical monuments that were shown to credulous visitors in Sicilian and Italian cities, and he insisted that the bull they were shown at Acragas was not a genuine archaeological exhibit. The bull that they were shown, he said, was really a statue of the river god Gelas, because the bull of Phalaris had been thrown into the sea. This at least is what the scholiast on Pindar says.[109] According to Diodorus (13.90.5), Timaeus denied that there had ever been such a bull. Perhaps what he said was that if such a bull had ever been used by Phalaris to torture his victims, the people of Acragas had not kept it, but had thrown it into the sea.[110]

Timaeus was equally scornful about a brazen bull that was preserved in Carthage, with a door set in its shoulders, so he says, through which victims could be lowered into the fire, supposed to have been carried off by Himilco with other art treasures when he sacked Acragas in 406. The door, whether it was really there or was merely added to improve the story, made it appear that this was the kind of bull in which Carthaginians burnt infants alive as an offering to Moloch. But when the Romans captured Carthage, and the younger Scipio, with Polybius by his side, saw a bronze bull in some public place, he said at once: "That must be the bull of Phalaris, it must be restored to its rightful owners." Polybius was happy to find such a good opportunity of discrediting Timaeus' claims to be an archaeological expert.[111] Cicero knew the story from Polybius, and used it to good advan-

---

[108] The references in Aristotle are *Pol.* 5.1310b, *Rhet.* 2.1393b. Scholars today are generally content with a brief summary of what we know or can conjecture about him; see, e.g., Dunbabin, *The Western Greeks* 314–23; T. Lenschau, *RE* XIX. 1649–52, s.v. Phalaris; H. Berve, *Die Tyrannis* I.129–32, II.593–95.

[109] F 28c—Schol. Pind. *Pyth.* 1.185: τὸν δὲ τοῦ Φαλάριδος ταῦρον οἱ Ἀκραγαντῖνοι κατεπόντωσαν, ὥς φησι Τίμαιος· τὸν γὰρ ἐν τῇ πόλει δεικνύμενον μὴ εἶναι τοῦ Φαλάριδος, καθάπερ ἡ πολλὴ κατέχει δόξα, ἀλλ᾽ εἴκονα Γέλα τοῦ ποταμοῦ.

[110] Much effort has been wasted in attempting to explain the contradictory accounts: for the latest discussion, see G. Schepens, *Ancient Society* 9 (1978) 117–48, with full bibliography.

[111] F 28b—Polyb. 12.25, 28a—Diod. 13.90: ὑπ᾽ αὐτῆς τῆς τύχης ἠλέγχθη, cf. Brown, *Timaeus* 54–57. According to Polybius, Timaeus denied that the bull in Carthage came from Acragas or that there had ever been a bull like this in Acragas.

tage in contrasting Scipio's efforts to recover Sicilian works of art with Verres' program of theft (*In Verr.* 2.4.73). Diodorus says the bull was on display in his time. Whatever the people of Acragas and their art critics may have thought, they could hardly insult the memory of the Scipios by consigning it to a basement.

Since Phalaris is well known to writers of later antiquity and presumably to their readers also, we may suspect that Timaeus, who was initially responsible for so much of the lore that appears in Hellenistic and Roman poetry, may be responsible here too for popularizing the image of the tyrant as a monster of cruelty. There are other writers, older contemporaries of Timaeus, equally hostile to tyranny in any form, who may have presented a similar picture of him—Phaeneas of Eresos, for example, in his book on "The Tyrants of Sicily," and Heraclides Ponticus,[112] but they are not authors whose influence on later literature, direct or indirect, can be compared with that of Timaeus. One may also suspect that the author of the *Epistles of Phalaris* had read Timaeus and learnt from him, for example, that Phalaris was a native of Astypalaea (*Ep.*4), that his wife was called Erytheia, that he was separated by exile from her and their son Paurolas (18, 19, 40, 67, 68), that he was on terms of close friendship with Stesichorus (*passim*), and that he quarrelled or actually fought wars with Leontini (4, 5, 30, 40), Messana (1, 21), Segesta (46), and Megara Hyblaea (2). But the writer reveals himself as a forger by speaking of the city of Tauromenium, which did not of course exist at the time.[113]

Polyaenus (5.1), who describes the device by which Phalaris seized power and secured his position with a bodyguard, as well as his stratagems in wars with the Sicans, probably did not use Timaeus or Philistus directly, but an occasional remark in Plutarch may be due to Timaeus, like the detail that the Acragantines never wore grey *himatia,* because that had been the uniform of Phalaris' servants (*Mor.* 821E). Stesichorus, according to Aristotle, warned the Acragantines against giving Phalaris a bodyguard by telling the fable of the horse and the deer, and Philistus seems to have borrowed the tale from him, but there is no evidence that Timaeus repeated it.[114] There is no mention of any of the less known early Sicilian tyrants in the authors who are likely to have read Timaeus.

---

[112] Phaeneas fr. 11–13 Wehrli; Heraclides fr.65, 132 Wehrli.

[113] The letters of Phalaris seem to have received little attention from scholars since Bentley's time. There is no edition of them more recent than that of R. Hercher, *Epistolographi Graeci* (Paris 1873)

[114] Stesichorus fr.104 Page—Aristot. *Rhet.* 2.1393b; cf. Philistus *FGrH* 556 F 6. For Polyaenus' Sicilian sources, see Chap. VIII, n.33.

One would expect that Timaeus had something to say about the sixth century tyrants in the Italian colonies, but the evidence is lacking. He will probably have recorded some of the actions of Telys of Sybaris, as well as those of Cylon and Cleinias in Croton.[115] But "King" Aristophilides at Taras is a mysterious figure,[116] and is not mentioned by any writer later than Herodotus (3.136). He can hardly be a tyrant in the accepted sense of the word, if Aristotle is correct in saying that the rule of the *gnorimoi* in Taras was not disturbed until after the Persian Wars.[117] At Heraclea, the colony between Siris and Metapontum, a tyrant, unnamed, is said to have been assassinated as the result of an ἐρωτικὴ συντυχία, a story like that of Harmodius and Aristogeiton in Athens. It is included in the *Romances* of Parthenius and attributed by him to Phaeneas of Eresos, noted by Aristotle and Plutarch (who set the story in Metapontum, not Heraclea), and repeated by Aelian.[118] It is the kind of story that would have appealed to Timaeus, and he is just as likely a source for Plutarch and Aelian as Phaeneas.

The tyrant of Elea called Nearchus by some authors, Diomedon or Demylus by others, must belong to the fifth century, if it is true that the philosopher Zenon attempted to assassinate him.[119] Aristodemus, however, is said to have established himself as tyrant of Cyme in 504, and since his story goes back twenty years before that, he may properly be regarded as a sixth century tyrant.

Our main account of him comes from Dionysius of Halicarnassus (*AR* 7.2–12), who dates his first rise to prominence, twenty years before he makes himself tyrant, in the sixty–fourth Olympiad (524–21 B.C.). The Olympic date is the first of many indications that he has taken the story from Timaeus, whose work of course he knew quite well, as did the other two authors who write about Aristodemus, viz. Diodorus, in a brief fragment (7.10), and Plutarch, who tells the story of the tyrant's consort, Xenokrite (*De Mulierum Virtutibus* 261E–262D). Plutarch has clearly adapted the story to suit his purposes in his collection of tales about courageous women: he portrays Xenokrite as a woman patriotic enough to help her countrymen assassinate the tyrant, but with mercy enough to see that he receives proper burial; she also admires him for being more of a

---

[115] Above, pp. 111–13, 115.
[116] Cf. Dunbabi *The Western Greeks.*
[117] *Pol.* 5.1303a, cf. Berve, *Die Tyrannis* II. 610.
[118] Parthenius 7; Aristot. *Eth.Eudem.* 3.1229a; Plut. *Mor.* 760C; Aelian fr.70.
[119] Diels–Kranz, *Fragmente der Vorsokratiker* I 29A 1, 2, 6–8—Diog.Laert. 9.25–27; *Suda,* s.v. Ζήνων; Diod. 10.18; Plut. *Mor.* 1126D; Clem.Alex. *Strom.* 4.56.

man than the unfortunate Cymaeans whom he humiliated by reducing them to the condition of common labourers.

In the tale as told by Dionysius, Aristodemus earned the title of ὁ Μαλακός as a foppish member of the ruling aristocracy of Cyme which was notorious for its τρυφή. Nevertheless, when the Etruscans attacked the country with a gigantic force (half a million infantry and eighteen thousand cavalry!), and they were held up by the miraculous stoppage and flooding of the Rivers Volturnus and Glanis, Aristodemus distinguished himself in the battle that destroyed the invading army, won great admiration among the common people, and turned himself into a radical demagogue (7.3–4). He was in consequence hated and feared by the aristocrats, and twenty years later, when the Latins of Aricia asked for help against the forces of Lars Porsena, the opportunity was taken of appointing him general of the force that was sent out, consisting mainly of persons they considered undesirable, in ships scarcely seaworthy, in the hope that they would not survive (7.5).

In fact, of course, a resounding victory was won in Latium, and they returned with an immense amount of loot and many Etruscan prisoners. Aristodemus won wide support by giving his men a generous share of the prizes, promised an attractive program of democratic reform if the people would give him full powers, and so established himself as tyrant, turning the Etruscan prisoners into his bodyguard. Instead of carrying out his promised reforms, he ruled in the most oppressive manner, forcing many into exile, confiscating property, disarming the population and doing his utmost to weaken and demoralize them; he tried to make the men effeminate, dressing the boys like girls and abolishing gymnasia and all manly exercises (7.6–11).

One need not deny that there was some kind of strong–armed autocrat in Cyme, but there is no need to take many details of this story very seriously. It is the usual highly coloured tale of a vicious tyrant, who humiliates common people and aristocrats alike, protecting himself with an armed bodyguard of foreigners. But it is exactly in the style that Timaeus cultivated. It has been argued, notably by Geffcken and Eduard Meyer and more recently by Alföldi,[120] that the story originated in a Cumaean chronicle which Timaeus used, but Jacoby with good reason rejects the hypothesis as unfounded and unnecessary.[121] The only so–called chron-

---

[120] Geffcken, *Timaios' Geographie* 44; E. Meyer, *Geschichte des Altertums* II (2nd ed., Berlin 1937) 809 (4th ed., Darmstadt 1957, III. 750); A.Alföldi, *Early Rome and the Latins* (Ann Arbor 1963) 56–72.

[121] *FGrH* IIIb, pp.606–7, with *Noten*, p. 333 n. 325.

icle of which he finds any trace is the work of Hyperochos, of which two or possibly three fragments survive. Athenaeus refers to this author as "Hyperochos or the man who wrote the *Cymaica* attributed to him,"[122] meaning evidently that the *Cymaica* purported to be an "early chronicle," but was of very doubtful authenticity. The odds and ends of antiquarian information in the fragments are quite in the style of some Hellenistic forgery, and Jacoby has good reason to date it "not earlier than the third century;" indeed, the author may be no older than Timaeus himself. It is as unprofitable to invent written sources for Timaeus as to imagine anonymous writers in place of the oral informants of Herodotus.[123]

Thucydides knew that it would be very hard and demand much ταλαιπωρία to put together an account of the seventh and sixth centuries in which he could have any confidence, and Timaeus must have known that it would be no easier in the West than in Aegean Greece. It may be doubted if any reader, except perhaps Polybius, looked for a work of accurate scholarship and scientific research about this period. For the fifth and fourth centuries they might expect something different. In writing about these centuries, Timaeus would have to imagine Herodotus and Thucydides looking over his shoulder as he wrote, when he was dealing with communities whose political feelings and moral attitudes he thought he understood, when he knew he would be expected to describe τὰ ἔργῳ γενόμενα.

---

[122] *FGrH* IIIB 576 F 1—Ath. 12.528 D–E.

[123] Alföldi remains unconvinced by Jacoby's argument, and Lasserre (note on Strabo 5.4.9) is also inclined to believe in the existence of this "Cymaean chronicle".

CHAPTER VI

THE FIFTH CENTURY: FROM GELON TO HERMOCRATES

In the fifth century, it is Sicily rather than South Italy that claims the attention of Greek historians. Sicilian history now becomes a significant part of Hellenic history, as Syracuse takes its place beside Athens and Sparta as a defender of Hellas against barbarian attack. We expect Timaeus to describe the careers of the tyrants who arose at the turn of the century, the rise of Syracuse to become the most powerful city in the island, its part in defeating the Carthaginians, and its history after the fall of the Deinomenids. We might also perhaps hope that he would describe how poetry and philosophy flourished in some cities on a scale fit to be compared with the contemporary splendour of Athens. But we cannot expect him to devote more attention to such matters than Herodotus and Thucydides. Herodotus does not even mention Aeschylus' *Persae* in his description of Salamis,[1] and his references to Ionian philosophers are confined to anecdotes about their part in political decisions.[2] Thucydides concerns himself with the sophists only in so far as their movement affects politics. There is no reason to believe that Timaeus gave poets a larger place in his history than his illustrious predecessors, while scientists and philosophers seem to have earned mention by him only if, like the Pythagoreans, they had some political importance or if there was something unusual about their way of life.

Timaeus found some occasion to mention Xenophanes;[3] he noted that Socrates had learnt the trade of a stone–mason,[4] and he may have had something to say about Socrates' friendship with Alcibiades.[5] He described

---

[1] The only reference to Aeschylus (2.156.6) is to an unidentified lost tragedy.

[2] 1.27.2,74.2,75.3,170.3 (Bias, Thales, Pittacus). In speaking about geography he never mentions by name any of the "Greeks who wanted to become famous for their wisdom" (2.20.1).

[3] F 133—Clem.Alex. *Strom.* 1.64.2: τῆς δὲ Ἐλεατικῆς ἀγωγῆς Ξενοφάνης ὁ Κολοφώνιος κατάρχει, ὅν φησι Τίμαιος κατὰ Ἱέρωνα τὸν Σικελίας δυνάστην καὶ Ἐπίχαρμον τὸν ποιητὴν γεγονέναι. The fragment does not tell us much, but the comparative dating is interesting.

[4] F 15—Cyril, *Contra Julianum* VI,p.208. Among various authors who noted the trade that Socrates had learned he cites Timaeus "in Book IX." Since this is a sixth century book, it can hardly have contained a discussion of Socrates and his circle.

[5] F 99—Nepos, *Alcib.* 11: Theopompus post aliquando natus et Timaeus, qui quidem duo maledicentissimi nescio quo modo in illo uno (sc. Alcibiade) laudando consentiunt.

Gorgias' visit to Athens and the speech which made such a great impression on the Assembly, when he asked for Athenian help in defending Leontini against Syracuse; but it does not follow that he went on to describe the Gorgianic style of rhetoric or even to say anything about the early development of rhetoric in Sicily.[6] If he had done so, later writers would surely have had more solid information to give us, instead of being content with the few remarks that they offer about Corax and Tisias.[7]

Some of Timaeus' remarks about Empedocles have been preserved. He denied emphatically that Empedocles committed suicide by leaping into the crater of Etna. "How can it be," he asked, "that he leapt into the craters, which he never mentioned, though they were not far away? We must conclude that he died in the Peloponnese. It is no reason for surprise that his grave was never found. He is not the only man of whom this can be said."[8] A legend had grown up round Empedocles (the various accounts of "How he became a god" are collected by Diogenes Laertius), and Timaeus ridiculed some of the writers who helped to establish the legend.

He found fault in particular with the Peripatetic writer Heraclides Ponticus, who, in one of his medical treatises, gave an account of the woman in a trance, whom Empedocles revived after people thought she was dead, thus earning the reputation of having supernatural powers. To celebrate his success, so Heraclides said, he invited a large number of guests to a sacrifice and feast on the farm of man called Peisianax, and in the middle of the night, when some of the guests were sleeping under the trees, a loud voice was heard (so it was said) summoning Empedocles, and there was a bright light in the sky; in the morning Empedocles had disappeared.[9] Timaeus evidently reported the whole story, but objected that Peisianax was a Syracusan, who had no farm near Acragas; and he also thought it curious that Pausanias, Empedocles' dear friend, who was wealthy, had not put up some monument in honour of the man who had become a god, if any such story had been current at the time.[10]

---

[6] F 137—Dion.Hal. *Lysias* 3: ἥψατο δὲ καὶ τῶν Ἀθήνησι ῥητόρων ἥ ποιητική τε καὶ τροπικὴ φράσις, ὡς μὲν Τίμαιός φησι, Γοργίου ἄρξαντος, ἡνίκ' Ἀθήναζε πρεσβεύων κατεπλήξατο τοὺς ἀκούοντας τῇ δημηγορίᾳ. Cf. Diod. 12.53.3 : καὶ τῷ ξενίζοντι τῆς λέξεως ἐξέπληξε τοὺς Ἀθηναίους ὄντας εὐφυεῖς καὶ φιλολόγους. This sentence may reflect Diodorus' reading of Timaeus, but the conventional remarks that follow about Gorgias' rhetoric are probably his own addition.

[7] Cf. *Artium Scriptores*, ed. L. Radermacher (Vienna 1951) 28–35.

[8] F 6—Diog.Laert. 8.71–72. Timaeus must have argued that, if Empedocles really intended to leap into Etna or wanted people to believe that he did, he would have given some hint in his poetry.

[9] Diog. Laert. 8.67–69—Heraclides Fr. 84 Wehrli.

[10] F 6—Diog.Laert. 8.71, cf. Timaeus' verdict (8.72): τοιαῦτά τινα εἰπὼν ὁ Τίμαιος

Timaeus very probably described the great success of Empedocles when he lectured at Olympia, just as he described Gorgias' reception in Athens, and he knew his arrogant verses:

χαίρετ', ἐγὼ δ' ὑμῖν θεὸς ἄμβροτος οὐκέτι θνητὸς
πωλεῦμαι.[11]

But he seems to have agreed with Aristotle that Empedocles was "a free spirit," averse to any kind of authority, calling him "modest and democratic" in his politics despite the boastful arrogance of his poetry;[12] and he told a story to illustrate his democratic attitude and explain how he came to play a part in politics.

Empedocles was invited to a party by one of the office holders, so the story runs, and when nothing to drink appeared as the dinner went on, he became impatient and demanded that some wine be served. His host, however, said that they were waiting for the Minister of the Council. The Minister finally appeared, and was appointed symposiarch, and he gave a hint of tyrannical authority by commanding them to drink unless they wanted the wine poured over their heads. Empedocles said nothing at the time, but next day he summoned his host and the Minister to court, secured a verdict of guilty against them, and had them put to death. This was how his career in politics started.[13]

Taken by itself the story gives the impression that the two men were sentenced to death, without any proof that they were guilty of any serious offence, simply because Empedocles resented their bad manners. But that cannot be right. They must be held guilty of plotting to establish a tyranny, and perhaps the intention of the story is to show that Empedocles was an independent and rather truculent man who could detect a tyrannical plot, when more tolerant persons might not suspect anything. Diogenes Laertius, in his effort to be brief, is fully capable of spoiling the point of a story, and we need the actual text of Timaeus to help us. We also need information about political conditions and institutions in Acragas. What kind of Council was this, and what sort of authority was wielded by its minister (the ὑπηρέτης τῆς βουλῆς)? It has to be supposed that this was a time of political crisis, with fear of tyranny in the air.[14]

ἐπιφέρει· "Ἀλλὰ διὰ παντός ἐστιν Ἡρακλείδης τοιοῦτος παραδοξολόγος, καὶ ἐκ τῆς σελήνης πεπτωκέναι ἄνθρωπον λέγων."

[11] Cf. Diels-Kranz, *Fragmente der Vorsokratiker* 31 B 112.

[12] F 2—Diog.Laert. 8.66 The references to Books I and II can hardly be right.

[13] F 134—Diog.Laert. 8.63–64.

[14] E.Bignone, *Empedocle* (Turin 1906) 302 n.1, admits that the story as told appears

Diogenes goes on to tell the story of the physician Acron and the epitaph that Empedocles composed for him beginning ἄκρον ἰατρὸν Ἄκρων'. Then he writes: "Later Empedocles abolished the group of The Thousand (τὸ χιλίων ἄθροισμα), which had been established for three years. Thus he was not only one of the wealthy citizens, but also one of the democratically minded. Timaeus, certainly, who refers to him frequently, says that his political attitude was quite different from the arrogant egotistical tone of his poetry."[15] All that we know about the political situation is that Theron, reconciled with Hiero of Syracuse, died in 474, and that his successor Thrasydaeus was quickly forced out of power by Hiero.[16] There is no record of any later effort to set up a new tyranny except for this story of the dinner party. Diodorus does not say what happened after the fall of Thrasydaeus. Clearly there was some account of the events in Timaeus.[17]

Heraclides Ponticus had reported that Empedocles' grandfather bred fine horses and won an Olympic victory. Timaeus agreed with him that Empedocles came from an old-established wealthy family in Acragas.[18] He also described one of his ingenious inventions, how to protect crops from high winds by spreading out the hides of donkeys on hillsides and promontories.[19] And he reported the story that he was excluded from Pythagorean discussions because he was suspected of divulging their secrets or "stealing their theories."[20] It seems that Diogenes Laertius was not able to find in Timaeus' history any serious continuous account of Empedocles which explained his great reputation as philosopher and scientific pioneer.

Diodorus begins Book XI with the year 480 B.C., and the surviving excerpts from the preceding book preserve hardly anything of his account of the rise of the Deinomenid tyrants. We are, therefore, dependent on fragments from other sources in attempting to recover Timaeus' account

---

"alquanto ridicolo." Brown, *Timaeus* 52, suggests that it may have been part of a caricature of Empedocles, not intended as serious history even by Timaeus, and misunderstood by Diogenes Laertius.

[15] F 2—Diog.Laert. 8.65–66.

[16] Diod. 11.53, cf. H.Berve, *Die Tyrannis bei den Griechen II*. 135–36, Glotz-Cohen, *Histoire grecque* II.679.

[17] The fragment of an epitome of Sicilian history in *P.Oxy.*IV.665—*FGrH* 577 F 1 mentions events not otherwise known, and it has been reasonably suggested that this epitome is based on Timaeus' history.

Some book numbers are almost certainly corrupt in the mss. of Diogenes Laertius. In F 2, Books I and II should perhaps be XI and XII, and in F 6, IV may be a mistake for XIV. XVIII in F 30 is very uncertain, but IX in F 14 may be correct.

[18] F 26b—Diog.Laert. 8.51.

[19] F 30—Diog.Laert. 8.60.

[20] F 14—Diog.Laert. 8.54.

and in comparing it with what Herodotus has to offer us. Timaeus was bitterly opposed to tyrants, but he made an exception in the case of Gelon, whose victory over the Carthaginians at Himera was much more decisive and lasting in its effect than any victory won by later tyrants. His account begins with a story of Gelon's childhood, how he escaped death when the school in which he was a student collapsed in an earthquake, because a wolf snatched his writing tablet from him and he ran out after it just in time before the earthquake shock came.[21] The story is clearly meant to have special significance as showing how good fortune or divine favour saved Gelon's life; the history of Sicily might have been different if he had not survived.

Timaeus regards most tyrants as impious and sacrilegious men whose acts cry out for divine punishment, but, like Herodotus, he seems to have taken the trouble to emphasize that Gelon came of a family whose members were hereditary hierophants of Demeter and Kore at Gela.[22] Pindar (*Ol.* 6.93) speaks of Hiero as καθαρῷ σκάπτῳ διέπων, and Didymus, citing Philistus and Timaeus, says this was because he was ἄνωθεν ἐκ προγόνων ἱεροφάντης τῶν θεῶν.[23] Timaeus was evidently content to follow Herodotus and Philistus in pointing to the family's hereditary privilege, though it does not follow that he gave the full account of Gelon's ancestry that we find in Herodotus.

When Herodotus describes how Gelon won the favour of Hippocrates, he notes that he was descended from the hierophant Telines, as though this

---

[21] F 95—Tzetzes *Chil.* 4.266:

Γέλωνα Συρακόσιον καθ᾽ ὕπνους δὲ βοῶντα
(κεραυνοβλὴς γὰρ ἔδοξεν ὀνείροις γεγονέναι)
ὁ κύων θορυβούμενον ἀμέτρως γνοὺς ἐκεῖνον,
καθυλακτῶν οὐκ ἔληξεν, ἕως ἐγείρει τοῦτον.
τοῦτον ἐξέσωσέ ποτε καὶ λύκος ἐκ θανάτου·
σχολῇ προσκαθημένου γὰρ ἔτι παιδίου ὄντος,
λύκος ἐλθὼν ἀφήρπαξε τὴν δέλτον τὴν ἐκείνου·
τοῦ δὲ δραμόντος πρὸς αὐτὸν τὸν λύκον καὶ τὴν δέλτον,
κατασεισθεῖσα ἡ σχολὴ βαθρόθεν καταπίπτει,
καὶ σύμπαντας ἀπέκτεινε παῖδας σὺν διδασκάλῳ.
τῶν παιδῶν δὲ τὸν ἀριθμὸν οἱ συγγραφεῖς βοῶσι,
Τίμαιοι, Διονύσιοι, Διόδωροι καὶ Δίων,
πλείω τελοῦντα ἑκατόν· τὸ δ᾽ ἀκριβὲς οὐκ οἶδα.

It is not important to know in exactly what form Timaeus told the story; it is the significance of the tale that counts.

[22] Cf. Hdt. 7.153.

[23] F 96—Schol. Pind. *Ol.* 6.158 (M. Schmidt, *Didymi Chalcenteri Fragmenta* [Leipzig, 1854] 219). Didymus gave the actual words of Philistus and Timaeus, παρατίθεται τὰ Φιλίστου καὶ τὰ Τιμαίου.

was one reason why Hippocrates thought well of him.[24] It cannot be proved that Timaeus represented Hippocrates also as a man with special respect for "sacred things," but there is a fragment from Diodorus' tenth book (10.28) which describes how, after Hippocrates had won a victory in the war against Syracuse, he made camp in the precinct of Zeus and "found the priest and some Syracusans removing the gold offerings that were kept there, in particular the gold cloak from the statue of the god." He rebuked them sternly for their sacrilege, and won a reputation for piety by not appropriating any of the offerings for himself. This is certainly the kind of story that would appeal to Timaeus.

Herodotus says that Gelon had been one of Hippocrates' personal guards, and was appointed cavalry commander δι' ἀρετήν when Hippocrates became tyrant after the assassination of his brother Cleandros. A sentence of Timaeus, quoted by Didymus, adds some useful detail: "After the death of Cleandros, Gelon had remained at his post; and since Hippocrates wanted to please the people of Gela, he sent for him, asked for his co–operation, and put him in charge of all the cavalry."[25] If "his post" was in the ranks of the bodyguard (of Cleandros or Hippocrates himself), this must mean that Gelon proved his loyalty by not turning against Hippocrates when he had the opportunity and that he was well–known and popular in the city.[26]

Timaeus also described the victory at the Elorus won by Hippocrates in his war against the Syracusans.[27] According to Herodotus (7.154.3) a truce was arranged by mediators from Corinth and Corcyra, and Camarina was surrendered to Hippocrates. As Thucydides tells the story (6.5.3), the Syracusans had destroyed the city some time earlier, as punishment for rebellious or disloyal behaviour, and Hippocrates now received only "the land of the Camarinaeans." He rebuilt the city, then destroyed it again, and in 460 it was re–established once again by the Geloans (Diod. 11.76.5),[28] so that Pindar, in an ode written a few years later, called it "new–founded" (τὰν νέοικον ἕδραν, Ol.5.8). The scholia inform us that Timaeus de-

---

[24] 7.154.1.

[25] F 18—Schol. Pind. Nem. 9.95a: βαθυκρήμνοισι δ' ἀμφ' ἀκταῖς Ἑλώρου. The scholiast quotes Didymus as saying that this was the battle in which Gelon was Hippocrates' cavalry commander, περὶ δὲ τούτου τοῦ πολέμου Τίμαιος ἐν τῇ ι' δεδήλωκε. And he takes from Didymus the sentence of ὁ Τίμαιος γράφων οὕτως· "Ἱπποκράτης δὲ μετὰ τὴν Κλεάνδρου τελευτήν, ἅμα μὲν τοῦ Γέλωνος ἐν τῇ τεταγμένῃ μεμενηκότος, ἅμα δὲ τοῖς Γελῴοις χαρίσασθαι βουλόμενος, μεταπεμψάμενος αὐτὸν καὶ παρακαλέσας ἐπὶ τὰς πράξεις, ἁπάντων τῶν ἱππέων τὴν ἐπιμέλειαν ἐκείνῳ παρέδωκεν."

[26] T. J. Dunbabin, The Western Greeks 378.

[27] Cf. n. 25.

[28] The text of Thuc. 6.5.3 has ὑπὸ Γέλωνος, corrected by editors to ὑπὸ Γελῴων.

scribed all these events, and that Hippocrates first became master of the ruined city "about the time of Darius' invasion" of Greece; the dates that they offer for the subsequent destruction and restoration are unfortunately corrupt.[29]

Timaeus also provided the scholiasts with the information that they needed in commenting on Pindar's *Second Olympian*, which honours Theron of Acragas.[30] They learnt from him that Acragas was named from the River Acragas and that it was a colony of Gela, but that Theron's ancestor, who was one of the original settlers, came directly from Rhodes to Acragas. "So much is clear from Pindar's own words, as Timaeus also says," is their comment.

Didymus is the immediate source of their information, and from the scholia in BCEHQ (29d), in explanation of the words of the first epode, we are told: "Didymus supplies some detail citing Timaeus." The note is clumsily written and looks like an unskilful attempt at summarizing a longer paragraph, but with the help of the version in A (29b) Timaeus' account can be reconstructed as follows:

Theron of Acragas was married to a daughter of Polyzelus, Hiero's younger brother, and gave his own daughter, Demarete, in marriage to the older brother Gelon. The Demaretean coinage is named after her. When Gelon died, his wish was that Hiero should succeed him in Syracuse, and Polyzelus was to be "general," that is, master of Gela, and to take over Demarete as wife. Polyzelus was well known and respected throughout Sicily, and had distinguished himself as a military leader. Hiero, however, was jealous of him and feared him as a rival. He therefore sent him off to conduct the war against the renascent Sybaris,[31] hoping that he would not return alive. But Polyzelus was successful in this war, and so Hiero, finding that accusations accomplished nothing, tried, unsuccessfully, to have him

---

[29] F 19—Schol. Pind. *Ol.* 5.19 (a, b). The text of the scholion is equally muddled and corrupt in both these recensions. According to recension c Philistus said that Hippocrates was given the city by the Syracusans in return for surrendering a large number of prisoners that he had taken in the battle (as in Thuc. 6.5.3: λύτρα ἀνδρῶν Συρακοσίων αἰχμαλώτων).

[30] F 92—Schol. Pind. *Ol.* 2.15(a): καμόντες, F 93a—Schol. *Ol.* 2 inscr., F 93b—Schol. *Ol.* 2.29d: τῶν δὲ πεπραγμένων.

[31] According to Diodorus (11.90.3, 12.10) the attempt to refound Sybaris was not made until 453, and the settlers were driven out by the Crotoniats a few years later. This war, in which Polyzelus is sent to fight, must be against the "Sybarites in exile" who settled on the West Coast at Laos and Scidrus (Hdt. 6.21). Strabo calls Laos ἄποικος Συβαριτῶν (6.1.1), but says nothing of its history. Its coinage may go as far back as 510 (J. Bérard, *La colonisation grecque* 147). Sybarites also seem to have found refuge in Poseidonia (P. Zancani Montuoro, "La fine di Sibari," *Rendiconti accad. Lincei,* Ser. 8.35 [1980] 149–56). Was that perhaps mentioned by Timaeus?

killed (ἐπειρᾶτο νεωτερισμοῦ is the euphemism in the text).[32] Theron was infuriated at this affront to his daughter and son–in–law, decided on war against Hiero, and advanced with his army as far as the River Gela. But the poet Simonides was able to reconcile them.[33]

This story differs in some details from the version in Diodorus (11.48), which can therefore be identified as coming from Ephorus.[34] Diodorus says nothing of Demarete, only that Hiero feared Polyzelus as a rival and wanted him out of the way; he therefore strengthened his own military forces, and prepared an army which Polyzelus was ordered to lead in defending the Sybarites against the Crotoniats, who were besieging their city (in Timaeus' account he is to fight against the Sybarites). Polyzelus, however, refused to go, and took refuge with Theron. Hiero, therefore, prepared to go to war with Theron, and the people of Himera, wishing to escape from the harsh rule of Theron's son Thrasydaeus, offered to hand over their city to him and help him in his war against Acragas. But Hiero refused their offer, and he and Theron patched up their quarrel. The final result is the same in both versions, and one is left wondering if the details are any less fictitious in one version than in the other.

Diodorus begins Book XI by saying that his preceding book (known to us only from excerpts) finished by describing the speeches that were made at the general congress of Greeks at Corinth with regard to obtaining Gelon's help in resisting the Persian invasion. Herodotus (7.145, 172) mentions this meeting "at the Isthmus" attended by leaders from "the right–minded cities." The meeting-place may have been the sanctuary of Poseidon at Isthmia, an eminently suitable place for such a meeting.[35] Herodotus

---

[32] The text here is ambiguous and possibly corrupt :ὁ δὲ μὴ φέρων γυμνότερον αὑτοῦ κατηγορεῖν, ἐπειρᾶτο νεωτερισμοῦ, καὶ οὕτω τὸν Θήρωνα, ὑπεραγανακτήσαντα θυγατρὸς ἅμα καὶ γαμβροῦ, συρρῆξαι πρὸς Ἱέρωνα πόλεμον, παρὰ Γέλᾳ τῷ Σικελιωτικῷ ποταμῷ. ὁ δὲ could be Polyzelus, not Hiero, and then the meaning would be that Polyzelus, rather than make a bare (or open) accusation, incited his father–in–law Theron to attack Hiero. Didymus with typical pedantry added that the River Gelas was mentioned by Callimachus (fr. 43.46 Pfeiffer).

[33] The scholiast writes φασὶ γὰρ τότε Σιμωνίδην . . . and may therefore be following another source. The poet's role as peacemaker recalls the part played by Stesichorus in the days of Phalaris (above, p. 120). On this whole story see now G. Vallet, "Note sur la 'maison' des Deinoménides," Φιλίας Χάριν. Miscellanea in onore di E. Manni VI (Rome 1980) 2153–56.

[34] Cf. Jacoby's note on F 93. He is right to reject the interpretation of Diod. 11.48 given by R. Laqueur, RE VIA, 1088.

[35] Since this sanctuary had not been excavated when Stein, How and Wells, and Legrand were writing, they are content to say that the meeting was probably at the Isthmus. Pausanias (3.12.6) cannot be right in saying that they met in Sparta at the Hellenion.

says nothing of any envoys from Gelon being present; according to him, one of the decisions taken at the congress was to send a delegation to Sicily, as well as to Corcyra and Crete; and he goes on to describe how the Greek envoys met with Gelon in Syracuse, who refused to help unless he was recognized as leader, a concession which neither the Spartan nor the Athenian delegate would grant (7.157–162). Polybius pays no attention to what Herodotus says,[36] and writes: "They say that the leaders of the Greeks made a thoroughly 'pragmatic' reply to Gelon's envoys. They asked that Gelon come as an ally with his forces, and let events decide the leadership; they would give it to the best men." This may mean that Ephorus as well as Timaeus brought envoys from Gelon to the congress, so that the story of his refusal could be told in a series of speeches.

Polybius thinks that the speeches in Timaeus' history show only too clearly his failure to understand how political argument was conducted and how decisions were reached in the real world. So he complains here that, instead of explaining the spirit in which the request for help was made, Timaeus took great trouble, when writing a speech for Gelon's envoys, to represent Sicily as a more important power than all the whole of Hellas, and to argue that its actions were more splendid and its wise men wiser than those anywhere else in the world, and the men in authority in Syracuse the most gifted leaders of their day, all with greater exaggeration than one might expect to find in a student's rhetorical exercise.[37]

Polybius' annoyance is understandable, but it is scarcely surprising that Timaeus should display his western pride in this way and want to acclaim Gelon as a leader to be matched with Themistocles and Pausanias. Indeed Polybius' remarks make it easy to identify Timaeus as the source of Diodorus' description (11.20–24), where the size of Gelon's fighting force is quite absurdly exaggerated. According to Herodotus (7.158), Gelon told the Greeks that he could offer them two hundred ships, two thousand cavalry, and twenty thousand hoplites, as well as two thousand archers, two thousand slingers, and two thousand light horse. Ephorus accepts this estimate,[38] except for the hoplite force, which he reduces to ten thousand. In

---

[36] Cf. Walbank, *Polybius* 38, n.30: "There is no firm evidence that he was acquainted with Herodotus."

[37] F 94—Polyb. 12.26b. After saying that the Greeks who asked for Gelon's help did not lack confidence in themselves, but wished to invite others to share "the crown of *arete*" with them, he adds: ἀλλ' ὅμως Τίμαιος εἰς ἕκαστα τῶν προειρημένων τοσούτους ἐντείνει λόγους καὶ τοσαύτην ποιεῖται σπουδὴν περὶ τοῦ τὴν μὲν Σικελίαν μεγαλοπρεπεστέραν ποιῆσαι τῆς συμπάσης Ἑλλάδος, τὰς δὲ ἐν αὐτῇ πράξεις ἐπιφανεστέρας . . .

[38] Schol. Pind. *Py.*1.146b—Ephorus, *FGrH* 70 F 186.

Diodorus, on the other hand, we find the enormous numbers that Polybius prepares us to expect, fifty thousand infantry and five thousand cavalry (11.21.1). There can be no doubt that he has these figures from Timaeus.[39]

These numbers, though quite impossible, still leave Gelon outnumbered six times, because, like Herodotus (7.165), this account gives the Carthaginians three hundred thousand men, two hundred fighting ships, and supply ships amounting to over three thousand (11.20.2). One must wonder if any reader took these figures seriously. But Timaeus' love for fantastic figures is shown in his account of Aristodemus of Cyme, who is said to have defeated an Etruscan force of half a million infantry and eighteen thousand cavalry.[40]

Herodotus has nothing to say about any agreement between Persia and Carthage to attack simultaneously, but Ephorus told of a Persian embassy coming to Carthage at the same time as the envoys came from Greece to Sicily asking Gelon to attend the congress in Corinth.[41] Although Aristotle does not believe that there was any collaboration between Persians and Carthaginians,[42] some scholars are prepared to believe Ephorus' story,[43] and it is likely that Timaeus accepted it. Diodorus says on two separate occasions that the Carthaginian attack was the result of previous arrangement with Persia.[44]

Herodotus makes no attempt to describe Hamilcar's advance to Himera or to describe the battle itself, except to say that they fought from dawn to dusk and that Hamilcar disappeared strangely in the course of the battle. He says that "the Carthaginians themselves" gave the explanation that he was making sacrifice before a huge fire in the camp, and threw himself into the fire when he recognized that the day was lost (7.167). The only description of the campaign and the battle that has survived is Diodorus' account, which is certainly taken from Timaeus.[45] It is the kind of account

---

[39] Jacoby, in his note on Ephorus F 186, recognizes these figures as coming from Timaeus, but in his later note on Timaeus F 94 he has (inexplicably) changed his mind and thinks that Diodorus has taken them from Ephorus.

[40] Above, p. 122.

[41] F 186—Schol. Pind. *Py.* 1.146b.

[42] *Poet.* 1459a.

[43] Hignett, *Xerxes' Invasion of Greece* (Oxford 1963), 17–18, rejects the story firmly, but see Jacoby's note on Ephorus F 186; Glotz–Cohen, *Histoire Grecque* II 45; How and Wells, in their notes on Hdt. 7.166.

[44] 11.1.4, 20.1, cf. Justin 19.1.10–13.

[45] There are no fragments of Timaeus, no remarks in other authors than can be offered in justification of this dogmatic statement. But as the argument proceeds it will be seen how clearly this narrative reveals the hand of Timaeus. For discussion and bibliography, see K. Meister, *Die sizilische Geschichte bei Diodor* 41–43.

that must have infuriated Polybius, though he never cites it as an example of incompetent military reporting. He thought Timaeus and Ephorus equally incompetent at describing military operations (12.25e–f), but although Ephorus and his predecessors, Antiochus and Philistus, must have given some account of the battle, it is impossible to believe that they offered anything like this astonishing story. And if no oral tradition supplied a convincing explanation for Gelon's victory, Timaeus was free to provide one of his own.

It is possible, of course, that some of the less outrageous details were borrowed by Timaeus from Ephorus, but even if we could identify them, they would give us only fragments of Ephorus' account and tell us little of its character. That is why Laqueur's analysis, in his long article in Pauly–Wissowa,[46] even if its method were sound, would not be very helpful in the present discussion. In fact, as I have argued elsewhere,[47] his method seems to me totally unsound. He believes that Diodorus began by copying or summarizing Ephorus, and then inserted excerpts from Timaeus into his original text, and that this clumsy method of composition was responsible for "contradictions" in his account as we have it. These so–called contradictions, however, are more apparent than real, as any reader can easily recognize who examines Diodorus' text with care and takes time to think out what he is trying to say, while not always expressing himself very well. His narrative may be ill–written, but it is neither illogical nor unintelligible.

Not everyone is willing to believe that it was the practice of Diodorus to follow one source at a time, i.e., Timaeus for his account of Sicilian events in Books XI–XIV, Ephorus for events in Aegean Greece in these books, Clitarchus for the history of Alexander, and Hieronymus for the twenty years after Alexander's death. Some scholars think it more probable that he regularly used more than one source at a time. A lengthy discussion of Diodorus' method cannot be undertaken here, but if a consistent picture of Timaeus' work emerges by supposing that Diodorus used him as his main source for Sicilian history in Books XI–XIV, it must be recognized that the "one–source" hypothesis cannot be discarded lightly for these books—the hypothesis that was proposed for the Sicilian sections over a century ago by Christian Volquardsen.[48] It must not be forgotten that Ti-

[46] *RE* VIA 1076 – 1203, s.v. Timaios (3).

[47] "Ephorus and Timaeus in Diodorus. Laqueur's thesis rejected," *Historia* 33 (1984) 1–20.

[48] C. Volquardsen, *Untersuchungen über die Quellen der griechischen und sicilischen Geschichte in Diodor, Buch XI bis XVI* (Kiel 1868). Cf. E. Schwartz, *RE* V.686, s.v. Diodoros

maeus himself knew and used (or adapted and altered) the work of Ephorus and Philistus, perhaps also that of Theopompus, and that when Diodorus mentions or appears to be following one of these writers for some detail, he may be quoting a reference that he has found in Timaeus; a second hand citation of this kind is often a more likely explanation than supposing that he has carried out bibliographical research of his own.

Historians in modern times have generally been content to offer a narrative that omits the more obviously fictitious items in Diodorus' account, on the assumption that Timaeus had at his disposal a traditional account which he proceeded to distort and elaborate. But there is no real reason to put much faith in this kind of rationalized or watered down version of Diodorus' Timaean account. My inclination is to agree with Eduard Meyer, who thinks that we cannot know what actually went on, that Diodorus' story is so utterly "phantastisch" that nothing can be got from it.[49] It includes incidents that must be intended as parallels to the Persian experience. Hamilcar suffers enormous losses in a storm that he meets on his voyage from Africa (a parallel to the storm that caused so much damage to the Persian fleet before Artemisium). All the ships carrying cavalry and chariots are lost (this is necessary to explain why Hamilcar has no cavalry in Sicily). He lands at Panormus, and in the space of three days repairs the damage to his ships, and gathers up his immense force, so that they can march towards Himera, escorted by the fleet sailing along the coast, as in the Persian advance on Thermopylae.[50]

After reaching Himera the army encamps in front of the city, and builds a wall from the sea to the foothills to protect itself. The fighting ships, all two hundred of them, are beached. They serve no purpose except to be set on fire by the Greeks. They are protected by a stockade, and the supplies are unloaded from the cargo vessels, which are then sent off to collect more supplies from Africa and Sardinia. With no ships to take the troops home again, their retreat is now cut off.

Hamilcar leads an attack against the Greeks, who conveniently come out to meet him, and inflicts great slaughter, "terrifying the people within the city." Theron now sends to Gelon asking for help, though Hamilcar has made no attempt to storm the city. Gelon comes to the rescue with fifty

---

(38): "So vereinigt sich alles, um T. als den Hauptgewährsmann für die sicilische Geschichte der Bücher XI–XIV zu erweisen." See also Jacoby, *FGrH* IIIb, pp.528–29 and Meister, op. cit. (n.45), who has little sympathy with the "Zweiquellen-theorie."

[49] *Geschichte des Altertums* IV. 1 (4th ed. Stuttgart 1944) 376–77. He considers the account unmistakeably Timaean in character.

[50] συμπαραπλέοντος τοῦ ναυτικοῦ, 11.20.3, cf. 11.5.1.

thousand infantry and five thousand cavalry. He makes the journey swiftly (no one apparently bothers him on the way). His men dig in in front of the city, defending themselves with a deep ditch and a stockade. The cavalry are then sent to attack the enemy who are roaming the countryside, and they take over ten thousand prisoners, whom they bring into the city. Gelon is given a tremendous reception, and fear of the enemy now changes to contempt. The necessary dramatic reversal has happened. The gates which had been built to protect the city are torn down, and new gates are built through which they can sally forth to the attack.

Gelon now decides that the proper thing to do is to set fire to the Carthaginian fleet. And "a fortuitous circumstance comes to his aid."[51] Hamilcar is in the "navy camp," preparing a splendid sacrifice to Poseidon, when a messenger arrives from Selinus and is duly captured by the Greeks. He brings a letter to tell Hamilcar that the Selinuntines will send "the cavalry" on the day appointed, apparently the very day fixed for the sacrifice. Gelon therefore sends cavalry of his own who can be mistaken for "allies of the Selinuntines," and be admitted to the Carthaginian navy camp, where they can kill Hamilcar and set fire to the ships. He posts scouts on the hills, who will signal to him when these horsemen enter the camp, and then he will attack the army camp with his main force. Everything goes according to plan, Hamilcar is killed, the ships are set on fire, the Carthaginian army comes out and there is a tremendous battle in which immense numbers of Carthaginians are killed; no quarter is given, and not a man escapes.[52]

It is hardly necessary to offer much comment on this preposterous story. On the other hand, if Timaeus had used his imagination with better judgment, and constructed a more credible account, could he have produced evidence to substantiate it? As Thucydides knew, very little of the information that Herodotus was able to gather about Xerxes' invasion was reliable. The sons and grandsons of men who had fought at Salamis or Platatea could only tell him what they, as individuals, had been able to observe. Thucydides, thanks to his exile and his opportunities to travel, could find out more, but it must be recognized that he did not report a "tradition" about events of the Peloponnesian War. It was he who established that tra-

---

[51] συνεβάλετο δὲ αὐτῷ καὶ τὸ αὐτόματον πρὸς τὴν ἐπίνοιαν μεγάλα, 11.21.3. Cf. Timoleon's sense of obligation to the goddess Automatia, Plut. *Tim.*36.6; Nepos, *Timol.* 4.4, where both are following Timaeus (below, p. 224).

[52] The Greeks take courage when they see the smoke from the burning ships, τῆς κατὰ τὰς ναῦς φλογὸς ἀρθείσης εἰς ὕψος (22.3). Variations of this phrase occur in other Timaean passages of Diodorus, 14.73.3, 20.67.2.

dition, and he established it so firmly that neither Ephorus nor any later writer rebelled against it. Likewise, it was Herodotus who established a "tradition" about Xerxes' invasion and its battles. If he had not written when he did, and if no history of these years had been written until over a century later, the result might have been very different.

But no one, neither Antiochus nor Philistus nor any other writer, seems to have established any "tradition" about the Carthaginian invasion until Ephorus made his attempt. And it seems that Timaeus was not prepared to show much respect for Ephorus. His object, so Polybius thought, was not to discover and describe what really happened, but to make the achievement of Gelon and his men appear as glorious as possible.

Herodotus (7.166) was told that the Battle of Himera took place on the same day as Salamis, but in Diodorus' account (11.24.1) it is said to coincide with Thermopylae, "the greatest victory with the most splendid defeat." If Timaeus (or Ephorus) could alter a "traditional" date without rousing indignant protests, the "tradition" cannot have been very strongly established. If Gelon's victory precedes the turn of the tide in Greece, it becomes more glorious as an omen of the ultimate Hellenic triumph, and this must be the object of putting it earlier in the year. "The men of Sicily by their victory put heart into the men of Greece" is what Diodorus says (23.2). The earlier date for Himera also gives Gelon the chance to be all ready to set sail for Greece "with a large force" to fight the Persians, only to be stopped when ships arrive from Corinth bringing the news of Salamis (26.5).

The victory at Himera is made to appear more complete even than the victory at Salamis, because, although Xerxes survived, the Carthaginian commander was killed and "not even a messenger, as the saying goes, reached Carthage to bring the news" (23.2). More exactly, as Diodorus describes in the next chapter (24.2), twenty of the Carthaginian fighting ships escaped the fire and put to sea overloaded with survivors, only to meet (inevitably) with a storm in which nearly all were lost, and "only a handful of men in a small boat reached Carthage to tell the tale".[53]

The account of what follows after the victory continues to show that Gelon achieved more at Himera than the victors of Salamis and Plataea. The Carthaginians are supposed to lose all of their three hundred thousand men. After a hundred and fifty thousand were slain in battle, the remainder were taken prisoner, and slaves were thus so plentiful in Sicily that some

---

[53] It is quite unnecessary to find any contradiction between these two stories, as Laqueur does (*RE* VIA. 1085–86), arguing that one is from Ephorus, the other from Timaeus. To have no messenger to tell the tale is proverbial of a great disaster, as in Diod. 13.21.3. Diodorus is careful here to say τὸ δὴ λεγόμενον, so that literal truth need not be expected.

individuals in Acragas had five hundred of them as their bondsmen (25.2). These Carthaginians were put to work to make Acragas into a splendid and beautiful city, although in Athens, as Timaeus would know, the great architectural projects had to wait until the time of Pericles. Could the Athenians say that they made Persians rebuild the temples that they had burnt? These contrasts are not pointed out by Diodorus, but they must have been intended for the reader to see for himself.

In Carthage, so we are told, when they heard the news of the battle, the fear of Gelon invading Africa was so great that they sent ambassadors with full powers to make any agreement that they could (24.4). And when they begged Gelon, with tears in their eyes, to treat them with humanity (26.2), he quickly established a peace treaty with them, setting an indemnity of only two thousand talents. He also specified that they should build two temples, where copies of the treaty would be preserved,[54] and they showed their relief at such fair treatment by sending a gold crown for Demarete. Thus the impression is given that the Greeks in Sicily achieved everything that they wanted in a single battle, whereas Athens had to continue fighting with the Persians for many years before a peace settlement was made. It is not pointed out that the Carthaginians were allowed to keep their holdings in the West of Sicily. It would diminish the Greek triumph if that were mentioned.

Furthermore, unlike Themistocles and Pausanias, Gelon did not fall into disgrace or suffer rejection at the hands of his countrymen. On the contrary, he was acclaimed throughout Sicily, and in Syracuse at a military assembly, when a great throng appeared in arms, he came before them "in civilian dress," wearing a himation without a chiton,[55] to show how democratic he was, and he was hailed as Euergetes, Soter, and King (26.5–6). This must be Timaeus giving him Ptolemaic titles; it is most unlikely that he received any of them. His gifts to Delphi and Olympia, however, can be documented,[56] and he maintained his reputation as one of the "good" tyrants in later centuries. Throughout Sicily, we are told, he not only main-

---

[54] No inscribed treaty is known and these temples have not been identified. For suggestions see Dunbabin, *The Western Greeks* 429, with the references given in his notes. Various versions were in circulation of the terms imposed by Gelon. Cf. Schol. Pind. *Py.* 2.2 (commenting on Syracuse as τέμενος Ἄρεος): τοῦτο εἴρηκε διὰ τὸ νεωστὶ Καρχηδονίους καὶ Λίβυας καὶ Τυρρηνοὺς ὑπὸ τῶν περὶ Γέλωνα καὶ Ἱέρωνα μὴ μόνον τῇ νήσῳ ἐπιπλεύσαντας καθῃρῆσθαι, ἀλλὰ καὶ ὑπ' αὐτοῖς τὴν Καρχηδόνα γενέσθαι ὥσθ' ὑπακούειν· τὸ γοῦν ἀνθρωποθυτεῖν φησιν ὁ Θεόφραστος ἐν τῷ περὶ Τυρρηνῶν παύεσθαι αὐτοὺς Γέλωνος προστάξαντος· ὅτι δὲ καὶ ἐκέλευσεν αὐτοὺς χρήματα εἰσφέρειν Τίμαιος διὰ τῆς ια´ ἀνέγραψεν (F 20). ια´ is a necessary emendation of ιδ´.

[55] Cf. Polyaen. 1.27.1, which must be based on Timaeus, even though altered in detail.

[56] Cf. R. Meiggs–D. Lewis, *Greek Historical Inscriptions* I no.28; Schol. Pind. *Py.* 1.152b; Paus. 6.19.7.

tained good relations with his allies, but re-established friendship with those who had fought against him, when they sought forgiveness of their errors (26.1). Athens could not say the same of her relations with the Thebans and Thessalians.

These chapters may not be an entirely accurate paraphrase of Timaeus, but they reveal many of his characteristics and make it easy to understand why Polybius was irritated by his whole treatment of Gelon. In the following chapters (27–37), Diodorus goes back to Ephorus for the story of Plataea, and the contrast in style deserves attention. There is more emphasis on the reasoning and the intentions of the combatants on both sides, and on the circumstances that influenced their decisions. And there is very little in the writing that could be called rhetorical or dramatic.

Diodorus then returns to the West to describe Gelon's death and his funeral (11.38). He says that Gelon did not want an elaborate monument and, before his death, insisted that the Syracusans must observe the restrictions on funeral expense that he had laid down. Nevertheless, they gave him a "noteworthy" (ἀξιόλογον) monument and showed him "heroic honours." The account would fit Ephorus or Timaeus equally well, since both admired Gelon as a "good" tyrant. Neither of them can have seen the monument, because it was destroyed by the Carthaginians on their next invasion, but Diodorus must be following Timaeus when he says that Agathocles destroyed the "nine towers" that stood near by (38.5), since Ephorus' history did not go beyond 335.[57]

When Diodorus describes Hiero's quarrel with Polyzelus and Theron, which very nearly results in war (11.48), he must be following Ephorus, since Timaeus is known to have given a quite different account of the quarrel.[58] And there is nothing noticeably Timaean in the other brief summaries of events in Sicily that appear at intervals in Book XI. There is no dramatic or rhetorical colouring in the narrative, even when the events are dramatic, and the contrasts in character between Theron and Thrasydaeus (48) and between Gelon and Hiero (67) are stated in commonplace general terms, without detail or illustration.

But Timaeus must have described the Sicel uprising led by Ducetius, which is known to us only through Diodorus, though accounts of it must

---

[57] Laqueur, *RE* VIA. 1087, maintains that Diodorus' narrative displays "nebeneinander zwei ganz verschiedene Fassungen; nach der einen erhielt Gelon eine bescheidene Grabstätte auf den Äckern seiner Frau, nach der anderen ein hervorragendes Denkmal." But why should not Gelon be given both the modest tomb and (later) the imposing monument? The attempt to distinguish Ephoran and Timaean elements in these chapters is not convincing.

[58] Above, pp. 131–32.

also have been given by Timaeus' predecessors. When Diodorus describes how Ducetius founded the city of Palike as a centre for the movement, "near the shrine of the gods called Palikoi" (88.6), and goes on to speak of the traditional lore connected with the place and the superstitious beliefs about the *krateres,* his dependence on Timaeus is easily recognized.[59] This is exactly the kind of topographical *parodoxon* that Timaeus loved to describe, a place where solemn oaths were sworn, a place of refuge for fugitives of all kinds, a place of *deisidaimonia* (89.8).

An account of the fighting and the final defeat of the rebellion follows, and the flight of Ducetius and the great scene in Syracuse when he comes into the agora, and takes refuge at the altar as a suppliant of the city (90–92). Here was an opportunity to give the speeches of those who were in favour of the death penalty or against it. Diodorus tells us that some speakers wanted Ducetius to be treated as an enemy, but it was the more thoughtful older men (οἱ χαριέστατοι τῶν πρεσβυτέρων) who persuaded the citizens that they should respect the suppliant and avoid the nemesis of the gods, and consider not what Ducetius deserved to suffer, but what it was fitting for Syracusans to do (δεῖν γὰρ σκοπεῖν οὐ τί παθεῖν ἄξιός ἐστι Δουκέτιος, ἀλλὰ τί πρέπει πρᾶξαι Συρακοσίοις, 92.3).

In similar fashion, according to Timaeus, [60] when the captured Athenian generals, Nicias and Demosthenes, were on trial in the Assembly of Syracuse, Hermocrates tried to save their lives by insisting that making proper use of a victory was more important than the victory itself, but the demagogue Diocles persuaded the Assembly to vote for the death sentence. Timaeus could hardly have failed to point the contrast between the two occasions, how the more moderate speakers saved the life of a suppliant and saved the good name of Syracuse, but all that Hermocrates could do, so he tells us,[61] was to save Nicias and Demosthenes from the ignominy of execution by giving them the opportunity to take their own lives.

It is Polybius who provides proof that Diodorus is following Timaeus in his account of the trial of Ducetius, when he rebukes Timaeus for his intemperate language in a later book about Demochares, the nephew of Demosthenes the orator, and reminds him of what he had written earlier, saying he should consider "what it is fitting for him to say, just as men of any intelligence consider first not what their enemy deserves to suffer, but what it is fitting for them to do" (καθάπερ οἱ νοῦν ἔχοντες, ἐπὰν ἀμύ-

---

[59] There is, however, no fragment of Timaeus that mentions Palike or the Palikoi. Macrobius (5.19.25) quotes his predecessor Callias (*FGrH* 564 F 1).

[60] F 100b—Plut. *Nic.* 28.3, cf. Diod. 13.19.5.

[61] F 101—Plut. *Nic.* 28.5.

νασθαι κρίνωσι τοὺς ἐχθρούς, οὐ τοῦτο πρῶτον σκοποῦνται τί
παθεῖν ἄξιός ἐστιν ὁ πλησίον, ἀλλὰ τί ποιεῖν αὐτοῖς πρέπει, τοῦτο
μᾶλλον , οὕτως καὶ περὶ τῶν λοιδοριῶν οὐ τί τοῖς ἐχθροῖς ἀκούειν
ἁρμόζει, τοῦτο πρῶτον ἡγητέον, ἀλλὰ τί λέγειν ἡμῖν πρέπει, τοῦτο
ἀναγκαιότατον λογιστέον, 12.14.2).

Timaeus must have written quite extensively about Sicilian events of
the Pentecontaetia in his eleventh and twelfth books,[62] but Diodorus gives
us only brief extracts from his account. The fragments of Didymus' *Commentary on Pindar* preserved in the Pindaric scholia tell us little of its content and character,[63] only what events he described, not how he described
them. No other account exists of events between 465 and 424, and he must
have written in some detail about these years. But his account has disappeared, leaving few traces.

Thucydides tells us, in a famous sentence, that when the Athenians
voted to send their expedition to Sicily, they had "no understanding of the
size of the island and the number of Greeks and barbarians who lived there"
(6.1). He also seems to tell us that he was ill–informed himself about the
recent history of the island. He has nothing to say about political events
since the fall of the tyrants, not a word about Ducetius or the relations
between Greeks and non–Greeks, no explanation of the situation in the
Carthaginian area of Western Sicily, although his story begins with the embassy from Egesta asking help against Selinus. There must have been
people who could have enlightened him if he went to Sicily, but was there
no other way of learning? Were Nicias and Alcibiades no better informed
than we are with our scraps of information from Diodorus? Were they entirely dependent on the carefully limited and biased reports given them by
the envoys from Egesta? Thucydides thought it necessary to give a careful
outline of events in Aegean Greece since 480. He said no written account
of these events was available except for the rather unsatisfactory version of
Hellanicus (1.97). He must surely be telling us that there was no adequate
account of the corresponding period in Sicily and Magna Graecia.

One must therefore conclude that no tradition of Western history in the
Pentecontaetia took shape until Ephorus attempted to establish it.
Antiochus must have had something to say about these years, but Thucy-

---

[62] The references are clear. Gelon's rise to power was described in Book X (F 18), the
Carthaginian invasion in XI (F 20, where the correction ια' for ιδ' seems certain), events of
the next generation in XII (F 21, 97).

[63] F 18–21, cf. Schmidt, *Didymi Chalcenteri Fragmenta* 214–41. The full text of Didymus' commentary might tell us more. It may have quoted from Ephorus and Timaeus to show
how they differed, like the quotations from historians in his *De Demosthene Commenta* (ed.
Diels-Schubart, Lepizig 1904; ed. Pearson-Stephens, Stuttgart 1982).

dides did not think it worth while to borrow anything from the later books of his history. Ephorus may have found them useful, but there is no evidence of his using them, nor is there any record of what Philistus had to say of this period. Ephorus must have been Timaeus' principal written source for the Pentecontaetia, and his task was to supplement Ephorus' account from his own imagination and such oral information as he might be able to collect.

It must be recognized that events in the West would not be considered as part of Hellenic history by Athenians until the West became involved in the Peloponnesian War. Until then, until the Congress of Gela, which offers a useful milestone, the West was hardly part of the world that they recognized as Hellenic. Thucydides, in his opening chapter, comes very near to saying that the Peloponnesian War marked a new stage in Greek history when it involved "almost the entire Hellenic world." We can perhaps complete his thought if we say that it was this war that brought the West into Hellenic history, and that Sicilian and Italian events before 424 B.C. seemed to him just as uncertain and hard to understand as events of earlier centuries which the passage of time made it almost impossible to recover. That could be his justification for not including them in his account of the Pentecontaetia.

The loss of this part of Timaeus' history, then, is a serious loss, not because it would have given us a very reliable account of these years, but because it would show us how he contrived to make the events intelligible and οὐκ ἄπιστα, even though they were perhaps, as Thucydides would say, ἀκοῇ μὲν λεγόμενα, ἔργῳ δὲ σπανιώτερον βεβαιούμενα (1.23). We can venture to say that Timaeus must have given a more interesting account than Ephorus, with more life in it than the account that Diodorus gives, even though he had to be content often with τεκμήρια for lack of μάρτυρες. And the element of τὸ μυθῶδες, as will be seen, was not entirely absent from his narrative.

For the Peloponnesian War, on the other hand, Thucydides set a pattern of narrative that was and is recognized as standard, and there is a general reluctance to disagree with what he wrote. Plutarch says that Timaeus "hoped to outdo Thucydides with his display of cleverness and to make Philistus look commonplace and unprofessional," but he gives no examples to show exactly what he means, saying only that "with his history he charges right through the conflicts and naval battles and debates which they described so well."[64] This seems to mean that, so far as Plutarch can see,

---

[64] ὃς ἐλπίσας τὸν μὲν Θουκυδίδην ὑπερβαλεῖσθαι δεινότητι, τὸν δὲ Φίλιστον

despite his clumsy pretensions to originality, he really has nothing new to say, no new details or interpretations. Such criticism may be unfair, but without more help from fragments it is as hard to counter as Polybius' contemptuous accusations.

Plutarch says that he disliked the malicious characterization for which Timaeus, like Theopompus, was famous. Some historian, whom he does not name, though it must be either Timaeus or Theopompus, offended him by calling Nicias a religious fanatic (θεόληπτος), though Thucydides had been content to say that he was "given to pious practices."[65] Nepos, in his *Alcibiades*, says that Timaeus and Theopompus were both *maledicentissimi*, but were nevertheless united *nescioquo modo* in their praise of Alcibiades.[66] He seems not to suspect that their praise was tinged with malice. They remarked, he tells us, on the ability of Alcibiades to adapt himself to circumstances. In Athens he stood out *splendore ac dignitate vitae,* but in Thebes, after he was exiled, he won admiration by showing off his remarkable physical strength, because Thebans admired bodily strength more than intelligence. In Sparta he amazed everyone by his gifts of endurance and his *parsimonia,* but he could adopt a different style *apud Thracas, homines vinolentos rebusque veneriis deditos,* and equally well win admiration in Persia, where extravagant display and a love of hunting were expected. This is perhaps the kind of adaptability that one might expect of a man who switched his allegiance so readily, and it is hard to believe that such a characterization is intended as genuine praise. It would be most interesting to know what exactly Timaeus did say.

Timaeus' verdict on Athenian leaders carries no particular authority, since it reflects only his interpretation of what he read in Thucydides and Ephorus. Fortunately, however, his judgment on the two leading figures on the other side at Syracuse has been preserved. Plutarch, who had read the account of Philistus as well as that of Timaeus, shows Philistus emphasizing how Gylippus on his arrival put new heart into the Syracusans.[67] This is hardly more than we find in Thucydides, who tells us little about the man himself.[68] It is Timaeus who explains that the Syracusans resented the authority claimed by this Spartan newcomer. He says that they laughed at his

---

ἀποδείξειν παντάπασι φορτικὸν καὶ ἰδιώτην, διὰ μέσων ὠθεῖται τῇ ἱστορίᾳ τῶν μάλιστα κατωρθωμένων ἐκείνοις ἀγώνων καὶ ναυμαχιῶν καὶ δημηγοριῶν (*Nic.*1—T 18). He characterizes Timaeus as ὅλως τις ὀψιμαθὴς καὶ μειρακιώδης φαινόμενος ἐν τούτοις.

[65] *De mal. Her.* 855B; Thuc. 7.50.4.
[66] *Alcib.* 11.1—F 99.
[67] *Nic.* 19—Philistus *FGrH* 555 F 56.
[68] H. D. Westlake, *Individuals in Thucydides* (Cambridge 1968) 277–89.

appearance when he first came, with his long hair and traditional Spartan costume, but even so he roused enthusiasm and there was no scarcity of men eager to serve under him. Later, however, he behaved like the traditional Spartan away from home, greedily taking every opportunity to enrich himself; and in his case, Timaeus says, this was a kind of hereditary weakness, because his father subsequently helped himself to thirty talents out of the thousand that Lysander sent to Sparta, and kept them hidden under the roof of his house until an informer exposed him and he was sentenced to exile.[69] Gylippus' meanness and greed, so Timaeus says, made him thoroughly unpopular, and after the victory he was allowed to go away without any honours or thanks.[70]

Timaeus described the special assembly of Syracusans and allies that met after the Athenian surrender. According to him, as in Thucydides (7.86.2), Gylippus opposed the sentence of death that was passed on Nicias and Demosthenes and asked that they be put in his charge, so that he could take them to Sparta; but his request was indignantly refused, naturally enough, Timaeus thinks, because many had found the Spartan discipline on which he insisted extremely irksome, and they were convinced that he had enriched himself quite shamelessly during the campaign. Hermocrates, on the other hand, was not well received when he showed himself opposed to the death sentence, saying ὡς κάλλιόν ἐστι τοῦ νικᾶν τὸ τὴν νίκην ἐνεγκεῖν ἀνθρωπίνως. But while the meeting was still in session he sent a message to Nicias and Demosthenes through one of the guards, and they were allowed to commit suicide and escape the indignity of execution. Thus Timaeus shows Hermocrates as having the final word (Plut. *Nic.* 28—F 100b, 101).

Diodorus' description of this assembly (13.19–33) ends with a speech by Gylippus, who persuades the Syracusans to adopt the proposal of Diocles that Nicias and Demosthenes be put to death and the rest of the Athenian captives be sent to the quarries; and he says that the sentence on the two generals was carried out immediately (33.1). It can be argued that this is a second speech given to Gylippus by Timaeus, after the failure of his first proposal. But it is equally possible that Diodorus has taken it from Ephorus. Diodorus also reports Hermocrates' attempt to save the lives of the generals. If he really spoke out in this way, it would have been remembered, and Ephorus is just as likely to have reported it as Timaeus.

Ephorus must certainly be recognized as Diodorus' source in the earlier

---

[69] F 100a, b—Plut.*Nic.* 19.5, 28.4.
[70] F 100c—Plut. *Timol.* 41.4.

chapters of Book XIII. In these chapters, he often differs from Thucydides, and offers a number of details that do not appear in the Thucydidean account. Ephorus may have some of them from Philistus,[71] and one can only conjecture how many of them may have been in Timaeus' version.

On the other hand it is more likely that Timaeus is the author of the speech of Nicolaus, who urges that mercy be shown to the Athenian generals (13.20–37). This long speech, full of conventional rhetoric and pathos, has some of the Timaean quality that Polybius disliked so much. Nicolaus is an old man who has to be helped on to the platform by his servants, and since he has lost his two sons in the war and might be expected to show great bitterness towards the Athenians, his plea for mercy has the element of paradox that might please Timaeus' readers. This is exactly the kind of speech that Polybius leads us to expect from him.[72]

If Diodorus took the speech of Nicolaus from Timaeus, while preserving some of Ephorus' description of the debate, we may suppose that, at some point in writing his narrative of the siege of Syracuse, he became dissatisfied with Ephorus' account and turned to Timaeus where he found something that he liked better. His account of the last battle in the Great Harbour (13.14–17) is quite unlike his descriptions of the earlier battles, where he seems to be following Ephorus, and it looks like an attempt, such as we might expect from Timaeus, to improve on the Thucydidean account by heightening the dramatic effect in rhetorical fashion. This may indeed be the passage which earned the rebuke of Plutarch, who disliked his attempt to improve upon one of Thucydides' most famous passages.[73]

It is possible that Syracusans in the years after the Athenian surrender wanted to defend themselves against the charge that they had treated the generals and the other captives with excessive cruelty, and that Ephorus is reporting their attempt to shift the blame on to the Spartan Gylippus, and that Timaeus goes one better when he says that the generals were not in fact put to death by them, but that they committed suicide, taking the hint that Hermocrates gave them (F 101). Alternatively, Timaeus may be responsible for both these attempts to excuse their severity.

Thucydides admired Hermocrates and thought that he deserved the credit for the Syracusan victory rather than Gylippus. But he does not give

---

[71] P.Pédech, "Philistos et l'expédition athénienne en Sicile," Φιλίας χάριν. *Miscellanea di studi in onore di E.Manni* V (Rome 1980) 1711–34.

[72] Cf. Meister, *Die sizilische Geschichte* 63–67. He also argues that Plutarch may be using Philistus as well as Timaeus in the *Nicias*.

[73] Plut. *Nic.* 1 (quoted in n.64). For further argument see R.Zoeppfel, *Untersuchungen zum Geschichtswerk des Philistos* (Freiburg 1965) 157–74.

his reasons for thinking so,[74] and Timaeus probably offered some discussion and gave a fuller characterization of the man. Like Thucydides, he introduced him by giving his speech at the Conference of Gela. According to Polybius, "he says that at the time when Eurymedon came to Sicily and tried to incite the cities against Syracuse, the people of Gela, being weary of war, sent envoys to Camarina proposing a truce, and the people of Camarina accepted their proposal gladly. Both sides then wrote to their own allies urging them to send trusted delegates to a conference at Gela, where they would discuss a settlement and consider the common interests of everyone. The conference assembled, and with the debate thrown open, Timaeus brings on Hermocrates with a speech to the following effect."[75]

This corresponds with the account in Thucydides (4.58), except that Thucydides does not describe Eurymedon's mission in quite such plain terms. But Polybius complains that the speech given to Hermocrates by Timaeus is absurdly inappropriate for a man who is one of the most highly respected statesmen in the history of Sicily: "The man begins by complimenting the people of Gela and Camarina, first for establishing the truce between themselves, then for their part in arranging the conference, and thirdly because they were careful not to have the whole citizen body discuss the peace settlement, but had restricted the conference to the political leaders in each community, who knew very well the difference between peace and war. Then, after two or three remarks of a general nature (ἐπιχειρήματα πραγματικά), he tells them they should stop and consider how different peace is from war."

Polybius remarks that this kind of writing reveals Timaeus' complete lack of political experience: he knows no more than he might have learnt in a school of rhetoric. Here he is insisting on the difference between peace and war, just after telling them that they know it only too well, making an experienced politician talk at length about matters that stood in no need of argument: "First he sees fit to remind them that in war it is trumpets that rouse sleepers in the morning, but in peace it is bird–song. Then he tells them how Heracles revealed his true purpose when he established the Olympic festival and the sacred truce, that when he was at war he harmed his enemies only because it could not be avoided or in obedience to an order, that he never caused harm to anyone willingly. And he goes on to quote the passage in Homer where Zeus rebukes Ares:

----

[74] He expresses his admiration only once, 6.72.3; cf. Westlake, *Individuals in Thucydides* 10, 289.

[75] F 22—Polyb. 12.25k.

'Most hateful art thou of all the gods in Olympus,'

and where Nestor curses the man who loves war, and then he quotes Euripides' *Ode to Peace*, Εἰρήνα βαθύπλουτε,[76] and cites some proverbial
sayings that are familiar to everyone—war is like sickness, peace like
health; peace cures the sick, but in war even the healthy perish; in peace
the young bury the old, but in war it is the opposite."

Must we believe that this report is accurate, that Timaeus gave
Hermocrates the kind of speech that most readers would find ridiculous? It
is certainly easier to believe it if he is responsible for the speech that
Diodorus gives to Nicocles, but Polybius is of course prejudiced against
Timaeus and fully capable of being quite unfair to him. He does not say
that the whole speech consisted of rhetorical commonplaces, only that they
occupied "the greater part of the speech." But there are only two or three
sentences here, not nearly enough for "the greater part" of a speech, and
they seem to be an enlarged version of what Thucydides makes Hermocrates say in the second sentence of the speech that he gives him (4.59.2):
"Why would anyone want to talk at length about the hardships of war to
people who know them so well?" Timaeus must have read the Thucydidean
speech (which Polybius never mentions), and if he made Hermocrates say
something like: "I need hardly remind you of the words of Homer and
Euripides or of the familiar proverbs that emphasize the hardships of war
and the blessings of peace . . .", he must have been deliberately following
the Thucydidean model. This is the only occasion when he is known to
have challenged comparison with a Thucydidean speech, but he may have
done so on other occasions. In any case, he may well have agreed with
Thucydides that a few conventional remarks of this kind were inevitable
and desirable (ἃ ἔδει λέγειν, as Thucydides would say) for the opening
speech at a conference of this kind.[77]

Timaeus must have asked himself the question whether the speeches
in Thucydides really were attempts at accurate reports, "keeping close to
the general sense of what was actually said" (ὅτι ἐγγύτατα τῆς συμπάσης
γνώμης τῶν ἀληθῶς λεχθέντων, as Thucydides says, 1.22.1), or more
imaginative compositions that left any later historian free to indulge his
own imagination. Polybius should have been able to tell us how Timaeus
answered this question, but he does not do so.[78]

---

[76] *Il.* 5.890, 9.63; Eur. fr. 453 Nauck.

[77] For further comment, see Walbank's note on Polyb. 12.25k.5. Brown, *Timaeus* 65–66,
is prepared to accept Polybius' summary as fair and thinks it must have been a bad speech.

[78] For discussion of Timaeus' speeches see "The Speeches in Timaeus' history," *AJP* 107
(1986) 350–68.

Unluckily, Timaeus' account of the Congress of Gela is lost except for what Polybius tells us. It would be interesting to know how he described the Syracusan reaction to the preliminary Athenian expeditions in 424 and earlier. He evidently thought Eurymedon's expedition was meant as preparation for an attack on Syracuse (so much at least Polybius tells us).[79] He also had something to say about a visit by the Athenian naval commander Diotimos to Naples, where he offered sacrifice to Parthenope in obedience to an oracle, and established the tradition of a torch race, which was still observed in Timaeus' time.[80] This Diotimos must be the Diotimos, son of Strombichos, who was one of the *strategoi* in command of the ships sent to Corcyra in 433.[81] His visit to Naples, whether in 433 or on some other occasion, is not mentioned elsewhere, and there is no record of Athenian triremes venturing as far as the Bay of Naples. It may perhaps be presumed that he went only with a single ship, in a diplomatic capacity, but his visit could have been interpreted as one more sign that the Athenians had serious plans for interference in the West.[82]

It is hardly likely that Timaeus had anything significant to add to Thucydides' account of the events of 415–13.[83] But, in his usual fashion, he

---

[79] Polybius 12.25k cites Timaeus as describing the circumstances in which the Congress of Gela was organized: ὁ δέ φησιν. . . . .καθ' ὃν καιρὸν Εὐρυμέδων παραγενόμενος εἰς Σικελίαν παρεκάλει τὰς πόλεις εἰς τὸν κατὰ τῶν Συρακοσίων πόλεμον, τότε τοὺς Γελῴους κάμνοντας τῷ πολέμῳ διαπέμψασθαι πρὸς τοὺς Καμαριναίους ὑπὲρ ἀνοχῶν κτλ. (F 22). Thucydides (4.65.3) reports that Eurymedon and his colleagues were found guilty of receiving bribes and failing to take advantage of their opportunity "to gain control of Sicily." It would be interesting to know what Timaeus thought of this verdict.

[80] F 98.

[81] Thuc. 1.45.2.

[82] Strabo writes (5.4.7): μετὰ δὲ Δικαιαρχίαν ἐστὶ Νεάπολις Κυμαίων· ὕστερον δὲ καὶ Χαλκιδεῖς ἐπῴκησαν καὶ Πιθηκουσσαίων τινὲς καὶ Ἀθηναίων, ὥστε καὶ Νεάπολις ἐκλήθη διὰ τοῦτο· ὅπου δείκνυται μνῆμα τῶν Σειρήνων μιᾶς, Παρθενόπης, καὶ ἀγὼν συντελεῖται γυμνικὸς κατὰ μαντείαν. No other source mentions this addition of Athenian settlers. It may have been mentioned by Timaeus, in connection perhaps with Diotimos' visit, and dated some time in the 440's or 430's after the settlement of Thurii. Jacoby (note on F 98) is sceptical, but see Lasserre's note on Strabo 5.4.7; K. J. Beloch, *Griechische Geschichte* II.1(2nd ed. Strasbourg 1914) 202–03; J. Bérard, *La Colonisation grecque,* 57–60; D. Kagan, *The Outbreak of the Peloponnesian War* (Ithaca 1969) 385–86, who lists various opinions about Diotimos' visit to Naples. Justin (4.3.4–7) says that an Athenian fleet was sent to Sicily at the invitation of Catana at some unspecified date before the expedition of 427, "ut sub specie ferendi Catiniensibus auxilii temptarent Siciliae imperium." But, since there is no trace of this expedition elsewhere, his report is generally ignored as unworthy of belief, as by G. E. M. de Ste.Croix, *Origins of the Pelop. War* (London 1972) 221–22. For Timaeus' account of the "Old City" and "New City" of Naples see pp. 94–95 above.

[83] Nevertheless, Philistus and Timaeus must have known more than Thucydides about events within Syracuse and tales that were told there. Some of the "stratagems" reported by Polyaenus that are attributed to Gylippus and Hermocrates and the Corinthian naval com-

noted some ominous signs that foretold the failure of the expedition. Nicias, whose name seemed to denote victory, was reluctant to take command, and when the Athenians incurred the anger of Hermes by their desecration of the Hermae, it was appropriate that a man called Hermocrates should help to carry out the will of Hermes. Heracles was also on the side of the Syracusans "for the sake of Kore, through whom he obtained Cerberus," and angry with the Athenians when they supported the people of Egesta, who were descended from the Trojans, whose city he had once destroyed.[84] Here we see more of the kind of argument that irritated Polybius.

Diodorus, however, says that a decision was taken by the Athenian commanders, in secret session with the *boule* before they left Athens, that "if they gained control of the island, they would enslave the people of Selinus and Syracuse and impose a *phoros* on everyone else, to be paid annually to Athens" (13.2.6). Plutarch says nothing of this "secret resolution," perhaps (very reasonably) dismissing it as a fiction, but it must have been mentioned by Timaeus, whether he invented the story himself or found it current in Syracuse among other tales of Athenian *hybris*.[85]

Timaeus also provided some details of the kind that interested Athenaeus. A small Sican community on the northern coast called Hyccara was captured by the Athenians because it was unfriendly to Egesta, and deserters from the Athenian fleet bought some of the men taken prisoner there and bribed their captains to accept these men as their substitutes in the ship's company (Thuc. 6.62.3, 7.13.2). Timaeus, in his usual manner, invented a Greek etymology for the name of the town, from fish called *hykes*, and (what was more important) said that it was the birthplace of the famous hetaira Lais.[86] This gave him the excuse to describe some of the episodes in her career, including her tragic death in Thessaly, where she became involved in a jealous quarrel with some women and was beaten to death with wooden footstools[87] in a sanctuary of Aphrodite, which in consequence became known as the sanctuary of Aphrodite the Unholy. He also

---

mander Ariston or Telesinicus (1.42–43, 5.13, 32) are probably derived from a Sicilian source, if not from Ephorus. Also perhaps some of the less creditable details about Nicias and Alcibiades (1.39–40). But Polyaenus' account cannot be regarded as "pure" Timaeus, cf. J.Melber, *Jahrbücher für classische Philologie*, Supp. 14 (1884–85) 484–95.

[84] F 102a—*De Sublim.* 4.3 (as an example of Timaeus' ψυχρότης); F 102b—Plut. *Nic.* 1.2 (also critical of Timaeus).

[85] R. Laqueur, *RE* VIA. 1097–98; K. Meister, *Gymnasium* 77 (1970) 511–12.

[86] F 23—Ath. 7.327B, one of many etymologies that Timaeus supplied for names that cannot be Greek (cf. above, p. 57); F 24—Ath. 13.588B–589A.

[87] ξυλίναις χελώναις τυπτομένην. Various heavy objects are called "tortoises," but "stools" seems the most likely meaning here.

pointed out where her grave was "shown,"[88] beside the River Peneius, with an inscription in verse.

It is likely that Timaeus also described how Diocles the Syracusan politician met his death. Diodorus finishes his account of the debate about the Athenian prisoners in the Syracusan Assembly by saying that Diocles' motion was adopted, the generals were put to death, and the rest of the Athenians sent to the quarries (13.33.1). Then he writes: "After the end of the war Diocles drafted his code of laws for the Syracusans, and it happened that this man met with a strange reversal of fortune." He explains that Diocles had himself introduced a law that anyone who entered the agora carrying a weapon must suffer the death penalty. But it happened that one time he was preparing to leave the city fully armed, ready to meet a rumoured enemy attack, when the alarm was raised of a disturbance in the agora. Without thinking he hurried there still wearing his sword. He was taxed with breaking his own laws, cried out "No, but I shall enforce them," drew his sword, and killed himself.

This is certainly the kind of story that would have appealed to Timaeus. It could be used to show either that Diocles was just as severe towards himself as towards the Athenians or that he was properly punished for his barbarous cruelty towards them.

Under the next year, 412 B.C., Diodorus describes the ultra–democratic constitution that Diocles devised as a safeguard against the threat of tyranny, and he says that Diocles was greatly admired during his lifetime throughout Sicily and given heroic honours after his death (13.35.1–2). Diocles was the leading opponent of Hermocrates, was responsible for his exile, and helped to have him killed when he tried to fight his way back into Syracuse. It is argued that Timaeus, who had great admiration for Hermocrates, would hardly speak in praise of such a man and that Diodorus has taken his account from Ephorus.[89]

The argument is false, because there is no praise of Diocles here, only a report that people admired him, rightly or wrongly, and there is no reason why Timaeus should try to suppress what could not be concealed. But it is likely that Timaeus himself was now more dependent than before on Ephorus and Philistus, since he no longer had Thucydides to guide him in his narrative. He would also inevitably find occasions to be critical of Ephorus, and this is how Diodorus' references to Ephorus can best be ex-

---

[88] For objects "shown" to visitors at sanctuaries or in cities by guides, cf. above, pp. 64, 77–79, 84.

[89] For more elaborate argument, see Laqueur *RE* VIA. 1103–05. He maintains, unconvincingly, that one source actually put the death of Diocles in 412, and did not recognize him as author of the radical legislation.

plained. It is quite unnecessary to believe, as Laqueur does, that he is trying to combine the accounts of the two authors.[90]

The quarrel between Selinus and Egesta, which had provided Athens with the opportunity to intervene in Sicily, now provided Carthage with its *prophasis,* and, at the invitation of Egesta, Hannibal attacked Selinus in 409 and captured it. According to Ephorus, so Diodorus says, he had two hundred thousand infantry and four thousand cavalry, but Timaeus cut down the size of his force to "not much more than a hundred thousand," and likewise in 406, when Ephorus gave the Carthaginians three hundred thousand men, matching the number given to Hamilcar in 480, Timaeus reduced the number to "not much more than a hundred and twenty thousand."[91] Comparisons of this kind cannot be taken as evidence that Diodorus compared the texts of both authors. If Timaeus reduced Ephorus' figures, he would have said what they were and found fault with them, thus providing Diodorus with his "fragment" of Ephorus.

Another indication of Timaeus' hand comes when Hannibal, in 409, lands near the site of the later city of Lilybaeum. Diodorus says that he made camp "starting at the well which was called Lilybaeum at that time and subsequently gave its name to the city, when it was founded many years later" (13.54.4).[92] This *aition* of the city's name would certainly have interested Timaeus.

Polybius warns us not to expect competent or intelligent description of military operations from either Ephorus or Timaeus, but Diodorus describes the sieges of Selinus, Himera, and Acragas in a more lively and dramatic style than would be expected if he were following Ephorus. There are some spectacular episodes, and numerous touches characteristic of Timaeus can be recognized.

For example, at Himera in 409 a sortie from the city comes near to inflicting a severe defeat on Hannibal, driving the Carthaginians back to the hills; it is only when Hannibal brings in fresh forces from his camp in the hills that the Greeks are driven back to the city. Diodorus quotes both Ephorus and Timaeus for this episode, but there is no proof that he actually read Ephorus' account.[93] And when Acragas is under siege in 406, the relief force of Syracusans under the command of Daphnaeus actually cap-

---

[90] His argument in *RE* VIA. 1105–06 will not stand up under scrutiny.

[91] F 103—Diod. 13.54.5; F 25—Diod. 13.80.5. Even with Timaeus' reductions these figures cannot be taken seriously.

[92] For the foundation of this city in 397 see Diod. 22.10.4.

[93] F 104—Diod. 13.60.5. Ephorus said that they killed twenty thousand of the enemy, but Timaeus reduced the figure to six thousand. He must have quoted Ephorus' figure.

tures one of the Carthaginian camps and drives the enemy to take refuge in its other camp; they might have stormed that camp too, it was believed, if they had not given the enemy time to strengthen their defences, because their commander was reluctant to attack it until he was overruled in a kind of disorderly *ecclesia* held in the captured camp (13.87).

Diodorus' account of these years resembles his account of the events of 480 in so many ways that it is hard to believe he is not using the same source as there. At Himera in 480, just as in all the three later sieges, it is explained that the Carthaginians are divided into two groups, usually with separate camps.[94] And just as the Syracusan relief force under Gelon makes victory possible in 480, it is a Syracusan relief force that nearly saves Acragas in 406. In 409 the Syracusans arrive too late to save Selinus (13.59.1), and at Himera the newly arrived Syracusan ships are sent back for fear that the Carthaginian fleet may attack Syracuse (13.61). The emphasis on the part played by Syracusans may be due to Timaeus, but it is very hard to determine when and how he differs from Ephorus. He may often be responsible for injecting some drama or pathos into the narrative, as when he describes the slaughter and looting in a captured city, the peculiar savagery and barbarity of the Carthaginians, or the part played by women and old men in the last stages of a siege and their unhappy plight and their thoughts when they are taken prisoner.[95]

At Selinus, we are told, the Carthaginians decided to spare the women who took refuge in temples. They were afraid, Diodorus says, that the women in their desperation might set fire to the buildings and destroy the rich treasure that they contained, and so "whereas others spared anyone who took refuge in a sanctuary for fear of offending the god by a sacrilegious act, the Carthaginians refrained from disturbing the refugees so that they could have the opportunity of despoiling the temples."[96] This cynical explanation of Carthaginian behaviour suits Timaeus better than the more conventional Ephorus, and it is in keeping with his bitter hatred of Carthage. Diodorus says that over two thousand persons from Selinus escaped to Acragas, where they were treated most hospitably (13.58.3). Later in Book XIII (81–84) there is an excursus on the wealth and lavish hospitality for which Acragas was famous, and Diodorus cites Timaeus as his source.[97] It may be assumed that he also described their generosity towards the refugees from Selinus.

[94] 11.20.3, 13.54.6, 59.6, 85.1.
[95] E.g., 13.55.4, 56.6, 57–58, 62.2–4, 89–90.
[96] 13.57.4–5.
[97] F 26a—Diod. 13.83.2; F 26c—Aelian, *VH* 12.29.

Timaeus could not have spoken himself with anyone who had lived through the wars of 409 and 406, and it is doubtful if Ephorus had either the opportunity or the inclination to do so. Inevitably, therefore, there is more imaginative writing here than historical record. If Philistus' account of these years had survived or been used by Diodorus, we might have a very different account of the sieges and the Syracusan effort.

Hermocrates' adventures in 409 and 408 are described by Diodorus (13. 63,75). Though the account is not perhaps credible in every detail, it is consistent and quite in the manner of Timaeus, and can be attributed to him with confidence. As an example of his way of writing, it will provide a fitting conclusion to this chapter. It seems to show that while Timaeus hated tyrants, he admired Hermocrates greatly, and thought he was ambitious to become a sort of "first citizen" in a democracy, like his own father at Tauromenium. And if Hermocrates' ambition was misunderstood and he was driven to attempt revolutionary violence, it may be that Timaeus thought this was for the good of the city. There is no need to suppose that the account, as it is reported by Diodorus, is in any way inconsistent with admiration for the man. Perhaps Timaeus regarded Hermocrates as in some ways a Syracusan equivalent of Alcibiades, but a man of much finer moral integrity and character.[98]

After Hermocrates was dismissed from his command of the Syracusan ships in the Aegean and sentenced to exile, he was at odds with Tissaphernes, but kept on good terms with Pharnazus,[99] obtaining money from him which he used to build five triremes for himself when he returned to Sicily, and to form a mercenary force of a thousand men (some of them presumably Campanians). He was joined by a thousand of the "exiled Himeraeans" (men in search of a new home) and made an attempt to enter Syracuse with the help of friends in the city. After failing in this attempt,

---

[98] R. Laqueur, *RE* VIA. (1112–13), finds inconsistencies in Diodorus' account, and thinks he attempted to combine a source less favourable to Hermocrates (Ephorus) with one more favourable to him (Timaeus). But the inconsistencies that he claims to find are imaginary.

[99] For Hermocrates' command, Thuc. 8.26.1. After the Battle of Cyzicus, the Syracusans burnt their ships rather than let them fall into the hands of the Athenians. The news then arrived that their *strategoi* had been sentenced to exile, and they had to submit, however unwillingly, when their appointed successors arrived (Xen. *Hell.* 1.1.18, 27–31). It has been argued that Hermocrates was exiled earlier, but see H. D. Westlake, "Hermocrates the Syracusan," *Bulletin of the John Rylands Library* 41 (1958) 259–61 (reprinted in his *Essays on the Greek Historians and Greek History* [Manchester—New York 1969] 174–202).

Timaeus could have learnt of Hermocrates' quarrel with Tissaphernes from Thucydides (8.29.2, 45.3, 85.2–4), and if he read Xenophon (*Hell.* 1.3.13), he would have known that he went on a diplomatic mission to the Great King with Pharnabazus and a Spartan delegation.

he moved westwards, gathered about him various persons who had survived the sack of Selinus, and built up a fortified post in "a part of Selinus."[100] One can imagine that the survivors of Selinus and Himera might
welcome the chance to join anyone who offered them the prospect of a new
home in Syracuse, and Western Sicily in 409, after Hannibal's withdrawal,
must have been full of desperate, homeless men. Even if Hermocrates'
force was never as large as six thouand, as Diodorus says it was (63.4), it
must have been a formidable little private army.

Hermocrates was able to keep them contented by letting them plunder
the territory that was now in Carthaginian hands, and he could claim that
he was helping the cause of Greek Sicily by harassing the barbarian. He is
said to have inflicted severe losses on enemy forces near Motya and
Panormus. Even if these battles are not completely fictitious, their scale is
doubtless exaggerated, but they are said to have won for him a great reputation among the Greeks of Sicily and caused a change of heart among
many in Syracuse, who repented of their folly in exiling such a man
ἀναξίως τῆς ἰδίας ἀρετῆς. Accordingly, he prepared for a triumphant
return, though he knew that his opponents would resist (63.4–6).

His first move was to organize a protest against Diocles for making no
effort to recover the remains of the Syracusan soldiers who fell outside the
walls of Himera. He inquired about the site of the battle, collected the
bones, and had them carried on decorated waggons towards Syracuse;
some of his men took them into the city, while he waited outside the borders of Syracusan territory, in obedience to the law which forbade any
meetings of exiles. A public funeral took place; when Diocles tried to stop
it, feeling was strong enough to pass sentence of exile on him; but there
was no vote to recall Hermocrates, because it was feared that he intended
to make himself tyrant, as indeed his private army and his spectacular bid
for support might suggest. So he withdrew to Selinus (75.2–6).

Soon afterwards, however, encouraged by supporters in Syracuse, he
made his final attempt to force his way in. He advanced through Geloan
territory, and a rendezvous was arranged for the entire force at a suitable
place. But something went wrong, and he had to enter the city with insufficient numbers to be sure of success. His opponents were ready to meet
him in the agora, and in the battle that followed he fell with most of his
party. One of those who survived and escaped was Dionysius (75.6–9).

---

[100] The walls of Selinus had been pulled down by Hannibal, but survivors from the city
were permitted to live there paying a tribute to the Carthaginians (Diod. 13.59.3).

It seems clear enough what Timaeus was trying to say. If only the Syracusans had refused to listen to Diocles and had never banished Hermocrates or had allowed him to return with honour and reestablish the traditional form of government, Dionysius would never have become tyrant.

CHAPTER VII

THE DIONYSII

i. Dionysius the Elder

A new epoch in Sicilian history begins with the rise of Dionysius I. When Timaeus recorded that Euripides was born on the day of Salamis and died on the day that Dionysius became tyrant,[1] he must have meant that the poet's life–span corresponded not only with the greatest period of Athens, but also with one of the best periods of Sicilian and Syracusan history. Euripides, according to this account, was born on a day of victory, when the freedom of Greece was saved, and died on the day when the freedom of Syracuse was lost, "with Fortune so timing it that the man who acted a tragic part came on the stage just as the poet who depicted scenes of tragedy withdrew." Thus the tragedy of Sicily begins with the death of Euripides.[2] Timaeus prided himself on his chronological exactness, and apparently liked to point out this kind of coincidence. He said that Alexander captured Tyre, a disaster for Carthage, on the same day of the month and at the same hour of the day as Carthaginians stole the bronze statue of Apollo that stood outside his temple at Gela, a statue which they sent to Tyre and which was recovered by the besiegers when the city fell. Here we have a Carthaginian triumph matched with a disaster to their mother city, though we are left wondering what calendar or what calculation led Timaeus to insist on the coincidence. The Carthaginians are punished for the sacrilege they committed at Gela and the Tyrians for their sacrilege at Tyre, where they "insulted" the statue and blamed Apollo for helping their enemies.[3] Passages of this sort would delight readers who had a taste for rhetoric. Timaeus knew the rhetorical value of coincidence[4] and contrast and

[1] F 105–Plut. *Quaest.Conviv.* 717C, cf. *Marm.Par.* 62–63. The mss. read ἀποθανόντος καθ᾽ ἣν ἐγεννήθη Διονύσιος, which must be a mistake for καθ᾽ ἣν τύραννος ἐγενήθη. Editors of Plutarch have not emended the text, thinking that the mistake is Plutarch's.

[2] K. F. Stroheker, *Dionysios I* (Wiesbaden 1958) 16.

[3] οἱ δὲ Τύριοι, καθ᾽ ὃν καιρὸν ὕστερον ὑπ᾽ Ἀλεξάνδρου τοῦ Μακεδόνος ἐπολιορκοῦντο, καθύβριζον ὡς συναγωνιζόμενον τοῖς πολεμίοις. Ἀλεξάνδρου δ᾽ ἑλόντος τὴν πόλιν, ὡς Τίμαιός φησι, κατὰ τὴν ὁμώνυμον ἡμέραν καὶ τὴν αὐτὴν ὥραν ἐν ᾗ Καρχηδόνιοι τὸν Ἀπόλλωνα περὶ Γέλαν ἐσύλησαν, συνέβη τιμηθῆναι θυσίαις καὶ προσόδοις ταῖς μεγίσταις τῶν Ἑλλήνων, ὡς αἴτιον γεγενημένον τῆς ἁλώσεως (F 106—Diod. 13.108.4).

[4] On the coincidence that the temple of Artemis in Ephesus burnt down on the night that

superstitious appeal. He also provided the ingredients for an epigram on Euripides, though it is not known that any poet used them.

It was the fall of Acragas that led directly to the rise of Dionysius, causing him to denounce the Syracusan generals as traitors, and, though he was fined for his disorderly manner in the Assembly, he persuaded the Syracusans to remove the generals from office and elect a new board which included himself. Philistus offered to pay his fines, no matter how often he incurred them,[5] and he must have described the scene in his history. Diodorus tells us that he ended the first part of his Sicilian history with the fall of Acragas,[6] and Timaeus seems to have followed him in representing the capture of this city as a turning–point in the history of the island. He took the opportunity to describe in his fifteenth book the wealth of its inhabitants before the city fell and their fine traditions of hospitality, thus "amplifying" the disaster in orthodox rhetorical style.[7]

This digression on the splendours of the city impressed Diodorus, who drew upon it extensively (13.81–84). Inevitably he reports some remarks of Timaeus about the τρυφή of the Acragantines; the children were spoiled by their wealthy parents and allowed to put up monuments to the animals that they kept as pets, just as their elders put up expensive memorials to their race–horses, and some of them combined their taste for luxury with a keen interest in athletics, using oil flasks and scrapers made of gold and silver (82.6–8). One might think that Timaeus, in conventional moralistic style, would represent Acragas as doomed to perish because of its decadent luxury, but he seems to have resisted this temptation. He gave some striking examples of Acragantine taste for elaborate display, describing the tremendous reception given to an Olympic victor at the Olympiad that preceded the Carthaginian attack (82.7) and the wedding feast given by Antisthenes for his daughter (84.1–5), and he also took the trouble to show that the wealthiest citizens could be both kind and shrewd: Antisthenes prevented his son from forcing an impoverished farmer to sell him his land, because he could achieve his purpose better by gentler methods (84.4); and

---

Alexander was born, Timaeus is said to have remarked: "No wonder, since Artemis was away, attending at Alexander's birth" (F 150a—Cic. *De Nat.Deor.* 2.69). Plutarch, rightly or wrongly, attributes the witticism to Hegesias, and thinks it "cold" enough to put out the fire (*Alex.* 3—*FGrH* 142 F 3). Timaeus also reported another anecdote about Alexander and the temple (F 150b—Strabo 14.1.22).

[5] *FGrH* 556 T 3—Diod. 13.91.4.

[6] Diod. 13.103.3—*FGrH* 556 T 11. Remarks of this kind do not prove that Diodorus knew Philistus' text and used him directly as a source, though this is maintained by Josef Hejnic, "Das Geschichtswerk des Philistos als Diodors Quelle," *Studia antiqua Antonio Salac oblata* (Prague 1955) 31–34. See also L. J. Sanders, "Diodorus Siculus and Dionysius I of Syracuse," *Historia* 30 (1981) 394–411.

[7] F 26a—Diod. 13.81–84.

the wealthy Gellias,[8] when called upon to entertain five hundred guests who arrived unexpectedly soaked to the skin, provided them all with fresh clothing as well as food and drink and shelter (83.2); and he was careful on another occasion not to embarrass the citizens of a less prosperous city by wearing his fine clothes when he appeared before their Assembly as an ambassador (83.4). Timaeus evidently wanted to show that men like Gellias were "kindly people in the old–fashioned manner" (ἀρχαϊκῶς καὶ φιλανθρώπως ὁμιλοῦντες, 83.1), quite different from the men who used their wealth to make themselves tyrants.

It may have been in this context that he told the story of a house in Acragas, called "the Trireme" because some young men once became so drunk there that they imagined they were at sea in a storm, and they threw all the furniture out of the window, supposing that the ship's captain had ordered them to throw the cargo overboard.[9] Perhaps also it was when Timaeus was describing the disaster of Selinus that he remembered the prosperous brothel–keeper of that city who created a proverb. During his lifetime he let it be known that he would leave all his property to the goddess Aphrodite, but when he died he left no will, only the statement ἁρπαγὰ τὰ Κιννάρου—"It's all theft, what Cinnarus left."[10]

Timaeus described the splendid vineyards and olive groves of Acragas as the main source of the city's wealth. Much of the wine and oil produced there was exported to Carthage in the years before the invasion, since the vine and the olive were not yet being grown in Africa (81.4–5). This is the kind of information that is found all too rarely in Greek historians, and there is no other evidence of trade between Sicily and North Africa in the fifth and fourth centuries.[11] Timaeus liked to notice what goods were imported and exported by the people of a city, even if only as an indication of their luxurious tastes. He noted that the Sybarites imported Milesian wool, and exported large quantities of their own wine.[12] And if Sybaris remained on friendly terms with other cities, he said this was because of their wish to exchange each other's produce and products.[13]

---

[8] Cf. Athenaeus 1. 4A. The name is given here as Tellias, and this may be the correct form. Valerius Maximus 4.8, Ext.2, knows him as Gillias.

[9] F 149—Ath. 2.37B–D.

[10] F 148—Zenobius, *Paroem.* 1.31.

[11] Rostovtzeff, *Social and Economic History of the Hellenistic World* I (Oxford 1941) 121–22, writing of the fourth century, says: "The economic history of South Italy and Sicily and the Etruscan federation is almost a blank." He notes that Sicily and South Italy were producing wine and oil of good quality (123), but says nothing of any export to Africa.

[12] Above, p.

[13] F 50—Ath. 12.519B: ἐφόρουν δ' οἱ Συβαρῖται καὶ ἱμάτια Μιλησίων ἐρίων πεποιημένα, ἀφ' ὧν δὴ αἱ φιλίαι ταῖς πόλεσι ἐγένοντο, ὡς ὁ Τίμαιος ἱστορεῖ· ἠγάπων γὰρ τῶν μὲν ἐξ Ἰταλίας Τυρρηνούς, τῶν δ' ἔξωθεν τοὺς Ἴωνας, ὅτι τρυφῇ προσεῖχον.

Diodorus, undoubtedly following Timaeus, says that the magnificent temples of Acragas offer the best indication of its wealth, as of course they still do. Timaeus had been in Acragas and seen the ruins of these temples, which the Carthaginians had ransacked and burnt. They had not been re-built when he was there,[14] and he probably took this as the surest sign that the city had not yet recovered from the disaster of 406. His description of the city, and of the temples in particular, was probably more detailed and extensive than the summary that Diodorus offers. His description of the temple of Olympian Zeus is incomplete, but accurate so far as it goes. The dimensions are given as three hundred and forty feet in length and sixty feet in breadth, thus making it the largest of all temples in Sicily and among the largest anywhere. Timaeus could have pointed out that it was fit to compare with the famous large temples of old Greece, and he has no need to exaggerate its size. He says it was never completed, and still lacked a roof in 406, but its design was clear: "While other temple–builders are content to enclose them with walls or with an outer circuit of columns built round the *cella,* this temple offers a combination of both styles. The columns were built into the walls, being rounded on the outside, but rectangular on the inside of the wall. These columns were twenty feet in circumference on the outside, and the flutings were on such a scale that a human body could fit into them" (82.3). A modern description adds clarification: "A massive platform about 350 feet long was first constructed on foundations nearly 20 feet deep, and around this was built, not the normal colonnade of free–standing columns, but a series of Doric half–columns of enormous size (13 feet in diameter) engaged to about half their height in a continuous screen wall."[15] It continues with detail that is not in Diodorus, but may have been in Timaeus' fuller account: "The top of this wall was finished with a shelf or belt–course upon which, in the 'windows' between each column, stood a giant *telamone* supporting the architrave with the help of invisible iron beams from column to column. These *telamones,* over twenty–five feet tall . . . are male figures, alternately bearded and beardless."

It is only in recent years that one of these *telamones* has been reconstituted from fragments,[16] but even if there were only fragments to be seen

---

[14] Diod. 13.82.1. Cf. 82.6—F 26a on the monuments that Timaeus found still standing.

[15] M. Guido, *Sicily: an archaeological guide* (London 1967) 124; cf. D.S. Robertson, *Greek and Roman Architecture* (Cambridge 1945) 122–24; P. Marconi, *Agrigento, Topografia ed Arte* (Florence 1929); W.B. Dinsmoor, *The Architecture of Ancient Greece* (3rd ed., London 1950) 101–05.

[16] M. Guido, (op. cit.) 119, Plate 7. For recent discussion of the Telamones and the

when Timaeus was there, there must have been people in Acragas who could have told him about them. Diodorus says nothing about these huge figures, but his text shows that Timaeus described the sculpture of the pediments: "The colonnades are on a very large scale. At the eastern end the sculpture represented the battle of the giants, with large and beautiful figures, and on the western end the capture of Troy; one can see each of the heroes depicted in a manner appropriate to the setting" (οἰκείως τῆς περιστάσεως δεδημιουργημένον, 82.4).

If this last phrase represents what Timaeus said, it deserves special attention. Few pediments from Greek temples have survived in good condition, and it is possible that in some pediment groups there were figures ill–matched with the composition and in a style different from the others. Even so, praise of this kind, which shows some appreciation of artistic design, must be noticed when it comes from an ancient author. Greek historians do not, as a rule, praise any work of art in terms other than "beautiful" or "life–like." If Timaeus had a genuine interest in sculpture and painting, one might expect him to describe or at least mention some of the art treasures looted by the Carthaginians. Diodorus (90.3) says that Himilco made a systematic search for works of art and had the most valuable paintings and sculpture sent to Carthage, but the only item that really interests him is the Bull of Phalaris. Timaeus insisted that there was no such object preserved in Acragas, but Diodorus believes he can refute him with his tale of the younger Scipio claiming to discover it after the capture of Carthage, when the Romans, in their turn, were looking for art treasures that might be worth taking back with them.[17]

If Timaeus' history included any account or description or appreciation of works of art looted from Acragas or preserved in temples and other public buildings elsewhere, it is possible that Cicero found it useful in compiling his catalogue of Verres' art thefts. One might indeed ask where else he could find a literary model for a description of the looting of art treasures. It would not be appropriate for him to mention Timaeus' history in an actual speech, but he refers to it several times in other works, and when he starts his description of Syracuse in the *Verrines* (2.4.117): "Urbem Syracusas maximam esse Graecarum, pulcherrimam omnium saepe audistis," he is quoting Timaeus, as he tells us elsewhere: "Urbs illa praeclara, quam ait Timaeus Graecarum maximam, omnium autem esse pul-

---

architecture of the temple see P. Griffo, "Note sul tempio di Zeus Olimpico di Agrigento," 'ΑΠΑΡΧΑΙ, *Studi in onore di P.E.Arias* I (Pisa 1982) 253–70; J.A de Waele, ibid. 271–78.
    [17] F 28a, b; cf. above, p.

cherrimam."[18] Where indeed except in Timaeus could he find help in
describing Syracuse or any other Greek city in Sicily? If Timaeus' description of Acragas were preserved complete, there is much that it might teach
us. Description or praise of a city was a recognized theme for orators of
later times. Did Timaeus or one of his predecessors establish a model or
pattern for others to follow?

Thanks to Diodorus we know that Timaeus not only described one or
more of the temples, but also gave a description of an artificial lake, which
is thought to have been to the south-west of the city.[19] He also described
the house in which Gellias dispensed lavish hospitality, taking from his
predecessor Polycritus the details of its cellar with three hundred storage
pithoi and a great tank, from which wine and oil could be channelled into
the *pithoi*.[20] And he gave a full account of the splendid feast that
Antisthenes offered to the city at his daughter's wedding: "When Antisthenes' daughter was married he provided food and drink for the city in the
streets where each person lived. In the bridal procession there were more
than eight hundred carriages, and besides these there were mounted men
forming an escort for the bride, cavalrymen from the city and in addition
many riders from places near by who had been invited for the wedding.
More remarkable than anything were the arrangements for lighting up the
scene. Antisthenes had firewood piled up on the altars in all the sanctuaries
and on the street altars all over the city, and he had distributed kindling
wood to men in the workshops, telling them that when the fire on the
acropolis was lit they should follow suit and get their fires started. Everyone obeyed the order when the bride was led out, and with large numbers
leading the procession carrying torches the city was filled with light. The
streets along the line of march could not contain the huge crowd that
wanted to follow the procession, everyone being eager to take part in Antisthenes' marvellous display" (84.1–3).

If there were many striking descriptions like this in Timaeus' history,
his popularity is easily explained. Outdoor festivities by torchlight, with
large numbers taking part, were common in Greek lands, but we have no
surviving description like this in any other prose author of this date. The
special interest of this description is the emphasis on numbers of horsemen,
as in the procession that honoured the Olympic victor Exaenetus, where

[18] *De Rep.* 3.43—F 40. For his other references to Timaeus, see T 9, 20, 21; F 119c,
138, 150a.
[19] M. Guido, op. cit. (n. 15) 109.
[20] Diodorus writes (83.3) καὶ Πολύκριτος ἐν ταῖς ἱστορίαις ἐξηγεῖται . . . , but he
must have found the reference in Timaeus. Πολύκριτος is Müller's emendation of the mss.
reading Πολύκλιτος or Πολύκλειτος.

there were three hundred teams of white horses (82.7). Timaeus reminds us that this part of Sicily was full of prosperous farmers who kept good horses. According to the text as preserved there were "more than twenty thousand" (πλείους τῶν δισμυρίων) citizens of Acragas, but if "foreigners" (ξένοι) were counted, the population would reach the figure of two hundred thousand (84.3). Twenty thousand seems too small a figure to suit the argument, and πλείους τῶν δεκακισμυρίων, "over a hundred thousand," has been suggested as an emendation, a figure too high for accuracy, but hardly too high for a writer like Timaeus who was often generous in estimating numbers.[21]

The account of the siege of Acragas that follows in Diodorus (85–89) needs only a brief discussion. As one might expect from the population figures, the Acragantines are not short of fighting men, and they are helped by a force of a thousand mercenaries, commanded by the Spartan Dexippus, whom they summon from Gela, reinforced by the Campanians who had fought under Hannibal in the previous invasion. Dexippus' force takes up its position on a hill near by, and nothing is heard of it again. Like Gylippus, as Timaeus described him in the defence of Syracuse against the Athenians, Dexippus seems to be a not very useful Spartan.

The narrative concentrates on the siege operations. The Carthaginian army, as in the earlier sieges, is divided into two camps, one on the hills, one near the city itself (85.1). Their men are attacked by a severe plague, which is supposed to be a punishment for their impiety in desecrating tombs as they clear the approach to the walls, despite warning from soothsayers. Hannibal had been appointed originally as sole commander of the expedition, but when he tried to refuse the appointment, saying he was too old, he was persuaded to change his mind when offered Himilco as his colleague.[22] Now, however, he is attacked by the plague and dies, and it is Himilco who is shown conducting the siege operations, after propitiating the gods (with success apparently) by sacrificing a child to Kronos (Moloch) and numerous victims to Poseidon. Some modern historians are prepared to accept this child–sacrifice as fact,[23] but it is perhaps more likely to be an invention of Timaeus, part of his picture of Carthaginian savagery and the evil effects of superstitious fear.

An effort to save Acragas is made by a relief force from Syracuse, com-

---

[21] On these figures, see now J. De Waele, "La popolazione di Akragas antica," Φιλίας χάριν, Misc. di studi classici in onore di E.Manni III (Rome 1980) 749–60.

[22] 80.2. Laqueur, RE VIA. 1115, believes that in Ephorus' account Himilco was sole commander from the beginning, that Hannibal refused the appointment and never came to Acragas; he thinks it is Timaeus who reports Hannibal's death from the plague.

[23] E.g., J. B. Bury, CAH VI. 111; Glotz- Cohen, Histoire grecque III 383.

manded by Daphnaeus. It contains men from various other cities and is said to number thirty thousand infantry and five thousand cavalry, as well as thirty triremes to keep the sea route open (86.4–5). Himilco sends a force of forty thousand to meet them, and near the River Himeras (or somewhere between Acragas and that river) there is said to be a battle in which the Syracusans are victorious and slay six thousand of the enemy. They overrun an enemy camp, which seems to be "the camp in the hills," and press on in pursuit, until they reach the city. Now their commander becomes cautious. He is afraid that, if they continue the pursuit, they will become disorganized and suffer a disastrous defeat when Himilco stages a counter–attack (87.2). He is supposed to remember what happened at Himera, when Hannibal called in his "men from the hills" and completely turned the tables on the Greeks who had pushed their attack too far.[24] So the Carthaginians are allowed to take refuge in their other camp ("near the city"), while Daphnaeus and his men settle down in the camp that they have captured.[25]

Meanwhile the fighting men in the city are restrained with difficulty from sallying forth in the hope of "destroying the enemy." Feeling runs high, and accusations of treachery and bribery are made. Many apparently have no difficulty in making their way to Daphnaeus' camp (87.4),[26] and a rowdy sort of "assembly" is held there. After some time Daphnaeus is persuaded to attack the other enemy camp, but it is too late. The defences have been strengthened in the meantime, and the attack has to be abandoned (88.1).

Himilco now takes charge of the situation. Nothing is said of further siege operations, but despite all the thousands who should be able to oppose him, he cuts the supply lines, captures the Syracusan ships that are bringing food, defeats the Syracusan triremes in a battle, and gains control of the sea (88.5). The city is doomed. Most of the Syracusans are able to get away, by land or sea, and many of the civilian population go with them. It is not explained how this is possible, if the Carthaginians have control of the sea and the blockade is effective, but the opportunity is not missed of describing the pathetic scenes when the sick and elderly members of a

[24] Cf. 13.60.6; above, p. 152.

[25] Diodorus' account leaves the topography vague. The battle is said to take place "after the Syracusans had crossed the River Himeras" (87.1). If the battlefield was near that river, which is 25 miles from Acragas, the pursuit might take several days before reaching the city. Since the Carthaginians take refuge in "the camp near the city" (87.3), the other camp, which Daphnaeus captures, must be "in the hills." But how far away is it?

[26] The story seems to assume that all the Carthaginians are shut up in "the camp near the city," and look on, without interfering, as Greeks go back and forth to "the hills."

family have to be left behind (89.2). In due time, Himilco enters the city, and the slaughter and the looting begin.

Evidently, Himilco starved Acragas into surrender after an eight months siege (91.1). But it is not at all clear how or why this happened. Ephorus may perhaps share the blame with Timaeus, who must have been in some degree dependent on him when he produced this account, which reads like a parody of military history.[27] As the subsequent narrative shows, many contemporaries outside Acragas found it difficult to understand the disaster. Treachery in high places was an attractive explanation. It was easy to suspect the Spartan Dexippus, and he was said to have received fifteen talents as the price of his treachery (88.7). But the Syracusans, provoked by bitter criticism from other cities, decided that their own generals must also have been corrupted, and Dionysius took advantage of the mounting suspicion to present himself as an incorruptible leader. Timaeus will have known how the historian Philistus was prepared to pay the fines imposed on Dionysius for his disorderly conduct in the Assembly when he denounced the generals,[28] and when Diodorus describes the incident (91.4), he is certainly following Timaeus' account, not quoting directly from Philistus' history. There seems to have been no dispute over what happened in the Assembly. But, as Diodorus shows, Timaeus (and possibly Ephorus before him) insisted that Dionysius "maligned the generals" (διέβαλλε τοὺς στρατηγούς, 91.4).

The account of the siege of Acragas, after the excursus on the wealth of the city, will have been in Timaeus' fifteenth book (F 26a—Diod. 13.83.2), and the narrative of Dionysius' career seems to have begun in his sixteenth book, preceded by the tale of a prophetic dream, which warned Syracusans how much they would suffer under his rule (F 29). A woman of Himera, so the story ran, dreamt that she was taken up to heaven to see the abode of the gods. When she saw a tall red–headed man securely chained to Zeus' throne, she asked her guide who he was and was told: "He is the scourge (ἀλάστωρ) of Italy and Sicily, and will ruin those countries if he is let loose." Some time afterwards, she saw Dionysius and his bodyguard for the first time, cried out: "That's the man who was pointed out as 'the scourge,'" and fell to the ground in a faint. Three months later she disappeared. Dionysius could not allow her to survive.

The dream is not original with Timaeus. Aeschines (2.10) says that Demosthenes compared him to Dionysius "and warned you to beware of

---

[27] Laqueur, *RE* VIA. 1116–19, tries to distinguish separate accounts of Ephorus and Timaeus, and blames Diodorus for producing an absurd combination of them.

[28] Above, p. 19.

me, telling the story of the dream of the priestess in Himera." There is in fact no such passage in the written version of Demosthenes' speech *On the Embassy* or in any other speech of his. The scholiast knows the dream from Timaeus,[29] but it was probably current in Syracuse when the tyrant was still alive and still remembered in Timaeus' day.[30] It was exactly what he needed as a reply to the dream recorded by Philistus that was supposed to foretell the great achievements of Dionysius.[31] And it was an effective counterpart to the miracle that saved the life of the boy Gelon so that he could grow up to be a "good" autocrat.[32]

It is likely that any Greek or Roman who was interested in the elder Dionysius would consult Timaeus' history, as the standard history of the Greek West. But there are not many direct references in later authors to his account of these years. All that has survived in Polybius' twelfth book is a complaint about his manner of criticism:[33] "Timaeus says that poets and historians reveal their character by the way they keep on repeating themselves in their writing—that Homer by "carving meat" in many episodes in his poems shows himself to be a glutton and that Aristotle, who is constantly preparing tasty food in his treatises, is a greedy gourmet.[34] Now if we apply the same standards to his own treatment of Dionysius, who is shown with a taste for decorative beds, always having unusual and elaborate fabrics made for their coverlets, we must come to the appropriate conclusion and criticize Timaeus in accordance with his theory. The fact is that, while he shows shameless ingenuity in criticizing others, his own narrative is full of dreams and portents and incredible stories. To sum him up, he is a mass of weak superstition and unmanly miracle–mongering."[35]

The passage shows that Timaeus was familiar with contemporary taste

---

[29] F 29—Schol. Aeschin. 2.10.

[30] He could have found it in Heraclides Ponticus, whose work he knew (F 6). Cf. Tertullian, *De Anima* 46, *P.Oxy.* 1012 fr.9 (if correctly restored). The dream is also recorded by Valerius Maximus 1.7, ext.6.

[31] *FGrH* 556 F 57a.

[32] F 95, cf. above, p. 129; R. Vattuone, *Riv. storica dell' antichità* 11 (1981) 139–45.

[33] Polyb. 12.24—T19, F152: ὅτι [οὐ] διαπορεῖν ἐστι περὶ τῆς αἱρέσεως Τιμαίου. φησὶ γὰρ τοὺς ποιητὰς . . . οὐ is Schweighaüser's addition, accepted by Pédech (Budé ed.), but the text is perhaps better without it: "One may wonder about his attitude towards writers and how they reveal their character."

[34] F156—Polyb.12.8.4; Cf. Ath. 8.342C: Τίμαιος δ' ὁ Ταυρομενίτης καὶ Ἀριστοτέλη τὸν φιλόσοφον ὀψοφάγον φησὶ γεγονέναι.

[35] The sentence that follows appears in the ms. tradition as οὐ μὴν ἀλλὰ διότι γε συμβαίνει διὰ τὴν ἀπειρίαν καὶ κακοκρισίαν πολλοὺς ἐνίοτε καθάπερ εἰς τὸν παρόντα τρόπον τινὰ μὴ παρεῖναι καὶ βλέποντας μὴ βλέπειν ἐκ τῶν εἰρημένων τε νῦν καὶ τῶν Τιμαίῳ συμβεβηκότων γέγονε φανερόν. Efforts to improve this sentence by emendation have not been happy and its meaning is quite obscure.

and fashion in literary criticism,[36] but it does not tell us what we really want to know about his treatment of Dionysius. Even without warning from Polybius, we should expect him to record many of the current anecdotes about the tyrant, especially those illustrating his expensive tastes, his fear of assassination, and his elaborate security measures, and it is no surprise to learn that Timaeus' narrative abounded in dreams and portents.[37]

For the rise of Dionysius and the events of 406 and 405 in Sicily, we have no continuous narrative except that of Diodorus (13.91–96, 108–12). His account is not repeated or summarized in any later author. His account of the following twenty years is supplemented by various other writers, but they never contradict it. Most of these authors were familiar with Timaeus' history, and they sometimes cite him for one detail or another.[38] It is likely, therefore, that they borrow quite often from him without citing him by name and that he is their source for most of what they have to say about Dionysius, if he continued to be regarded as the standard authority for the history of these years.[39] Some readers knew that Philistus admired Dionysius. He must have characterized him differently. But we have no way of recovering his account. It is likely that many knew it only through allusions to it in Timaeus.[40]

There is no doubt that Diodorus is following Timaeus in the chapters that describe the events of the years 406 and 405. He refers to Timaeus twice, recording his story about the statue of Apollo at Gela (13.108—F 106),[41] and noting how he estimated the size of the force commanded by Dionysius in 405: he reduced Ephorus' figure of fifty thousand to thirty thousand (13.109—F 107). Polybius reminds us that Timaeus is still finding fault with details in Ephorus, complaining of his inaccuracy when he says that Dionysius was twenty–three when he became tyrant and that he held power for forty–two years (12.4a—F 110). Remarks in later authors show that the reign was normally reckoned as lasting thirty–eight years (405–367),[42] and Timaeus' criticism shows this is what he believed, that

---

[36] See the notes of Walbank and Pédech (Budé ed.) on Polyb. 12.8.4.

[37] The anecdotes can be found in Cicero, Plutarch, Athenaeus, and Valerius Maximus, as well as in other writers; see Stroheker, *Dionysios I* 13, 188.

[38] E.g., Cicero, Strabo, Dionysius of Halicarnassus, Plutarch. Polyaenus does not tell us about his sources for the Dionysii. Though some details in the *Strategemata* can be traced back to Timaeus, it is only because other writers have enabled us to identify them.

[39] See Stroheker's good discussion, "Timaios und Philistos," *Satura Otto Weinreich dargebracht* (Baden–Baden 1952) 139–61.

[40] Though Cicero and Plutarch had probably looked into Philistus' history, it does not follow that they checked every reference that they found in Timaeus.

[41] Above, p. 157.

[42] E.g., Cic. *Tusc.Disp.* 5.57; Dion.Hal. *AR* 7.1.5.

Dionysius was twenty–five when he seized power and sixty–three when he died. Polybius did not check the reference in Ephorus.[43] There is no reason to suppose that Diodorus was more conscientious.

These chapters in Diodorus are much better written than chapters that appear to be based on or adapted from Ephorus. They have well–defined shorter cola than in the rather straggling style that we find in Diodorus elsewhere, and they fulfil their rhetorical purpose admirably.[44] If Timaeus wanted to represent Dionysius as a typical tyrant, this is how we should expect him to describe his sudden rise to power. First, he accuses the generals and other leading citizens of treason and oligarchic designs; and though the more intelligent citizens (οἱ χαριέστατοι) understand very well what he is doing, the δημοτικὸς ὄχλος is not alarmed by his behaviour (92.3). He is elected a member of the new board of generals, and at once proceeds to act as though he was the only one with any authority. He asks that all exiles be recalled, feeling sure that they will be on his side when they return and will support any measures that enable them to recover their property. At Gela, he has wealthy men condemned in the courts and uses the money from their estates to satisfy the soldiers' demands for pay (93.2). On his return to Syracuse, he makes further accusations, showing his distrust in anyone else who holds office, and so has himself appointed *strategos autocrator*. The next step is to ask for a bodyguard, when he maintains that he is threatened with attack (95.4–6).

One may suspect that the truth was not quite so simple as this narrative makes it appear. But this is good rhetorical writing, which reveals the purpose of Dionysius, without any necessity for constant explanation and interpretation. It is a very different kind of narrative from what can be found in the early chapters of Diodorus Book XIV, where the events as described do not reveal any continuity, and specific motivation for each individual action has to be given. This seems to be the kind of narrative that Ephorus preferred. The acknowledged quotations from Timaeus[45] show a style more like what we find here.

Dionysius had been one of the supporters of Hermocrates when he tried to force his way into Syracuse in 407 and was killed. He escaped trial and death himself only because he was so badly wounded that he was reported

---

[43] Polybius thinks Timaeus' criticism of Ephorus unwarranted. He was puzzled by the arithmetic, since 23 plus 42 should be 65, not 63, and he thought there must have been a copyist's error in Timaeus' text of Ephorus. He evidently did not look up the reference in Ephorus himself.

[44] With no better evidence than this it is scarcely profitable to attempt any serious discussion of Timaeus' narrative style.

[45] F 6, 11, 13, 16, 18, 31, 57, 93, 102, 139, 158.

as killed. Timaeus must have said something about his family and his early years when he first introduced him, and when Diodorus introduces him here, he calls him simply "son of Hermocrates," without explaining that this is a different Hermocrates.[46] The correct form of the father's name may perhaps be Hermocritus, since that is the name that Dionysius gave to one of his sons.[47] Most sources take for granted that he came of an undistinguished family and had not acquired any reputation until he pushed himself forward in 406, though Cicero speaks of him as "bonis parentibus atque honesto loco natus" (*Tusc.Disp.* 5.58). Timaeus would prefer the less creditable account, calling him an ἰδιώτης, a γραμματεύς,[48] and it is possible that Cicero's source is Philistus, who is more likely to be both fair and accurate. If Dionysius had been a *grammateus,* this might mean that he had been secretary to the generals or some other board of officers,[49] an honourable and responsible position. But when Demosthenes (18.127, 19.95) calls Aeschines an ill–educated *grammateus,* he means something more like an office–boy, as though that kind of work was all that Aeschines was fit for, despite his fine speaking voice. Timaeus may have used the word in the Demosthenic sense, following Demosthenes' example and trying to stamp Dionysius as an ignorant rabble–rouser with no qualifications to govern a great city. We have no more reason to believe that he was telling the truth than to believe Demosthenes.[50]

Diodorus describes how Dionysius connected himself by marriage with the family of Hermocrates, marrying Hermocrates' daughter and giving his own daughter in marriage to Hermocrates' brother–in–law, and how he dealt with the men who opposed him or failed to help him, having Daphnaeus and Demarchus killed and the Spartan Dexippus, who had been in command at Gela, sent back to Greece (13.96.1–4). All of this will have been in Timaeus. He may also have said something about the help given him by his future father–in–law Hipparinus, who, according to Aristotle, acted as a kind of manager for him.[51]

[46] 13.91.3 He explains later that he married the daughter of the more famous Hermocrates (13.96.3). And some thought that Heloris was his adoptive father (14.8.5).

[47] *SIG*³ 159; cf. K. J. Beloch, *Griechische Geschichte* III.2 (2nd ed. Berlin–Leipzig 1923) 102; Stroheker, *Dionysios I* 196 n.29.

[48] E.g. Isoc. *Philippus* 65; Diod. 13.96.4; Polyb. 15.35.2; Plut. *Regum Apophthegm.* 176D.

[49] As Stroheker thinks likely, *Dionysios I* 38–39.

[50] Cicero seems to take it for granted that Dionysius received a good education, "doctus a puero et artibus ingenuis eruditus" (*Tusc.Disp.* 5.63).

[51] *Pol.* 5.1306a, cf. Plato, *Ep.* 8.353b. Hipparinus, the father of Andromache, must be meant (Plut. *Dion* 3). O. Immisch, *Philologus* 72 (1913) 1–41, thought that Plato, *Ep.* 1 (an obviously spurious letter) might have been an adaptation of a letter in Timaeus' history, a letter

When Diodorus describes Himilco's attack on Gela and the unsuccessful attempt of Dionysius to save the city, he tells us himself that he is following Timaeus' account.[52] The military description is noteworthy. Dionysius' three–pronged attack is clearly and intelligently explained, and also the reason for its failure to achieve its purpose (109.4–110.7). It is likely that Philistus was one of the "friends" who acted as Dionysius' advisory staff (111.1), and that Timaeus made good use of his account of the battle.[53] Diodorus (108.3) says that Himilco established his main camp near the River Gelas, east of the city. Archaeologists claim to have discovered traces of this camp, but no such camp is mentioned during the battle, only a camp on the west side of the city near the sea. It seems that the Carthaginians moved their camp before the battle, and that Diodorus omitted to mention this.[54] No more elaborate explanation is needed.

After the battle, Dionysius holds a conference with his "friends," and gives the order that Gela is to be evacuated and Camarina also. The description of the plight of the refugees streaming eastwards and the brutality of the Carthaginians towards all who fall into their hands is in true Timaean style (111.4–5). There is strong feeling against Dionysius. His bodyguard protects him, but his house in Syracuse is open to attack and his wife is cruelly maltreated (112.3–4). But when Dionysius with his personal troops arrives and forces his way into the city by burning down the Achradina gate, all who do not retire in fear to Leontini are surrounded and cut down (113.1–3).

All of this description seems to be in Timaeus' imaginative "fantastic" style.[55] Unluckily, Diodorus' text is corrupt in more than one place,[56] and any attempt at correction is purely conjectural. There is evidently a lacuna at the end of Chapter 113, where an explanation is needed of the circumstances which compel Himilco to send a herald "inviting the defeated to

from Dexippus to Dionysius complaining of his abrupt dismissal, which the forger adapted to make it look like a letter of Plato. This theory is dismissed by Pasquali as "del tutto fantastica" (*Le Lettere di Platone* [Florence 1938] 227–29).

[52] F 107—Diod. 13.109.2.

[53] Stroheker, *Dionysios I* 45; Meister, *Die sizilische Geschichte bei Diodor* 83.

[54] D. Adamesteanu, "Osservazioni sulla battaglia di Gela di 405 A.C.," *Kokalos* 2 (1956) 142–57; P. Griffo–L. von Matt, *Gela* (Engl. trans., New York 1968) 182–83. Laqueur, *RE* VIA. 1121–23, as usual, devises different stories for Ephorus and Timaeus, with Ephorus putting the Carthaginian camp on the river north–east of the town, and Timaeus putting it west of the city.

[55] Meister, op.cit. (n. 53) 84. It does not deserve to be treated as a precise factual account, though it is apparently accepted as such by Bury, *CAH* VI.113 and Glotz–Cohen, *Histoire grecque* III.385–86.

[56] 112.4 and 6.

reach a settlement with him." The explanation must be the plague that is devastating the Carthaginian camp, because in the next chapter Diodorus says they have lost more than half their total force from it. Dionysius accepts the offer gladly and peace is signed, but Diodorus does not record any comment of Timaeus on the tyrant's motives in accepting the offer so readily.[57]

After this dramatic account of the early years of Dionysius, the beginning of Book XIV is a great disappointment. Some of the Sicilian chapters are written in a flat undistinguished style, providing only a year by year outline of events. This sort of summarized account tells the reader very little about the source on which it is based. Diodorus tells us, in his usual way, that Timaeus reduced the numbers of Himilco's invasion force in 396 as estimated by Ephorus,[58] but this is the only occasion in Book XIV when he cites either author.

A search in the text of authors who record miscellaneous details about Dionysius results in a few tentative additions to the fragments, but they are not of any great significance. It is arguable that Timaeus told the story of the flatterer who laughed when the tyrant laughed, even though he could not hear what the joke was.[59] He may also be responsible for the tale that Dionysius stole an elaborate *himation* that had been displayed in Hera's temple on the Lacinian promontory and sold it to a Carthaginian for a high price[60]—one of the many sacrilegious thefts of which he was accused.

Timaeus was interested in the origins of unusual words and expressions, as also of proverbs and aphorisms, and he noted (with scorn, no doubt) some of the words that Dionysius used in his poetic compositions— like μέναvδϱος for a maiden ("waiting for a husband"). Athenaeus cites an earlier Syracusan writer, Athanis, for this newly coined word, but it is likely that he has found the reference to this obscure historian in Timaeus

---

[57] Scholars today have their comments ready, e.g., Bury, *CAH* VI.113: "There can be little question that in abandoning the defence of Gela and Camarina Dionysius was deliberately playing into the hand of Himilco;" Glotz–Cohen, *Histoire grecque* III.386: "Vaincu par l'étranger, mais vainqueur de ses concitoyens, il va justifier les soupçons auxquels avait donné lieu la retraite de Géla." Timaeus would surely have agreed with them.

[58] F 108—Diod. 14.54.5–6.

[59] Athenaeus (6.249E) cites as his authority for this story a little known historian, who is thought to be a contemporary of Timaeus, Hegesander of Delphi. But since he goes on to record two stories of flatterers of the younger Dionysius, and finally cites Timaeus as his source for the last story, one may suspect that Timaeus told all three stories, giving Hegesander as his source for the first two.

[60] Ath. 12.541A–B (his source is *Mir.Ausc.*96). Later in the paragraph he cites Timaeus for another detail (F 9). The whole paragraph seems to be based on Timaeus, the reference to Herodotus (6.127) included.

(and that Diodorus and Plutarch, who also mention Athanis, are equally indebted to Timaeus for their references).[61]

Two sayings recorded by Diodorus in Book XIV can be identified as coming from Timaeus because they also appear in authors who are known to have used Timaeus as a source. When Dionysius, in 404, was blockaded by his opponents on the Island of Syracuse, he is told that tyranny "makes a good winding sheet" (14.8.5, καλὸν ἐντάφιόν ἐστιν ἡ τυραννίς). Since Aelian, who cites Timaeus elsewhere, also records this saying, one can be reasonably sure that it was in his history, though the story was already known to Isocrates.[62] On the same occasion, according to Diodorus, Philistus told Dionysius that, far from "leaping on a horse to flee from the tyranny," as Philoxenus advised, he should wait until he was dragged away by the leg. This piece of advice was in Timaeus, as a passage in Plutarch shows.[63]

Far more interesting than anecdotes of this kind are the details of the tyrant's economic measures and unusual ways of raising money that are described by Aristotle and in the pseudo–Aristotelian *Economica* Book II.[64] There is no trace of these measures in Diodorus, and hence it cannot be claimed that Timaeus said anything about them.

Every time that Diodorus turns from "affairs of Hellas" to "affairs of Sicily" in Book XIV, it has to be asked afresh: "Is he using Ephorus or Timaeus?" When we find something in the text that recalls Timaeus' manner, his special interests or opinions, or indeed his special familiarity with a city like Acragas or Syracuse, we shall probably not be wrong in concluding that we have identified a fragment of his work. We can be sure that, if Timaeus knew the city of Syracuse well, he must have described the building programme of Dionysius fully and intelligently, the fortifications of the Island, as a place apart for himself and his "friends," with a well protected acropolis and harbour, the new buildings and stoas intended for public use (14.7.2–5), and the subsequent fortification of Epipolae, which was accomplished by organizing a citizens' work force (14.18.2–8). But Diodorus reveals nothing of his source's style in this description. In these chapters of Book XIV (7–10, 14–16, 18), he writes in his own peculiarly unattractive style which tells us nothing about his source.

[61] Ath. 3.98 D—Athanis, *FGrH* 562 F 1; Diod. 15.94.4; Plut. *Timol.* 23.6, 37.9.

[62] Aelian, *VH* 4.8; Isoc. *Archidamus* 44–45. Aelian quotes from Timaeus' description of Acragas, *VH* 12.29—F 26c. For the story, see also Diod. 20.78; Plut. *Mor.* 783D, with a variation in 175D.

[63] F 115—Plut. *Dion* 35. M. Sordi, *Aevum* 54 (1980) 23–26, claims to have found the "pre–Timaean" form of these anecdotes.

[64] *Pol.*1.1259a, 5.1313b, *Econ.* 2.1349a.

If Timaeus described the remarkable escape of Dionysius after the Gela campaign, when he seemed almost certain to lose control (13.113), he must also have explained how he escaped from his difficulties in 404, when he was blockaded in the Island and some of his advisers thought he should abandon the tyranny and seek refuge in Carthaginian territory; he obtained permission from his opponents to sail out of the harbour with five ships, and was able to organize the Campanian mercenaries to help him recover his position, settling them at Entella when he was securely in power again. Diodorus compresses the story into a single chapter (14.9),[65] and explains the success of Dionysius by saying that "the Syracusans became rather careless" (ῥᾳθυμότεροι καθειστήκεσαν). This is the third miraculous escape of the tyrant that Timaeus must have described; he had been left for dead in the streets of Syracuse in 408 when Hermocrates' *putsch* failed, and he narrowly escaped death in 405, when his wife was attacked and killed, and he had to burn down the gate of the city to force his way in. Timaeus probably took pains to make his plight seem particularly hopeless on this occasion, and to show how his craftiness and good luck enabled him to survive.

Dionysius had another lucky escape a few years later, when an army from Rhegium and Messana was advancing towards Syracuse, but abandoned its plan of attack when it was pointed out to the men from Messana how foolish it was to attack Dionysius unsupported by any vote of their popular Assembly. The Rhegines, who had the support of their Assembly, were not strong enough to undertake the war on their own, and so the army dispersed. Diodorus (40.4) says that it was Laomedon of Messana who addressed them and convinced them that it would be inadvisable to attack Dionysius. The historian whom Diodorus is following must have written a formal speech for Laomedon, and it is more likely to have been Timaeus than Ephorus.

The military operations of 403 are described in outline by Diodorus, and sometimes his narrative is so severely abbreviated as to be scarcely intelligible.[66] But in his account of the year 399 he describes and explains the decision of Dionysius to go to war with Carthage and devotes three

---

[65] This chapter is written in good Attic Greek, without Hellenistic circumlocutions, and with short cola—not at all in his 'Ephoran' style. There may be many phrases here taken straight out of Timaeus; cf. Laqueur *RE* VIA. 1124, though his choice of examples is questionable. Repetition of a phrase used earlier is not necessarily repetition of a Timaean phrase, because Diodorus is prone to repetition of his own phrases.

[66] For example, the betrayal of Naxos is described in a short sentence (14.15.2). It cannot be determined whether Timaeus showed Dionysius using the stratagem described by Polyaenus(5.2.5).

chapters to his preparations (41–44). He emphasizes the personal interest of the tyrant in any unusual good work done by manufacturers and designers of arms and how he rewarded individuals and paid good wages to all (42.1), just as he had tried to encourage workers on the Epipolae fortifications by visiting the site and praising any outstanding performance (18.7). If it was Timaeus who reported his attention to individual workers then, it must be Timaeus again here.[67] But Timaeus' hand is revealed more clearly when Diodorus explains that Dionysius wanted to do better than the Corinthians, who built the first triremes, by producing quadriremes and quinquiremes in a colony of Corinth. This must be Timaeus in his usual style trying to show that the Greek West can match or outdo anything that old Greece can offer.[68]

Thus with each succeeding chapter Diodorus' use of Timaeus becomes clearer. He records that Dionysius made some concessions of territory to Messana and Rhegium, to make sure that they would not help the Carthaginians when war started. This information would come naturally from the source that described the earlier abortive attack by these two cities. His proposal of a marriage alliance with Rhegium is rejected by the Rhegines after a debate in their Assembly (44.3–5), but he obtains a bride from Locri and sends a quinquireme to fetch her, marrying her on the same day that he marries Aristomache, daughter of a prominent Syracusan. He celebrates the double wedding with a series of feasts offered to the army and the general public (44.6–8). These feasts are of course reminiscent of the feast offered by Antisthenes of Acragas at his daughter's wedding, which Timaeus described (Diod. 13.84).[69]

Diodorus goes on to describe a speech that Dionysius made to the Assembly, explaining his decision to go to war, and he says it was received favourably, not only because the people hated the Carthaginians, but because they hoped that his government would be less harsh when he had the enemy to fear as well as his own subjects, but above all because they hoped that they could make a bid for freedom once they had weapons in their hands, if the opportunity came (14.45.5). This interpretation must come from Timaeus. As a true tyrant–hater he would be unwilling to believe that the people's support for a tyrant was genuine, and would feel the need to

---

[67] Meister, *Sizilische Geschichte* 87.

[68] The report that Dionysius built quinquiremes has been doubted. If the report is due to Timaeus, in whose time such ships were no longer a novelty, it has no value. If it goes back to Ephorus or Philistus, it cannot be discarded so easily. This point seems not to be understood by writers who have studied ancient ships and ship–building.

[69] Cf. Plut. *Dion* 3.3; Aelian *VH* 13.10. For discussion of the date of these marriages and other chronological questions of these years, see M.Sordi, *Aevum* 54 (1980) 23–35.

excuse it.[70] Likewise, if Dionysius now discarded some of his tyrannical severity and took on a more kindly character, showing more *philanthropia* to his subjects, "instead of killing and sending men into exile, as he had been doing", as Diodorus says (45.1), Timaeus would want to insist that the transformation of the tyrant was more apparent than real.

As Dionysius marched westwards forces from other cities joined him, and when he reached Eryx, so Diodorus says (47.4–7), his army was eighty thousand strong. No difference is cited between figures given by Timaeus and Ephorus, and it could well be that eighty thousand is Timaeus' figure. He maintained that in 405 Dionysius could not raise more than thirty thousand (F 107—Diod.13.109), and he might want to give him more than twice as many now. He gave Gelon fifty thousand in 480 (Diod. 11.21), and he would surely want to show that Dionysius had a better opportunity and an easier task than Gelon.

The siege of Motya follows (14.48–53). If Timaeus had read about Alexander's siege of Tyre, in Callisthenes or Clitarchus,[71] he would have recognized that Dionysius was facing a somewhat similar task at Motya and found a similar solution to his problem, building a series of mounds (χώματα). The narrative is interrupted by an account of the Carthaginian raid on Syracuse, when their ships enter the Great Harbour and do great damage—only to sail away again. Then Himilco appears out of the blue (ἀνελπίστως, 50.2) at Motya, but the Greeks use their catapult artillery so effectively that he has to withdraw, leaving the city to its fate. This was the first time that catapults were used in any action, so Diodorus says (50.4). The night attack and the capture of the city follow, with the inevitable description of butchery and plunder, when the Greeks show the same savagery that Carthaginians had shown when cities fell into their hands (53.1).

The whole story of the siege is certainly remarkable enough for Timaeus, and the reader is left wondering whether more detail and explanation would make the strange tale credible. Diodorus reminds us that he has had the text of Timaeus at hand when he describes the great armament that Himilco collects next year, and in his usual ways contrasts the figures given by Ephorus, three hundred thousand infantry and four hundred fighting

[70] Stroheker, *Dionysios I* 69–70; Meister, *Sizilische Geschichte* 88.
[71] He had read about the siege of Tyre and knew the tale of the statue of Apollo from Gela that the Carthaginians sent there (F 106—Diod. 13.108.4). Some version of this tale was in Clitarchus (Diod. 17.41.8; Q.Curt. 4.3.21–22), and a borrowing from Clitarchus by Timaeus seems to me more likely than the reverse, which was proposed by F.Reuss, *Rh.Mus.* 63 (1908) 65–67.

ships, with Timaeus' reduced figure of a hundred thousand men, which leaves Dionysius not so seriously outnumbered (F 108—14.54.5).

The summer of 397 ends with Dionysius returning to Syracuse, leaving Leptines in command of a hundred and twenty ships at Motya to keep watch against any Carthaginian crossing from Africa in the spring. He is also ordered to lay siege to Egesta and Entella. The Egestaeans resist vigorously, and when Dionysius returns in the spring, he brings his main force to Egesta (53.5–54.4). Meanwhile Himilco's huge invasion force has set sail with sealed orders (55.1). Leptines, with a mere thirty ships, intercepts it at sea, and sinks fifty of the transport ships, but is not able to prevent the rest of the force from reaching Panormus, and there is no opposition to the landing.

Eryx is now betrayed to Himilco, and he advances to Motya. Diodorus describes what follows: "At this time Dionysius with his force was in the neighbourhood of Egesta, and Himilco attacked and captured Motya. The Siceliots were eager to fight, but as Dionysius was isolated from his allies and his supply of food was running low, he decided that it would be best to continue the war in a different part of Sicily" (55.4–5). And so he withdraws to Syracuse.

Taken as it stands, without explanation or further detail, this brief narrative makes it appear that Dionysius was prepared to leave his allies to their fate and unwilling to take advantage of the successes of the previous summer. It is possible, though it cannot be proved, that this was the impression Timaeus wished to convey.[72] Himilco now advances eastwards along the north coast, "with his fleet sailing alongside" (56.2), as usual, and proceeds to capture Messana and destroy it, though most of the population succeeds in escaping. He now proposes to advance on Syracuse.

Meanwhile, Dionysius makes preparations to resist him, freeing slaves so as to provide crews for sixty ships (58.1), sending to Sparta for mercenaries, building up his supply of food, moving the Campanians from Catana to Aetna "since this was a very strong place." He is said to have thirty thousand infantry, more than three thousand cavalry, and a hundred and eighty ships, "but few of them triremes" (58.2).[73] More than half of the previous year's allied army seems to have melted away.

---

[72] Meister, *Sizilische Geschichte* 90. One may say, as some critics do, that Dionysius had hoped to secure his hold on Western Sicily before a new Carthaginian force arrived, and that he did not dare face such superior numbers in open country. But one must also ask if he deserted his allies or was deserted by them.

[73] This could mean either that most of the ships were old–fashioned, smaller vessels, or that most were quadriremes and quinquiremes, as believed by Bury, *CAH* VI.124, and Stro-

In an account written by Timaeus an omen or an oracle predicting the fall of Messana can be expected, and Diodorus duly records an "old oracle" (56.5) of ambiguous meaning which said that Carthaginians would be water–bearers in the city—not making it clear whether they would be drawing water as masters or as slaves. But Timaeus' more unmistakeable signature is seen in the etymology of Tauromenium. The Sicels who settled on Mount Taurus and established the beginnings of a city there called their settlement Tauromenium because "they stayed on Taurus" (διὰ τὸ μεῖναι τοὺς ἐπὶ τὸν Ταῦρον ἀθροισθέντας, 59.2).

Himilco orders his fleet to sail southwards to Tauromenium, but when he arrives there[74] with the army he finds that his advance to the south along the coast is blocked by the flow of lava from Etna, so that his men have to make a long circuit to the west of the volcanic area and his fleet is near Catana long before they arrive there. Meanwhile, Dionysius has advanced northwards from Syracuse as far as Catana, and sees the opportunity to attack the Carthaginian fleet when it is without support from land. He sends in Leptines with orders to keep his ships together. But Leptines allows his fastest ships to become separated from the rest, and after some initial success inevitable defeat follows. The Carthaginians with their superior numbers are able to surround the Greek ships, and what follows is described as being more like a battle on land than a proper naval battle (60.3). Even though the seamanship of the Greeks was better, the Carthaginians prevailed because of superior numbers. The description recalls Thucydidean accounts of battles in confined space, like battles in the Great Harbour of Syracuse, and it is likely that Timaeus drew upon the Thucydidean Philistus in writing this battle description.

Dionysius is urged to fight a land battle with Himilco's advancing army, and win a victory to compensate for the defeat at sea, but he is warned by his "friends" that this may give Mago's fleet the opportunity to attack Syracuse when there is no one to defend it, just as they had captured Messana; and so he withdraws to Syracuse (61.2). Here too Timaeus has evidently followed the account of Philistus, who will have been one of the

---

heker, *Dionysios I* 75. It is hard to believe that this fleet was so far above or below normal standards. Diodorus may have misunderstood or misrepresented his source.

[74] Dionysius on his march north encamps at another Taurus, Monte Tauro near Augusta, "160 stades from Syracuse" (58.2). Laqueur, *RE* VIA.1136–37, believes that in Ephorus' version (Diodorus' earlier version, as he thinks) it was to this more southerly Taurus that Mago was bidden to sail (59.1); that it was Timaeus who took it to be Tauromenium; and that Diodorus in a clumsy attempt to combine both versions has produced mere nonsense. But Diodorus' narrative is clear and without confusion, unless one accepts this perverse interpretation. There is every reason to believe that he is following Timaeus.

advisers. Nothing is done to stop the whole Carthaginian fleet from entering the Great Harbour, cargo ships as well as fighting ships, and the description of the scene—the whole space filled with all the various kinds of
craft, nothing but masts to be seen[75]—must be taken from Philistus' account of what he had seen with his own eyes. Then Himilco's land force
approaches, "more than three hundred thousand, as some reported," clearly
a reference to Ephorus again (62.3), but this time Diodorus does not tell
us what Timaeus had to say about this exaggerated estimate of Carthaginian numbers.

A modern reader might think that the huge Carthaginian fleet had
doomed itself to destruction by "bottling itself up" in the Great Harbour,
its ships packed so tight that they can scarcely move. Even though
Dionysius' fleet has melted away, one expects him to do great damage with
his famous artillery or to make some attempt to cause a fire. But disease
breaks out in the Carthaginian camps on the marshy ground (63.2, 70.4),
just as it did when the Athenians were there in 413, and, as one might
expect in a Timaean account, this is represented as the inevitable result of
Himilco's sacrilegious behaviour. He takes up his quarters in the Olym-
pieium (62.3), and after capturing Achradina pillages the temples of Demeter and Kore (63.1). He even goes so far as to desecrate the tombs of
Gelon and Demarete (63.3), forgetting the plague that broke out at Acragas
and took the life of Hannibal, when they started to dismantle the tomb of
Theron (13.86.2). The gods swiftly exact due punishment.[76]

The tide now begins to turn. Some reinforcements arrive from Italy and
the Peloponnese (14.63.4), and there is an encounter at sea in which the
Syracusans sink twenty–four Carthaginian ships (64.1–3). Dionysius and
Leptines are both away at the time, seeking necessary supplies,[77] and the
Syracusans gain new confidence from their success when "acting on their
own." When Dionysius returns, he praises their exploit in a meeting of the
Assembly, and before he can dissolve the meeting, a prominent citizen by
the name of Theodorus rises to his feet and delivers a vigorous harangue,

---

[75] διὸ καὶ συνέβαινε τὸν λιμένα τῶν Συρακοσίων, καίπερ ὄντα μέγαν, ἐμπε-
φράχθαι μὲν τοῖς σκάφεσι, συγκαλύπτεσθαι δὲ σχεδὸν ἅπαντα τοῖς ἱστίοις (62.2).
The text of the preceding sentence is very uncertain, but the total number of ships seems to
have been estimated at over two thousand.

[76] ὑπὲρ ὧν ταχὺ τῆς εἰς τὸ θεῖον ἀσεβείας ἀξίαν ὑπέσχε τιμωρίαν (63.1).

[77] The verb or verbal phrase indicating their departure is missing from the text (64.1), but
it is clear that they were absent. The Greeks have access to the sea by the Little Harbour,
where their ships were secure from attack (cf. Diod. 14.7.3). Laqueur, RE VIA. 1141, thinks
that it was only in Ephorus' account that the Carthaginians occupied the Great Harbour, that
in Timaeus' version they had their ships outside, to the south and west of the Great Harbour.
As so often, he is unwilling to believe that Diodorus' account is intelligible as it stands.

attacking Dionysius and calling on the people to assert their claim to liberty. The speech must be taken almost word for word from Timaeus,[78] and can be claimed as "pure Timaeus" with much greater confidence than the speeches of Nicocles and Gylippus in Book XIII. It is Timaeus' way of expressing his opinion about the previous ten years of the tyrant's rule, and as a sample of his style it deserves particular attention.[79]

Hiatus is avoided as strictly as by Isocrates, even at the end of a sentence, and the sentence structure is such that an orator would find no difficulty in delivering the text as it stands. It is written with careful economy of words, and each sentence leads inexorably to the next; new points for consideration, explanations, and conclusions come one after the other.

It begins without any formal introduction, taking up the declaration of Dionysius that he will bring the war to an end quickly. Of course he will, says the speaker, if only he gives us our freedom, gives us some incentive to fight the enemy. At present, we have no incentive, because he is treating us worse than the Carthaginians would treat us, if we were left to their tender mercies (λειφθέντας γὰρ Καρχηδονίοις δεήσει ποιεῖν τὸ προσταττόμενον, νικήσαντας δὲ Διονύσιον ἔχειν βαρύτερον ἐκείνων δεσπότην, 65.2). What must first be brought to an end, therefore, is not the war against Carthage, but the tyrant's rule within our walls. Soon there is an appeal to their sense of shame, in good Demosthenic style:[80] Are we to face death bravely in battle with the Carthaginians, but not dare raise a voice against the tyrant in defence of liberty? are we to face all the thousands of the enemy, but shake with fear before this tyrant, who does not even possess the good qualities of a useful slave?[81]

The comparison with Gelon follows, to show that Dionysius is not even effective as a tyrant. Gelon fought the war in the far West of Sicily; Dionysius fled the whole length of the island from Motya, and shut himself up behind the walls of Syracuse. Dionysius brought ruin on his allies as well as his fellow citizens, lost Gela and Camarina, allowed Messana to be destroyed, fought a battle at sea that cost us twenty thousand lives, and enslaved Naxos and Catana. When the Syracusans entrusted him with the command of their fighting forces, he responded by taking their freedom from them, killing anyone who spoke up to defend the rule of law, exiling

---

[78] Laqueur agrees: "Am Timaeischen Ursprung kann überhaupt kein Zweifel sein" (*RE* VIA. 1142); cf. Stroheker, *Dionysios I* 17, 78; Meister, *Sizilische Geschichte* 93.

[79] For fuller discussion of this and other Timaean speeches, see L. Pearson, "The Speeches in Timaeus' history," *AJP* 107 (1986) 350–68.

[80] Cf. Dem. 3.20,30–32, 4.10.

[81] A Greek reader might remember what Demosthenes said of Philip, that he came from Macedonia where you could not even buy a slave that was worth anything (9.31).

all who had any property, and dishonouring their wives by giving them to slaves and other men of mixed blood. And who is Dionysius after all, but a despicable creature who ran errands in a government office (ὑπηρέτης ἀρχείων, 66.5)?

Readers would recognize the echo of Demosthenes' sneering references to Aeschines.[82] And they would also recognize the Demosthenic style of his appeals to *paradeigmata:* Where is the Syracusan spirit of freedom? where are the deeds of our ancestors? I am not thinking of our glorious victory at Himera or how we drove out the tyrants that came after Gelon, but only yesterday when the Athenians came . . .

Having come so far, Theodorus can now venture to make his final accusation, that Dionysius does not want peace or victory, because it may mean the end of his rule. He is afraid that, once victory has given us confidence, we will strike a blow for freedom when we still have arms in our hands. This must be the reason why he betrayed Gela and Camarina and agreed to a peace settlement that gave away so many Greek cities, why he destroyed Naxos and gave Catana to the Campanians, and started a new war with the Carthaginians when he thought his tyranny was threatened. He might have fought the enemy when they were in disorder near Panormus after the landing, but he let them take Messana, so that they could prevent any help reaching us from Italy or the Peloponnese (68.2–6). He fought the sea battle off the coast near Catana, when we should have fought it near our own harbour. And after the battle he neglected the splendid opportunity to attack their army on land. The final appeal is to the superstitious belief of the people. So long as they have for their leader a man who has robbed temples of their treasure, the gods will be against them. Now, in the absence of Dionysius, they have won a notable success. Could the gods have made their presence more plain?

Polybius complains that Timaeus' speeches could never have been delivered by the persons to whom they are attributed,[83] and here the complaint would be just. No Greek tyrant would have permitted such an attack on himself; if Theodorus had attempted to make a speech of this kind, the tyrant's guards would have suppressed him before he made much progress. Polybius, however, does not spend much time complaining about the historical improbability of Timaeus' speeches. He seems to be concerned rather to explain their rhetorical shortcomings. Orthodox rhetoricians expected a speaker to develop one or two arguments in support of his thesis

---

[82] Dem. 18.127, 19.95.
[83] 12.25i–26b.

and to leave aside other less immediately pertinent arguments that an inexperienced speaker might want to use. Polybius thinks Timaeus is inept because he regularly tries to use "all the available arguments," like some student in a rhetorical school who has no judgment, but wants to show that he is aware of the arguments—that he has "done his homework," as we should say.[84] This speech illustrates Polybius' criticism perfectly, because Theodorus gives his complaints against Dionysius one after the other, instead of choosing one or two for consideration in detail. A modern reader may not think that this is a fault, but Polybius expects the orthodox standards of rhetoric to be observed.

Timaeus is not writing a Thucydidean speech, giving arguments that were or must have been used by the speaker. His purpose is to present a case against Dionysius. The preceding narrative supplies the material for the speaker's accusations, and if the narrative has been designed so as to lead up to the speech, it should be treated with great caution by historians. When the speech is finished, there is no outbreak of violence, no repressive action by the tyrant's guards, but the newly arrived Spartan commander walks to the *bema* and says he has come to help Dionysius fight the Carthaginians, not to remove him from power (70.1–2). Since the Spartans fail to support this attempt to start a revolution, it ends peacefully without anyone getting hurt. It is hardly a convincing story.

Timaeus must have been unwilling to give Dionysius credit for saving Syracuse, arguing that the city would have fallen if it had not been for the arrival of the Spartans and the devastating plague that broke out among the Carthaginians. The description of this plague in Diodorus (70.4–71.4) is adapted from Thucydides' famous description of the plague at Athens, and the adaptation is most probably the work of Philistus, doing his best to write like Thucydides, which Timaeus took over rather than attempt a description of his own.

Diodorus then describes the operations against the Carthaginians, which lead to a Carthaginian disaster comparable to the Athenian disaster of 413 (14.72–75). It is one of the best written passages of military writing in all his history. The tactical plan is clearly understood and explained, a simultaneous attack on the camp by two forces, one coming by ship into the Great Harbour, the other in a long circular night march from the upper

---

[84] πάντας διεξιέναι τοὺς ἐνόντας λόγους, ὃ ποιεῖ Τίμαιος, πρὸς πᾶσαν ὑπόθεσιν εὑρεσιλογῶν, τελέως ἀνάληθες καὶ μειρακιῶδες καὶ διατριβικὸν φαίνεται, καὶ πολλοῖς ἀποτυχίας αἴτιον ἤδη τοῦτο γέγονεν καὶ καταφρονήσεως· τὸ δὲ τοὺς ἁρμόζοντας καὶ καιρίους ἀεὶ λαμβάνειν, τοῦτ' ἀναγκαῖον (12.25i.5). For further discussion of this passage see Pearson, op.cit. (n. 79) 354–58.

part of the city to attack the Carthaginian camp from the landward side. When this force, with Dionysius himself riding among them, reaches the bay, it starts a fire among some Carthaginian ships, which soon spreads to other ships. A third force, consisting of men whom Dionysius is quite prepared to lose, is sent inland to keep the enemy groups there occupied.[85]

The description must go back to an eye–witness' account. If it was Philistus who described the appearance of the Great Harbour completely covered by ships' masts (62.2), it must be the same man who described the astonishing sight of the blazing Carthaginian ships as seen by an onlooker in the city, "like something in the theatre, a sight that made it look as though the barbarians were being destroyed by lightning because of their wickedness" (73.5), and "from a distance it looked like a battle between gods" (74.4).

Philistus would be able to write with good understanding of the topography, and we find that places are mentioned by name without any explanation of where they are, so that the modern reader is left to decide for himself the exact site of the temple of Cyane (72.1), and of Polichna and Dascon (72.3). One may suppose that he knew the topography from walking over the ground as well as from reading Thucydides' account of the Athenian defeat in the same area. One can imagine him saying to himself that if the Carthaginians had read their Thucydides, they would have known that disease and failure were bound to follow if they camped on the marshy ground near the Anapus. And if his account was well written, with Thucydidean detail and accuracy, Timaeus would have no need to attempt any improvement.

When night came on, Diodorus says, the Carthaginians opened secret negotiations with Dionysius, offering him the three hundred talents that they had in their camp if he would let the survivors escape. Dionysius replied that he could allow only the Carthaginian citizen force to escape, that it would be impossible for everyone to get away. He knew that the Syracusans and the allies would not permit any such concession to the enemy. But he made the concession because he did not want Carthaginian power to be completely destroyed. He wanted to be sure that fear of the Carthaginians would keep the Syracusans occupied, so that they would not have the opportunity to make a bid for their freedom. He fixed the next night but two ("the fourth night") as the time for their escape, and Himilco

---

[85] They are mercenaries whom he distrusts and who have constantly made trouble (72.2). He instructs the cavalry to leave them in the lurch and let them be wiped out by the enemy. Diodorus does not say that they will serve their purpose by dying, but this is evidently what they do. If it were not for them, Dionysius might have been attacked from the rear.

brought the three hundred talents into the acropolis and handed all of it over to the men on the Island appointed by Dionysius (75.1–4).

Timaeus, the "tyrant–hater," can be identified fairly confidently as the source of this highly improbable story,[86] as well as for what follows in Diodorus' account. At the time arranged, he tells us, Himilco loaded forty ships with men from the citizen force, and set out. They were not noticed, it seems, until they were nearly out of the harbour, and even then Dionysius "took his time" in organizing any counter–action. The Corinthians, however, without waiting for him, gave chase and sank some of the ships (75.3–5). Dionysius wasted no time in blocking all escape routes for the land army, though he was not quick enough to prevent the Sicels from getting away. He let his soldiers take all the prisoners that they wanted, but took the Iberians into his service as mercenaries (75.6–9).

Diodorus goes on to offer some pious reflections on the changed fortunes of the Carthaginians. They destroyed Syracusan graves only to see a hundred and fifty thousand of their own men[87] lying in heaps unburied because of the plague; and after burning the Syracusan countryside, they soon had to watch their own fleet go up in flames. Their commander, who had encamped in the temple of Zeus and robbed temples to enrich himself, escaped the immediate death that he deserved for such wickedness, but he returned to his own country in disgrace and confessed his own offences wandering from one Carthaginian temple to another in rags, finally committing suicide (76.1–4). All of this is in Timaeus' usual manner. There is a similar emphasis on *deisidaimonia* in the account that follows (77.1–6) of the revolt of Carthage's Libyan subjects. Here too Timaeus must be the source. When Polybius described the troubles that beset the Carthaginians in their war with discontented mercenaries in Africa after the First Roman Punic War (1.65–88), he must have been familiar with Timaeus' account of this earlier rebellion, though he does not see fit to mention it.

Diodorus ends his description of four eventful years in Sicily (399–396 B.C.) with a chapter (78) describing the efforts of Dionysius to find homes

---

[86] Modern historians may agree that Dionysius was perfectly capable of taking a bribe and "the last man to refuse payment for doing what he wished to do"; see Glotz–Cohen, *Histoire grecque III* 396; Bury, *CAH* VI.125; Stroheker, *Dionysios I* 79 n. 101. But was he "capable" of having three hundred sacks of money carried into the acropolis unnoticed? Or is Timaeus providing Syracusans with a story to match the Harpalus scandal and the bribe supposed to have been taken by Demosthenes?

[87] How could Timaeus say that they lost 150,000 men if their total force was only 130,000 (F 108—Diod.14.54.5)? K. J. Beloch, *Neue Jahrbücher* 119 (1879) 599–600, has a good explanation. He thinks that Timaeus' figure of 130,000 does not include the crews of the 208 fighting ships (40,000 men) and the non–combatants (at least 50,000).

for mercenaries and other displaced persons in various cities. But, in contrast with what has preceded, he offers little more than a summary account in pedestrian style. It is the same when he returns to Sicilian affairs in 14.87, and takes up the events of 394. He describes various activities of Dionysius in brief, but gives more detail of his unsuccessful attempt to take Tauromenium from the Sicels, when he suffered severely from the cold weather, which injured his eyes, and had a narrow escape from death or capture when he fell and had to abandon his arms. Timaeus may be presumed as a source for anything that concerns Tauromenium.[88] This may be an occasion when he is dependent on local informants.[89]

In Diodorus' account Dionysius is shown as unable to exercise any control over western Sicily, so that, in 393, when Mago invades, "most of the Sicels" (90.3) are ready to become his allies, and he meets with no opposition until he is in Messenian territory and Dionysius defeats him in a battle near Abacene (90.4). Instead of pursuing his advantage, Dionysius leaves Mago alone, withdraws to Syracuse, and sets off with a hundred ships to attack Rhegium. His attack is unsuccessful, and his interference in Italy produces the opposite effect to what he intended: "The Greeks in Italy saw that the *pleonexia* of Dionysius was advancing into their territory, and they grouped themselves together in an alliance" (91.1). Timaeus' prejudice against Dionysius is easily recognizable here. His attack on Rhegium, which must have been intended to prevent any help reaching the Carthaginians from Italy, is interpreted as mere *pleonexia*.

When Mago returns with a larger force in the next year (392),[90] he meets no opposition until his progress is checked at Agyrium by the powerful tyrant Agyris. Dionysius advances to meet him and makes Agyris his ally. By skilful guerrilla tactics, they succeed in cutting Mago's supply lines, and without ever meeting him in any major pitched battle (despite Syracusan demands for a "quick battle to settle the issue"), they make his position so difficult that he agrees to a peace settlement, abandoning any

---

[88] Timaeus may have made a point of recording all Dionysius' narrow escapes from death. Perhaps he also emphasized his readiness to suffer hardship and injury, as when he injured his eyes in the winter cold at Tauromenium, just as Demosthenes liked to remind people of all the injuries that Philip suffered in his pursuit of power (e.g., 18.67).

[89] Note especially 88.1, where it is noted that the Sicels "heard from their fathers" how the early Greek settlers on Naxos drove out the Sicels from the hill of Tauromenium; and now the Sicels claim their right to recover it as an ancient possession.

[90] M. Sordi, *Aevum* 52 (1978) 1–26, claims to find a "contradiction" ("as though Mago were now being sent for the first time"), and argues that Diodorus has produced a series of "doublets" in the chapters that narrate the movements of Dionysius in the rest of Book XIV, trying to combine divergent accounts in Timaeus and Ephorus. Her arguments seem to me no more convincing than those of Laqueur.

claim to control the Sicels. They are now said to be "subject to Dionysius" (96.4). Timaeus must have thought this a severe blow to the freedom of Sicily (95.4–5). And one detail of the year must have seemed particularly important to him. Dionysius expelled the Sicels from Tauromenium and installed his own mercenaries there (96.4).

Diodorus provides more detail of the fighting in Italy between 390 and 387. In 390, after an unopposed landing "on the borders of Locrian territory," the army of Dionysius marches towards Rhegium (100.1). Dionysius himself is with the fleet, which attacks the ships from Croton that are coming to help the Rhegines. They capture some of these ships,[91] but a storm breaks out and some of their own ships are wrecked. Dionysius gets away safely in his quinquireme—yet another of his lucky escapes.

Before returning to Syracuse, Dionysius negotiates an alliance with the Lucanians, intending to use them to conquer the Greeks in Italy for him. Timaeus must have had some comment on this plan,[92] and it must have seemed unwise because, as Diodorus notes (101.1), the Greek cities of Italy were bound by treaty to come to the help of the Thurians when the Lucanians invaded their territory.[93] Unfortunately the Thurians did not wait for allied help to arrive, but took the field on their own with disastrous results. They let themselves be trapped in an enclosed plain where the Lucanians attacked them and "more than ten thousand fell" (102.1), a rhetorical estimate in Timaeus' familiar style. Some of the survivors reached the sea, and swam out towards some warships that were passing, only to find that they were Syracusan ships under the command of Leptines, the tyrant's brother. He sees the opportunity to arrange with the Lucanians for the ransom of about a thousand prisoners at the low rate of one mina per man,[94] advancing the money himself, and charging the Greeks no doubt an exorbitant rate of interest. The Italiots are grateful none the less,

---

[91] They are fired on by Crotoniat land forces when they approach the shore. Their own land force must have been far away, marching to Rhegium. Timaeus may have given some account of its activities.

[92] Using barbarian allies to help conquer Greeks would have been thought monstrous in earlier times, but both Spartans and Athenians had set an example for Dionysius to follow.

[93] Perhaps in the following spring (Stroheker, *Dionysios* I 114). But Diodorus merely says μετὰ δὲ ταῦτα and records the event under 390 (101.1).

[94] This must at one time have been a conventional rate, since Aristotle gives it as an example of custom, οἷον τὸ μνᾶς λυτροῦσθαι (*Eth.Nic.* 5.1134b). Actual rates seem always to have been higher, for example, two minas in Hdt. 5.77 and 6.79, even ten minas, as agreed between Demetrius Poliorcetes and the Rhodians (Diod.20.84). More could be asked for individuals, e.g. 26 minas in [Dem]. 53.7. Prisoners of war and persons kidnapped by pirates might owe their release to public-spirited individuals who advanced the money either as a loan or a free gift, cf. M. Rostovtzeff, *Social and Economic History of the Hellenistic World* 202, 1364–65 (n. 24, n. 26.). No other example is known to me of a person or organization

and to make sure that he can collect what they owe him, he encourages them to make peace with the Lucanians. Dionysius is not at all pleased to find that his brother's rapacity has wrecked his plan of using the Lucanians to make himself master of all Greek Italy, and he removes him from command of the fleet (102.3).

Dionysius invades Italy again the next year (389) and lays siege to Caulonia. He wins a decisive victory over an Italiot army, and when the survivors take refuge on a hill–top, lack of water soon forces them to surrender (as will be seen, this happens more than once in Timaeus' battles).[95] There are said to be "more than ten thousand" of them, the same rhetorical figure as before (one can imagine Polybius' comment). Diodorus says that he let these men go without demanding ransom (104.2–105.4), and the story can be identified as coming from Timaeus since it also appears in Dionysius of Halicarnassus (*AR* 20.7). Diodorus comments that this release of the prisoners was thought to be "the finest thing that Dionysius ever did" (105.4). Timaeus may have been more cynical in his interpretation, if this generosity enabled Dionysius to obtain the terms he wanted from Italiot cities. He made peace with the Rhegines, but imposed an indemnity of three hundred talents (is this another rhetorical estimate?),[96] took over all their ships, and demanded hostages as a pledge of their good behaviour. He destroyed the city of Caulonia,[97] removed its inhabitants to Syracuse, where they were granted citizenship (106.3), and gave their land to the Locrians.

Next year (388), Dionysius treated the citizens of Hipponium in the same way, destroying their city and giving their land to the Locrians. Strabo records that he also added Scylacium to the Locrian territory, and made an attempt to build a wall across the isthmus from this city to the sea on the west. And he gives the tyrant's reason for this grandiose scheme: "Ostensibly this was to protect the communities south of the isthmus from the barbarians to the north, but his real purpose was to break up the unity that held the Greek cities together, so that he could be securely in control

---

lending or guaranteeing the money in the hope of profiting by the transaction, advancing the money as a business venture, not an act of charity. But this must be what Diodorus means: γενόμενος δὲ τῶν χρημάτων ἐγγυητὴς καὶ διαλλάξας τοὺς Ἰταλιώτας τοῖς Λευκανοῖς ἔπεισεν εἰρήνην ποιήσασθαι, καὶ μεγάλης ἀποδοχῆς ἔτυχε παρὰ τοῖς Ἰταλιώταις, συμφερόντως αὐτῷ, οὐ λυσιτελῶς δὲ Διονυσίῳ συντεθεικὼς τὸν πόλεμον (102.3).

[95] Below, pp. 249, 253.

[96] Compare the 300 talents that Himilco is supposed to have given Dionysius, Diod. 14.75.1–3.

[97] The supposed etymology of Caulonia, "previously called Aulonia διὰ τὸν προκείμενον αὐλῶνα" (Strabo 6.1.10), may well have been noted by Timaeus, but it is as old as Hecataeus (*FGrH* 1 F 84).

of everything south of the isthmus. An attack by people from the north put an end to this scheme" (6.1.10). Although not mentioned by Diodorus, this plan for a wall was probably described by Timaeus. Philistus and other advisers must have tried to dissuade Dionysius from such an impracticable project, if it was ever seriously considered.

Dionysius is said to have been well disposed towards Locri because it had sent him a suitable bride, but he was determined to punish the Rhegines for the insult they offered him when, in reply to his request, they told him that he could have the executioner's daughter (107.2–3). After making a peace treaty with them that left them without ships, he found an excuse to repudiate the treaty, and laid siege to the city. There is the usual collection of stories about the hardships of the siege, and when the city finally surrendered, ten months later, Diodorus says that the six thousand survivors were more dead than alive. All who could not raise a mina to buy their freedom[98] were sold as slaves, and Dionysius is said to have treated their military commander Phyton with the most astonishing brutality (111.1–112.5).[99] Strabo (6.1.6) says that the city was destroyed, and partially rebuilt by Dionysius II. His information must come ultimately from Timaeus. He explains that the tyrant was angered by the offer of the executioner's daughter as a bride.[100]

Diodorus says that the Gauls invaded Italy while Dionysius was besieging Rhegium (113.1). Polybius not only dates these events in the same year as Diodorus (387–6, the year of the King's Peace), but uses the same form of phrase.[101] It is hard to resist the conclusion that he is echoing Timaeus' words. Justin (20.5.4) says that when Dionysius was in Italy, he was approached by a Gallic delegation, after the burning of Rome, and that a pact with the Gauls was arranged. This information also might come from Timaeus. Diodorus devotes five chapters (113–117) to the familiar tale of the Gauls in Rome, the cackling geese on the Capitol and so on, but one cannot be at all confident that he found any of this in Timaeus, because the story must have been familiar to Greeks as well as Romans in Diodorus' time, and it is unnecessary to seek any particular written source for it. It is also very difficult to determine what kind of contribution Timaeus

---

[98] A different version is given by [Aristot.] *Econ.* 2.20g (1349b). For discussion, see B.A. Van Groningen, *Mnemosyne,* N.S. 59 (1931) 336.

[99] An entirely different story about Phyton is told by Philostratus, *Vit.Apoll.* 7.2. Diodorus says many poets treated the subject (112.5).

[100] The story is confirmed as coming from Timaeus when Strabo reports it as well as Diodorus. For Strabo's use of Timaeus, see Chapter VI.

[101] καθ' ὃν καιρὸν μάλιστα Ῥήγιον ἐπολιόρκει Διονύσιος (Diod. 113.1), ἐν ᾧ. . . . ἐπολιόρκει Ῥήγιον (Polyb. 1.6.2).

made in shaping the tradition of early Rome, or how much interest he actually took in early Roman history. Since he thought it worthwhile to write about the origins of Rome and to fix a date for its foundation,[102] his interest may have continued into historical times. But there is no real evidence that this was so.

Books XIII and XIV of Diodorus enable us to understand fairly well how Timaeus described the first twenty years of the reign of Dionysius. We know far less about the second half of his reign (386–368), because in Book XV Diodorus returns to his summary manner of writing, and he gives us no reason to believe that he is still following Timaeus. But we should not blame Diodorus exclusively for our lack of information. We may reasonably believe that there was no good account of these years in Philistus' history, because this was when he was in exile and could not write about events from personal knowledge. Without an adequate account from Philistus, both Ephorus and Timaeus would be helpless.[103]

It seems to have been accepted in later times that Dionysius began to turn against his advisers at the time when he became seriously interested in writing poetry. Timaeus, whom Diodorus is certainly following in 14.109, evidently thought that the tyrant was trying to match the successes of Hiero and Theron in the Olympic games, entering his horses in the races and making a lavish display at the festival of 388 B.C.[104] And while the earlier tyrants had been content to offer patronage and hospitality to the poets of their day, Dionysius had his own compositions performed at Olympia, only to find that the audience jeered at them. He was equally unsuccessful on the race course, when his chariots not only failed to win, but broke down or collided with others. The disaster was complete when the ship bringing his delegation back to Sicily met with bad weather and was blown off its course to Taras.

Inevitably, Dionysius had flatterers who urged him not to be discouraged, but to persevere with his writing and disregard the criticism of so-called experts (109.5–6). This is as far as Diodorus goes in Book XIV. It is not until Book XV, under the year 386, that he tells the famous stories of Dionysius sending Philoxenus to the quarries and trying to sell Plato as a slave, and here he seems to be following Ephorus (15.6–7). He repeats

---

[102] Above, p. 85.

[103] Stroheker, *Dionysios I* 119–20, says that if Philistus spent his exile on the Adriatic coast, he must have been familiar with the plans and operations of Dionysius in that area. But if he wrote about them, his account was apparently neglected by Ephorus.

[104] In 15.7.2 Diodorus dates this Olympic festival in 386 instead of 388. This may be Timaeus' mistake.

details that he took from Timaeus in his account of 388 B.C., but he writes in the flatter, less vivid style that he commonly uses when he is dependent on Ephorus, and he represents the tyrant as turning against "all his friends," suspecting them of plots against him and complaining that they envy him his artistic talent (15.7.3). Timaeus' narrative gave better reasons for his distrust of them. Leptines had thwarted his plan to gain control of the Italiot cities, and Philistus may have been among those who wanted him to challenge Mago to a pitched battle when the chances of a decisive victory seemed good, only to have their advice rejected.[105]

Timaeus represented Dionysius as shamelessly sacrilegious, but he cannot be held responsible for the rumour that he planned to rob Delphi of its treasures,[106] or for the tale that he stole the golden cloak from Zeus' statue in the temple of Olympian Zeus at Olympia.[107] He had quite enough examples of sacrilegious theft nearer home and had no need to strain his readers' credulity too far.

Diodorus devotes only ten chapters in Book XV to Sicilian affairs, and there is nothing in them that can be traced to Timaeus. It might be thought that his remarks about the plague at Carthage are taken from Timaeus (15.24), because they are similar in style to his descriptions of such epidemics in earlier books, with strong emphasis on the theme of divine punishment.[108] But it is equally likely that he is merely recalling and re-phrasing what he wrote on earlier occasions himself.[109]

Diodorus finishes his account of Dionysius I by describing his death. He says that after receiving the news that his tragedy had won the prize at the Lenaean festival in Athens, he drank very heavily at the festivities celebrating the victory, became ill, and never recovered. He had been warned by an oracle that he would die ὅταν τῶν κρειττόνων περιγένηται, "when he got the better of those who were better (or stronger) than he was." He had been careful, in the past, to avoid making his victory over the Car-

---

[105] Above, pp. 184–85.

[106] Diodorus, 15.13.1, mentions the plan without any explanation, except that he appears to connect it with his proposed conquest of Epirus: ἔσπευδε γὰρ ἄφνω μεγάλαις δυνάμεσιν ἐπιπλεῦσαι τοῖς κατὰ τὴν Ἤπειρον τόποις καὶ συλῆσαι τὸ ἐν Δελφοῖς τέμενος, γέμον πολλῶν χρημάτων. This sentence can hardly be a fair representation of what his source wrote. Laqueur, RE VIA. 1149, thinks the source is Timaeus, but there is no real reason to think so.

[107] Cic. De nat.deorum 3.83, together with other stories of thefts from temples.

[108] Cf. Laqueur, RE VIA. 1150; Meister, Sizilische Geschichte 103.

[109] Cf. Diod. 13.59.5, where Hannibal at Himera is represented as remembering what happened to his grandfather Hamilcar, who lost 150,000 men at the Battle of Himera in 480. Diodorus can be remembering what he wrote in 11.22.4, and is not necessarily copying out something that he has just read in Timaeus.

thaginians complete, but now he had completely disregarded the warning by winning a victory over poets who were certainly better than he was (74.2–4).

Though the story cannot properly be attributed to Timaeus, it has a certain Timaean quality.[110] There was also some point in showing that Dionysius died like Alexander, who drank heavily for several days before his death and, according to one report, when asked to whom he bequeathed his kingdom, replied τῷ κρατίστῳ, "to the best (or strongest)."[111] Plutarch wanted to show that Dionysius, like Alexander, never made it clear whom he wanted as his successor, his eldest son, the young Dionysius, who was the child of his Locrian wife, Doris, or one of his sons by his Syracusan wife, Aristomache. He says that Dion tried to ask him his preference when he was near death, but was prevented by the physicians, who wanted to keep in favour with young Dionysius, "and, so Timaeus says, when the sick man asked for a hypnotic drug, they gave it to him," and he never recovered consciousness.[112] The story may not have been invented or "revealed" until later, inspired perhaps by the tales about Alexander's death. Other authors tell us nothing of what Timaeus had to say about the last days of Dionysius. Athenaeus says only that he gave a splendid description of the funeral pyre.[113]

Diodorus decided to concentrate in Book XV on affairs of mainland Greece and the Aegean, and one may perhaps suppose that Ephorus did the same. We are left wondering how much more we should know about the elder Dionysius if we had the books of Philistus and Timaeus dealing with these years. If Plutarch, for example, had chosen to write a *Life* of Dionysius, could he have found enough material about his later years to make the effort worth while? There really is no way of answering the question.

Thanks to Book XIV of Diodorus, we can see how Timaeus established his version of the first twenty years of Dionysius' career, showing him as a man who followed the traditional pattern of a tyrant's behaviour—taking advantage of a crisis to put himself forward as an autocratic leader, narrowly escaping death or disaster on several occasions, but making himself secure from attack by recruiting mercenary soldiers and using mercenaries

---

[110] Meister, *Sizilische Geschichte* 104, says it cannot come from Timaeus, because he gave an entirely different reason for the unwillingness of Dionysius to exploit his victories. The reason given here may be a note added by Diodorus himself.

[111] Arr. *Anab.* 7.25–26.

[112] F 109—Plut. *Dion* 6.3.

[113] F 112—Ath. 5.206 E.

as guards, deciding questions of national policy in the way that suited his personal interest rather than the interests of Syracuse and Sicily, building a Syracusan empire beyond the limits that his advisers thought safe or desirable, rejecting the advice of his friends when he found it unpalatable, and accumulating enormous wealth by unscrupulous and often sacrilegious methods. What we cannot discover with any certainty is how much Timaeus altered this portrait in describing the years from 386 to 368.

ii. Dionysius II and Dion

Plutarch cites Timaeus several times in the *Dion,* and much as he disliked his manner of writing, he must have found him a more sympathetic source than the "tyrant–lovers" Philistus and Ephorus in describing Dion's defence of free government against tyranny.[114] Diodorus, on the other hand, never mentions Timaeus in Book XV or XVI, and there is good reason to suppose that he has abandoned him in favour of Ephorus as his source for Sicilian affairs.[115] He mentions Ephorus only once in these two books, but he continues to write in his "Ephoran" style even in his chapters that are concerned with the West, and there is one passage in his text that corresponds very closely with a fragment of Ephorus.[116] It has also been suggested that he has turned his attention to Theopompus, who covered this period in his three books devoted to Sicilian history, as Diodorus informs us himself (16.71.3).[117] Some critics, on the other hand, are unwilling to believe that Diodorus has abandoned Timaeus, and Laqueur still believes that he can identify "extracts" from Timaeus "inserted" into an account based on Ephorus.[118]

For present purposes, it will not be necessary to prove that Diodorus is actually following Ephorus. It will be enough to point out the differences

---

[114] Cf. *Dion* 35–36 (he calls Ephorus φιλοτυραννότατος)—F 115, 154. He cites Timaeus also at *Dion* 6,14, 31—F 109, 113,114.

[115] Cf. W. H. Porter, *Plutarch: Life of Dion* (Dublin 1952), xxviii–xxix; E. Schwartz, *RE* V. 681–82, s.v. Diodoros (38) (though he believes that for the story of Dion Diodorus followed a later source who knew Timaeus' account).

[116] 16.16.3–4, which corresponds with Ephorus *FGrH* 70 F 219, 220; cf. Meister, *Sizilische Geschichte* 108; M. Sordi, *Diodori Liber XVI* (Florence 1969) xxxvi–xxxviii.

[117] N. G. L. Hammond, *CQ* 32 (1938) 137–51. He thinks Diodorus' account not dull and flat enough to be based on Ephorus, with more life than is usual in his Ephoran sections. But, as Porter points out, it is the events, not the style, that make this narrative interesting and readable.

[118] R. Laqueur, *RE* VIA. 1150–56; E. Meyer, *Geschichte des Altertums V* (4th. ed., 1958) 500–01; H. Berve, *Dion* (*Abh. d. Akad. Mainz,* Geistes–u.Sozialwissensch. *Kl.* 1956, 10) 756–57, who seems unwilling to reach a decision.

between Plutarch and Diodorus which warn us that we can no longer look to Diodorus for Timaeus' version.[119]

Nepos, on the other hand, certainly followed Timaeus, whose work he mentions in his *Alcibiades*.[120] Nepos' narrative corresponds closely enough with Plutarch's to make no other explanation possible, and the minor discrepancies are easily explicable, once one recognizes that the two biographers are likely to treat their source differently. Plutarch may add some explanations of his own, but it is Nepos who is the more likely to distort or misrepresent what he has read, whether from carelessness or deliberate intention.

Plutarch had read the Platonic letters and relies mainly on them in writing about Plato's experience at Syracuse. There is unfortunately no record of what Timaeus had to say about Plato's visits. He had little respect for Plato or Aristotle,[121] but he might at least have respected Plato for his attitude towards tyranny. It is perhaps unlikely that he had read the Platonic letters,[122] but he had read Philistus' account of his relations with Plato, and probably also Timonides' *Letter to Speusippus,* which gave a report of Dion's expedition to Syracuse.[123] Since nothing is known of Timonides apart from the references in the *Dion* and a brief mention in Diogenes Laertius,[124] it is possible that Plutarch knew of his report only through references to it in Timaeus.[125]

[119] For a good discussion, see K. F. Stroheker, "Timaios und Philistos," *Satura Otto Weinreich dargebracht* (Baden–Baden 1952) 139–61. Various opinions have been expressed about the sources of Diodorus, Plutarch, and Nepos for the history of these years. In addition to the works cited in preceding notes, see C. Volquardsen, *Untersuchungen über die Quellen bei Diodor* (Kiel 1868); G. Morrow, *Studies in the Platonic Epistles (Illinois Studies in Language and Literature* 18, 1935) 34–36, and the works of Bachof, Biedenweg, Hejnic, Pasquali, Voit, and Westlake listed in the Bibliography. I am not prepared to take seriously the theory propounded by Bachof, Pasquali, and Voit, that Nepos and Plutarch were dependent on a biography of Dion written in Hellenistic times, a theory that Berve, *Dion* 753–55, seems disposed to accept. My views on imaginary *Zwischenquellen* were expressed in *Historia* 11 (1962) 424–25.

[120] *Alcib.* 11.1—F 99.

[121] T 18, F.11, 12, 14; above, pp. 99–100.

[122] It might be argued that he could have seen copies, of some, if not all, in Athens. No one actually cites any of the letters before Cicero, who quotes from the Seventh Letter, calling it "praeclara epistula Platonis" (*Tusc.Disp.* 5.100), though Diogenes Laertius (3.61–62) tells us that letters were included among the works of Plato in the library of Alexandria in the third century, and were recognized by Aristophanes the Grammarian as forming part of his fifth tetralogy; cf. J. Harward, *The Platonic Epistles* (Cambridge 1932) 60–61. But those who believe that Timaeus made use of the letters, like Morrow, op. cit. (n. 119) 27–28, cannot produce evidence to support their contention.

[123] Above, p. 31.

[124] *Dion* 22, 30, 31, 35; Diog.Laert.4.5; cf. *FGrH.* 561.

[125] It is usually, though needlessly, taken for granted that Plutarch had seen the text of

Plutarch cites Theopompus (*Dion* 24.5–10),[126] and even if he had not done so, it might be taken for granted that he made some effort to discover what this author had to say in his Sicilian books. Unluckily, except for this one passage, there is no way of identifying any detail or episode in the *Dion* as Theopompan. But as the narrative of the *Dion* is studied chapter by chapter, it will become clear how much Plutarch owes to Timaeus, while no positive evidence of his use of Theopompus will emerge.[127] Perhaps he looked into Ephorus' account, and decided that it was not much use to him. We need not believe that he carried bibliographic research any further than this.

Plutarch begins his narrative (*Dion* 3) by describing the two marriages of Dionysius I after the death of his first wife, marrying Doris the Locrian and the Syracusan Aristomache on the same day. This corresponds with Diodorus' version (14.44–45), which is certainly based on Timaeus, and Plutarch must still be following Timaeus when he adds that it was customary for both women to dine together with Dionysius and that they took turns to spend the night with him; that Doris soon bore him a son, but it was some time before Aristomache became pregnant, though he was particularly anxious to have a son by her; he suspected Doris' mother of giving her a drug to prevent conception, and had her put to death. All this is exactly what one might expect from Timaeus.

Plutarch also seems to be following Timaeus when he says that Dion won the favour and confidence of the elder Dionysius by giving proof of his intelligence (4.1), because Nepos says the same thing: "Erat intimus Dionysio priori, neque minus propter mores quam affinitatem" (*Dion* 1.3). And when Plutarch reports the tyrant's order that Dion is to be given anything that he wants, "but after giving it they must tell him of it the very same day," we are being shown Timaeus' typical tyrant, suspicious and distrustful of his "friends." It is also essential for Timaeus' story that Dion should be allowed full independence by the younger Dionysius in dealing with the Carthaginians, as Plutarch (5.8) and Nepos (1.4–5) both report.

Plutarch quotes and appears to accept Timaeus' account of the last hours of the elder Dionysius. According to Timaeus, the tyrant died in his sleep, after asking his physician for a sleeping draught so as to avoid talking with Dion, who had sought an interview, hoping to persuade him to

---

Timonides, e.g. by Porter, op. cit. (n.115) xiv, xx–xxii; Berve, op. cit. (n.118) 748–49; Morrow, op. cit. (n.119) 36–46. But see H. D. Westlake, *Historia* 2 (1953) 295 n. 2.

[126] Below, p. 197.

[127] For attempts to identify fragments of Theopompus in Plutarch, see W. Biedenweg, *Plutarchs Quellen in den Lebensbeschreibungen des Dion und Timoleon* (Leipzig 1884).

nominate one of the sons of Aristomache as his successor, instead of his eldest son Dionysius, Doris' child.[128] If Timaeus in his earlier narrative had shown Dionysius particularly anxious to have a son by Aristomache who could succeed him, he might now want to explain why his eldest son Dionysius was preferred. He could have pointed out that Aristomache's sons were still very young, and that the tyrant did not want Dion to have the powers of a regent acting for his nephews, that he feared his influence and his ambition. Dion's request for an interview would appear to confirm the dying man's fears, and Plutarch's account of what followed gives further confirmation. Once the younger Dionysius is accepted as tyrant, Dion tries to assert himself as the only competent adviser with the courage to speak his mind (6.4–5), explaining that he has the "Carthaginian question" completely under control, with plans ready made to put into effect immediately, according as peace or war is desired.

It is not surprising that the "friends" of the elder Dionysius should take offence at such assertiveness, and it looks as though Timaeus represented him as a man with ambitions to be the strong power behind the throne. If Plutarch thought Timaeus had misjudged Dion's character, it is understandable that he should be constantly critical of him and quick to find fault. But he seems to have accepted his account of the deathbed scene and its immediate sequel.

Equally, he seems to have adopted Timaeus' account of the way in which Dion was forced into exile. Timaeus represented the young Dionysius as a heavy drinker and "a slave to his sensual passions,"[129] and Plutarch (7.1–4) says that the "friends" of the elder Dionysius established their power over him by gratifying his tastes, providing him with every opportunity to indulge himself, in the hope that they would counteract the influence of Dion. They were afraid that Plato, whom Dion had invited back to Syracuse, would exercise his spell over the impressionable young man and persuade him to abdicate in favour of the sons of Aristomache, leaving all the power and wealth to Dion and his nephews, while he sought "the Good" in the Academy and found "happiness" in geometry (14.2–3).

---

[128] F 109—Plut. *Dion* 6.2–3. Ancient writers naturally assumed that the drug hastened his death. In Nepos' version (*Dion* 2.4–5), it is the younger Dionysius who keeps Dion away and orders the sleeping draught, and Justin, another writer who often follows Timaeus, says "insidiis ad postremum suorum interficitur" (20.5.14). It is possible that Timaeus spoke simply of "Dionysius" asking for the drug, and that some readers took this to mean the father, others the son. But Berve, *Dion* 766, thinks that Nepos' version is a later adaptation of Timaeus' story, designed to put the blame on the younger Dionysius.

[129] F 158a, b—Ath. 10. 437B; Philodem. *Index Acad. Herculanensis* 8, p. 43 Mekler; cf. Aelian, *VH* 2.41.

They prevailed on Dionysius to recall Philistus,[130] and it was not long before Dion was sent away in disgrace.

Some of the language that Plutarch uses in describing these developments may be taken from Timaeus,[131] and he acknowledges that he is following him as he tells the story of the plan devised by Philistus and the others: "Dionysius first became suspicious, and then, as suspicion turned into anger and the breach between them became more open, a letter was brought secretly to him which Dion had written to the Carthaginian overseers (ἐπιμεληταί), telling them that whenever they wished to discuss terms of peace with Dionysius, they should never arrange a conference without him, that if they worked through him they would be able to overcome all difficulties without trouble. After reading this to Philistus and discussing it with him, so Timaeus says, Dionysius approached Dion saying that he wished to discuss whatever differences they had. After alleging some reasonable grounds for complaint and agreeing to settle them, he drew him away unaccompanied along the foot of the acropolis towards the sea, and then showed him the letter and accused him of conspiring with the Carthaginians against him. He refused to listen to any explanation, but without further ado thrust him, just as he was, into a boat and ordered the sailors to take charge of him and set him ashore somewhere on the Italian coast."[132]

In the next chapter (15) Plutarch describes the public protest at Dion's banishment and how Dionysius tried to explain it as not really banishment but "a change of abode," and sent two ships after him loaded with his possessions. He points out how wealthy Dion was, as he could have learnt from Plato's seventh letter (347b), and how he lived in "almost tyrannical style." Timaeus would not have failed to describe Dion's pretentious manner of living, and he would certainly have mentioned the lavish gifts of the

---

[130] Timaeus evidently believed that Philistus remained in exile until 368, but Diodorus (15.7.3–4) says that Dionysius I recalled him soon after banishing him. This is one of the indications that Diodorus is no longer following Timaeus in Book XV.

[131] Notably λέγοντες ὡς οὐ λέληθε κατεπάδων καὶ καταφαρμάσσων τῷ Πλάτωνος λόγῳ Διονύσιον, and the rhetorical point that the Athenians in the past with their great armament failed to capture Syracuse, but now, it seems, δι᾽ ἑνὸς σοφιστοῦ καταλύσουσι τὴν Διονυσίου τυραννίδα, if they persuade him to abandon his ships and hoplites and cavalry and ἐν ᾽Ακαδημίᾳ τὸ σιωπώμενον ἀγαθὸν ζητεῖν καὶ διὰ γεωμετρίας εὐδαίμονα γενέσθαι (Dion 14.1–3).

[132] F 113—Dion 14.4–5. The account in Plato, Ep.7.329b–c has none of this detail, only that Dion was the victim of slanderous accusations and that Dionysius accused him of plotting against the tyranny and σμικρὸν ἐς πλοῖον ἐμβιβάσας ἐξέβαλεν ἀτίμως. Nepos (4.1) says that Dionysius gave him a trireme to take him to Corinth. This is probably his own interpretation (or inaccurate memory) of Timaeus' story.

elder Dionysius which made it possible.[133] But when Plutarch goes on to describe the relations between Dionysius and Plato after Dion's departure, he has abandoned Timaeus for the Platonic letters.[134] When he describes events in Greece after Plato joins Dion there, and events in Syracuse after Plato returns for his third visit, he seems to have a source that supplements the letters, but there is no positive reason to think that it is Timaeus. The only help that he gives us is to say, as he finishes the tale of Plato's final departure: "Plato's own account is not quite the same as this."[135]

Diodorus never mentions Plato and he compresses all the events of these years into a single chapter (16.6). His source must be Ephorus, since he represents Dion as hiding and taking flight from Syracuse to avoid arrest, instead of being "thrust into a boat" by Dionysius. In the next chapter he mentions the founding of the city of Tauromenium by Timaeus' father Andromachus (16.7—T 3a), as a home for the survivors from Naxos, which Dionysius had destroyed in 403 (Diod. 14.15.2). Timaeus must have described his father's foundation,[136] but it does not follow that Diodorus is borrowing from his account here.[137] He says that Andromachus gave the city its name ἀπὸ τῆς ἐπὶ Ταύρου μονῆς, "because they stayed on Taurus," but Timaeus did not credit his father with inventing the name. He says it was given to the place when the Sicels established their settlement there in 396 (Diod. 14.59.2).[138] This may be one of the many inaccuracies that Timaeus claimed to find in Ephorus.

Plutarch is not concerned with events in Sicily and Italy during the absence of Dion, and Diodorus has very little to say about them (16.5.1–3). Philistus is supposed to have made a start on his history of the times of Dionysius II, "covering five years in two books," and coming down as far as 363,[139] and Timaeus could have borrowed from it. But since neither Plutarch nor Diodorus seems to have been interested, Timaeus' account of these years is completely lost.

Timaeus or Timonides may have provided Plutarch with some of the information about Dion's preparations for his expedition, but it cannot be proved. When we read of the omens that disturbed superstitious members

[133] Nepos (1.2) says that Dion inherited great wealth from his father "quas ipse tyranni muneribus auxerat."

[134] Cf. especially *Ep*.7.329d–330b.

[135] *Dion* 20.4, cf. Plato, *Ep*.3.319a–c, 7.350a–b.

[136] He will also have given the exact date. Diodorus' date, ἅμα τούτοις πραττομένοις, is vague, because the preceding chapter covers events of ten years.

[137] As is maintained by Laqueur, *RE* VIA. 1151; Meister, *Sizilische Geschichte* 113.

[138] Above, p. 177.

[139] T 11b—Diod. 15.89.3

of the expedition at Zacynthus, and further portents that seemed to warn Dionysius of his impending disaster, we might think that here at last is a piece of Timaeus' narrative. But Plutarch says that he found the story in Theopompus.[140]

In the next chapter (25), Plutarch describes Dion's strange Odyssey after he sails from Zacynthus. His ships are well stocked with food, because they intend to sail directly to Sicily across the open sea so as to avoid detection. It takes them twelve days before they sight Cape Pachynus, the south–eastern point of Sicily, and their navigator warns them that if they do not land soon a north wind may rise and drive them out to sea. Dion is unwilling to land so near Syracuse, and as they sail westward, a north wind does indeed rise, and in a fierce storm they are driven towards Africa, where they narrowly escape shipwreck on the Syrtes. The storm dies down, a south wind, which they could not dare hope for, comes up, and on the fifth day they land unopposed at Minoa, half–way between Selinus and Acragas.

Plutarch's description has quite an epic quality, and readers may be reminded of the storm in the first book of the *Aeneid* that drove Aeneas from Sicily to Carthage. There can be no objection to claiming Timaeus as Plutarch's source. Timaeus had brought many heroes on their *Nostoi* across stormy seas from Troy to Italy or Sicily, and he might well be tempted to treat Dion as another hero bringing freedom to Sicily, and to write in a style appropriate to a heroic theme. Some of Plutarch's language is worth quoting:

ἐκ δὲ τούτου τραχὺς μὲν ἀπαρκτίας ἐπιπεσὼν ἤλαυνε πολλῷ κλύδωνι τὰς ναῦς ἀπὸ τῆς Σικελίας. ἀστραπαὶ δὲ καὶ βρονταὶ φανέντος Ἀρκτούρου συμπεσοῦσαι πολὺν ἐξ οὐρανοῦ χειμῶνα καὶ ῥαγδαῖον ὄμβρον ἐξέχεαν,

and when the storm finally dies down,

ἀθυμοῦσι δ' αὐτοῖς πρὸς τὴν γαλῆνην καὶ διαφερομένοις αὖραν τινὰ κατέσπειρεν ἡ χώρα νότιον.[141]

---

[140] *Dion* 24: ταῦτα μὲν οὖν Θεόπομπος ἱστόρηκε. This need not mean that everything in the chapter is taken from Theopompus.

[141] This is not the language of dactylic hexameter, but it can be adapted for a messenger's speech in a tragedy:

τραχὺς γὰρ ἄνεμος ἐπιπεσὼν ἀπαρκτίας
πολλῷ κλύδωνι πλοῖα Σικελίας ἄπο
ἤλαυνεν, ἀστραπαὶ δὲ καὶ βρονταί. . . .

This is highly romantic writing, recalling some of the "fantasy" of Timaeus' account of the Battle of Himera,[142] and modern historians usually content themselves with speaking in general terms of Dion's "hazardous voyage."[143]

Diodorus (16.6.5) says Dion had given instructions for Heraclides to follow later with some triremes[144] and merchant ships, but Plutarch does not even mention Heraclides until he arrives at Syracuse and sets himself up as a political rival to Dion (32.3). He says that Dion quarrelled with him before leaving Greece, and that he organized his expedition entirely on his own initiative (ἰδιόστολος), that he was a man with talent for command (στρατηγικὸς ἄνθρωπος), but of unstable character and unreliable as a colleague. It can be argued that Diodorus, presumably following Ephorus, has the better version here, and that Dion was not relying on his own small number of men and ships to achieve his purpose.[145]

The hazards of the voyage play no part in Diodorus' account (16.9–11). He says that Dion landed with two merchant ships at Minoa, where he was welcomed by the "overseer" of the town, a friend of his called Paralus, and as he marched eastwards so many volunteers from Acragas and Gela and elsewhere joined him that there were twenty thousand of them when they reached Syracuse. Dionysius was far away in Italy, attempts to organize resistance failed completely, and Dion was welcomed into the city by the populace. Plutarch, on the other hand, shows fortune still playing a part in the story (25.12–26.10). A Carthaginian called Synalus,[146] a good friend of Dion's, was in charge of the town of Minoa. Not knowing who these armed men from the sea might be, he was preparing to oppose their landing, and it was lucky that no one was killed before he realized who they were. But once they were recognized he gave them a hospitable welcome.

Dion had wanted to wait a few days to give his men a chance to recover

---

[142] Chapter VI.

[143] E.g., I. Hackforth, *CAH* VI.278. Others, like G. Glotz–R. Cohen, *Histoire grecque III* (Paris 1936) 410, and Berve, *Dion* 810, seem to find no difficulty in believing this story of an epic *Nostos*.

[144] He had twenty triremes when he reached Syracuse, according to Diod. 16.16.2.

[145] J. H. Thiel, *Mededel. d.Akad. Amsterdam*, Afd. Letterkunde, N.R.4 (1941) 157–170, believes that Dion's plan was to arrive at Syracuse unexpectedly by sailing across the open sea, and thus to draw Philistus and his ships back from Italy and leave the coastal voyage clear for Heraclides. It is difficult to believe that such a plan would ever have been considered without modern means of communication. Philistus would in fact gain nothing by bringing his ships back to Sicily once Dion's force had landed.

[146] Synalus and Paralus are probably alternative translations of a Punic name.

from the hardships of the voyage before starting on the march to Syracuse, but they insisted on starting at once. Luck was with them, because Dionysius had just set sail for Italy with eighty ships (26.1–2). But for their delay at sea, he might not have left when they arrived, and another piece of luck delayed the news of their arrival from reaching him. The messenger who was sent to overtake him by the land route had crossed to Italy and was on the road from Rhegium to Caulonia, when he met a man returning from a sacrificial feast, who gave him a piece of meat. Being in no hurry to eat it, he stopped to sleep in a wood by the side of the road, and when he woke found that a wolf had run off with the meat and taken the despatches as well. Not daring to face Dionysius empty–handed, he ran away and was never heard of again (26.5–10). So a wolf helped Dion, just as one had once saved the life of Gelon.[147] It is not difficult to decide that Plutarch has this story from Timaeus, as there is no trace of it in Diodorus.[148]

Timaeus must have described the march to Syracuse and Dion's triumphant entry into the city, welcomed by the populace as military resistance melted away. Plutarch's account may not always represent exactly what Timaeus wrote, but it contains at least two details not mentioned by Diodorus which can confidently be identified as derived from him. Timaeus liked to use and explain local words and slang terms,[149] and as Dion approached the city Plutarch describes how the more respectable citizens came out to meet him wearing their best clothes, while οἱ πολλοί took the opportunity to attack the various spies and *agents provocateurs* of Dionysius, the so–called προσαγωγίδες ("go–betweens") who reported to him any seditious talk that they overheard.[150] Then as Dion marched through the city, he mounted a sun–dial, "a large and conspicuous monument beneath the acropolis and the Pentapyla,"[151] in order to make a speech. Here was the inevitable ominous incident for Timaeus to describe and explain. It presented the soothsayers with a problem. They thought it was a good

---

[147] F 95, cf. above, p. 129. Both stories deserve a place in a commentary on Horace's "Namque me silva lupus in Sabina;" see E. Fraenkel, *Horace* (Oxford 1957) 186.

[148] Laqueur, *RE* VIA. 1151 and Meister, *Sizilische Geschichte,* 113–14 claim to find small "inserts" from Timaeus in these chapters of Diodorus, but their argument is not convincing. They express no opinion on the source of Plutarch here. Jacoby is reluctant to discuss Plutarch's sources, but admits that "he seems to have used Timaeus" in the *Dion* (*FGrH* IIIb, p. 529).

[149] E.g., F 8, 49, 51.

[150] *Dion* 28.1, cf. Aristot. *Pol.* 5.1313b; Plut. *Mor.* 523A. Are the προσαγωγίδες women, or are they given this name because their occupation is considered unmanly?

[151] *Dion* 29.3–5. This description of the monument must come from a writer who knew Syracuse well, as Timaeus did.

omen that Dion made his speech standing on a monument set up by Dionysius, but standing on a sun–dial (ἡλιοτρόπιον) might be a sign that there would be a quick change (τροπή) in his fortunes.

After Dionysius returns to Syracuse and is safe in the shelter of his acropolis on the Island, there are negotiations with him as well as some fighting in which the Syracusans win a "splendid victory" in the first encounter (30–31). Finally, Plutarch has a reference to Timaeus. He says that heralds came from Dionysius bringing letters for Dion from members of his family, and he writes: "One of the letters was marked outside 'To father from Hipparinos.' This was the name of Dion's son. Timaeus says he was called Aretaeus after his mother Arete, but I think we should believe Timonides, as he was a dear friend of Dion and was with him on the expedition" (*Dion* 31.3—F 114)

This need not mean that Plutarch had read Timonides' account of the arrival of this letter.[152] The argument about the boy's name could have been reported by Timaeus.[153] In any case, the letter is not from his son, but from Dionysius himself, threatening harm to Dion's wife and son and sister unless he preserves the tyranny by taking over the power himself, warning him against giving freedom to a population full of hatred and resentment.

Dion insists on opening the letter, though the heralds want him to keep it for himself to read privately. It is of course designed to undermine his position and rouse suspicion against him, συγκειμένη πρὸς διαβολὴν τοῦ Δίωνος. His popularity does in fact diminish, and Plutarch describes the failure of the Syracusan populace to appreciate his true character or to see how right he was to use diplomatic tact in dealing with Dionysius (32.1–3).

This may be Plutarch's own judgment, but he certainly owes something to Timaeus when he characterizes Dion's rival Heraclides as "a man of unstable disposition, susceptible to any kind of influence, and particularly unreliable as a partner in any situation where authority and a good reputation are needed."[154] Timaeus may also be his source for the story of Sosis, the agent of Dionysius, who wounds himself and tries to convince people

---

[152] Above, p. 192. Meister, *Sizilische Geschichte* 114, believes that Diodorus 11.4–12.5 is from Timaeus, and that Plutarch is following Timonides.

[153] Polyaenus 5.2.7 has παρὰ Ἱππαρίωνος, "little Hipparinus," perhaps the name that he was called in the family, to distinguish him from his grandfather Hipparinus, after whom he was named (like little Tommy to distinguish him from his grandfather Tom). If he was also called Aretaeus that would mean "Arete's Hipparinus;" cf. Porter op. cit. (n. 115) xxi.

[154] ἥκιστα δὲ βέβαιος ἐν κοινωνίᾳ πραγμάτων ἀρχὴν ἐχόντων καὶ δόξαν (32.3). The precise meaning of the Greek is open to doubt and the reading ἀρχήν has been questioned.

that Dion attempted to kill him as part of a murderous purge. And he tells us himself that he is following Timaeus as he describes the victory over Philistus' fleet and the savage treatment of Philistus when he is taken prisoner:

"Ephorus says that he killed himself when his ship was captured,[155] but Timonides, who had been with Dion since the start of the expedition and sent his report to the philosopher Speusippus, says that Philistus was taken alive when his ship ran aground; first the Syracusans stripped him of his breastplate, and when they had him naked and defenceless, treated him outrageously, old man though he was; then they cut off his head, handed over his body to a group of boys, and told them to drag it through Achradina and throw it down into the quarries. Timaeus shows even less respect for the poor man (ἔτι μᾶλλον ἐφυβρίζων), saying that the youngsters caught hold of the dead man's lame leg and dragged him through the city, while everyone jeered at the sight of the man being dragged by the leg who had told Dionysius that, if he had to take flight from his tyranny, instead of mounting a swift horse, he should wait to be dragged out by his leg.

"Philistus, in fact, reports this advice as given by someone else to Dionysius, not as something he said himself. But Timaeus seizes on the vigorous and faithful support given to the tyranny by Philistus as a fair excuse for attacking him, and indulges his feelings to the full. One could pardon someone who had actually suffered under the tyranny for being resentful to the point of savagery, but when people are writing a history of the events in later years, who were never hurt by the man in his lifetime, common decency demands that they should refrain from using vulgar abusive language in exulting over the sufferings that accompany his fall—sufferings that fortune might compel even the best of men to endure" (*Dion* 35.4–36.2—F 115, 154).

Plutarch adds that in his opinion Ephorus is equally at fault for praising Philistus to the skies,[156] that he is no judge of character and seems to admire tyranny and all its extravagant luxury. In his moralizing way, Plutarch seems to be telling us that both Timaeus and Ephorus showed themselves better rhetoricians than historians in passing judgment on Philistus.

Dionysius escaped by ship, leaving his mercenaries still in command of the acropolis, and Heraclides again stirred up popular opposition to

---

[155] Cf. Diod. 16.16.3.

[156] Diodorus is clearly following Ephorus when he writes ὁ δὲ Φίλιστος εὐλαβηθεὶς τὴν ἐκ τῆς αἰχμαλωσίας αἰκίαν ἑαυτὸν ἀπέσφαξεν, πλείστας μέν καὶ μεγίστας χρείας παρεσχημένος τοῖς τυράννοις, πιστότατος δὲ τῶν φίλων τοῖς δυνάσταις γεγονώς (16.16.3).

Dion. There is no disagreement over this, but it is Plutarch (38), not Diodorus, who describes the portents that delayed the election of a new board of *strategoi*. There are summer thunderstorms and other omens in the sky, which disturbed the voters, and a strange incident follows: a carter's ox turns against its driver, breaks loose from its harness, and dashes into the theatre, causing the Assembly to scatter in dismay. Timaeus is warning his readers that disaster will follow when the omens are disregarded and twenty–five new *strategoi* are elected, including Heraclides, but not Dion. Dion has to leave the city.

Further comparison of the narrative in Plutarch and Diodorus seems to show Timaeus generally agreeing with Ephorus, but making changes and additions such as one might expect from him.[157] He described the loyalty of Dion's mercenaries, who were ready to escort him out of the city peacefully; and when the Syracusans were so foolish as to oppose them, they made a token attack, at Dion's command, which caused no bloodshed, but showed how absurdly helpless the Syracusans were when it came to fighting. On the road to Leontini, however, at a river crossing, the Syracusans forced them into regular battle. According to Ephorus, as appears from Diodorus, the Syracusans were defeated with severe loss of life, but Timaeus, if Plutarch is following him, maintained that "not many" were killed.[158] And he described the welcome given to Dion and his men at Leontini.

Like Ephorus, Timaeus described how Nypsius arrived at Syracuse, with ships bringing much needed supplies to Dionysius' men on the Island. The Syracusans attacked their ships with some success, but their drunken celebration of the victory rendered them unable to put up much resistance when Nypsius attacked the city itself. He looked like gaining control of it, and in desperate fear they sent word to Dion, asking for help. Here was Timaeus' opportunity for one of his great scenes. Seven men galloped through the night to Leontini, arriving just as day was breaking, and "leaping from their horses they threw themselves on the ground in front of Dion, telling him in tears of the plight of Syracuse." A great crowd gathers in the theatre, Dion rises to speak, and after the sympathy and encouragement of his men help him to control his tears, a few sentences from him are enough

---

[157] Despite these constant indications that Plutarch is following Timaeus, Laqueur, *RE* VIA. 1154–56, pays no attention to Plutarch but continues to look for scraps of Timaeus "inserted" into Diodorus' account. And he never considers the possibility that Timaeus may sometimes adopt Ephorus' account.

[158] *Dion* 39; Diod. 16.17.

to make the mercenaries leap to their feet, demanding to be led to Syracuse to rescue the city.[159]

Plutarch was clearly moved by Timaeus' dramatic story. But all that Diodorus has to say is that Dion, great–hearted man that he was, bore no grudge against his fellow citizens and soon had his men on the way to Syracuse. And he describes Dion's triumphant success in recovering possession of the city quite briefly, finishing with an account of the election of Dion as *strategos autocrator* and his reconciliation with his Syracusan opponents (16.20.2–6).

Plutarch's account is much fuller and more elaborate (44–47). He shows all the difficulties that Dion has to meet one after another. When Nypsius' men retire to their acropolis and the immediate danger seems to have passed, the Syracusan "demagogues" renew their opposition to Dion and propose to prevent him from entering the city, but they change their mind and send for him when Apollocrates, the son of Dionysius, decides to set fire to Syracuse. There is a vivid description of Dion's men fighting the fire as well as the enemy, until the enemy all withdraw again to the Island, and Dion, with fine generosity, forgives Heraclides and the others for their bad faith towards him. It may be Plutarch, not Timaeus, who represents Dion as influenced by his training in the Academy, when he decides against exacting vengeance (47.4–9).

Diodorus does not continue his story beyond this point, and Plutarch is the only authority for what follows, the continued *stasis* in Syracuse and the renewed faithlessness of Heraclides when he tries to sail against Syracuse with his fleet, taking advantage of the absence of Dion, who has led out an army to meet the Spartan soldiers of fortune, Pharax and Gaesylus, who have appeared in the Acragas area (49–50). Since there is no other account with which to compare it, there is no proof that Plutarch's story is based on Timaeus, but one must suspect that it was he who provided Plutarch with the story of Dion's wild ride through the night to save Syracuse from Heraclides' fleet, when he covered seven hundred stades, reaching the city at the third hour of the day (49.4), and that it was he who compared the Spartan adventurer, Gaesylus, with Gylippus (49.5). And who but Timaeus can be responsible for describing the climactic scene when Apollocrates finally despairs of holding the Acropolis any longer, and by agreement with Dion leaves under safe conduct? "There was not a

[159] *Dion* 42.6–43.7. The few sentences that Plutarch gives to Dion may be part of a longer speech in Timaeus.

single individual in Syracuse who failed to watch him go, as they cried out against anyone who was not there to see the sun of freedom rising over Syracuse" (50.3).

Plutarch must also have found in Timaeus the description of Dion's meeting with Aristomache and Arete when he entered the Acropolis: "They rushed to the door, Aristomache leading Dion's son by the hand and Arete following behind in tears, wondering how she should greet and speak to her husband after she had been living with another man. Dion welcomed first his sister and his son, and then Aristomache brought Arete to him and said: 'We suffered much, Dion, when you were in exile; now by your return and your victory you have taken away every trace of our unhappiness except hers, this woman whom I unhappily saw forced into union with another man while you still lived.' At these words of Aristomache, Dion burst into tears and embraced his wife fondly . . ." (51). One cannot be sure how far Plutarch borrowed or adapted passages of dialogue from his source, though he certainly made good use of the speeches that he found in Timaeus.[160]

In describing Dion's modest behaviour after his victory and his attempt to introduce a "true aristocratic *politeia*" at Syracuse, Plutarch is clearly influenced by his Platonic feelings; he cites the Platonic letters and the *Republic* to show that Dion tried to be a good son of the Academy (52). But the account of the final quarrel with Heraclides can be attributed to Timaeus: Dion refuses to tear down the fortifications on the Island or to destroy the tomb of the elder Dionysius, he sends to Corinth for advisers, and in the end he decides to have Heraclides murdered (53). The speech at Heraclides' funeral (53.6), which is supposed to convince the people that no peace would have been possible if Heraclides had remained alive, must certainly be a composition of Timaeus.

The conspiracy that leads to Dion's murder is described in similar terms by Plutarch (54–57) and Nepos (*Dion* 8–9), and the story is also told very briefly in the seventh Platonic letter (333e–334c). Plutarch reminds his readers (54.1) that the arch–conspirator Callippus and his brother are the two brothers mentioned in this letter as companions of Dion in Athens. Nepos calls these two men Callicrates and Philostratus,[161] but he is just as severe as Plutarch in his judgment, thinking Callicrates a despicable scoun-

---

[160] Some examples of dialogue may be indicated in F 18, 43, 48, 109, 115.

[161] No name is mentioned in the Platonic letter, but Diogenes Laertius (3.46) and Athenaeus (11.508E), both of them readers of Timaeus, call him Callippus, like Plutarch. Nepos may have quoted incorrectly from memory; see Porter, op. cit. (n.115) 96.

drel, and the two agree on so many details that they must be following the same source—who cannot be any one but Timaeus.

Nepos says nothing of Dion's efforts to rule in philosophic "aristocratic" style, as reported by Plutarch, and he is presumably following Timaeus when he describes how Dion, after the murder of Heraclides, found money to pay his mercenaries by confiscating the property of Heraclides' supporters, until that source ran dry and he had to use his friends' money, with the inevitable result "ut, cum milites reconciliasset, amitteret optimates" (7.2). It was in this situation that Callippus (or Callicrates) saw his opportunity. By talking individually to Dion's mercenaries, he found out those whose loyalty was wavering, and at the same time he won Dion's confidence by pretending to act as an *agent provocateur* in his interest, reporting to him subversive remarks that he heard or invented.

Inevitably, with Timaeus telling the story, there is a portent of impending disaster. One evening as Dion was sitting outside he heard a noise in the far corner of the colonnade, and looking there saw a woman "dressed like a tragic Fury" sweeping the floor. Terrified, he asked some of his friends to spend the night with him, in fear of being alone if the vision should reappear. It did not reappear, but a few days later his young son, in a fit of boyish anger or distress, killed himself by jumping from the roof of the house.[162]

Dion was seized by deep depression, thinking that he was being punished for the murder of Heraclides, and Callippus took full advantage of the situation, spreading the rumour that, since Dion had lost his son, he was planning to adopt the tyrant's son, Apollocrates. He went to the women of Dion's household, when they became suspicious of him, telling them in tears that he was their friend and offering to give them any assurance of his friendship that they asked. At their request, he swore "the great oath" in the underground temple of the Thesmophoroi, putting on the robe of the goddess and holding a burning torch in his hand; and then, as Plutarch says, he made a mockery of the two goddesses by waiting for their festival before committing murder, murdering the man whom he himself, as mystagogue, had admitted into the Eleusinian mysteries (56.1–6).

It took a team of murderers to carry out the plot. They surrounded the house, guarding all doors and windows, and sent in some men from Zacynthus to the room where Dion was entertaining a few guests. They were unarmed, as could be seen since they were not wearing himatia, and

---

[162] The story, as told by Plutarch (55), must come from Timaeus, but it is absent in Nepos' *Dion* and is not found elsewhere.

they tried to strangle Dion with their bare hands; but, despite little opposition from the guests, who hoped to save their own lives by letting their host die, they found the task too difficult, and called for a sword, which was handed in through a door. Plutarch does not think it necessary to point out that Dion, unlike a tyrant, had no armed guards in the house.

So Dion was killed, and his pregnant wife, together with his sister, was thrown into prison, where she gave birth to a son. Hicetas, one of Dion's former circle, tried to save their lives, but he was bribed to have them put on a ship, supposedly bound for the Peloponnese; and they were all drowned at sea. Appropriately, however, Callippus came to a bad end. After attempting to establish himself in one city after another (Catana, Messana, Rhegium) with the aid of some of the mercenaries, he was duly murdered, with the same sword, "so they say," that was used to kill Dion.

Plutarch tells the story well, and if Timaeus' version was equally well written, it must have been widely read and admired. Nepos reproduces it rather clumsily (*Dion* 9), adding a few details that Plutarch, showing good judgment, prefers to omit, but there is no trace of it in Aelian or Polyaenus or anywhere else in ancient literature. No rival or alternative account is known, and it has held its place as the definitive story of Dion's murder. Only a rash story–teller would attempt to improve on it.

Timaeus' account of Dion's life, so far as we can reconstruct it, seems to have been arranged as a series of highly dramatic episodes, each one raising more than one question which the reader is left to answer for himself, if he wants to make up his mind what really happened, or what kind of man Dion really was, what his real purposes were, how sincere he was as a disciple of Plato and a fighter for political freedom. Plutarch had hoped, perhaps, that Timaeus' narrative would help him answer the questions that Plato's letters raised. But he evidently found that it did not provide him with the answers.[163] And so what he gives us must be not much more than Timaeus' account rewritten, with the questions still unresolved. Timaeus had no love for either the elder or the younger Dionysius, but he may have left Dion's character ill–defined, showing him only as a man with many enemies.

Plutarch does not carry the story of Dionysius II beyond Dion's death, and in consequence Timaeus' account of the ten years (354–344) that intervene before the coming of Timoleon is completely lost. All that we have, apart from a brief summary in Plutarch,[164] is the kind of gossip that

---

[163] Cf. especially *Alex*.1.
[164] Below, p. 209.

Athenaeus preserves about the flatterers and the heavy drinking at the tyrant's court.

Numerous stories were current about the flatterers of both Dionysii. Cicero (*Tusc. Disp.* 5.61) tells the familiar story of the sword of Damocles, setting the scene at the court of the elder Dionysius; but Athenaeus cites Timaeus for a story about Damocles as a flatterer of the younger tyrant:[165] "It was customary in Sicily to offer sacrifice to the Nymphs in private houses and to stay awake all night by their statues, drinking and dancing around them. But Damocles would have nothing to do with the Nymphs. He said it was a mistake to honour "lifeless goddesses," and he came up to Dionysius and started to dance round him. On another occasion, he had been a member of an embassy, and when they were all returning to Dionysius on board a trireme,[166] he was accused by the others of subversive behaviour when they were abroad, of acting in a manner contrary to the public interest. This accusation made Dionysius very angry, but Damocles explained how the difference arose between him and his fellow ambassadors. After their dinner, they had been singing compositions of Phrynichus and Stesichorus, and some of the crew followed by singing a paean of Pindar, while he, and anyone who wanted to join him, went through the collection of paeans composed by Dionysius. He offered to give clear proof that what he said was true. His accusers, he said, could not even say how many paeans there were, but he was prepared to sing all of them, one after the other. So Dionysius' anger was appeased, and Damocles said: 'You would be doing me a favour, Dionysius, if you would tell someone who knows your paean to Asclepius to teach it to me.'"

Then, one time when the "friends" had been invited to dinner, Dionysius came into the room saying: "My dear friends, I have just received a report from the officers that were sent to Naples." Damocles was quick to say: "Yes, by the gods, they have done well." And when the tyrant looked at him and said: "How do you know if their report is favourable or not?", Damocles had to reply: "Yes, I must admit, your rebuke is just."

These stories fit the elder Dionysius better than the younger, since it is not elsewhere recorded that the younger was a persistent writer of poetry and music, and no other example is ever quoted of the younger Dionysius actually putting a flatterer in his place.[167]

Athenaeus also cites Timaeus for a drinking contest that the younger

---

[165] F 32—Ath. 6.250A–D. Athenaeus calls him Democles.
[166] The text is uncertain at this point.
[167] See Jacoby's note on F 32.

Dionysius held at the feast of Choes.[168] He offered a prize of a golden crown to the man who was quickest at drinking off a *chous* of wine (about two quarts), and it was Xenocrates, Plato's pupil, the "sluggish" philosopher, whom not even Lais could tempt, who won but showed his lack of concern for worldly things by leaving his prize on a herm in the courtyard when he left the party.

Stories of this kind are not normally assigned to any particular date, and so the impression is given that the younger Dionysius did not change his habits as he grew older. A tale is told of his "tyrannical" behaviour at Locri, which should belong to the years of his exile after 354, when he established himself for a time at Locri, before moving to Rhegium; it may reasonably be attributed to Timaeus, since it is recorded by his contemporary Clearchus of Soli, as well as by Aelian and Justin, and it is known to Plutarch, though not told in full by him.[169] In earlier years, when the Locrians were at war with Rhegium and things were going badly for them, they made a vow, so Justin says, that if they were victorious they would offer their daughters as sacred prostitutes on Aphrodite's feast day.[170] But they failed to keep their promise to the goddess, and when Dionysius, in later years, came to Locri with his army, he insisted that they do so, in order that he and his soldiers might take advantage of it. The Locrians could not refuse to obey the tyrant's order, but they took a terrible revenge on him when he finally fell from power, subjecting his wife and daughters to the same outrage that their daughters had suffered and then putting them to death.

Timaeus' account of the elder Dionysius established him in tradition as the typical tyrant, with the appropriate strengths and weaknesses that such a ruler was supposed to display. His son, on the other hand, seems to have been given no positive qualities at all, except as the type of a strong tyrant's successor, who is worthless, weak, and ineffectual, and is bound to lose his position in the end.

---

[168] F 158a.

[169] Clearchus fr.47 Wehrli—Ath. 12.541C–E; Aelian, *VH* 9.8 (cf. also 6.12); Justin 21.3; Plut. *Timol.* 13; *Mor.* 821D; Strabo 6.1.8.

[170] The story has sometimes been taken as evidence that sacred prostitution was practised at Locri (above, p. 104).

VIII

Timoleon, Agathocles, and Pyrrhus

i. Timoleon

The only surviving account of the ten stormy years in Sicily that followed the murder of Dion is the summary narrative in the first chapter of Plutarch's *Timoleon:* "After Dion was murdered and dissension arose among the men who had won freedom for Syracuse under his leadership, the city endured a series of tyrants one after another, and under the weight of its sufferings came near to becoming a deserted place. Elsewhere in Sicily, the wars rendered the population homeless and deprived them of civic life, while the cities were for the most part in the hands of a motley collection of barbarians and mercenary soldiers out of employment. It took very little to bring about a change in a city's ruler, and Dionysius was able to collect a body of mercenaries and in the tenth year after his expulsion from Syracuse succeeded in driving out Nysaeus who was in power there, so as to recover his former position and make himself tyrant again. It had been a great surprise when an attack by a small force had made him lose the mightiest tyranny that the world had seen, and it was an even greater surprise when this despised exile overcame the party that had thrown him out.

"The surviving population in the city of Syracuse now found themselves subject to a man who had never been a benevolent despot and was now embittered and brutalized by his misfortunes. The better citizens who had some standing looked for help toward Hicetas, who was master of Leontini; they entrusted themselves to him and chose him as leader of the rebellion. He was no better than any of the openly professed tyrants, but there was no other recourse open to them, and they had some faith in him, as he was a Syracusan by birth and had at his disposal a military force sufficient to face Dionysius.

"In the meantime the Carthaginians had landed in Sicily with a huge armament and were waiting to take advantage of events. The Greeks in Sicily were in great fear and decided to send an embassy to Greece and ask help from Corinth."

Diodorus has only a few isolated sentences referring to events in Sicily during these years, but he adds some details that are not in Plutarch—that

Hipparinus ruled for two years between Callippus and Nysaeus (16.36.5), and that Dionysius was for some time in control of Rhegium until ousted by Callippus and Leptines in 351 (16.45.9). Justin, on the other hand, has Dionysius as tyrant of Locri, where he behaves in grossly hybristic fashion until he is expelled by a Locrian uprising (21.3).[1]

One might reasonably suppose that Plutarch, who used Timaeus extensively in his *Dion*, has summarized Timaeus' account here, and that Diodorus, as before, has taken his pieces of information from Ephorus. Ephorus carried his historical narrative down to 340,[2] and appears to have given some account of Sicilian affairs at least up to the time when Timoleon enters the story, since he spoke of Timoleon's soothsayer Orthagoras.[3] Theopompus also had something to say about these years in Sicily, because Athenaeus refers to him for stories about the members of Dionysius' family when they became tyrants—Hipparinus, Nysaeus, and Apollocrates.[4]

Even if Plutarch has in fact summarized Timaeus' account and summarized it accurately, he has given us very little notion of the quality or tendency of Timaeus' narrative. His purpose in this introductory chapter is to show the state of chaos into which Sicily has fallen, not to tell us about the events and persons responsible for this sorry state of affairs. If Timaeus gave such an account, it might be more valuable and trustworthy than anything in the earlier books of his history, since he could have spoken with men who were politically active or personally involved in Syracuse or other cities, and as the son of a supposedly benevolent autocrat, he is likely to have listened to much conversation about current developments as soon as he was capable of understanding it. It is indeed possible that he met Timoleon himself, and that his admiration for him, which Polybius thought almost absurdly excessive,[5] was based on personal acquaintance. Or perhaps he never forgot the deep impression made upon him as a child, when what seemed like a genuinely heroic figure first appeared at Tauromenium and was welcomed by his father Andromachus.

Plutarch's narrative reveals some of the devices Timaeus used to magnify Timoleon's stature. Ephorus and Theopompus had described the mur-

---

[1] Above, p. 208.

[2] T 10—Diod. 16.76.5: Ἔφορος μὲν ὁ Κυμαῖος τὴν ἱστορίαν ἐνθάδε κατέστροφεν εἰς τὴν Περίνθου πολιορκίαν.

[3] Ephorus, *FGrH* 70 F 221, Timaeus, *FGrH* 566 F 116—Plut. *Timol.* 4.6: τὸν μάντιν, ὃν Σάτυρον μὲν Θεόπομπος, Ἔφορος δὲ καὶ Τίμαιος Ὀρθαγόραν ὀνομάζουσιν.

[4] F 185–188—Ath. 10.435E–436B. Laqueur, *RE* VIA. 1156, thinks that Diodorus' *Grundquelle* for his account of Timoleon is Theopompus.

[5] F 119a—Polyb. 12.23.4; cf. F 119b—Plut. *Timol.* 36.1–2, F 119c—Cic. *Ad Fam.* 5.12.7, T.13—Marcellinus, *Vit.Thuc.* 27.

der of his brother Timophanes, the tyrant: how Timoleon took a soothsayer with him when he went to confront his brother and killed him with his own hands when he refused to listen to the demands made of him. But in Timaeus' account, Timoleon turns aside and veils his head while his companions draw their swords and do the deed.[6] Plutarch must be quoting Timaeus almost word for word when he says that the deed was approved by the "best citizens," and regarded with horror only by those who were "unable to live under democratic government" (*Timol.* 5.1–2). Even Timoleon himself seems to feel little remorse, until his mother refuses to speak to him or let him enter the house, and his friends have to intervene to prevent him from committing suicide. Like Himilco oppressed by the disgrace of his defeat at Syracuse, who went wandering from one temple to another confessing his impiety,[7] he retires to the most desolate part of the country and spends many years wandering about in despair. Only the prospect of renewing the fight against tyranny recalls him to the city. The moralizing remarks must be added by Plutarch himself (6), who seems to think that some comment of his own is required.

When the embassy from Sicily comes to Corinth, and a commander has to be appointed for the expedition to Sicily, it is an anonymous speaker (εἷς τῶν πολλῶν) who is "divinely inspired, so it seems," to propose that Timoleon be appointed: "So brightly did the favour of Fortune shine upon their choice, and her grace her accompanied all his future deeds, embellishing the *arete* of this man."[8] This is the kind of exalted language that would have infuriated Polybius, and Plutarch may well be quoting Timaeus' own words.

Timaeus does not usually let an expedition set out without an omen of success or disaster,[9] and when Timoleon goes to Delphi to consult the oracle, he receives his answer before even asking his question. As he walks into the oracular chamber, some ribbons from the offerings hanging on the wall fall upon his head, and they are embroidered with crowns and victory symbols. Not only Apollo but Demeter and Kore also soon show their sup-

---

[6] F 116—Plut. *Timol.* 4.5–8.

[7] Diod. 14.76.3–4.

[8] τοσαύτη καὶ περὶ τὴν αἵρεσιν εὐθὺς ἀνέλαμψε τύχης εὐμένεια, καὶ ταῖς ἄλλαις πράξεσιν ἐπηκολούθησε χάρις, ἐπικοσμοῦσα τὴν ἀρετὴν τοῦ ἀνδρός (*Timol.* 3.3). This is the language of tragedy, and can be rewritten as iambic trimeter:

ἤδη τοσαύτη τοῦδε περὶ τὴν αἵρεσιν
ἔλαμψεν εὐθὺς εὐμένεια τῆς τύχης
ἐπηκολούθησεν δὲ πράξεσιν χάρις.

[9] See above, pp. 149–50, 196–97.

port for the voyage. The priestesses of Kore have a dream in which they see the two goddesses preparing for a journey and saying they will be sailing to Sicily with Timoleon (Plut. *Timol.* 8.1–3). This could only mean that they had left Sicily, disgusted no doubt by the impious and sacrilegious practices of the tyrants, but are now ready to return to their beloved land, bringing peace and prosperity with them. So the Corinthians prepare a special sacred trireme in which the goddesses can travel, and Timaeus' readers would remember how he described the ship prepared for the Spartans by Locrian envoys to carry the Dioscuri to Italy, where they could fight against the Crotoniats at the Battle of the Sagra.[10] And when the ships are on their way, a fire blazes out in the sky, a burning torch appears above the sacred ship, and fire points the way to Italy, a sure sign, the soothsayers think, that Demeter and Kore are indeed returning to their homeland.

The dream, the sacred trireme, and the divine light pointing the way are in Diodorus (16.66.3–5) as well as in Plutarch, but the narrative is arranged differently and neither the language nor the style is such as to suggest that Diodorus is following Timaeus (which would in any case be unlikely, since he seems to have paid no attention to him since the end of Book XIV). It should follow, therefore, that he found the story in Ephorus or Dyillus, who took up Ephorus' narrative at the point where he left off.[11] In that case Timaeus will not have devised or "discovered" the story himself, but it must have been current at the time of the expedition, reported perhaps by Theopompus, as well as by Ephorus or Dyillus. The tragic language in Plutarch's text may be Timaeus' special contribution to lend it dignity.[12]

A message from Hicetas warns Timoleon that he is now allied with the Carthaginians and that they will block his passage and prevent him from

---

[10] Diod. 8.32, cf. above p. 109.

[11] *FGrH* 73 T 1, 2—Diod. 16.14.5, 76.6. Critics, rather curiously, have generally resisted this conclusion. For their different views see K. Meister, *Die Sizilische Geschichte bei Diodor* (Munich 1967) 121–22. Meister himself believes that Diodorus follows a *Zwischenquelle* that is based on Timaeus (123–29). It is not necessary for present purposes to enter into argument about Diodorus' source here, only to recognize that it may well be an author earlier than Timaeus.

[12] As before (see n. 8; above p. 210), Plutarch's text can be adapted so as to produce iambic trimeter:

καλῷ δ'ἀνήχθη χρώμενος τῷ πνεύματι,
καὶ νυκτὸς εὐθὺς εἰς τὸ πέλαγος ἐμβαλὼν
τὸν οὐρανὸν ῥαγέντ' ἔδοξεν ἐκχέαι
ὑπὲρ νεὼς πῦρ περιφανές τε καὶ πολύ·
λαμπὰς γὰρ ἀρθεῖσ' ἐμφερὴς ταῖς μυστικαῖς
συμπαραθέουσα τὸν δρόμον. . . . . .

reaching Sicily. Diodorus describes how Timoleon sails up the coast ἐν παράπλῳ, and is joined by ships from Leucas and Corcyra; when they reach Metapontum, a Carthaginian ship meets them with envoys who warn them not to go any further. Timoleon disregards the warning and continues on to Rhegium, where twenty Carthaginian ships are waiting to block his way. In Plutarch's account, on the other hand, which is certainly based on Timaeus, Timoleon, like Dion before him, takes the more direct route across the open sea and meets no Carthaginian ship until he reaches Rhegium.

At Rhegium (in both accounts), he outwits the Carthaginians, keeping the Rhegines and the Carthaginian officers listening to speeches at a protracted meeting of the Assembly, while his ships set sail, and he slips away from the meeting to board the ship that is waiting for him after the others have gone. The trick is evidently known to earlier writers, but some of the circumstantial detail in Plutarch's version, which makes the tale more credible, must be taken from Timaeus. Timoleon makes sure that the gates of the city are closed, to prevent any of the Carthaginian officers from reaching the harbour, and as he slips away through the throng, the Rhegines who are crowded round the *bema* help to conceal his movement (10.4–5). It must also be Timaeus who explained that Andromachus had invited him to Tauromenium some time before, so that, like Dion again, he lands within reach of Syracuse with only a small force, but is warmly welcomed by a good friend.

Both sources describe the forced march to Adranum and the successful surprise attack on the much larger force that Hicetas had brought there. But Plutarch has additional detail that can be recognized as coming from Timaeus. Timoleon will not allow his men to stop for a meal, and for the last few miles, he marches at the head of the line, carrying a shield, "like a man leading them to certain victory." The people of Adranum open their gates and join forces with Timoleon's men, describing with amazement the sign they have seen that their local god, Adranus, is on their side—his spear has been shaking and the face of his statue streaming with sweat (12.6–9). Timaeus might have learnt of this portent from local sources, if he did not invent it itself.

Plutarch describes how this initial success earned Timoleon the support of several cities, including that of the tyrant of Catana, a Campanian called Mamercus,[13] and how Dionysius decided to surrender to him, allowing Corinthian soldiers to enter his acropolis in small groups until there were

---

[13] Or Marcus, as Diodorus calls him (16.69.4)

four hundred of them there, while he himself escaped by sea to Timoleon's camp and put himself in his hands. Caught as he was between the forces of Hicetas and Timoleon, with a Carthaginian attack imminent, he is evidently supposed to decide that Timoleon was more likely to spare his life than Hicetas.[14] Timoleon allowed him to set sail for Corinth in a single ship, taking only a few possessions with him. Once he was gone, the mercenaries on the Island agreed to serve under Timoleon, and the enormous armory of weapons stored there was at his disposal (13.1–8).

Diodorus' story is quite different. In his version, Dionysius does not surrender until the following year,[15] after the Carthaginian force under Mago has sailed into the Great Harbour with its hundred and fifty ships, and lands its huge army of fifty or sixty thousand men.[16] Diodorus' account of the previous year breaks off after describing how Timoleon hurried on to Syracuse immediately after the battle at Adranum, hoping to take the city by surprise (68.11), instead of remaining at Adranum, as Plutarch supposes. The next year's narrative begins by showing him in possession of the old part of the city on the mainland (without ever describing how he won it), while Dionysius is still on the Island, Hicetas in possession of Achradina and the New Town, and the Carthaginians are encamped outside the city, presumably in the ill–omened marshy area of the Anapus, if they had sailed into the Great Harbour.[17] Timoleon has thus let himself be caught in a trap, but fortunately he is saved by "a remarkable and quite unexpected change in the situation." The arrival of ten ships from Corinth causes the entire Carthaginian force to withdraw "in irrational fear".[18] With Hicetas deprived of Carthaginian support, Timoleon quickly gets the upper hand, wins control of the entire city, and soon persuades Dionysius to surrender (69.6,70.1).

If this was the version that Timaeus found in Ephorus or some other earlier writer, it is not surprising that he was dissatisfied with it and substi-

---

[14] This is the explanation that seems to be demanded of Dionysius' conduct, though Plutarch says only that he was full of admiration for Timoleon and had no respect for Hicetas after he had been ignominiously defeated (13.3).

[15] The chronological table which says that Dionysius sailed to Corinth in *Ol.*109.2 (343–42 B.C, *P.Oxy.* I.12, col.ii—*FGrH* 255) seems to be following the same source as Diodorus.

[16] As described by Plutarch in 17.1–3. He gives the Carthaginians 60,000 men, while Diodorus (69.3) gives them 50,000 foot soldiers.

[17] The text as preserved (69.3) does not say where they were camped, but editors have suspected a lacuna.

[18] φοβηθέντες ἀπέπλευσαν ἐκ τοῦ λιμένος ἀλόγως (69.5). Cf. [Aristot.] *Rhetorica ad Alex.* 1429b (as an example of "the unexpected"): ὡσαύτως δὲ Κορίνθιοι Συρακοσίοις ἐννέα τριήρεσι βοηθήσαντες Καρχηδονίους ἑκατὸν καὶ πεντήκοντα ναυσὶν ἐπὶ τοῖς λιμέσι τῶν Συρακοσίων ἐφορμοῦντας τὴν δὲ πόλιν ἅπασαν πλὴν τῆς ἀκροπόλεως ἔχοντας οὐδὲν ἧττον κατεπολέμησαν. This could be an inaccurate version of Diodorus' source.

tuted something more credible. In his version, as we find it in Plutarch, Dionysius has left and the Corinthians are in possession of the Island before Hicetas invites Mago to bring his main force to Syracuse, and it is only then that they sail into the Great Harbour; and they camp in the city itself, making people think that here at last is the terrible barbarization of Syracuse that they have been dreading (*Timol.* 17.1–3). The Corinthians on the Island, commanded by Neon, are now under siege and their supply of food runs low, though Timoleon, who is still at Catana, is able to get some supplies to them in small boats that slip through the Carthaginian blockade. The situation improves, however, when Mago and Hicetas set off with a large force to attack Timoleon at Catana, and Neon takes advantage of the enemy's poor discipline in their absence to capture Achradina, where he has command of a plentiful supply of food and money; since it is a strongly fortified place, he makes his headquarters there instead of on the Island (17.4–18.5). The Corinthian reinforcements arrive, despite Carthaginian efforts to block their way, and Mago finally decides that he can no longer rely on the loyalty of his Greek allies, that they cannot match the *arete* and *tyche* of Timoleon's men. Although Hicetas pleads with him to stay, he withdraws with his entire force and returns to Africa αἰσχρῶς κατ᾽ οὐ-δένα λογισμὸν ἀνθρώπινον ἐκ τῶν χειρῶν ἀφεὶς Σικελίαν (19.2.–20.11).

This is the version of events that has generally been accepted in outline by modern historians and will be found in the standard histories.[19] It may not be a strictly correct or accurate account,[20] but we must at least recognize that Timaeus was more likely to have been well–informed than writers who had never been to Syracuse.

Plutarch's dependence on Timaeus becomes clearer with every chapter. After describing the surrender of Dionysius and his departure for Greece, he devotes two chapters (14–15) to an account of the life that he led in Corinth as an ex–tyrant. This digression, with its numerous anecdotes, is hardly relevant to a biography of Timoleon, and Plutarch must have included it because he found it in Timaeus' history, where it would come naturally at the end of the account of Dionysius II, with a selection of the tales about him and some of his sayings.

Equally reminiscent of Timaeus is the emphasis on the good fortune of

---

[19] E.g., R. Hackforth, *CAH* VI.290–91; M. L. W. Laistner, *History of the Gk. World 479 to 323*, 286–87; G. Glotz–R. Cohen, *Histoire grecque* III (Paris 1936) 413–14.

[20] For criticism of both accounts, see H. D. Westlake, *Timoleon and his relations with tyrants* (Manchester 1952) 17–26. He thinks the version of Diodorus "palpably false," but also finds difficulties in Plutarch's version. For a different opinion, M. Sordi, *Timoleonte* (Palermo 1961) 96–101.

Timoleon. Like Dion, he enjoyed more than his fair share of it when he first landed in Sicily, and Plutarch reminds his readers of this several times.[21] For one thing, guile served him much better than it served his enemies. This was seen first at Rhegium (10.3–5), and again at Thurii, where Carthaginian ships held up the Corinthian relief force. The Corinthians, after landing there, first found themselves free to perform a worthy deed, guarding the city from the Carthaginians while the Thurians took the field against the Bruttians (16.4), and then they were able to make their way to Rhegium overland, apparently without the Carthaginians even being aware that they had gone. Luck was with them because, after a long spell of bad weather, the sea calmed down as they reached Rhegium, and they were able to cross the strait to Sicily in small boats, their horses swimming behind them. Meanwhile, the Carthaginian naval commander thought he had devised a splendid stratagem. Thinking that the Corinthians were still at or near Thurii, he took some of his triremes to Syracuse decorated with what appeared to be spoils of victory and sailed past the Island in a victorious display, his sailors crowned with garlands, while he called out to everyone on land that he had defeated the Corinthians at sea and captured their ships. The result, of course, was that no one kept watch for Corinthian ships or Corinthian soldiers by land or sea, and they were able to join their compatriots without difficulty—a piece of Punic deceit backfired (19.1–6).

Timoleon had another stroke of luck when the attempt to murder him failed. Hicetas sent two men to Adranum to assassinate him, thinking that the task would be easy, because he took no particular care to protect himself. They came into the sanctuary where he was preparing to offer sacrifice, with daggers hidden under their himatia, pushed their way through the crowd to the altar, and were almost ready to strike him down, when one of them fell dead to the ground, struck on the head with a sword by someone who recognized him as his father's murderer. His companion saved his own life by revealing details of the plot to murder Timoleon, and everyone marvelled at the strange ways of luck and coincidence, how one man's act of vengeance saved another man's life. Plutarch is certainly following Timaeus when he remarks on the effect of this stroke of luck, how it raised everyone's hopes and made them look upon Timoleon as "a holy man who had come with divine help as an avenger of Sicily" (16.5–12). Timaeus'

---

[21] He remarks that while the ill–fortune of Dionysius II took everyone by surprise, the good fortune of Timoleon had a large element of the marvellous also (16.1). Compare his language in 16.10–12, 19.1, 20.1, 21.7. For the theme, cf. M. J. Fontana, "Fortuna di Timoleonte," *Kokalos* 4 (1958) 3–23.

display of sententious piety seems to have appealed to Plutarch, but it irritated Polybius, who disapproved of any efforts to present Timoleon as a semi-heroic figure.[22]

Timoleon was lucky that Mago and Hicetas never made the attack on him at Catana that they had planned; they returned to Syracuse when they heard that Achradina had fallen into the hands of Neon's Corinthians (18.7). It was an even greater stroke of luck when Mago actually withdrew from Syracuse altogether before Timoleon reached the city on his advance. The Carthaginian withdrawal came as a complete surprise to everyone, but Plutarch provides an explanation for Mago's decision. He describes how, in the intervals between fighting, the Greek soldiers on both sides fraternized when they went fishing in the pools and streams outside the city. On one occasion, a Corinthian asked some men from the other side how they could be so foolish as to help the Carthaginians barbarize a Greek city. This conversation was duly reported to Mago (who is presumed to rely heavily on spies and informers), and it increased his doubts about the reliability of his Greek mercenaries and the wisdom of allying himself with Hicetas. His informer's report supplies the *prophasis* which explains his withdrawal.

If this story comes from Timaeus, and it is unnecessary to imagine any other source, it illustrates his familiarity with the surroundings of Syracuse, where perhaps he went fishing as a boy. The description of Timoleon's plan of attack in the next chapter (21), a three-pronged attack, as in earlier battle narratives,[23] also implies familiarity with the terrain, as well probably as oral information from men who took part in the operation, since the names of several Corinthian officers are given. In earlier books, Timaeus could fall back on Philistus, as a witness who had been on the spot himself, when he wanted to describe battle plans,[24] but this is not possible now, and Timaeus himself must be given the credit for good reporting of military detail. His descriptions of battles are not always as incompetent as Polybius says they were.

Plutarch shows his continued dependence on Timaeus by the lavish praise that he bestows on Timoleon in commenting on this victory. His ἀρετή is supposed to match his τύχη, and it is hailed as a special mark of his good fortune that no Corinthian was killed or even wounded in this action. As with another famous victory reported by Timaeus,[25] the good

[22] F 119a—Polyb. 12.23.7.

[23] Cf. Diod. 13.109.4–5, 14.72.1–2.

[24] Above, p. 110.

[25] The victory of the Locrians at the Sagra (above, pp. 170, 181–82). In *Aemilius* 24.3–25.1, the parallel Life to *Timoleon*, Plutarch describes how word of the victory at Pydna

news is said to travel with remarkable speed, so that "within a few days" Greece resounded to the greatness of his achievements, and Corinth learnt of his victory almost before hearing that the relief expedition had reached Sicily. Here was another example of "good fortune contributing something" to increase the splendour of his success (τοσοῦτο τῷ κάλλει τῶν ἔργων τὸ τάχος ἡ τύχη προσέθηκεν, 21.7). This kind of comment must have irritated Polybius.

Unlike Dion, who refrained from destroying the fortifications of the Island and the tyrant's palace, Timoleon invited the citizens to bring their own tools and demolish everything, and after destroying every trace of the tyrant's buildings and monuments, he constructed law–courts on the site. This was his way of symbolizing the victory of democracy over autocracy (22.1–3). Timaeus clearly approved of these measures. Plutarch, remembering how brutally the Romans had destroyed the city of Corinth in later years, may have felt some sympathy for Dion who "spared the palace because of its beauty" (22.1). But he seems ready to agree with Timaeus that Timoleon showed himself a wiser man and a sterner tyrant–hater than Dion.

There are two characteristically Timaean details in Plutarch's narrative that deserve mention. When Mago reaches Carthage, he commits suicide, as Himilco did in 396 (Diod. 14.76.4), but Mago's disgrace is greater, because the Carthaginians impale (or crucify) his dead body (22.8).[26] Thus Timoleon's victory is seen to be greater even than the triumph of Dionysius I. And while statues of tyrants everywhere are pulled down and sold to anybody who wants them, "they say that the Syracusans kept the statue of Gelon, honouring the man who won the victory of Himera" (23.8). Timaeus did not miss the opportunity of reminding readers that Gelon was a good tyrant.

Plutarch describes how Timoleon raised money for Syracuse by selling houses and statues (presumably those which had belonged to the tyrants or members of their families or their party), and many of the purchasers must have been the new settlers brought to Sicily under the ambitious resettlement scheme organized by the Corinthians. Our only information about this remarkable enterprise, quite without parallel in Greek history, comes from a chapter in Plutarch (23) and some brief references to it in Diodorus (16.82.3, 83.2–3). No inscriptions have been found to add documentary

---

reached Rome "on the fourth day," and recalls the even faster speed with which news of the Sagra reached the Peloponnese. His reading of Timaeus is still fresh in his mind.

[26] Plutarch uses the verb ἀνασταυρόω, leaving it to his readers to decide which meaning he intended.

detail. We are told that no fewer than fifty thousand settlers were collected by the Corinthians and sent to Sicily, but nothing is said about how long it took to settle them. Diodorus says that ten thousand were actually settled in the territory of his own native city of Agyrium (82.5), and here he is probably speaking on his own authority, not repeating something he found in his source.

Timaeus should have been able to tell us a great deal more about this scheme of resettlement, which apparently succeeded not only in restoring prosperity and stability to many cities and to the countryside, but also offered large numbers of emigrants an opportunity to find land and a new citizenship overseas, such as had not been available since the great days of colonization. If he provided adequate description and explanation, we must regret that Plutarch suppressed it.

Plutarch has no wish to record all the details of fighting with Hicetas and Leptines and other tyrants, nor does he make any effort to explain the chronology of events between 344 and 340, contenting himself with a brief summary (24.1–4). Diodorus, under the year 343, gives further detail about the fighting with Hicetas at Leontini and with Leptines at Engyum and Apollonia, and the sending of mercenaries to overrun the Carthaginian *epikrateia* (16.72–73). The interval which his account shows before the Carthaginian invasion in 340 explains how it was possible for Timoleon to build up a fighting force to face the invaders and to collect the necessary money by plundering the *epikrateia* as well as by other means. Whatever source Diodorus may have been following here,[27] it is unlikely that there was substantial difference between the accounts of Diyllus, Athanis, or even Theopompus, since information must have been easy to obtain when they were writing. Nor is there any reason why Timaeus should want to quarrel with their versions, unless he found reason to disagree with their interpretations.

Diodorus says nothing of the political arrangements that Timoleon made in Syracuse, though the restoration of some form of stable government was one of the most important tasks that he faced. Plutarch also leaves us wondering if Timaeus had much to say about Timoleon's efforts in this direction, because all that he says about it is this: "He returned to Syracuse so as to devote himself to organizing the political constitution, to

---

[27] Meister, *Sizilische Geschichte* 123–29, thinks he may have used a *Zwischenquelle* that was based on Timaeus. But why should he have done so, if he had access to an actual text of Timaeus? If he does not reproduce his source exactly, the reason may be that he tried to recall what he had read without going back to the text. Later in his narrative, as will be seen, he agrees closely with Plutarch and seems to be reproducing Timaeus' account.

work with the lawgivers who had come from Corinth, Cephalus and Dionysius, in making the best possible arrangements" (24.3). Quite contrary to his usual practice, he seems in a hurry to move on to the events of the Carthaginian invasion.

The war narrative is simpler than usual, because nothing is said about any operations at sea. There is no mention of any ships under Timoleon's command, though the Carthaginians are said to have two hundred fighting ships, in addition to the thousand vessels needed to bring their huge force to Sicily, seventy thousand infantry and ten thousand cavalry.[28] The numbers on the Greek side are kept very low, so as to make Timoleon's victory more remarkable than those of Gelon and Dionysius, and his chances of success seem very poor when many of his mercenaries refuse to fight after learning what heavy odds they will have to face, a mere five thousand against seventy thousand (25.5). Diodorus gives more detail about this mutiny led by a man called Thrasius who had fought on the Phocian side in the Sacred War, and hence was a man guilty of sacrilege (a liability, therefore, if he remained with them). He also notes that Timoleon (unlike Dionysius I) was determined to fight in the Carthaginian *epikrateia,* so as to save the land of his allies from pillage.[29]

Plutarch says that there was great alarm in Syracuse when it became known how large the Carthaginian army was, and that "there were barely three thousand brave enough to take arms and follow Timoleon." And there were only four thousand mercenaries. He agrees that they were near Acragas on their march westward when the mutiny occurred.[30] Diodorus gives Thrasius a speech in which he complains that Timoleon is gambling with their lives[31] and is also behindhand with their pay. Timoleon, thankful that they had not waited until the battle to show their attitude, made no attempt to inflict any punishment, and allowed a thousand of them to return to Syracuse with Thrasius, where they could "ask for their pay."[32]

The remainder advanced until they were near the Crimisus, when the inevitable portent occurred, identified elsewhere by Plutarch as mentioned by Timaeus.[33] Some mules met them, loaded with burdens of wild celery

---

[28] The figures are similar in Plutarch (25.1) and Diodorus (77.4).

[29] 78.1–4. These details must have been in Timaeus.

[30] Plut. *Timol.* 25.4–5; Diod. 78.3.

[31] ἐναποκυβεύων ταῖς τῶν μισθοφόρων ψυχαῖς (78.5). This verbal compound is a *hapax,* and the expression may well be taken from the speech in Timaeus. There is no conflict now between Diodorus and Plutarch, and both seem to be giving an equally "Timaean" account.

[32] Diod. 16.79.1–2; Plut. *Timol.* 25.6.

[33] F 118—Plut. *Quaest. Conviv.* 676D. Cf. Polyaen. 5.12.1, where Timaeus is clearly the ultimate source for the three "stratagems" of Timoleon.

(σέλινον), and this could be interpreted as an evil omen, because celery was used as a funeral decoration. But Timoleon replied by reminding them that the victors' wreaths at the Isthmian Games were made from this plant, and he made garlands of it for himself and others to wear, supposing that the sign of victory given to him at Delphi was being renewed. Here was an ambiguous omen for Timaeus to explain, as when Dion stood on a sundial. Meanwhile the soothsayers caught sight of two eagles in the sky, one with a snake in its claws, while the other flew around "making loud and confident noises."[34]

Timaeus evidently took the opportunity to expand Timoleon's speech into a formal "address before battle,"[35] which Polybius thinks as inept and ill–written as his speech for Hermocrates at the Congress of Gela.[36] He finds it ridiculous that the speaker should begin by saying that the whole world is divided into three continents and that the proverbial saying "Emptier than Libya" means not that Libya is empty of inhabitants but "empty of real men."[37] He seems unwilling to recognize the literary convention that Timaeus is following when he represents Timoleon as giving his men the courage and confidence to face an enemy that outnumbers them, explaining the meaning of the omens and reminding them that Carthaginians are men of an inferior breed, who like to keep their hands hidden in folds of their clothing and are so prudish that they wear loin-cloths under their tunics.[38] Polybius is disgusted that such a dignified speaker as Timoleon should have any soldierly coarseness attributed to him. But Timaeus, of course, wanted to give Timoleon the kind of speech that he thought was needed in the situation, just as he thought that the situation demanded omens. It is not necessary that a reader should believe that omens or portents actually oc-

---

[34] Plut. *Timol.* 26.1–6; Diod. 16.76.3–4. For the omen of Dion's speech as he stood on a sundial, above, pp. 199–200.

[35] Plutarch (26.3) says that Timoleon stopped their march and "among other remarks suited to the occasion told them that the crown of victory had come into his hands of its own accord." Diodorus (79.2), like Polyaenus (5.12.3), has him "gathering the army for an assembly." He also gave him a speech before leaving Syracuse (78.2).

[36] F 31a, b—Polyb. 12.25.7, 26a.1–4.

[37] It has been argued, as by Pédech, *Polybe, Histoires Livre XII* (Budé ed. 1961), 123, that Polybius is complaining because Timaeus speaks of "the world" being divided into continents, when he should have said "the *oikoumene*," but Walbank, in his note on 25.7, points out that this technical inaccuracy is often found in ancient writers, even in Isocrates (*Paneg.* 179), and more probably Polybius is complaining that it is pedantic to give simple soldiers a lesson in geography (cf. Laqueur *RE* VIA. 1080).

[38] καθόλου δέ, φησι, τίς ἂν φοβηθείη τοὺς ἄνδρας, οἵτινες τῆς φύσεως τοῦτο τοῖς ἀνθρώποις δεδωκυίας ἴδιον παρὰ τὰ λοιπὰ τῶν ζῴων, λέγω δὲ τὰς χεῖρας, ταύτας παρ' ὅλον τὸν βίον ἐντὸς τῶν χιτώνων ἔχοντες ἀπράκτους περιφοροῦσι; τὸ δὲ μέγιστον οἵ γε καὶ ὑπὸ τοῖς χιτωνίσκοις, φησί, περιζώματα φοροῦσιν, ἵνα μηδ'ὅταν ἀποθάνωσιν ἐν ταῖς μάχαις φανεροὶ γένωνται τοῖς ὑπεναντίοις (12.26a.3).

curred. But he should understand what might happen if people at the time thought they had occurred.[39]

Polybius tells us nothing about Timaeus' description of the Battle of the Crimisus. Plutarch's account, however, is long and quite elaborate, and he must have taken trouble writing it. He might not want to copy his source slavishly, but on the other hand he would not invent military detail. He must have set to work to adapt Timaeus' version, rewriting it in his own language and style. In fact, comparison with Diodorus' briefer version (16.79.5–80.6), which is clearly based on the same source, makes it easy to reconstruct the outline of Timaeus' description.

As the early morning mist began to clear, the Greeks on the high ground could see the enemy starting to cross the river below them. Timoleon saw the opportunity to attack while only part of their force was across; taking up his position in the centre of the line, he led an effective attack, with his cavalry on the wings outflanking the Carthaginian chariots.[40] Plutarch has retained what seems a typically Timaean touch: Timoleon's shouts of command and encouragement were so loud that many thought some god was giving extra power to his voice (27.9).

A surer sign of divine intervention was to come. As enemy reinforcements crossed the river and it was feared that their superior numbers might turn the tide,[41] a violent storm broke out, with rain and hail blowing in the faces of the enemy, but on the backs of the Greeks, while dazzling lightning and thunder added to the confusion and noise of the battle. The river and all the streams overflowed, and the plain became a sea of mud, in which the heavily–armed Carthaginians were at a hopeless disadvantage. Huge numbers were killed and taken prisoner, and the loot was beyond belief, because the Carthaginians brought so much gold and silver in their baggage. Plutarch (29) takes particular pains to explain how Timoleon disposed of it, much finding its way into temples (cf. Diod. 80.6). If Timaeus did not write this part of his history until 280 or later, he can hardly have escaped being influenced by the accounts of Alexander's battles and the tale of the enormously rich loot captured in the Persian camp at Gaugamela.[42] There is much more emphasis on the luxury of the Carthaginian camp here than in accounts of earlier campaigns.

[39] Thucydides makes no great effort to investigate the mutilation of the herms; it is the unhappy consequences of the incident that interest him.

[40] Plut. *Timol.* 27; Diod. 16.79.5–6.

[41] Cf. Diod. 79.6. Plutarch (28.2) writes as though he were describing a battle of Roman legions: ἐπεὶ δ᾽εἰς ξίφη συνῆλθεν ὁ ἀγών, καὶ τέχνης οὐχ ἧττον ἢ ῥώμης ἐγεγόνει τὸ ἔργον, ἐξαίφνης ἀπὸ ὀρῶν βρονταί κτλ.

[42] The same may be said of Plutarch. It is believed that the *Timoleon* and the *Alexander*

There is one more sign that the gods punish the wicked. When Timoleon returns to Syracuse, he finds the mutinous mercenaries still there, and
he orders them to leave the city before sunset. They cross to Italy and are
treacherously killed by the Bruttians. "Divine justice punished them for
betraying Timoleon" is Plutarch's comment (30.1–3).[43] It seems not to have
disturbed him that Timaeus laid on the piety with such a heavy hand.

The gods are shown punishing temple–robbers with equal severity.
Among the mercenaries serving with Timoleon was a group who had
fought in the Sacred War under Philomelus and taken part in the pillage of
Delphi. They shared in Timoleon's victories (apparently the gods forgave
Timoleon for employing them), but when they were sent out on their own,
they were caught in an ambush and all killed.[44] Plutarch has the appropriate
pious comment: "One must marvel at the favour that the gods showed to
Timoleon, in his misfortunes as well as in his success."

The years following the Battle of the Crimisus appear to have been
taken up with military operations, often apparently on quite a small scale,
against Hicetas and Mamercus and other tyrants in different parts of Sicily,
as result of which all, or very nearly all, tyrants were removed from power
and freedom was restored to their cities. If any other "benevolent despots"
besides Andromachus were allowed to retain their position, nothing is said
about it. Plutarch and Diodorus select only a few isolated incidents for
brief description, and we cannot tell how Timaeus arranged his account.
Plutarch shows that in at least one instance he introduced his favourite motif of a victory promised by the unexpected appearance of a victory symbol. On one occasion, when Timoleon drew lots to determine which of his
ilarchae should have the honour of being first to lead his men across a river
to attack the enemy, after shaking up their rings in his chlamys he drew one
out and it had a trophy for its seal emblem. Speedy victory of course followed (31.6–8).

Hicetas and Mamercus were in due course taken prisoner and put to
death, and the women of Mamercus' family also, a barbaric act which
obliged Timaeus to find an explanation, since Timoleon could not be
allowed to behave with unreasonable cruelty.[45] The death of Mamercus provided a dramatic scene for Timaeus to describe. When he finally sur-

---

belong to the same period of his literary activity; see K. Ziegler, *Plutarchos von Chaironeia*
(Stuttgart 1949) 263–65

[43] Cf. *Mor.* 552F; Diod. 82.1–2. Diodorus explained the victory at the Crimisus as due
"not only to their own bravery, but also to the help given by the gods."

[44] Cf. *Mor.* 552F.

[45] Plut. *Timol.* 33.1–4. It is explained that he gave in to the Syracusans who wanted to
punish Hicetas for killing the wife and child of Dion (cf. *Dion* 58.8–9).

rendered, it was on condition that he should stand trial "among the Syracusans," and that Timoleon should not prosecute himself. Mamercus, though a Campanian, is represented as priding himself on his literary ability, writing poetry like Dionysius the Elder (31.1). So, when he appears before the people in the theatre, he tries to deliver a prepared speech in his defence. Of course, he is shouted down, and recognizing that his case is hopeless, he tries to kill himself by dashing his head against the stone benches. But he is not allowed the privilege of suicide, is carried off still breathing, and "suffers a pirate's punishment" (34.5–7). For Plutarch and his readers, that would mean that he was crucified. But it is not clear what Timaeus would mean by this expression.

Plutarch is full of praise for Timoleon in the closing chapters of his *Life*. The words may be his own, but he expresses his approval of Timaeus' high praise and applauds his application of Sophocles' words to Timoleon:

ὦ θεοί. τίς ἄρα Κύπρις ἢ τίς ἵμερος
τοῦδε ξυνήψατο;[46]

He argues that, in comparison with men like Epaminondas and Agesilaus, Timoleon seemed to achieve his purpose with a kind of effortless ease, and that his success should be attributed not just to good fortune but to *arete* blessed with good fortune (36.4), a remark that must be borrowed from Timaeus, whose account was full of allusions to *arete* and *tyche*. Nepos found a simpler way of explaining what Timaeus meant: "Quod ceteri reges imperio potuerunt, hic benevolentia tenuit" (3.5).

Plutarch (36.6)[47] and Nepos (4.4) both mention Timoleon's cult of Automatia, "the goddess who makes things happen of themselves," as evidence of his modesty, when he claimed no credit for his own successes, and also his refusal to allow any public protest or obstacle when Laphystius and Demaenetus brought actions against him, because it was his special pride that he had restored the right of free speech to Syracusan citizens (37.1–7). Evidently, Timaeus thought it specially noteworthy that Timoleon was able to enjoy his later years as a private citizen, with no more serious threats to his safety than mere civil lawsuits. It could hardly be maintained that he had done nothing to expose himself to the threat of vengeance, because the families and supporters of deposed and assassinated tyrants would not forgive him readily. But since killing tyrants was not supposed to involve any blood–guilt, it could be maintained that he had

---

46 36.2–F 119b; Sophocles fr. 874 Radt.
47 Cf. *Mor.* 542E, 816E.

done nothing to rouse the anger of the gods. Plutarch notes that he suffered from failing eyesight in his later years, but insists that this affliction could not be considered a "judgment" on him or even one of the "slings of outrageous fortune," but was merely the result of heredity, because many members of his family suffered from blindness in old age.[48] Timaeus seems to have worked very hard to explain that fortune was kind to Timoleon and that this kindness was well deserved.

Timaeus described Timoleon's funeral, and his account was followed by Plutarch (39.1–6) and Diodorus (16.90.1). Instead of writing a funeral oration to be delivered by some admirer, he reported the proclamation read out by a herald, announcing the musical and racing festivals that were to be established in his honour, "because he put down tyrants and conquered the Carthaginians, because he restored cities that had been destroyed and restored the rule of law to Siceliots."

It is probable that Timaeus' constant attempt to praise Timoleon would be irritating to modern taste, just as it offended Polybius, because of his pietistic moralizing, his sententiousness, and his sentimentality. But his admiration for Timoleon seems to have been genuine. There was no one else whom he was prepared to praise without reserve.

ii. Agathocles

The twenty years from Timoleon's retirement in 337 to the rise of Agathocles in 317 are no better recorded than the ten years between Dion's death and Timoleon's arrival in Sicily (354–344). No author offers even a brief summary comparable to the introductory chapter of Plutarch's *Timoleon*, and there is not a word about Sicilian affairs in the seventeenth and eighteenth books of Diodorus.[49] Alexander's conquests and events immediately following his death occupy him fully until he reaches the year 317, and it is only with the first chapter of Book XIX that he turns his attention again to Sicily.

---

[48] οὔτ' αὐτὸς ἑαυτῷ πρόφασιν παρασχών, οὔτε παροινηθεὶς ὑπο τῆς τύχης, ἀλλὰ συγγενικῆς τινος ὡς ἔοικεν αἰτίας καὶ καταβολῆς ἅμα τοῦ χρόνου συνεπιθεμένης (37.7). Plutarch must mean that he did not give the gods any reason to blind him; it could not therefore be divine punishment, because the gods do not punish unless they have a *prophasis*. The expression is probably taken from Timaeus. Nepos evidently knows it, but shows his imperfect mastery of Greek by misunderstanding it, when he writes "sine ullo morbo lumina oculorum amisit" (4.1).

[49] Twice in Book XIX (3.3 and 10.3) Diodorus refers the reader to the preceding book for Sicilian detail, but the references are false. He must have thought he had written or intended to write some account of Sicilian affairs in Book XVIII.

While Timaeus' account of 354–344 would be valuable, because he must have known many men who were politically active in those years, his account of 337–317 would be even more valuable if he was personally involved in events of the time. His father, Andromachus, was permitted by Timoleon to retain his position as ruler of Tauromenium,[50] but we do not know how many years he remained in power or how long he lived, whether he was succeeded in his position by some member of his family before 317 or if he (or his successor) was removed from power by Agathocles. Nor do we know whether Timaeus inherited or expected to inherit any position of authority or privilege from his father or for what precise reason Agathocles decided to exile him from Sicily; there is no direct evidence of the date of his exile, though it probably was later than 317 rather than earlier.[51] We might have the answers to all these questions if Timaeus' history had survived.

Timaeus seems to have written in some detail about these years. If the numerals in the text of Polybius and Athenaeus are correct, he described the Battle of the Crimisus in Book XXI, while comment about Dionysius II continued on into XXII, where there was perhaps a final discussion of his life and character.[52] The treatment of Timoleon's activity must have required several books. Athenaeus quotes Book XXVIII for the following sentence: "A man called Polyxenus, one of the people who were removed from Tauromenium, was appointed as envoy, and he came back bringing various gifts from Nicodemus, including a Thericlean cup (by the Corinthian potter Thericles)."[53] Athenaeus gives no indication of context, but the sentence seems to belong to a description of the diplomatic negotiation and bargaining that went on in Timoleon's later years (340–337). Nicodemus is presumably the tyrant of Centuripe, who was removed from power by Timoleon, and the persons "removed from Tauromenium" may be opponents of Andromachus who had to seek refuge elsewhere.[54]

If the twenty–eighth book was the last book to deal with the conflict between Timoleon and the tyrants, this leaves five books (XXIX–XXXIII) for the twenty years that follow,[55] because Diodorus tells us that the last five books (which appear to be XXXIV–XXXVIII) were devoted to the

[50] T 3b—Plut. *Timol.* 10.6, T 13—Marcellinus, *Vita Thuc.* 27.

[51] Above, p. 37.

[52] T 8—Diod. 21.17.3.

[53] F 31b—Polyb. 12.26a, F 32—Ath. 6.250A–D.

[54] F 33—Ath. 11.471F:Πολύξενός τις τῶν ἐκ Ταυρομενίου μεθεστηκότων ταχθεὶς ἐπὶ τὴν πρεσβείαν ἕτερά τε δῶρα παρὰ τοῦ Νικοδήμου καὶ κύλικα θηρικλείαν λαβὼν ἐπανῆκεν.

[55] See Jacoby's note on F 33.

career of Agathocles.[56] Unfortunately, no extant author refers to Books XXIX–XXXIII or to any event that can be assigned to them. The events in Sicily during these years must have seemed unimportant to any student of history in comparison with what was happening in Aegean Greece and the Near East.

For his account of Agathocles, Diodorus could no longer obtain any help from Ephorus, and it would be natural for him to rely mainly, if not exclusively, on Timaeus, who would now be writing about events of his own time. But he is not at all satisfied with the way Timaeus wrote about Agathocles, and he expresses his disapproval in quite strong terms:

"He was exiled from Sicily by Agathocles, and as long as the tyrant was alive was unable to take vengeance on him; but after his death he blackened his name for ever in his history. In addition to any failings that this king may have possessed, the historian attributed others of his own invention to him. He grudged him his successes, and not content with re-counting the failures which were really his fault, he held him responsible for other misfortunes that were pure accidents, due to nothing except ill–luck. Although Agathocles was by general consent a gifted military com-mander, vigorous, bold, and full of courage on the field of battle, through-out his history Timaeus never ceases calling him a coward and a weakling. Everyone knows, however, that no ruler in all history started from such small beginnings and won a greater empire for himself. The son of ordi-nary working class parents he had to earn his living as a boy by working with his hands as a potter; but subsequently by his own efforts and ability he won control not only of all Sicily, but also of a large part of Italy and Libya by armed conquest. The writer's lack of consistency is really amaz-ing. All through his work he is full of praise for the bravery of the Syra-cusan people, but he calls the man who became their ruler the greatest coward in the world. Caught in his self-contradiction his guilt is clear. A personal quarrel and hatred of a single individual made him a traitor to the candour and truthfulness of history. One has good reason to be dissatisfied with the last five books of his history, which include his account of the career of Agathocles."[57]

Diodorus does not offer comparable criticism of any historian else-where, and he is not telling us here that he has found another source whom he prefers. Nevertheless, some critics believe that this is what he means, and that for his account of Agathocles he follows Callias or Antander, Syr-

---

[56] Jacoby *FGrH* IIIb, p. 545.
[57] F 124d—Diod. 21.17.1–3.

acusan writers whom he mentions in the course of Books XIX–XXI, or Duris of Samos,[58] or later writers who used the earlier sources.[59]

Diodorus expresses an opinion on Callias, and is just as severe on him as on Timaeus: "Callias the Syracusan might justly and properly be thought to deserve criticism. He was taken under Agathocles' protection, and in return for the lavish gifts that he received, was false to history, the mouthpiece of truth. He never ceases heaping undeserved praise on his benefactor. Despite all the wickedness of Agathocles, his offences of impiety against the gods and his lawless conduct towards men, this historian says he was by far the most god–fearing and kindly man of his time. Taking a general view, one may say that just as Agathocles robbed citizens of their property and gave the historian improper gifts that he did not deserve, so this worthy writer had no difficulty in making full repayment to his royal master by bestowing every virtue on him in his history."[60]

This is hardly the language that an author uses in describing one of his principal sources, unless there is other strong evidence that he made use of him,[61] and the only evidence is what he says himself after describing the death of Agathocles and noting that "he reigned for twenty–eight years and lived for seventy–two, as is recorded by Timaeus the Syracusan and Callias, also a Syracusan and author of twenty–two books, and Antander, the brother of Agathocles, also a writer of history."[62] In fact, these references to authors who support Timaeus are probably taken from the text of Timaeus.[63] So also, when Josephus says that Timaeus frequently disagrees with Antiochus, Philistus, and Callias,[64] he is not telling us that he is familiar with all three authors, but that he knows Timaeus' work and how often he quarrels with his predecessors. The severe verdict on Callias may also be borrowed from Timaeus;[65] it is exactly what one expects Timaeus

[58] 19.3.3, 20.4.1, 16.1, 72.1, 21.6.2, 16.5, 17.4.

[59] E.g., H. J. W. Tillyard, *Agathocles* (Cambridge 1908), Chap. I; H. Berve, "Die Herrschaft des Agathokles," *SB. d.Akad. München* 1952.5, 4–21; Meister, *Sizilische Geschichte* 131–36; E. Manni, *Kokalos* 6 (1960) 167–73. No attempt can be made here to review or even to list all the work of those who believe that some author other than Timaeus was Diodorus' source in Book XX. No one has proved that Timaeus *cannot* be the source.

[60] 21.17.4—*FGrH* 564 T 3, F 7.

[61] But see Tillyard, *Agathocles* 9–12, who compares Diod. 22.42.2 with Callias, *FGrH* 564 F 3—Aelian, *NA* 16.28 and thinks that Diodorus' information about Africa must come from Callias.

[62] 21.16.5—Callias, *FGrH* 564 F 6, Timaeus, *FGrH* 566 F 123a; cf. F 123b—[Lucian] *Macrob.* 10

[63] Above, pp. 18, 93.

[64] *Contra Apionem* 1.17—Callias, *FGrH* 564 T 4, Timaeus, *FGrH* 566 T 17: ἀλλ'οὐδὲ περὶ τῶν Σικελικῶν τοῖς περὶ Ἀντίοχον καὶ Φίλιστον ἢ Καλλίαν Τίμαιος συμφωνεῖν ἠξίωσεν.

[65] The criticism of Timaeus, on the other hand, must come from Diodorus himself, a rare

to have said—that no one would praise Agathocles unless his praise had been bought.

Callias and Antander are little known authors, but Duris was widely known and widely read. He wrote Τὰ περὶ ʼΑγαθοκλέα in four books or more,[66] and it would certainly have been easier for Diodorus to find a copy of this work than a text of Callias or Antander. He mentions Duris twice. Under the year 370 B.C. (15.60.5) he points out that his *Hellenica* started in that year; and he says that according to Duris the Romans slew a hundred thousand of the Etruscans, Gauls, and Samnites in the Battle of Sentinum in 295 B.C. (21.6).[67] Decius Mus, the Roman commander, is supposed to have known the oracle that promised victory to the Romans if their commander was killed, and to have sacrificed himself, like the Athenian king Codrus. This was a tale that would have appealed to Timaeus, and if Duris had already told the story, it would be typical of him to complain that the numbers of men slain were too high. It is possible, therefore, that Diodorus has this reference from Timaeus, and that he never actually read anything of Duris. Duris and Timaeus were contemporaries, and one cannot hope to know the precise date when Duris wrote his study of Agathocles.[68]

The theory that Diodorus used a later *Zwischenquelle*, an unknown author who drew on earlier work,[69] has even less to recommend it. So far as we know, it was not the habit of Diodorus to follow a later writer when earlier sources were available.

Duris shared many interests with Timaeus.[70] He is supposed to have

---

example of his personal judgment, though it has been argued that both criticisms, those of Timaeus and of Callias, come from Diodorus' "late source," who would have known the complaints of Polybius about Timaeus; see F. Bizière, *Diodore de Sicile, Bibliothèque Historique, Livre XIX* (Budé ed. 1975) xvii–xix.

[66] *FGrH* 76 F 16–21, 56–59.

[67] Duris *FGrH* 76 F 56a, cf. F 56b—Tzetzes, ad Lyc. 1378 (he knows the Duris reference from Diodorus). For the belief that Diodorus used Duris, see E. Schwartz, *RE* V.687–88; Jacoby, *FGrH* IIC, p. 120; Pédech, note on Polyb. 12.15.2, all following the lead of A. F. Roesiger, *De Duride Samio Diodori Siculi et Plutarchi auctore* (Göttingen 1874). See also now S. N. Consolo Langher "*Quellenfrage* o ricostruzione storica," *Scritti in onore di Salvatore Pugliatti* V (Milan 1978) 349–69, and a further paper (not yet published); R. Vattuone, *Ricerche su Timeo: la "pueritia" di Agatocle* (Bologna 1983) 25 n.1.

[68] It is easier to believe that Timaeus knew and used Duris' account than the reverse. But Roesiger, *De Duride Samio* 8–10, believes that Duris quoted Timaeus and that Diodorus' criticism of Timaeus and the references to him in 20.79.5, 89.5, and 21.16.5 are copied from Duris. Unfortunately not one of the fragments that can be assigned to Duris' book about Agathocles refers to Agathocles; all are concerned with topography. We do not know the dates of Duris' birth and death, only that he was still writing after 281; cf. F 55 with Jacoby's note; R. B. Kebric, *In the Shadow of Macedon: Duris of Samos* (Historia Einzelschriften 29, 1977) 70–80.

[69] As argued by C. Dolce, "Diodoro e la storia di Agatocle," *Kokalos* 6 (1960) 124–67.

[70] Cf. Berve, "Die Herrschaft des Agathokles," 16–19. Nevertheless he concludes: "Es

written in a dramatic style, and he liked unorthodox mythology and topographical oddities, and if there were positive evidence that Diodorus took
any details from Duris, there are many places where he might seem to be
as likely a source as Timaeus. But since there is no such evidence,[71] the
most reasonable conclusion seems to be that Diodorus still continues to
rely on Timaeus, but rejects or modifies some of his judgments. His attitude towards Agathocles is certainly not "favourable," but he may occa-
sionally disagree with Timaeus on some detail, as when he claims that
Agathocles was considered brave and adventurous on the battlefield
(19.3.2).[72]

Justin devotes Book XXII and part of XXIII to Agathocles, so that
Pompeius Trogus must have given quite a full account. After he has used
Timaeus as his source for earlier Sicilian history,[73] there is no reason to
think that he would turn to someone else now, and there is no sign of dependence on Duris. Justin is as hostile to Agathocles as Diodorus, and the
same can be said of the extracts in Aelian and Polyaenus.[74] If these writers
disagree in detail from Diodorus or among themselves, this is no sign that
they are following different sources. Timaeus spent five books on the life
and times of Agathocles, and it is not surprising that later writers should
select their material from him differently or make changes to suit their purposes.

Polybius tells us that Timaeus made numerous slanderous remarks
about Agathocles, saying he was a κοινὸς πόρνος as a boy and a noto-

---

kann nach alledem keine Frage sein, dass Diodor auch den Duris benutzt hat. In welchem
Umfang dass geschah, ist kaum auszumachen."

[71] Diodorus (20.104.3) describes how Cleonymus in 303 B.C. took two hundred girls
from Metapontum as hostages, and the story was in Duris (FGrH 76 F 18—Ath. 13.605D–
E). Meister, Sizilische Geschichte 163 n.91, takes this correspondence as proof that Diodorus
was using Duris. But the same story may have been in Timaeus.

[72] Laqueur, in his usual manner (RE VIA. 1161–63), and T. Orlandini, "Duride in Diodoro XIX-XXI," Parola del Passato 19 (1964) 216–26, claim to find "contradictions" in Diodorus' text, indications that he is sometimes using a source less hostile to Agathocles than
Timaeus. But these "contradictions" are illusory. It is a mistake to think that 20.63 reveals a
brighter side of the tyrant's character; the final sentence of the chapter shows that his display
of geniality has a sinister purpose. Nor is the description of Sosistratus as a "capable commander" in 19.71.4 inconsistent with 19.3.3, where he and Heraclides are called murderers.
Cf. the good remarks of F. Bizière, op. cit. (n. 65) xviii. Berve, op. cit. (n. 59) 5–6, however,
like Tillyard, Agathocles 38 n.2, thinks that Diodorus is really inconsistent in his attitude.

[73] Cf. Chapter VII above.

[74] Polyaenus describes stratagems of Agathocles in 5.3.1–8. Aelian describes his rather
absurd efforts to conceal his baldness by wearing a wreath (like Julius Caesar). Everyone, it
seems, knew what he was doing, but pretended not to notice, διὰ τὸ τῶν τολμημάτων αὐτοῦ
καὶ ἀσεβημάτων ἐμμανές (VH 11.4). Diodorus might think it beneath his dignity to notice
such things, but Timaeus would not miss the opportunity to make Agathocles look ridiculous.

rious seducer of women in adult life, hinting also that he had a taste for unorthodox and sadistic sexual practices.[75] Accusations of this kind were common enough in Greek politics, and Polybius appears to be surprised that any historian should take them seriously.[76] He finds it equally disgraceful that Timaeus makes comparable accusations against Demosthenes' nephew Demochares,[77] who was certainly no tyrant–lover, either as politician or historian.[78] Polybius (12.14) says he had no occasion to turn against him, but there must have been some cause for disagreement.[79] Perhaps Timaeus wrote some brief description of the Athenian resistance to Macedon, as he had observed it in Athens, comparing it with contemporary developments in Sicily.

Diodorus begins his account of Agathocles with the story of his birth (19.2.2–9). Carcinus, an exile from Rhegium living in Western Sicily, asks some Carthaginians, who are going to Delphi, to consult the oracle for him. A woman who is a native of the area is bearing his child, and he has had disquieting dreams about it. The answer comes back from Delphi that the child will be the cause of great suffering to the Carthaginians and all Sicily (as in the woman's prophetic dream about Dionysius I).[80] Carcinus,

[75] F 124b—Polyb. 12.15.1–3. Polybius expresses his severe disapproval of such λοιδορίαι, λέγω δὲ τούτοις, ἐν οἷς ἐπὶ καταστροφῇ τῆς ὅλης ἱστορίας φησὶ γεγονέναι τὸν Ἀγαθοκλέα κατὰ τὴν πρώτην ἡλικίαν κοινὸν πόρνον, ἕτοιμον τοῖς ἀκρατεστάτοις, κόλοιον, τριόρχην, πάντων τῶν βουλομένων τοὺς ὄπισθεν ἔμπροσθεν γεγονότα. πρὸς δὲ τούτοις, ὅτ' ἀπέθανε, τὴν γυναῖκά φησι κατακλαιομένην αὐτὸν οὕτω θρηνεῖν. τί δ'οὐκ ἐγώ σε; τί δ'οὐκ ἐμὲ σύ; Walbank, in his note, is certainly right in saying that the wife is supposed to be talking of their sexual experiences. Timaeus would expect his readers to draw whatever conclusions they wanted.

[76] Diodorus ignores them, but they are duly reported by Justin (22.1.2–5): Non honestiorem pueritiam quam principia originis habuit, siquidem, forma et corporis pulchritudine egregius, diu vitam stupri patientia exhibuit. Annos deinde pubertatis egressus libidinem a viris ad feminas transtulit. Post haec, apud utrumque sexum famosus, vitam latrociniis mutavit.

[77] F 35b—Polyb. 12.13.1–4: ὅτι Τίμαιός φησι Δημοχάρην ἡταιρηκέναι μὲν τοῖς ἄνω μέρεσι τοῦ σώματος, οὐκ εἶναι δ'ἄξιον τὸ ἱερὸν πῦρ φυσᾶν, ὑπερβεβηκέναι δὲ τοῖς ἐπιτηδεύμασι τὰ Βότρυος ὑπομνήματα καὶ τὰ Φιλαινίδος καὶ τῶν ἄλλων ἀναισχυντογράφων. ταύτην δὲ τὴν λοιδορίαν καὶ τὰς ἐμφάσεις οὐχ οἷον ἄν τις διέθετο πεπαιδευμένος ἀνήρ, ἀλλ'οὐδὲ τῶν ἀπὸ τοῦ τέγους ἀπὸ τοῦ σώματος εἰργασμένων οὐδείς.

[78] FGrH 75 F 2—Ath. 6.253B–D.

[79] They may have disagreed violently in their accounts of Agathocles, since Demochares is supposed to have written about him; see FGrH 75 F 5—[Lucian] Macrob. 10: Ἀγαθοκλῆς δὲ ὁ Σικελίας τύραννος ἐτῶν ἐνενήκοντα πέντε τελευτᾷ, καθάπερ Δημοχάρης καὶ Τίμαιος (F.123b) ἱστοροῦσιν. The text cannot be trusted. According to Diodorus Timaeus gave Agathocles only 72 years (21.16.5—F 123a).

[80] For this dream, cf. above, pp. 165–66. Originally the tale of the oracle may have been intended as a compliment to Agathocles, with its message that he would cause great suffering

therefore, exposes the child when it is born. But it is rescued by its mother, and brought up in her brother's house; she names it Agathocles after her own father. Carcinus sees the boy there when he is seven years old, admires his good looks, and is told the truth by the boy's mother. They decide to take their son back after all; as he grows up, he is trained to be a potter. Carcinus dies soon after they move to Syracuse, but the mother dedicates a stone image of her son in some sanctuary, and when a swarm of bees gathers round it, the orthodox interpretation is given: the boy will grow up to be a great personage.[81]

The dreams, the oracle, and the portent are in Timaeus' best style. The story, moreover, has special point if Agathocles had claimed, rightly or wrongly, to come from a well–established family, and Timaeus wanted to show him as base–born and not of pure Greek origin (if his mother was Sican or Sicel or Punic), and marked out from birth as "the scourge of Sicily."[82]

As the story continues, the malice of Timaeus becomes clearer. Agathocles is said to obtain quick advancement in his military career because the *strategos* Damas (whom Justin calls Damasco) has been his lover and has lavished gifts on him, and promoted him to be chiliarch. When Damas dies, Agathocles marries the wealthy widow, but Justin insists on his continued moral depravity ("in omne facinus promptissimus"), and says that he seduced her while her husband was still living.[83]

According to Diodorus (19.3.3), after Damas' death Agathocles served as chiliarch in a Syracusan force sent to help Croton against the Bruttii, who were besieging the city. His brother Antander was one of the *strategoi*, and the force was commanded by Sosistratus and Heraclides.[84] Diodorus says that these two men had spent most of their lives "in plots and murders and gross acts of sacrilege," and that he had given details of their activity

---

"to the Carthaginians." By adding "and to all Sicily" Timaeus could change its effect and turn it against Agathocles.

[81] This tale also must originally have been intended as a compliment. But if it is combined with the altered version of the oracle, it has the opposite effect, suggesting a great power to do harm. Aelian (*VH* 12.46) has a story of Dionysius I finding bees in his horse's mane and being told by the Galeotae that "this is a sign of monarchy." Timaeus could have turned this story also against Dionysius, if he prepared the way with the dream in which he is revealed as "the scourge of Sicily."

[82] Justin (22.1) offers a somewhat rationalized version: Ad regni maiestatem ex humili et sordido genere pervenit, quippe in Sicilia patre figulo natus.

[83] Diod, 19.3.1–3; Justin 22.1.8–13; cf. F 122—*De Sublim.* 4.5 for another tale showing him as a shameless seducer.

[84] Sosistratus appears as Sostratus in some mss.

in the preceding book. In fact, Book XVIII has nothing whatever about Sicily,[85] but the false reference tells us that he had found the details in Timaeus. Timaeus will have described the political reorganization in Syracuse that followed the downfall of the tyranny, and he must have explained, among other things, how the body known as the Six Hundred came into being and what sort of group it was, whether a regular Council or an oligarchic *hetairia*.[86]

As Diodorus tells the story (19.3–4), Agathocles quarrels with his commanders Sosistratus and Heraclides when they refuse to award him the prize of *aristeia* in recognition of his distinguished service. He accuses them of aiming at tyranny; when he finds no popular support for his accusation, he remains in Italy, where he builds up a strong group of supporters among Syracusan exiles. He fails in an attempt to seize control of Croton, serves for a time with the mercenaries employed by the Tarentines, until they become suspicious of him, and then with his group of exiles joins the Rhegines in fighting the *dynasteia* of Sosistratus and Heraclides which is in control of Syracuse. He is able to return to Syracuse when this *dynasteia* falls from power. Its members are forced into exile, but they receive support from the Carthaginians, and Agathocles continues his military career in the forces that are determined to prevent their return.

It is appropriate that Agathocles should have some narrow escapes like Dionysius the Elder,[87] and Diodorus (19.4.4–6) describes how, on one occasion, after fighting his way into Gela with a thousand men, he appeared to be trapped, but despite receiving seven wounds saved himself and his companions by ordering the trumpeters to sound the call to battle outside the walls, thus leading the enemy to believe that a large Syracusan force was near.[88] Diodorus describes (19.5.1–3) how he escaped being murdered by Acestorides, the Corinthian general who was sent out from Corinth to help the Syracusans in their wars, in accordance with an agreement made in honour of Timoleon.[89] Acestorides suspected that he was plotting to make himself tyrant, and decided to have him killed rather than risk an accusation without substantial proof. But Agathocles escaped his killers by

---

[85] Above, p. 225.

[86] For the various opinions that have been expressed about the Six Hundred, see Berve, "Die Herrschaft des Agathokles," 23 n. 17.

[87] For the narrow escapes of Dionysius I, see above, p. 173.

[88] Justin describes how he escaped capture, when he was practising piracy "contra patriam" in younger days: Saluti ei fuit quod socii capti tortique de illo negaverunt (22.1.15).

[89] Plut. *Timol*. 38.

dressing up a slave in his armour and leaving him to be killed in his place, while he escaped in ragged clothing into a second exile.[90].

"After this," Diodorus continues, "the Syracusans received back the men who had gone into exile with Sosistratus, and made peace with the Carthaginians; but Agathocles in exile had gathered together a private army in the interior of the island." Justin's account is similar: Agathocles, in exile after an unsuccessful attempt to seize power, sought refuge at Morgantina, then established himself at Leontini and laid siege to Syracuse; and the Syracusans asked the Carthaginian commander to help them against him (22.2.1–4).

Justin and Diodorus give quite different accounts of what followed. According to Justin, Agathocles persuaded Hamilcar to act as mediator, promising to return the favour by giving Hamilcar support when he needed it; and after he had sworn on the sacred symbols of Demeter that he would do whatever the Carthaginians asked of him, a settlement was arranged which allowed him to return and actually hold office as *strategos*. Then both men men showed what black–hearted villains they were. Hamilcar lent Agathocles five thousand Libyan soldiers. This enabled him to surround meetings of the Assembly and the Council that he summoned, and slaughter democrats and oligarchs alike, and to attack neighbouring cities, including some that were allied with Carthage. Hamilcar did nothing to stop him, and when word of this reached Carthage, he was condemned in absentia, but died before any action could be taken against him (22.2.5–3.7).

In Diodorus' account (19.5.4–8.6), both Syracusans and Carthaginians are afraid of Agathocles, and it is decided to conciliate him. He is invited into the city,[91] and the citizens make him swear an oath in the temple of Demeter that he will not do anything to overturn the democracy.[92] The sharp political division between the *demos* and the oligarchic faction led by the Six Hundred still prevails, but by his display of democratic sentiment Agathocles persuades the voters to appoint him as *strategos* and temporary Guardian of Peace "until the factions reach a proper agreement with one another." He is of course seeking to establish a personal *dynasteia*, and he uses the powers of his office to build up an army composed of

---

[90] Justin says, without giving details: Bis occupare imperium Syracusarum voluit, bis in exilium actus est (22.1.16).

[91] By ἐπείσθη κατελθεῖν εἰς τὴν πόλιν (5.4) Diodorus does not mean that Agathocles had to be "persuaded" to return, but that satisfactory conditions had to be offered to him.

[92] This oath, in the temple of Demeter or "expositis insignibus Cereris tactisque" (Justin 2.8) recalls the equally false oath that Callippus swore to the women of Dion's family.

men who will support him in a revolution—men from Morgantina and other cities in the centre of the island who have served under him before, and all the impoverished malcontents in the city. He gives orders for the army to assemble at daybreak at the Timoleonteum and invites leaders of the Six Hundred to a conference. Then, when they arrive, he has them arrested, and cries out that they have plotted against him because of his democratic sympathies. The anti-oligarchic feelings of the crowd become clear, and when he orders the trumpeters to sound the call to battle, the inevitable massacre begins.

These different versions are best understood as different attempts to abbreviate or simplify a more complex account given by Timaeus, in which Agathocles reaches separate agreements with Hamilcar and the demos, swears that he will keep faith with both, and deceives them both. Timaeus must also have explained the part that Hamilcar played. Previously it had been Carthaginian policy to support the oligarchs; perhaps Hamilcar thought he could control Agathocles more easily than the *demos,* and so helped him to seize power, as Justin describes.

Diodorus has a long description of the frightful massacre, one of the longest *ecphraseis* of this kind in his history. There was *hybris* everywhere, the women were not spared (19.8.3–5), and the temples were no protection to those who took refuge there (7.3). Many respectable law-abiding citizens perished when they came out into the streets wondering what was the cause of the tumult, many of them persons against whom no one had any grievance except that they were χαριέστεροι τῶν ἄλλων.[93] Houses were pillaged by the soldiers, who were as thirsty for loot as for blood (6.6), and there was fighting even on the roof–tops (7.3). Some four thousand persons were killed, but even though all the city gates were closed, more than six thousand escaped, mostly by leaping from the walls; most of those who got away took refuge in Acragas, where they were well treated.[94] Timaeus described the horrors of slaughter and pillage in a captured city on many occasions,[95] but he seems to have insisted that this was a specially horrible disaster because it was Greeks fighting Greeks, in time of peace, in their own native city (7.4).

The massacre leaves Agathocles undisputed master of Syracuse, and

---

[93] 8.1; cf. οἱ χαριέστατοι τῶν πολιτῶν (6.6). Timaeus seems to have used this adjective regularly to describe the more respectable and intelligent citizens.

[94] 8.2. Those who escaped from Selinus before it was captured by Hannibal were also well treated in Acragas (13.58.3). Timaeus liked to emphasize the generosity and kind hospitality of the Acragantines; cf. the excursus on Acragas in Diod. 13.81–84. For other echoes of Timaeus in this passage see Meister, *Sizilische Geschichte* 139–40.

[95] Most notably at Selinus (13.57), Himera (13.62), Acragas (13.90), and Motya (14.53).

Diodorus (9.1), still certainly following Timaeus, shows him addressing the Assembly, "playing the part of a democratic man," and with magnificent hypocrisy claiming that he has purged the city of the persons who wanted to establish a *dynasteia*. He steps down, discarding his military chlamys for a civilian himation, saying that he wishes to be an ordinary citizen henceforth,[96] though he knows quite well that they will not allow anyone else to be *strategos* except the man with whom they share the guilt for the massacre. They are dependent on him, just as he is dependent on them. The tyrant is established by a kind of criminal pact.

This is not the way the story is told in the standard histories, but this is what Timaeus said, if Diodorus is a trustworthy guide: "Agathocles knew very well that the majority of the men in the Assembly had taken part in the criminal outrages and hence would not be willing to confer the *strategia* on anybody else. Immediately, therefore, the men who had looted the property of their victims cried out to him not to desert them, but to take charge of everything. For a while he said nothing, then, as the crowd became more insistent, he said he would accept the *strategia,* but could not have a colleague in this office. He said he could not endure, as co–ruler with others, to be held legally responsible for crimes that others might commit. So the crowd agreed that he could be sole ruler, and he was elected *strategos autocrator*" (9.2–4).

Whether accurate or not, this is a remarkable and extremely frightening description. No one dared oppose Agathocles now. He won over the penniless and the debtors by promising to cancel all outstanding debts, and, like Octavian in Rome, he seemed to be on the way towards transforming himself into a just and highly respected ruler (9.6–7). Diodorus does not date any of the incidents in the rise of Agathocles. He does not even say how long the periods of exile were. He seems to have made a selection from Timaeus' narrative, not summarized it, but there is no doubt of the tendency of the account. It represented Agathocles as a murderous tyrant, totally unscrupulous and treacherous. It is easy to see why Polybius and Diodorus complain of Timaeus' prejudice, but there is no other witness to whom they can appeal. Unlike Dionysius, Agathocles has no Philistus to speak in his favour.

---

[96] According to Polyaenus 5.3.7–8, the massacre follows the attempt of Agathocles to present himself as a "simple citizen," instead of preceding it, as in Diod. 19.9.1–2, and the meeting at the Timoleonteum, when he accuses the leaders of the Six Hundred of plotting against him and has "more than two hundred" killed by his soldiers, is kept separate from the massacre that results in thousands of deaths. This version may come from another source, or it may in fact be a more accurate summary of Timaeus' account than Diodorus gives.

When Diodorus returns to Sicilian affairs again (19.65), there is no sign of any change of source. Agathocles wanted to get control of Messana, where many Syracusan exiles had taken refuge, and he already had possession of a stronghold in the territory. Despite an agreement to give up this fort if he was paid thirty talents (which he received), he did not withdraw, and actually made a surprise night attack on the city. This attempt failed, as did a more open attack later in the summer, and he agreed to a peace settlement that was drawn up by a Carthaginian mediator. But his behaviour did not change. He moved on to Abacaenum and had forty men killed there who were opposed to him (65.5–6).

Next year the Syracusan exiles in Acragas decide that something must be done to stop Agathocles (70.1–3). They send to Sparta, hoping to find a man like Timoleon who will help them, and they find Cleomenes' son Acrotatus happy to undertake some task away from home. Unluckily, like other Spartans before him, like Gylippus in Sicily, as Timaeus had described,[97] he is corrupted by the temptations of an un–Spartan life, misuses the money that is put at his disposal, and finally murders Sosistratus because he seems to be a capable man who will be an inconvenient colleague and mentor.[98] Once this crime is discovered, he has to leave and, thanks to Hamilcar's mediation, an agreement is reached which establishes the autonomy of all Sicilian cities except those that are subject to Carthaginian rule.

The hand of Timaeus can easily be recognized in the characterization of Acrotatus, and also in Diodorus' account of events in 312 and 311. In 312, Agathocles sends his general Pasiphilus to Messana, and when he advises them to conciliate Agathocles by expelling the Syracusan exiles, they obey (19.102). Agathocles now comes himself, and when he asks them to take in some other exiles, "exiled by due process of law, but serving in the army," they dare not disobey. He then carries out a search in Messana and Tauromenium for men whom he knows to have opposed him in the past, and has about six hundred of them put to death.[99] The affront to Tauromenium helps to explain the strong feelings of Timaeus about Agathocles. This may in fact be the year when he was obliged to leave Sicily.

---

[97] Above, pp. 144–45.

[98] 71.3–4. When Diodorus says that Acrotatus was anxious ἐκ ποδῶν ποιήσασθαι δραστικὸν ἄνδρα καὶ δυνάμενον ἐφεδρεῦσαι τοῖς κακῶς προισταμένοις τῆς ἡγεμονίας, he is not contradicting what he said about Sosistratus in 3.3; cf. F. Bizière's note on the passage.

[99] Cf. Polyaenus 5.3.6.

After making sure that Messana will no longer be a centre of resistance, he goes to Acragas, hoping to "regulate the situation" here also,[100] but is prevented by the arrival of sixty Carthaginian ships. He does succeed, however, in foiling an attempt to make Centuripe a new centre for the exiles' activity, and he carries out similar bloody executions there. During his absence from Syracuse, fifty Carthaginian ships sail into the Great Harbour. Though unable to do any real damage, they sink an Athenian merchant ship and cut off the hands of its crew. In revenge, therefore, when Agathocles' men capture some of their ships off the coast of Bruttium, they treat the Punic crews in the same way. In Timaeus' proper style this is considered as divine punishment for Carthaginian barbarity.[101]

Deinocrates, the exiles' commander, now gains possession of "a place called Galeria" (otherwise unknown) and concentrates his force there. It is said to number at least three thousand infantry and two thousand cavalry (104.1). These figures deserve attention, because even if Timaeus was no longer in Sicily by now, he could have been in touch with people who took part in this action. The high proportion of cavalry to infantry suggests that many of these men were quite wealthy. Agathocles sends an army of five thousand against them, under his generals Pasiphilus and Philonides, and after a hard fought battle they are routed, Galeria is recaptured, and "the persons responsible for the rebellion" are put to death. Agathocles now sees the opportunity for a full–scale battle with a Carthaginian army encamped near Gela, but his challenge is refused and he returns to Syracuse where he dedicates "the spoils" in the principal temples (104.2–4). Timaeus must have explained what these spoils were, since there had been no battle with the Carthaginians; and if they were spoils taken from Greeks, he may have protested that Agathocles was not honouring the gods, if he dedicated such spoils in temples.

The next year, the Carthaginians send an invading force to Sicily commanded by Hamilcar, the son of Gisgon, who, as Justin warns his readers, must be distinguished from the Hamilcar who has appeared in the preceding narrative and is now dead.[102] As had happened in one of the earlier Carthaginian invasions, this expedition suffers serious losses in a storm, losing sixty triremes and two hundred supply ships, according to Diodorus.[103] These figures may be mere conventional conjecture, but the

---

[100] καὶ ταύτην τὴν πόλιν συσκευάσασθαι (102.8). The phrase may be borrowed from Timaeus. It recalls similar euphemisms for savage repression used in our own time.

[101] δοξάντων δ'αὐτῶν ὠμῶς κεχρῆσθαι μηδ'ὁτιοῦν ἀδικοῦσι ταχὺ τὸ δαιμόνιον αὐτοῖς ἐπεσήμαινεν (103.5).

[102] Justin 22.3.6–8.

[103] Cf. Diod. 11.20.2, and the prototype of such storms in Hdt. 7.188.

numbers given for the fighting men are credible enough, a grand total of forty thousand infantry, after Hamilcar has made up for his losses by recruiting mercenaries in Sicily (106.3–5).

The Carthaginians concentrate their forces in the area of Gela, and Agathocles uses a combination of guile and brutality to make sure that the city, where many of his personal enemies have found shelter, is not betrayed to the Carthaginians. Instead of alarming them by sending in a large force, he sends in a few men at a time (κατ'ὀλίγους), just as Timoleon did in order to secure the acropolis in Syracuse.[104] Then, when he has sufficient men inside the walls, he accuses the Geloans of treachery, carries out wholesale executions (over four thousand), and forces the survivors to bring him all the money and uncoined gold and silver that they have (107.3–5). Now he prepares for battle with the Carthaginians, who are encamped on Ecnomus, the "Lawless" Hill, so called, says Diodorus (108.1), because Phalaris set up the brazen bull there. The hill Phalarion, where Agathocles encamped, was also said to be named after Phalaris. These etymologies (which may not really be traditional) are a sure sign that Timaeus is Diodorus' source here. He loved to find such explanations of place names and pretend that they were traditional.[105]

Timaean battle descriptions usually begin with an omen or a portent, as before the Battle of the Crimisus.[106] A stream, the Himeras, separated the two armies, and an old tradition gave warning that "a great number of men were destined to perish in battle there" (108.2). The omen was suitably ambiguous, and men on both sides were assailed by *deisidaimonia* and unwilling to fight. Only by taking advantage of a chance incident was Agathocles able to bring on a full–scale battle.[107] A Greek foraging party was assailed by some Carthaginians, and Agathocles set an ambush to catch them at the river crossing, drove them back towards their camp, and brought out his main force in the hope of making his way into the Carthaginian camp on their heels (108.3–5).

One does not expect a soldier's description of a battle from Diodorus, and the result may not have been quite as disastrous as he describes it, with more than seven thousand Greeks killed and only five hundred barbarians (109.5).[108] Polybius and Diodorus give us fair warning that Timaeus exaggerated the defeats that Agathocles suffered and blamed him for disasters

[104] Plut. *Timol.* 13.5

[105] Berve, "Die Herrschaft des Agathokles" 9, following Laqueur, *RE* VIA. 1169.

[106] F 118—Plut. *Mor.* 676D, cf. Diod. 16.79.3–4.

[107] παραλόγος τις αἰτία προεκαλέσατο αὐτοὺς εἰς τὸν ὁλοσχερῆ κίνδυνον (108.3).

[108] M. Cary, *CAH* VII. 624, rather surprisingly considers these figures "a credible estimate."

that resulted from ill–fortune, not bad generalship.[109] Here Diodorus may have omitted some pungent remarks of Timaeus criticizing Agathocles. He attributes the defeat himself to a stroke of ill–luck, the unexpected arrival of Carthaginian ships with fresh troops. He offers an explanation also for the difficulty which the Greeks experienced in forcing their way into the Carthaginian camp, saying that Hamilcar used the slingers from the Balearic Islands with particularly good effect. He notes that these slingers were trained from boyhood in the islands and could shoot stones as heavy as a mina (109.2). He had described the training of these boys in an earlier book (5.17–18), in a context where his dependence on Timaeus is unquestionable.[110] Timaeus must certainly have emphasized their value to Hamilcar in the battle.

After the battle, Agathocles and what was left of his army took refuge in the city of Gela, where supplies were plentiful, in order to keep Hamilcar's army busy in a useless siege, while Syracuse was got ready to face attack. Hamilcar, so Diodorus explains, soon gave up the attempt to capture Gela, and apparently allowed Agathocles' army to reach Syracuse and prepare to face the siege there. The defeat at the River Himeras was evidently serious enough to convince Agathocles that he could not face Hamilcar in another battle,[111] and it persuaded many of the cities to join the Carthaginians in fighting him. Tauromenium was one of the cities that made overtures to Hamilcar, and one can imagine that when Timaeus heard the news (he may have been in Athens by this time), he might think that Agathocles was finished, but also that eastern Sicily would now be controlled by the Carthaginians instead of by a Greek tyrant—a dismal prospect indeed.

This was when Agathocles made his bold decision to carry the war into Africa. From Timaeus' point of view, this had the advantage that it took him away from Sicily: he would not hurt Acragas or Tauromenium by winning victories there. But he was extremely brutal in raising money for the expedition and in "ridding the city of persons ill–disposed towards him" (20.4.5–8). His procedure is condemned as "unholy,"[112] and it can hardly be maintained that the account of the African campaigns is too favourable to Agathocles to be based on Timaeus. It shows considerable malice

---

[109] F 124c, d—Polyb. 15.35.10; Diod. 21.17.2.

[110] Cf. also F 66—Schol. Lyc. 633.

[111] Justin (22.3.9–10) speaks of a second battle, just as disastrous as the first, but this is not reliable evidence that there was such a battle.

[112] διὰ μιᾶς ἀνοσίου πράξεως εὐπορήσας καὶ τῶν ἀλλοτρίως διακειμένων καθαρὰν ποιήσας τὴν πόλιν (20.4.8). Henceforth references to Diodorus are to Book XX unless otherwise noted.

towards him, as will be seen. It also contains a number of episodes that seem like repetitions of improbable incidents recorded by Timaeus in earlier wars.[113]

There is an air of unreality about the story from the beginning. First comes the carefully guarded secret. No one is supposed to know where the ships are going.[114] And it is only by pure luck that they reach Africa. Everything is ready for departure, but Carthaginian warships, outnumbering the Greek fleet, are outside the harbour waiting for them (Diod. 20.5.2). Some merchant ships are sighted bringing food for Syracuse, and the entire Carthaginian fleet goes after them, leaving the way clear for Agathocles' sixty ships to emerge from the harbour. But just as the Carthaginians are in reach of the cargo ships, they see the Greek fleet out in the open and turn to give chase. The result is that the supply ships are allowed to reach Syracuse safely, where they are sorely needed, and Agathocles' ships escape because night comes on.

They sail for Africa, but their troubles are not over, because there is an eclipse of the sun, which causes great alarm among the men (5.4–5). Diodorus does not record what explanation Agathocles devised to calm their fears, but in Justin's account, which must be based on Timaeus, he assures them that eclipses always mean a change of some kind, an end to Carthaginian success therefore (6.2–3).

The eclipse has been identified as historical (though there is some doubt whether 311 or 310 is the correct year for it), but since it could not have been observed off the south coast of Sicily, it has been suggested that the ships may have taken the longer route through the straits of Messina and along the north coast.[115] It is just as likely that they took the normal direct route to Carthage and were not aware of the eclipse at all, but that Timaeus thought they must have seen it; or perhaps he considered it appropriate that they should see it and be alarmed by it.

A more serious difficulty in the story is that a substantial fighting force is supposed to be carried in sixty fast–sailing triremes. Timaeus must have known that triremes alone were insufficient to carry a large army. But if there had been slower-sailing vessels besides the triremes, στρατιωδίδες or ὁπλιταγωγοὶ νῆες and other πλοῖα, how did they escape the pursuing

---

[113] It is hardly correct to say, as Berve does ("Die Herrschaft des Agathokles" 12–13), that Diodorus' account "shows few traces" of dependence on Timaeus.

[114] "Mira prorsus audacia" is Justin's comment and "Huius consilii non minus admirabile silentium quam commentum fuit" (22.4.2–3).

[115] Cary *CAH* VII.625; P. Roussel, *Histoire grecque* IV (Paris 1939) 383, and the references given there.

Carthaginian ships? The abbreviated account of Diodorus leaves questions of this kind unanswered.

There is no storm, and after six days at sea they land in Africa and beach their ships despite an attempt by the Carthaginians to prevent them (6.2–3). They are safe from attack on land, because no preparation has been made to meet them, and Agathocles insists that they must burn their ships, which will be a burden to them now that they are on land. Diodorus describes the ceremonial burning of the fleet: "After offering sacrifice to Demeter and Kore, Agathocles summoned an assembly, and came forward to speak with a garland on his head, clothed in a shining himation. After a few suitable words of introduction,[116] he said that when they were being pursued by the Carthaginians he had made a vow to Demeter and Kore, the goddesses of Sicily, that he would set fire to all their ships, and since they had found safety, it was right and proper to carry out this promise. He assured them that he would give them back many times this number of ships if they fought bravely, because the goddesses, when he offered them sacrifice, foretold victory in the whole war.

"While he was speaking, a serving man brought him a burning torch, and taking this in his hand he commanded a similar torch to be given to each ship's captain, and crying out an invocation to the goddesses he led the way to his flagship, and standing on the poop commanded all the others to do as he did. Then, as all the trierarchs put the torch to their ships and the flames rose up in the air, the trumpets sounded the call to battle, the whole army cried out, and all prayed together for a safe return home" (20.7.1–4).

Those who believe that Duris is the source of Diodorus in Book XX may want to hail this description as a good example of his so–called tragic style. But Timaeus was equally capable of writing in this manner, and if he had already described the burning of two Carthaginian fleets,[117] he would hardly refuse the opportunity of describing this scene. He would also take pleasure in showing such a display of rhetorical showmanship (γοητεία) by Agathocles, which made the men accept the loss of their fleet with equanimity for the moment, until its effect wore off and he had to find some other way of reviving their spirits, letting them loot the well–tilled countryside and the defenceless towns on their advance.[118]

---

[116] Justin gives him a longer speech (5.2–13) as Timaeus may have done.

[117] Diod. 11.22, 14.73; cf. above, pp. 000, 000. The phrase τῆς φλογὸς εἰς ὕψος ἀρθείσης appears with slight variation in all three passages, and also in 20.67.2, in describing the fire in the Carthaginian camp. Timaeus may have used the phrase.

[118] Diod. 20.8.1–5.

The Greeks meet no opposition until they are near the city of Carthage, and the Carthaginian citizen army, forty thousand strong (10.5), comes out to meet them, under the joint command of Hanno and Bomilcar. Bomilcar is introduced as a man anxious to make himself tyrant (10.2), and it is explained that the Carthaginian habit of turning against their generals once a war was over seemed to invite ambitious men to aim at tyranny. This is a natural enough remark for Timaeus to make, since he hated and despised the Carthaginians as much as he hated tyranny.

The battle is preceded by a good omen, carefully arranged by the crafty Agathocles. He releases a number of owls who fly through the ranks and perch on the shields and helmets of the men, making everyone believe that Athena will be fighting on their side (11.3–4).

The description of the Greek battle order tells us for the first time how large their force is. They have thirteen thousand infantry, five hundred archers and slingers, and an unstated number of cavalrymen, but no horses for them.[119] Not all the infantrymen, however, have proper hoplite equipment. It appears that the ships' crews—rowers, steersmen, and so on—have been drafted into the ranks without shields, but only shield cases which are useless as protection, but which will look like shields from a distance (11.1–2). Here is another example of Agathocles' attempts at deceit.

After hard fighting, the enemy are driven back towards the city: "Agathocles pursued them for a time, but then turned back and looted the Carthaginian camp" (12.8). This perhaps means that Timaeus censured Agathocles for not taking full advantage of the victory.[120] Diodorus says that about two hundred Greeks fell in the battle, "but not more than a thousand Carthaginians, though some writers say six thousand" (13.1). This must mean that Timaeus cut down the figures given by some admirer of Agathocles, Callias probably.[121] It also looks as though he represented the victory as due in great part to sheer good luck. Diodorus explains that Bomilcar, after Hanno was killed, ordered his men to retreat because he wanted Agathocles to win a victory, so that he could take advantage of the citizens' fears to make himself tyrant.

The narrative that follows is equally in the Timaean manner. It is said that waggons were found in the Carthaginian camp loaded with shackles, intended for the numerous Greeks whom they expected to take prisoner,

---

[119] Cf. Diod. 20.4.1–2. Agathocles could not bring horses, but he wanted to have men ready to mount them ὅταν ἵππων κυριεύσῃ.

[120] Cf. below, p. 255.

[121] Justin (22.6.6) says the Greeks lost two thousand, the Carthaginians three thousand.

clear evidence of arrogant over–confidence, which was duly punished by the gods. Indeed, the Carthaginians are supposed to recognize that their defeat was a divine punishment, and they appease Melkart and Moloch with lavish gifts and human sacrifice.[122]

Diodorus goes on to describe how messengers were sent to Syracuse bringing the news to Hamilcar. They took with them the bronze beaks that they had recovered from the ashes of the Greek ships, and by displaying them Hamilcar was able to make the Syracusans believe that Agathocles and all his men were lost together with their ships. These two chapters of Diodorus (20.15–16) preserve something of the quality of Timaeus' dramatic narrative. They describe the distress and terror caused in Syracuse and the expulsion of all relatives and friends of the exiles and numerous other persons, and a debate by the leading political figures, at which a decision is taken to wait for confirmation of the news. Then the situation changes when a triaconter arrives from Africa, sent by Agathocles and manned by an élite crew. As it approaches land at daybreak, Carthaginian ships give chase, and with the population watching, it just manages to escape its pursuers and reach the safety of the harbour, bringing news of Agathocles' victory. Hamilcar tries to take advantage of unguarded places in the walls, when so many are streaming to the harbour to watch the ship arrive, but his attempt fails, he withdraws from the city, and sends five thousand men to Carthage to meet their need there.

In his account of the following year (309 B.C.), Diodorus describes another attempt to break into the city, led by Hamilcar himself, by narrow tracks up the slope of Euryalus (29.2–11). He is clearly following a description written by someone who is familiar with the hillside. A Syracusan party is waiting for them on Euryalus, the Carthaginians apparently have no competent guides and allow themselves to be trapped helplessly in the narrow lanes, and Hamilcar, who had been told by a soothsayer that he would dine in Syracuse that evening (29.3), is cut off from the rest and captured. Timaeus would have known what these lanes and tracks were like, just as he seems to have known the pools and streams near the city,[123] and the misleading prophecy is also quite in his style.

Since Timaeus seems to have been greatly attached to Acragas and per-

---

[122] Historians today seem unduly credulous when they accept as literal truth Timaeus' gruesome tales of children of noble families thrown into the furnace to appease Moloch (Cary, *CAH* VII.626; Roussel, *Histoire grecque* IV. 384). Even if human sacrifice was sometimes practised by the Carthaginians, it is hardly necessary to take seriously each instance of it reported by Timaeus.

[123] Above, p. 217.

haps knew the city as well as he knew Syracuse, it is likely that he took some trouble to describe the new effort made there to organize a freedom movement, with Xenodicus as leader, and to explain how Xenodicus was able to gain control of Gela and to free several other cities from the Carthaginians, though he apparently did nothing to help Syracuse where food was running short (32.3). Indeed the ὁρμὴ πρὸς τὴν ἐλευθερίαν is shown to be directed equally against the Carthaginians and Agathocles' Syracuse (31.5), and Sicily appears now to be in the throes of a three–sided war, in which each side faces two separate enemies. This is where we need the help of a contemporary writer to help us; Diodorus' summary is quite inadequate (20.31–32).

In two earlier chapters (17–18) Diodorus offered only an outline of the progress made by Agathocles in 310, and it has been supposed that the fragment of historical narrative preserved in a papyrus text (*P.Oxy* 2399) refers to events of that year. The account, however, bears hardly any relation to Diodorus' summary, and those who believe that Duris is the author of the fragment and also that he is Diodorus' source in Book XX can justify their belief only by supposing that Diodorus made his source's account unrecognizable by incompetent excerpting. If, on the other hand, Timaeus is Diodorus' source, as argued here, it remains quite possible, if unprovable, that Duris is the author of the papyrus text. The style of narrative does not suggest the manner of Timaeus, and no one has seriously proposed to identify him as the author, though Callias and Antander have both been proposed.

There is nothing in Diodorus' preceding chapters (15–16), as described above, that corresponds to the story partially preserved here (*P.Oxy.* 2399, cols. ii–iv) of how a man called Diognetus, not otherwise known, "corrupted by Hamilcar," spoke up in the Syracusan Assembly in an attempt to persuade the Syracusans to surrender, and was duly interrupted and arrested by Antander. Indeed, Antander's decisive action is quite inconsistent with the narrative of Diodorus, who represents him as despondent and ready to surrender until Erymnon the Aetolian exerts his counter–pressure.[124]

When Diodorus resumes his African narrative (20.33), it comes to life again and shows the influence of Timaeus quite clearly. The head of Hamilcar had been brought from Syracuse as a proof of his death for Agathocles to show the enemy, and he rode up to their camp to display it.

---

[124] See E. G. Turner's introduction, *Oxyrhynchus Papyri* xxiv (1957) 99–102. For further discussion, see W. S. Barrett, *Gnomon* 33 (1961) 691–92; E. Manni, *Kokalos* 12 (1966) 163–71; M. A. Cavallaro, *Historia* 26 (1977) 54–59; W. Huss, *ZPE* 39 (1980) 63–71.

Here was the counterpart to the bronze ships' beaks that the Carthaginians had sent to Hamilcar at Syracuse. The Carthaginian reaction is properly barbaric and they are plunged into deep gloom, while the Greeks are elated. But in regular rhetorical style we are shown how Fortune changes the course of her stream. Agathocles now has to face trouble from his own men. One of his officers, Lyciscus, makes some offensive remarks about Agathocles when he is a guest at his table, and picks a quarrel with Agathocles' son Archagathus, who, in furious anger, snatches a spear from one of the guards, thrusts it into Lyciscus' ribs, and kills him instantly. The incident might remind readers of Alexander's quarrel with Cleitus, but the sequel is entirely different. Lyciscus has many supporters in the army, and a mutiny breaks out when Agathocles refuses to surrender his son to them. He saves the day, however, by appearing before the angry throng in simple civilian dress, offering to take his own life, if that is what they wish. He draws his sword, as though to stab himself, but of course he is prevented, good feeling is restored, and he leads them out to win a victory over the Carthaginians (33.3–34.7).

Here we have another highly dramatic incident, a display of showmanship, like the ship–burning, but also a display of great courage. It has commonly been thought that Timaeus would not tell a story that reflected so much credit on Agathocles, and it has been assigned to Duris.[125] But bitterly as Timaeus may have hated Agathocles, he recognized his abilities as an orator who could control and "bewitch" a crowd. It is also probably fair to say that description of "the marvellous and the unexpected" was always more important to him (and to his readers) than consistent characterization.[126] It is also possible that Diodorus has altered his version slightly, perhaps omitting some details discreditable to Agathocles.[127]

If the Lyciscus episode invited readers to admire Agathocles, events of the next two years made up for it by revealing how treacherous he could be. He enticed the Syracusans who had fought in the Carthaginian ranks to surrender "under a truce," and then had them killed (39.6), and he turned against Ophellas, who had come from Cyrene at his invitation, bringing a substantial army to support him in fighting Carthage. In an address to the army he is shown accusing Ophellas of a plot to kill him (clever rhetoric

---

[125] E.g. Berve, "Die Herrschaft des Agathokles" 17; R. Schubert, *Geschichte des Agathokles* (Breslau 1887) 137; Meister, *Sizilische Geschichte* 150–51.

[126] Above, pp.

[127] The purple "royal garb" that Diodorus gives Agathocles (34.3) cannot be in Timaeus' account, since Agathocles has not yet declared himself to be a king. Tillyard, *Agathocles* 129, calls this "careless" of Diodorus. It is also a good indication that he is not reproducing his source exactly. But Timaeus must be responsible for the trumpet call and the insistence on "paradox" (34.6, cf. 7.4, 42.4).

again), and taking advantage of τὸ παράδοξον he leads the murderous attack against him (42.3–5). The attack is all the more deplorable, as Diodorus notes (42.5), because Ophellas had trusted Agathocles and put himself in his hands. Justin adds (22.7.5) that Agathocles had permitted him to adopt one of his sons, an important detail that Diodorus omits. It must have been part of the story as Timaeus told it.[128]

Agathocles is supposed to have offered Ophellas all the territory that they could acquire from Carthage, saying he did not want any of it for himself. It is not clear whether Timaeus or Duris or any other author represented this as a genuine offer, or merely as a bait to entice him to his doom and put his army in the hands of Agathocles. In fact, of course, like any other mercenary army, when their employer was killed, the men took service with his killer.

Bomilcar's attempt to seize power in Carthage is supposed to take place at the same time as the murder of Ophellas. Diodorus remarks that if Agathocles had known of the disorder and confusion in the city, he might easily have taken possession of it, and that if he and Bomilcar had known of each other's plans, they might have combined forces and been sure of success against their common enemies; or if the Carthaginians had known that Agathocles planned to murder Ophellas and Ophellas' army had joined them, they could easily have defeated Agathocles. He also regrets the inadequate *mimesis* of history which cannot describe simultaneous events simultaneously and thus reproduce the *pathos* of reality (43.1–7). Some may think that remarks of this kind are more typical of the "tragic" historian Duris than of Timaeus, but the description of Bomilcar's attempted *coup* has true Timaean quality. Bomilcar marches into the city with the army that is supporting him, but once they are in the city streets, they are at the mercy of the defenders, who have occupied the tall buildings round the agora. Bomilcar is tricked into surrender and killed in the most brutal manner (44.1–6). Timaeus does not miss an opportunity to describe street fighting and to dwell on Carthaginian savagery and cruelty.

Justin (22.7.8–11) adds a detail that must certainly be attributed to Timaeus. Bomilcar is crucified "in medio foro . . . ut idem locus monumentum suppliciorum esset, qui ante fuerat ornamentum honorum," and he makes a speech from the cross "quasi a tribunali," denouncing the Carthaginians for their acts of folly and faithlessness in the past.

Diodorus apparently thinks that Agathocles assumed the title of king in 307, following the example of Antigonus and Ptolemy and the other dy-

---

[128] Polyaenus 5.3.4 has an even more malicious version, in which Ophellas is represented as a paederast.

nasts, and that he undertook the campaign against the Itycaeans in order to justify the title by winning some victories (54.1–2). His dating, however, is at fault. None of the dynasts can have taken the title until at least two years later, when Antigonus and Demetrius set the fashion after their victory at sea off Cyprus, and if Agathocles followed their example, it must have been in 304 after his successes in Sicily.[129] It is unlikely that Timaeus was confused about these dates, since he must have been in Athens when Antigonus and Demetrius declared themselves kings. Diodorus must be responsible for the error.

But Diodorus is certainly following Timaeus in his account of the campaign against the Itycaeans, when Agathocles attacks their city with captives hanging from his siege engines, so that the defenders are forced to shoot at their fellow citizens,[130] and Agathocles shows his usual brutality when the city falls (54.3–55.2). Then, after successes at Hippo and elsewhere, he returns to Sicily leaving his son Archagathus in charge in Africa. He takes two thousand troops with him (55.5), and there is some hard fighting with the liberators, but when their numbers increase and he finds himself outnumbered, he refuses all invitations to a regular battle (57.2–3).

Meanwhile, Archagathus meets with complete disaster in Africa. All went well at first. His general Eumachus took part of the army into the interior, winning easy victories against cities and peoples with Greek names and against Meschela, "a city founded in ancient times by Greeks on their return from Troy" (a true Timaean touch).[131] After his triumphant return, he sets out again and penetrates even further inland, only to meet with strong resistance, and he has to make his way back after heavy losses through a mountainous area where there are so many cats that no bird nests there (58.2), and through the Monkey Country, where monkeys are regarded as gods and maintained at the expense of the community (58.3–5). Timaeus would not miss the opportunity to write about strange country and

---

[129] Berve, "Die Herrschaft des Agathokles" 61–63; E. Will, *Histoire politique du monde hellénistique* I (Nancy 1966) 64, 101–03.

[130] Diodorus seems to be borrowing the language of Timaeus when he writes that Agathocles by this device ταῖς ψυχαῖς τῶν ἔνδον ὥσπερ καυτήριά τινα προσῆγεν, but that the Itycaeans shot down some of these men, τινὰς δὲ τοῖς ὀξυβέλεσιν πρὸς τῇ μηχανῇ προσκαθήλωσαν καθ' οὕς ποτε τύχοι τοῦ σώματος τόπους, ὥστε σταυρῷ παραπλησίαν εἶναι τὴν ὕβριν ἅμα καί τήν τιμωρίαν (54.5–7).

[131] 57.6. Diodorus says he has already spoken of this place in Book III. There is no trace of it there, and it seems to be a false reference. But like the false references to Book XVIII (above, n. 49) it indicates that Diodorus is recalling a passage in Timaeus of which he thought he had made some record. Timaeus had evidently written about this mythical colony in an earlier book.

strange peoples, gratifying the appetite for "marvels and *paradoxa*" that the historians of Alexander had whetted. This is the kind of writing that Polybius despised.

Once the Carthaginians organize a counter–offensive and induce Archagathus to divide his forces to meet their newly formed armies in three different areas, disaster follows quickly (59–60). Eumachus and Archagathus are revealed as totally incompetent commanders. Eumachus is shown committing the blunder that is so common in Timaean battle descriptions. He seeks refuge for his men—more than eight thousand of them—"on a hill short of water," and waits for the enemy to surround the place.[132]

Archagathus sends word of his troubles to his father (61.1), who decides to come to his aid. According to Justin's brief account, Agathocles has made excellent progress since coming back from Africa and the Carthaginians have withdrawn from Sicily before he is recalled (22.8.3). But Diodorus' story is confusing. He shows Agathocles preparing to send seventeen fighting ships to Africa when the outlook in Sicily is still very bleak (ἐν ἀθυμίᾳ δεινῇ πάντων ὄντων), and as before[133] a lucky chance gives him the opportunity to put to sea. Some Etruscan ships have arrived and slipped into the harbour at night, unnoticed by the Carthaginians; with their help, he wins a notable victory at sea, which breaks the blockade and solves their food-supply problem.[134] But though one expects him to be at sea, with the way to Africa clear, he is shown giving orders to Leptines to take the field against Xenodicus; he celebrates Leptines' successes with a display of genial hospitality (hoping to make false friends reveal their true feelings in their cups), and sets off for Africa only when he is satisfied that his authority is secure (61.5–63.7).

Did Timaeus make Agathocles repeat his earlier performance, leaving Syracuse still under siege and evading the Carthaginian ships thanks to a stroke of luck, or did he make him wait until things improved in Sicily before leaving? Unless Diodorus has misunderstood him or has tried to combine different stories from different sources, Timaeus himself seems to have combined the two alternatives, so that the ships are sent off at once, while Agathocles remains behind, watches Leptines win his victories, and then sets out for Africa himself.

---

[132] Cf. Diod. 14.105.1 (above, p. 186), where ten thousand men are said to seek refuge on a waterless hill top in Italy. Diodorus must have both these instances from Timaeus.

[133] Cf. Diod. 20.4–5 (above, p. 241).

[134] 61.5–62.1: τὸ λοιπὸν θαλασσοκρατῶν παρείχετο τοῖς ἐμπόροις τὴν ἀσφάλειαν.

Justin and Diodorus also give different accounts of what happened after Agathocles reached Africa. They show how differently Trogus and Diodorus selected their material from their source. Justin describes a speech of Agathocles to the soldiers, who have to be pacified because they have received no pay (22.8.5–6): "Stipendia illis non a se flagitanda esse, sed ab hoste quaerenda." Diodorus says nothing of this speech,[135] but both authors describe the attack that follows, which is disastrous.[136] In Justin's version, Agathocles and Archagathus take flight from the camp that night in despair. Archagathus becomes separated from his father in the darkness, is caught by the pursuers and killed, but Agathocles reaches the ships and sails away to Sicily, "exemplum flagitii singulare, rex exercitus sui desertor, filiorumque pater traditor" (8.12).

As before, this seems to be a simplified version of Timaeus' account, which is better represented by Diodorus; it is only in his version that Agathocles is really "filiorum traditor." He describes the παράλογος συμφορά of that night. The Carthaginians were burning some captives as a sacrifice of thanksgiving for their victory (Timaeus never misses a chance to remind his readers that the Carthaginians sacrificed human beings), when the sacred tent and other temporary shelters caught fire (it was of course a windy night), and before long the whole camp was ablaze and many perished in the flames (a proper punishment for their crimes, says Diodorus—exactly the comment one might expect from Timaeus). The panic was aggravated when five thousand Libyans, who had been fighting on the Greek side, now came over to join them, but were mistaken for a hostile force, so that a disorderly sort of battle and stampede resulted, in which "more than five thousand" lost their lives before the survivors reached safety in the city of Carthage (64.5–66.4). Timaeus liked to describe fires and the panic or excitement that they caused,[137] and he seems to have thought it specially fitting that Carthaginians should suffer from fire.[138]

A similar panic arises in the Greek camp when the Libyan deserters, finding themselves not welcomed by the Carthaginians, try to return and

---

[135] Justin in 22.5.2–13 seems to be describing the speech that Diodorus summarizes in 20.7.1–3, but Justin 22.4.3 and 7.9–10 have no counterparts in Diodorus. Justin calls Agathocles "in contionibus perfacundus" (22.1.9), but he does not describe or mention the speeches to which Diodorus refers in 19.3.5, 6.4, 9.3, 70.8, 107.4, 20.4.5–6, 16.1, 34.3–4, 42.3. On some of these occasions Timaeus must have written a formal speech for the speaker.

[136] Diod. 64.3–5; Justin 22.8.7.

[137] Above, p. 242.

[138] Cf. Diod. 14.73.5.

are mistaken for an enemy force. The outbreak of fire and the wild cries in the Carthaginian camp are supposed to confirm this suspicion,[139] it is thought that the enemy is coming in full force, and four thousand die in the fighting before the mistake is discovered. Meanwhile, Agathocles has decided to slip away to a ship with a small party, taking his younger son Heraclides with him, but leaving Archagathus behind.[140] Archagathus, however, discovers the plan in time, the party is arrested, and Agathocles is put in chains. But in the "panic fear" and confusion that result from the false alarm of an enemy attack, the soldiers are seized with pity when they see their commander in chains. "All cried out that he must be released", and he finds his way to a ship and sets sail despite the stormy weather, abandoning both his sons, who are promptly slaughtered by the soldiers. New commanders are elected, who arrange peace with the Carthaginians on humiliating terms. "Thus the Carthaginians recovered their freedom" (68.4–69.5).

One would think that Agathocles' authority as a ruler must be at an end after his ignominious flight and with the final failure of the African expedition acknowledged. Diodorus does not describe his landing in Sicily, but, after a chapter of moralizing (70.1–4), shows him arriving at Egesta, which is described as an "allied city" with a population of ten thousand.[141] He sends for "a part of his military force" and is strong enough to annihilate the citizenry. He kills off those that have no money and extorts everything that they possess from the more prosperous, using the most brutal tortures, including a "brazen bed" that recalls the brazen bull of Phalaris. Men and women are treated alike, and he raises even more money by selling the children to the Bruttii. It is said that he even changes the name of the place, calling it Dicaeopolis and inviting all "deserters" (that is, anyone in Deinocrates' force who wishes to join him) to settle there (71.1–5).

If the story has any historical value, it means that Agathocles has not dared show his face in Syracuse, but has landed in the Carthaginian *epikrateia* and is trying to make a fresh start in an area that is beyond the reach of Deinocrates' liberation forces. It seems, however, that Antander is still in control in Syracuse, and when Agathocles hears that his sons have been killed, he sends word to him to see to it that all relatives of the men

---

[139] For the phrase τῆς φλογὸς εἰς ὕψος ἀρθείσης (67.2), see above, n. 117.

[140] He is supposed to fear Agatharchus and to suspect his relations with his stepmother.

[141] Nothing is reported of Egesta since it was under Carthaginian control in 309. It is difficult to see how it can be an ally of Agathocles or Deinocrates. Perhaps τῶν Καρχηδονίων is missing in the text at 71.1.

who served on the African expedition are put to death, and the order is carried out so thoroughly that the sea is stained red with their blood (72.1–5).

In his account of the following year (306), Diodorus represents Agathocles as completely disheartened and attempting to reach an agreement with Deinocrates; he offers to give up his *dynasteia* if he can be allowed to keep Therma and Cephaloedium with their territory (77.3).[142] But Deinocrates is in no hurry to accept this offer or to make any move towards a settlement. It is explained that he has ambitions of becoming a monarch himself (79.2), since he now has an army of more than twenty thousand men under his command. When he makes further demands of Agathocles, asking for his sons as hostages (does he not know that they are dead?), and insisting that he must leave Sicily, Agathocles retaliates by complaining to the "exiles" (as Deinocrates' force is still called) about these delays and by making his own peace with the Carthaginians. He offers them peace if they are allowed to recover all the cities formerly subject to them and in return receives the sum of three hundred talents—or according to Timaeus only half that sum together with two hundred thousand medimni of wheat (which, no doubt, he needed even more urgently than money if he was to maintain his army).[143]

The reference to Timaeus is extremely welcome. It seems to tell us that Timaeus reduced the sum of money mentioned by some earlier writer in order to show how Agathocles was ready to abandon many Greek cities to the Carthaginians in return for quite a modest sum. It would be reasonable for Timaeus to reduce the sum in order to emphasize how desperate Agathocles was, and how little he cared about the freedom of the Greeks in Sicily.[144] And Timaeus might well think, as Diodorus does, that Deino-

---

[142] Diodorus (20.77.3–78.3) expresses surprise that Agathocles sank so low (οὕτως ἐταπεινώθη τὴν ψυχήν) after weathering many crises in his earlier career, and he recalls the advice given to Dionysius I when he contemplated flight. The comparison with Dionysius would be appropriate for Timaeus.

[143] F 120—Diod. 20.79.5. It is simplest to suppose that Diodorus took the reference to another source, and to "other sources" in 20.89.4—F 121, from the text of Timaeus, and that he has in fact been relying on Timaeus in his narrative. This is preferable to other solutions—that he is using a later *Mittelquelle* (K. J. Beloch *Griechische Geschichte* ed. 2, Berlin and Leipzig 1927, 8–9) or trying to combine Timaeus and Duris (Jacoby, note on F 120–124).

[144] Cf. Justin 22.8.15: Poeni. . . . duces in Siciliam miserunt, cum quibus Agathocles pacem aequis condicionibus fecit. It seems to be assumed that the Carthaginians still consider Agathocles the only competent authority with whom to negotiate, despite his present condition, and that they put little trust in the earlier agreement supposedly reached with the army in Africa. Or was it "another source" that described this earlier agreement? If so, it might well have been reported by Timaeus, and there is no proof in Diodorus' narrative that he is using another source directly.

crates was responsible for allowing Agathocles to recover his authority (79.3). The next year, Agathocles decides to risk a direct encounter with him, and after his own force has been increased by a good many deserters from the "exiles," he wins a victory in battle, and proposes that they cease fighting and "return to their own native cities." He actually hopes that he may be permitted to return to Syracuse.[145]

The proposal is supposed to be made after Agathocles calls off the pursuit of the enemy and orders a "cease–fire." As has happened before in Timaean battle descriptions, some of Deinocrates' infantry have taken refuge on a hill top.[146] Though they should know better, they accept the word of Agathocles that their lives will be spared, and when they come down from the hill, they are surrounded, disarmed, and shot down, "seven thousand of them, according to Timaeus, though only about four thousand, so others say."[147] Here we have one more example of the tyrant's contempt for oaths and promises. Deinocrates, on the other hand, is treated with respect, accepts an appointment as one of the tyrant's generals, and "betrays his allies," handing over to Agathocles the fortresses and cities that he had controlled (90.1–2).

Agathocles, thus miraculously restored to power, secures a further fifty talents by a completely unprovoked attack on the Liparaean islands. In his usual sacrilegious way, he steals treasure marked with the names of the gods of the islands, Aeolus and Hephaestus, and they take their revenge. The god of the winds sees to it that eleven of the ships carrying off the treasure are wrecked in a storm, but Hephaestus bides his time, waiting until Agathocles is near death and having him burnt alive (101.1–3).

It may seem excessive to trace every tale of divine punishment back to Timaeus, but here his signature is unusually clear. Diodorus describes the death of Agathocles in Book XXI (16.4–5). He was suffering from a painful disease, apparently cancer of the jaw, which rendered him unable to speak; he was taken for dead when he was still living, and carried to his funeral pyre by Oxythemis, who was an envoy from Demetrius Poliorcetes, and so burnt alive, unable to utter a sound. "A fitting punishment for such a man," is Diodorus' comment, "after he had reigned for twenty–eight years and lived for seventy–two, as Timaeus the Syracusan records in his History,[148] as well as Callias and Antander."

---

[145] Diod. 20, 89.1–3. All that Justin says is: Agathocles, rex Siciliae, pacificatus cum Carthaginiensibus, partem civitatium a se fiducia virium dissidentem armis subegit (23.1.1).
[146] Diod. 20.89.4.
[147] F 121–Diod. 20.89.4.
[148] F 123a—Diod. 21.16.5, cf. F 123b—[Lucian] Macrob. 10.

Diodorus appears to have said that Hephaestus burnt Agathocles συνωνύμως.[149] This might mean that he used the agency of a man bearing his own name to punish him, just as, according to Timaeus, Hermes punished the Athenians for the mutilation of the Hermae using Hermocrates as his agent.[150] But extant literature does not provide a man with a name like Hephaestion as the tyrant's killer, and the expression remains a puzzle.[151] Diodorus adds that Hephaestus showed equally just judgment when he provided protection from his fire to the men who saved their parents from being burnt to death by Etna's fire, meaning Amphinomos and Anapias, whom the god helped to carry their father and mother to safety during an eruption of Etna.[152] It would be in Timaeus' manner to introduce this local myth of a god rewarding filial piety, after he had told how Agathocles' grandson Agatharchus murdered (or at least did his best to murder) his grandfather, arranging for Menon of Egesta to smear poison on the tyrant's toothpick and so bring on the painful infection that would have killed him if he had not been burnt alive first.[153]

Agathocles, so the story runs, wanted his surviving adult son Agathocles to succeed him, but young Agatharchus murdered him, determined as he was to assert his claim as son of the eldest son. The tyrant had two more sons, small children still, by his latest wife, Theoxena, the daughter of Berenice. For fear that they would be murdered too he sent Theoxena to Egypt with them. Justin tells the story of her unwillingness to leave and the tearful parting from Agathocles, who was already a sick man (23.2.6–12). All this must have been in Timaeus, and also the full story of what happened after the tyrant died. All that Justin says is: "Regnum nepos occupavit" (23.2.5).

Under the year 303 (20.104–105), Diodorus tells how Cleonymus, the brother of Acrotatus, was sent out from Sparta to help the Tarentines in their wars, and the hand of Timaeus can be seen clearly in the description of his behaviour and character. He is one more Spartan corrupted by the luxury of the Greek West, like Acrotatus and Gylippus.[154] He is also guilty of gross *hybris,* like Dionysius II, when he extorts a payment of two hun-

---

[149] οἰκείως τῆς ἀσεβείας κολάσας τὸν τύραννον ἐν τῇ πατρίδι, συνωνύμως ἐπὶ θερμοῖς τοῖς ἄνθραξι κατακαύσας ζῶντα (20.101.3).

[150] F 102a, b, cf. above, p. 150. The connection with this fragment is pointed out by Meister, *Sizilische Geschichte* 162.

[151] No one connected with the incident seems to have a suitable name.

[152] The earliest known reference to the story is in Lycurgus, *In Leocr.* 95. For other references, see *Der Kleine Pauly,* s.v.Amphinomos.

[153] Diod. 21.16.4.

[154] Above, pp. 144–45, 237.

dred talents from Metapontum, together with two hundred girls from the best families as "hostages."[155] The full story must have been told by Timaeus, and he must have given a proper consecutive account of Agathocles' wars in Italy. The excerpts from Diodorus Book XXI give only a few incidents.

One of Agathocles' notable achievements was rescuing Corcyra when it was attacked by Cassander. He is said to have destroyed the entire Macedonian fleet by fire—another great conflagration for Timaeus to describe. Agathocles must also have been criticized, as before, for not pressing his advantage home: he is said to have missed the chance of annihilating the Macedonian forces, and thus to have illustrated the proverb "πολλὰ τὰ κενὰ τοῦ πολέμου." Timaeus had quoted this proverb on an earlier occasion.[156]

There were also great feats of siegecraft and deceit at Croton (21.4) and Hipponium (21.8) for Timaeus to describe. For more interesting, if it could be recovered, would be his description of Agathocles' relations with the great dynasts, Cassander, Demetrius Poliorcetes, and Ptolemy. The years that Timaeus spent in Athens, when Athens alternately resisted the dynasts and tried to please them by subservience, gave him some qualification to understand and evaluate the efforts of Agathocles to be accepted as a dynast himself. We may agree with Polybius that he had no understanding of military affairs or of the older style politics of city states in the fifth and fourth centuries. It is possible that he understood the contemporary world, as he observed it from Athens, rather better.

Despite the scepticism of some scholars, it seems hard to deny that the story of Agathocles, as we know it from Diodorus and Justin, is Timaeus' version. Timaeus' story may have been read with avidity by generations of readers, to whom the world of those days was a totally strange world. It is not a version that we can accept with any confidence as good history.

iii. Pyrrhus

There is not much that can be said about Timaeus' treatment of Pyrrhus,[157] because it seems not to have attracted much attention from the writers who tell us so much about the earlier books of his history. Cicero and Dionysius of Halicarnassus tell us that he wrote a separate monograph

---

[155] Diod. 20.104.3–4.
[156] Diod. 21.2–3, cf. 20.67.4.
[157] Above, pp. 49–50.

(πραγματεία) on the wars of Pyrrhus,[158] but they do not say whether this was in one or several books or what wars of Pyrrhus it described—his wars in Italy and Sicily or his whole career. Polybius refers to his "treatment of Pyrrhus" (ἐν τοῖς περὶ Πύρρου) only for a detail that has nothing to do with Pyrrhus,[159] and there are no other attested fragments. There is no mention of Timaeus in Plutarch's *Pyrrhus,* and though it might seem reasonable for him to rely on Timaeus here as in his *Dion* and *Timoleon,* it is impossible to escape the evidence that his main source for Pyrrhus was Hieronymus of Cardia, whom he quotes in three passages, and whom he certainly used in his *Eumenes* and *Demetrius.*[160] When he cites another author to point out a difference in detail, it is Phylarchus whom he quotes, not Timaeus (*Pyrrhus* 27.8).

Hieronymus seems to have been regarded as the standard authority for the history of the Diadochi, and he is generally recognized as the principal source of Diodorus in Books XVIII–XX. In Book XXI, Diodorus shows himself familiar with Timaeus' treatment of Agathocles, complaining of his bitterness and hostility towards the man who forced him into exile,[161] but there is no word of Timaeus in any fragment from his later books, and the presumption must be that, like Plutarch, he was content to rely on Hieronymus for the story of Pyrrhus. One good reason for thinking that neither of them is following Timaeus is that there is far less emphasis here on τὸ θεῖον than when they are known to be following him. Although Pyrrhus is an over–adventurous character who gambles with Fortune, the kind of man whose behaviour might seem to call for divine intervention no less regularly than the tyrannical *hybris* of Agathocles or Dionysius the Elder, the moralizing that occurs so frequently when Diodorus and Plutarch write about these tyrants is largely lacking here. There is little trace of the *deisidaimonia* of Timaeus, which offended Polybius so much,[162] and which left its mark on Plutarch's *Lives* of Nicias, Dion, and Timoleon. The difference in tone between these *Lives* and his *Pyrrhus, Eumenes,* and *Demetrius* is easily understood if he followed Timaeus in the former three *Lives,* and Hieronymus in the latter three.

Nonetheless, even if neither Plutarch nor Diodorus ever looked into Timaeus' account of Pyrrhus, it is likely enough that their accounts will

---

[158] T 9a, b—Cic. *Ad Fam.* 5.12.2; Dion. Hal. *AR* 1.6.1.
[159] F 36—Polyb. 12.4b.1.
[160] Plut. *Pyrrhus* 17.7, 21.12, 27.8; cf. Jacoby *FGrH* IID, pp. 544–45; R. Flacelière–E. Chambry, *Plutarque, Vies* VI (Budé ed. 1971) 7–14.
[161] 21.16.5, 17.1–F 123a, 124d.
[162] 12.24.5

include some events that were described by him, some details, some anecdotes and sayings that found mention in his text. Timaeus, Hieronymus, Phylarchus, and Duris were all roughly contemporary, and if all of them wrote about Pyrrhus, it is impossible to be sure of the order in which their work appeared or to decide how far one borrowed from the other, or how independent they were of each other, agreeing perhaps as often as they disagreed over various details. Even if we feel quite sure that some description or some item in Plutarch or Diodorus was in Timaeus, there is no reason why they should not have found it in Hieronymus or Phylarchus or Duris. There is no reason to believe that Plutarch consulted all four sources and tried to combine them or reconcile them with each other.[163]

This chapter is not concerned with Plutarch's methods. Its purpose is to find out how much can be recovered of what Timaeus had to say about Pyrrhus, and since attested fragments are lacking, all that can be done is to pick out from Plutarch and Diodorus items of which one can say: "This must have been in Timaeus, here is something that would have interested him." Plutarch begins his *Life* by saying that Pyrrhus is descended from Achilles, whose son Neoptolemus, also called Pyrrhus, founded a line of kings in Epirus. We are at once reminded of Timaeus when we are told that after several generations the dynasty reverted to barbarism (μετὰ τοὺς πρώτους τῶν διὰ μέσου βασιλέων ἐκβαρβαρωθέντων, 1.4), as happened in Sardinia, according to Timaeus, and in the kingdoms founded by the sons of Aeolus in Sicily.[164]

Just as Timaeus described Gelon's almost miraculous escape from death in his boyhood, when he ran out of the schoolhouse chasing a wolf that snatched his writing tablet just before the building collapsed in an earthquake,[165] he would certainly want to describe how narrowly Pyrrhus escaped death as a baby. Plutarch tells how the infant Pyrrhus had to be smuggled out of Epirus when Molossians took over the country, how the party of fugitives was held up by a river in flood until men from across the river came to their help, and the man who carried the baby in his arms was called Achilles—a splendid omen that would have delighted Timaeus (2.3–8). Pyrrhus is taken to Glaucias, king of the Illyrians; when Glaucias hesitates to give him shelter, for fear of offending Cassander, the little boy

---

[163] For full discussion of the literary sources of the life of Pyrrhus see Pierre Lévêque, *Pyrrhos* (Paris 1957) 18–77. He believes that Plutarch tried to 'harmonize' the various accounts that he had read (65), and he perhaps exaggerates the influence on Plutarch of Proxenos, a writer of whom very little is known; see *FGrH* IIIC 703, with Flacelière—Chambry, op. cit. (n. 160) 12.

[164] Above, pp. 66–67.

[165] Above p. 129.

charms him so completely that he takes him into his household and refuses to surrender him even when Cassander offers him two hundred talents (3.1–5). The whole story is in Justin also (17.3.16–20), and when Plutarch and Justin seem to be following the same source, it is usually Timaeus.

Plutarch's story of Pyrrhus' life, though full of drama and excitement, lacks real Timaean touches. There are of course some omens and portents; there is Pyrrhus' dream, in which he speaks with Alexander (11.4–6), and there are occasional moralizing paragraphs. But we cannot discover what part Cineas played in Timaeus' account or if he gave any speeches to Romans or if Ennius made any use of him when writing his *Annales*.

It is only in the Sicilian episodes that more convincing traces of Timaeus can be found. According to Plutarch, the delegation that invites Pyrrhus to Sicily, "to help in driving out the Carthaginians and freeing the island of tyrants" (22.2), seems to hope that he will prove to be more like Timoleon than Agathocles. This is how Timaeus must have presented their attitude, and a fragment of Diodorus reports conditions in Sicily as similar to what they had been when Timoleon came, with tyrants in control almost everywhere, "Hicetas in Syracuse, Phintias in Acragas, Tyndarion in Tauromenium, and others in the smaller cities" (22.2.1). We are reminded strongly of Timaeus when we learn that a tyrant of Tauromenium was ready to receive Pyrrhus' forces into the city and that Pyrrhus made his first landing in Sicily there (Diod. 22.7.4), just as Timoleon had been welcomed by Timaeus' father Andromachus.[166] Plutarch's version never mentions Tyndarion; he says that Thoenon and Sostratus[167] in Syracuse "were the first who persuaded Pyrrhus to come to Sicily and they put the city in his hands when he arrived" (23).

It is likely enough that all the excerpts of Diodorus that describe Pyrrhus' activities in Sicily derive ultimately from Timaeus, but without the full text of Book XXII one cannot hope to prove direct use of him. One sentence of Diodorus, however, deserves quotation. As a comment on the behaviour of Pyrrhus' Gallic mercenaries, he writes: "Recognizing what sort of impious acts they had committed, it was natural that they should expect to be suitably punished for their wickedness" (22.11.2). Here at least is a genuinely Timaean sentiment.

Timaeus wrote about the wars of Pyrrhus, in his History and in his separate monograph, at a time when memories of the events were fresh.

---

[166] Cf. Plut. *Timol*. 10.

[167] The alternative form of the name, Sosistratus, is found in some mss. of Plutarch and Diodorus.

He was probably in Athens when Pyrrhus paid his visit to the city,[168] and there must have been many people in Athens who could give him reliable reports of what went on in Epirus and Macedonia. Visitors from Sicily and Magna Graecia could give him fresh news of events there, and if he returned himself to Sicily about 260 B.C., or perhaps even earlier, there would be no scarcity of informants in Syracuse and Tauromenium who had been personally involved and had perhaps actually spoken or worked with Pyrrhus.

Timaeus' account of Pyrrhus must have been one of the very first to be made public, perhaps the first by a writer with an established reputation. It must have been the nearest thing available to an account by an actual eye–witness of the events. It therefore deserves a quite different kind of respect from the rest of his work. The various authors who followed him, thinking no doubt that readers would not be lacking for another version of the story, must have borrowed extensively from him, with or without acknowledgment. It is surprising that so few recognizable or identifiable fragments of "The Wars of Pyrrhus" have survived.

---

[168] As described by Plutarch, *Pyrrhus* 12.7.

IX

Epilogue

One of the tasks of a final chapter is to summarize and compare the conclusions of earlier chapters, reconciling and comparing differences in detail, to give some appearance of unity and finality to the argument of the book. Sometimes this task may be very difficult. But it presents no great difficulty here, if the character of Timaeus as an historian has already emerged clearly.

Timaeus irritated Polybius by his pride and patriotism as a Sicilian Greek, which showed itself in various ways. In his treatment of the heroic age he brought many figures from Greek mythology to the West, and described settlements that they were supposed to establish there. The innovative poets of Alexandria welcomed this new mythology. And when Greek heroes, and gods and goddesses, were shown treading the soil of Sicily and Italy in early times, this could be taken as proof that the Greek West had been part of Hellas from the beginning. A clear historical argument seems to be intended. The colonists who came in the eighth century can be presented as recovering land that is part of the Hellenic heritage, and it will seem only natural that the Delphic oracle should command them to found colonies there.

Modern scholarship is unwilling to believe that Delphi played any significant part in encouraging colonial enterprise.[1] But by the fifth century, if not earlier, colonies were ready to claim that their foundation had been sanctioned by Apollo, and Timaeus certainly found these claims recorded by the historians of the West who preceded him. Like the Greek colonies of Asia Minor, the colonies of the West developed and probably proclaimed belief in a divinely inspired *ktisis,* sometimes in a wholly imaginary *ktisis* by some god or hero in pre–historic times.[2] It is customary to call beliefs of this kind "traditions." But we have no proof that such so–called traditions had taken shape before the fifth century. And when we start asking how much citizens of Syracuse or Acragas or Croton or Locri in Timaeus' time really knew about their early history, we are thrown back on pure speculation.

[1] See J. Fontenrose, *The Delphic oracle* (Berkeley 1978) 137–44.
[2] E.g., Heracles at Eryx (above p. 60), Daedalus near Acragas (pp. 67–68), Jason at Paestum (p. 64).

Since Timaeus wrote most of his history, if not all of it, during the fifty years that he lived in Athens, he had no opportunity of seeking information, in the Herodotean manner, by inquiry among people in different colonies. It is possible, of course, that he returned to Sicily in later life and made some effort to discover what "traditions" were current in the cities. But there is no proof of this, and Polybius complains of his failure to seek information in this way.[3] It is true that he seems to have made inquiries among the Locrians of old Greece in his determination to disprove Aristotle's story of the foundation of Locri Epizephyrii. He was offended by Aristotle's declaration that this Italian colony was founded by the children of irregular unions between Locrian women and slaves, and he insisted that Locri was a perfectly normal Greek colony, with members of the leading families in old Locris among its founders.[4] But we do not know what kind of "tradition" he might have found current there.

Polybius tells us that Timaeus prided himself on his accuracy in chronological detail,[5] and this statement may lead us to believe that he gave numerous dates (in Olympiads) for events of the seventh and sixth centuries. We have no proof at all that he did so: if he had offered many such dates, we should expect to find some trace of them in Diodorus, even in the excerpts that survive of Books VI–X. The fragments offer us only a handful of Olympic dates. We may believe that he gave a good many more, but there is quite insufficient evidence to construct a chronological framework for Timaeus' history, or to reach any conclusions about his chronological method. It is all very well for critics to complain that no one has provided the necessary discussion of his method, but without further evidence any such discussion would be unprofitable.

In fact it must be doubted if the chronological table of the Greek West in archaic times would be much improved if we had his history intact. We must wonder if he knew much more about the history of these centuries than we do, and we can only hope that archaeological investigation will enable us to be more exact than he was.

When he reached the fifth century he appears to have started writing as though only the history of Sicily claimed his attention. And now that Syracuse became the most powerful city on the island, Sicilian history

---

[3] Polyb. 12.27–28—T 19.

[4] F 12—Polyb. 12.9; cf. above, pp. 98–101.

[5] F 12—Polyb. 12.10.4. Some remarks from the Preliminary Survey (above, pp. 44–48) are repeated here as a reminder that the fuller investigation of the intervening chapters has confirmed them.

meant the history of Syracuse and its tyrants. The result was that he touched upon the history of Magna Graecia only when a Syracusan tyrant invaded Italy. And if there were other historians who wrote about events in Locri and Croton after the fall of Sybaris in 510 B.C., their work has left hardly any trace.

Timaeus of course indulged his Siceliot pride to the full in writing about Gelon's victory at Himera. Polybius found this intolerable, complaining that he exaggerated the size of Gelon's fighting force to an absurd degree and did his best to represent everything in Syracuse as better than anywhere in the world.[6] He may have complained also about the "fantastic" story of the battle, but if he did, the complaint has not survived in the excerpts from Book XII. Polybius probably looked down on Sicily as a mere province of Rome; and if it had taken the Romans over twenty years to expel the Carthaginians from the island, he would not take very seriously any Sicilian claim to have crippled them in a single battle. Nonetheless the story of Gelon's victory, as told by Timaeus and handed on by Diodorus, seems to have established itself as the standard account. Herodotus gave only a brief outline. Nothing has survived of any more sober version, such as Antiochus or Philistus or Ephorus may have given, and no later historian is known to have tried to rationalize the story, as modern historians are obliged to do. This is perhaps the clearest illustration of the secure position that Timaeus occupied as the recognized authority on the history of the Greek West.

Timaeus had some successors who wrote *Sicelica* and *Italica* in the third and second centuries, but references to them are not frequent, and in comparison with Timaeus they seem not to have attracted much attention. They are quoted by the writers who also refer to Timaeus, by scholiasts in their notes on the poets, and by Aelian, Antigonus of Carystus, and Athenaeus, mostly for the same sort of detail these collectors of strange customs and topographical curiosities found in Timaeus. If these historians had abandoned Timaeus' standards and treated their theme in an entirely different way, there would be some indication of it in one or another of these sources.

Lycus of Rhegium received some attention, partly because he was thought to be the father or adoptive father of Lycophron. He is very probably a contemporary rather than a successor of Timaeus. He is said to have been the victim of a plot made by Demetrius of Phalerum, and so the pre-

---

[6] F 94—Polyb. 12.26b; cf. above, pp. 133–35.

sumption is that he was one of the scholars who sought employment at Alexandria early in the third century.[7] But all that we learn from the fragments is his concern with mythology and with tales about birds and animals and "wonders of nature."

The *Sicilian Genealogies* of Hippostratus were devoted to tracing descent from heroic ancestors (he maintained that the Emmenidae were descended from Telemachus),[8] and this sort of interest is very much in the Timaean manner. The interest in etymologies, such as are recorded in the fragments of Timaeus, continued. Silenus of Cale Acte suggested an etymology that is as deplorable as anything that Timaeus offered. He said that the Palikoi were so called διὰ τὸ ἀποθανόντας πάλιν εἰς ἀνθρώπους ἱκέσθαι.[9]

Some notes of Artemon of Pergamum on Sicilian place–names and personages are quoted, and geographical descriptions of Sicily were written in Hellenistic times, either *Periegeseis* or books about particular features of the country, about the rivers, for example. There was a book on *The Wonders of Sicily* by Nymphodorus. One might think there would be a demand for books about the more noteworthy cities of Sicily and Magna Graecia, and we hear of books about Syracuse, Sybaris, and Cumae.[10] The works of Polemon of Ilion, a prolific writer, included Κτίσεις Ἰταλικῶν καὶ Σικελικῶν πόλεων. He must have drawn extensively on earlier historians, and in fact wrote a *Reply to Timaeus* (Πρὸς Τίμαιον), which may have anticipated some of Polybius' criticisms.[11] A book of this kind is a good indication that Timaeus' history was still being read

Just as Herodotus blackened the reputation of Greek tyrants in general, though he had some respect for the more constitutional Peisistratus, so also Timaeus must be held responsible for the picture of Sicilian tyrants that has prevailed. Pindar dutifully praised Hiero and Theron as well as Gelon, but Timaeus made no exceptions apart from Gelon and of course his own father, Andromachus, whom Timoleon allowed to remain in power as autocrat of Tauromenium. Though nothing is preserved of what he had to say about earlier tyrants like Phalaris, the presumption is that he was just as severe on them as on Gelon's successors in Syracuse.

It is the tyrants who are the dominant figures during the fifth and fourth centuries at Syracuse, and Timaeus appears to have concentrated attention

[7] *FGrH* 570–T 1–2.
[8] *FGrH* 568 F 2.
[9] *FGrH* 175 F 3.
[10] *FGrH* 569, 572, 573, 575.
[11] *FHG* III, pp. 126–29, fr. 38–46.

on them, showing how and why they were able to seize power, and he reserves his highest praise for Timoleon, who set out to free Sicily from the yoke of tyranny. He may, for all we know, have given an extensive description of political developments in Sicily during the Pentecontaetia, but his account has been completely lost, because Diodorus pays little attention to Sicily in writing about these years, devoting only a brief chapter to the debate in the agora of Syracuse when Ducetius takes refuge at the altar there.[12] The loss of this part of Timaeus' history is much to be regretted, and nothing has survived of the earlier accounts by Antiochus, Ephorus, Philistus, or any others.

It is unlikely that Timaeus or any Greek writer showed sympathy with the Sicel movement of which Ducetius was the leader, or that he was willing to regard Sicels or Sicans as the equals of the Greek colonists. No writer seems to have said anything about Greeks intermarrying with them or to have admitted that the citizen population of cities in the interior and the west of the island may have contained half–Greek members. But if some Greek from Magna Graecia described the expansion of the Greek colonies in Italy, the founding of Paestum, for example, and its development, he could hardly avoid describing the relations, friendly or otherwise, with Samnites and Etruscans, and with Romans, as their power spread southwards. Here was a subject that should have attracted a writer from one of the Italiot cities. Unfortunately no trace has survived of any history of Magna Graecia in the fourth and third centuries. Timaeus spoke of the Gallic invasion of 390 and the capture of Rome by the Gauls, and he gave quite a detailed account, so it seems, of the wars of Pyrrhus. But what of the long interval between the coming of the Gauls and Pyrrhus' invasion of Italy?

Except for tyrants and their opponents, there is little indication that Timaeus described or discussed the careers and achievements of many individuals at length. In the earlier period, he evidently wrote extensively about Pythagoras and his influence at Croton, while he seems to have belittled the importance of the lawgivers Zaleucus and Charondas.[13] But the man whom he particularly admired in the fifth century was Hermocrates of Syracuse. He may have argued that if the Syracusans had only appreciated his high ability he could have been the most powerful man in their city instead of Dionysius I, a good autocrat instead of a vicious tyrant. He was ready to disagree with his predecessors in their judgment of individuals,

[12] Diod. 11. 92; cf. above, pp. 141–42.
[13] F 130, cf. above, pp. 106–07.

representing Gylippus, for example, as a contemptible character, just as he seems to have differed from Thucydides on other matters.[14]

He could not, of course, displace Thucydides as the standard authority on the Athenian siege of Syracuse. But his account of the siege by the Carthaginians and the disaster that they suffered in 396 must have been quickly accepted as a worthy counterpart to the story told by Thucydides. The description of the Great Harbour filled with ships, the attack planned by Dionysius from the land, and the spectacle to be seen from the city as the ships were set on fire—this passage gives perhaps the best example of Timaeus' talent for vivid and dramatic writing.[15]

Not that a modern critical reader can accept it as an exact or truthful piece of historical writing, or feel the same respect for it as for Thucydides' account of the naval battle in the harbour. Thucydides was more concerned to be accurate than to stir the emotions of his readers. He had the opportunity to talk with men who had taken part in the battle or watched it from the shore. Philistus probably watched it from the city as a boy, and when he came to describe the siege of 396 he must have been conscious that he was challenging comparison with the famous Thucydidean description. We can only guess how much Timaeus borrowed from Philistus' account or from that of Ephorus. But if readers preferred his account to theirs, it must have been because of the imaginative touches that he added.

If Philistus was conscientious in attempting to write in Thucydidean style, he will have tried to give his characters speeches that reproduced as closely as possible "what was actually said," the arguments, if not the actual language, that they used. Thucydides does not tell us what his object was in inserting so many speeches in his history, but modern critics will not quarrel with Polybius when he says that it is important for historians to report what was actually said on various occasions, in debates, diplomatic negotiations, speeches before battle, and so on, so that readers will understand how and why certain results occurred. He maintains that speeches, if accurately reported, "give coherence to the historian's exposition" (συνέχει τὴν ὅλην ἱστορίαν). He does not say how far he thinks Thucydides succeeded in discovering and reporting "what was actually said." But he insists that Timaeus destroys the whole purpose of history when he offers fictitious compositions instead of the actual speeches which could explain how things turned out as they did.[16]

---

[14] Above, pp. 144–48.

[15] Diod. 14.72–74, cf. above, p. 182.

[16] Polyb. 12.25a–b—T 19. For fuller discussion of Timaeus' speeches, see "The Speeches in Timaeus' history," *AJP* 107 (1986), 350–68.

One might reply that a shrewdly written fictitious speech may help a reader to reconstruct the course of events by appealing to his imagination. And one may also remember that though Philistus should have been able to report with some degree of accuracy speeches that were made in Syracuse during his lifetime, it could not be expected that Timaeus would recover the arguments and the language used by speakers in the fifth and the first half of the fourth century, though he might have had accurate reports for the times of Timoleon and Agathocles. Nor do we know that Timaeus made any claim to be giving accurate or trustworthy reports of actual speeches in the Thucydidean manner. His readers must have been well aware that in many cases he was offering them pure fiction.

Polybius complains that the speeches are not even good fiction, that Timaeus seemed not to understand what kinds of argument were used in practice by politicians in real life, and, as has already been shown,[17] in at least one instance Timaeus offered a speech that does not fit the context at all. The speech of Theodorus, as reported by Diodorus (14.65–69), is an attack on the elder Dionysius such as would not have been tolerated for a moment in any city under tyrannical government. Its only purpose seems to be to reveal the historian's own strong feelings about the evils of tyranny. And if Timaeus is also to be held responsible for the speech of the elderly Nicolaus (Diod. 13.20–27), with its long series of conventional arguments urging clemency for Nicias and Demosthenes after their capture at Syracuse, any modern reader who has the patience to read it through to the end will gladly admit that Polybius has not been too severe in his criticism. He complains that Timaeus often writes as no historian should write, but more like a student in a rhetorical school carrying out a prescribed exercise, who brings out all the possible arguments that might be used in support of his thesis.[18] The speech of Nicolaus illustrates his complaint remarkably well.

Thucydides sometimes offers several of the speeches made in a debate

---

[17] Above pp. 178–181.

[18] Polyb. 25a.5: οὐ γὰρ τὰ ῥηθέντα γέγραφεν, οὐδ'ὡς ἐρρήθη κατ'ἀλήθειαν, ἀλλὰ προθέμενος ὡς δεῖ ῥηθῆναι, πάντας ἀριθμεῖται τοὺς ῥηθέντας λόγους καὶ τὰ παρεπόμενα τοῖς πράγμασιν οὕτως ὡσανεί τις ἐν διατριβῇ πρὸς ὑπόθεσιν ἐπιχειροίη, ὥσπερ ἀπόδειξιν τῆς ἑαυτοῦ δυνάμεως ποιούμενος, ἀλλ'οὐκ ἐξήγησιν τῶν κατ'ἀλήθειαν εἰρημένων. The ῥηθέντες λόγοι are usually taken as "the speeches according to the historian's version" (cf. Walbank's note), but the choice of the verb ἐξαριθμεῖται is important, and both λόγοι and τὰ παρεπόμενα τοῖς πράγμασιν ("the circumstances and consequences") are its object. What Polybius must mean is that Timaeus makes up his mind ὡς δεῖ ῥηθῆναι, then carefully lists all the arguments used by his speaker or speakers ("numbering them from one to ten," as we might say), and fits the circumstances and consequences to match the arguments. Thus he has an elaborate rhetorical structure, in which his arguments are shown as confirmed, but a complete falsification of both λόγοι and πράγματα.

or discussion, and Timaeus seems to have done the same. To balance the speech of Nicolaus he almost certainly gave some of the speeches of those who wanted the death penalty,[19] and likewise in the debate about Ducetius he must have introduced speakers who called for the severest punishment before the final speaker who persuaded the Assembly to spare his life.[20] In describing the congress at Corinth at the time of Xerxes' invasion, he will have given or at least described other speeches besides that of Gelon's envoy[21]—a speech that Polybius thought rather absurd, because it exaggerated the strength of Gelon's fighting force so grossly. And it is also likely that he brought on other speakers besides Hermocrates at the Congress of Gela in 424. Polybius is extremely scornful of Hermocrates' speech, but his criticism may not be entirely fair.[22] Timaeus must have known the speech that Thucydides gives to Hermocrates and would expect many of his readers to be familiar with it. He must be inviting comparison with the Thucydidean speech, and it would be most interesting to see his actual text.

If Timaeus offered detail about the congress in Corinth that was lacking in Herodotus and a fuller account of the Congress of Gela than was offered by Thucydides, less critical readers might think that he had improved on the accounts of his predecessors, giving them information that had not been previously available. But Polybius knew better than that. He says that Timaeus would decide for himself how the discussion should have gone, and here we should probably accept his criticism.

Polybius, however, was in some ways rather literal–minded, and as a "pragmatic" historian he saw no difficulty in laying down the rule that history should describe things as they really happened. He evidently thought that he himself always followed his own rule, and he disapproved strongly of a writer who offered a speculative or imaginative reconstruction of events. In our own time, a student of history is warned that this kind of reconstruction should be "treated with caution." But there will always be less critical readers who will not only be attracted by it, but will accept it without question.

Thucydides cannot be accused of literal–mindedness, but when he expresses disapproval of any historian who provides an ἀγώνισμα ἐς τὸ

---

[19] But the speech that Diodorus gives to Gylippus (13.28–32) seems to be taken from Ephorus (above, p. 145).

[20] Diodorus (11.92) seems to be following Timaeus this time, when he says: ἔνιοι μὲν οὖν τῶν δημηγορεῖν εἰωθότων συνεβούλευον κολάζειν ὡς πολέμιον.

[21] Diodorus (11.1) says that his preceding book finished with "the speeches made at this congress."

[22] Above, pp. 147–48.

παραχρῆμα ἀκούειν (1.22.4), "a performance that will give immediate pleasure," he is clearly thinking of the history of Herodotus. Herodotus is said to have introduced his work to the public in a series of lectures, which were enthusiastically received, like musical or dramatic performances at a festival. Thucydides does not expect his work to be considered suitable for this kind of performance. He wants it to be read and reread carefully.

But it cannot have found many readers when it first appeared. In the fifth century there were many listeners, and some of them undoubtedly had good memories, but readers who would acquire written books and read them with care cannot have been very numerous. Even if copies of Anaxagoras' book could be bought "in the orchestra," as Socrates tells the jury (Plato, *Apol.* 26d), it does not follow that copies were being sold by the hundred. Private reading, whether for study or for entertainment and relaxation, cannot have been a common practice. Dionysus in the *Frogs* (52–53) talks of "reading the *Andromeda* to himself," but we have no evidence that many mortals followed his example.

A century later, things were already very different, and by the time that Timaeus was writing, poets as well as historians, at Alexandria and elsewhere, were looking for readers rather than for opportunities of public performance. Papyrus fragments show that there were plenty of readers even in Oxyrhynchus. This new reading public was not made up solely of critical readers, such as Thucydides hoped to find, but included many who wanted to be entertained, excited, or amused by what they read. They read prose as well as poetry, and if some preferred the romances that were now being offered them, others found what they wanted in the accounts of Alexander's expedition that historians provided for them. These were the readers whom Timaeus and his contemporaries were hoping to attract.

Some of Timaeus' contemporaries have acquired the title of "tragic" historians, and it has been suggested that they were applying Aristotle's theories of tragedy to the writing of history.[23] Timaeus was contemptuous of Aristotle, and there is no reason to think that he concerned himself with these theories, but Polybius complains that he introduced "tragic" elements into his history, which had no place there, like the story of the Heliades transformed into poplars weeping tears of amber beside the Po. He had no patience with Timaeus' use of divine intervention, with the gods giving warning through signs and portents and punishing impiety, perjury, and sacrilege. We may be inclined to sympathize with Polybius' feelings, but

---

[23] E.g., K. von Fritz, "Die Bedeutung des Aristoteles für die Geschichtsschreibung," *Histoire et historiens dans l'Atiquité, Entretiens Hardt* 4, 1956) 85–128.

we need not believe, as he does, that Timaeus was addicted to "unmanly superstition" or pietistic credulity.[24] We need not suppose that either he or many of his readers accepted every detail of his narrative as something that really happened.

Even Thucydides found occasion to remind his readers of mythological details. Mythology had its traditional place in historical discussion, but it is more pertinent to the present argument to remember that myth and geography were constantly blended in Hellenistic epic, and that the readers who enjoyed reading Timaeus probably also enjoyed Apollonius' *Argonautica*. Indeed the popularity of Timaeus is best explained if we suppose that many enjoyed reading history and epic and romance for similar reasons, without constantly asking themselves "Could this have really happened?" Nor were they perhaps unduly concerned whether they were reading "What was actually said" when they read the speeches in Timaeus' history. Greek readers were passionately interested in rhetoric, and we may well believe that what really interested them in reading a speech was its rhetorical technique, how it faced rhetorical problems and applied rhetorical precepts, rather than whether it was historically convincing and appropriate to its context. We need the actual text of some of Timaeus' speeches to be sure of this, but even if Polybius is sometimes excessive in his criticisms, we must agree that speeches in Timaeus and other Hellenistic historians failed to present either what the speakers must have said or what they ought to have said if they were to convince their hearers.[25]

Timaeus was without any doubt a successful and popular writer, and his history continued to be read when other histories of the Greek West were forgotten. This does not mean that he was the most accurate recorder of events or their most intelligent interpreter. Diodorus does not tell us why he preferred Timaeus to Ephorus as historian of the West, though he knew the history of Ephorus very well. Plutarch is equally uncommunicative in his *Dion* and *Timoleon*, not telling us why he has drawn so heavily on Timaeus' account, though he has said very plainly elsewhere (*Nicias* 1) how much he dislikes his way of writing. Would it be a possible answer to say that Timaeus' account of these two men appealed to Plutarch's romantic imagination? that rather than calling Timaeus "tragic" or "rhetorical" in his style and manner, we might call him a "romantic" historian? and that we should compare the appeal of his narrative with the appeal of the romances that were beginning to attract many readers?

---

[24] F 68—Polyb. 2.16.3, T 19—Polyb. 12.24.5.

[25] We may wonder what Timaeus thought Thucydides meant by τὰ δέοντα μάλιστ'εἰπεῖν (1.22.1).

One may certainly say that Dion and Timoleon are presented to us as heroes who would have appealed to the poets of the romantic movement, as men whose idealistic love of liberty led them into strange actions and whose success against great odds made people believe that they were divinely inspired or divinely led. It is also true that the whole history of Sicily since the beginning of the fifth century is presented by Timaeus as a struggle for freedom, freedom from the foreign conqueror and from their own tyrants. And the peculiar tragedy of Sicily was that Dionysius I, the man who spent most of his life trying to repel the foreign invader, was himself an enemy of their freedom.

Without the actual text of Timaeus it would be foolish to press the point. But Polybius calls his own style of history "pragmatic," and Timaeus seems to represent the exact opposite of this. Indeed, he sets us a problem that requires an answer. He maintained his position as the standard authority on the history of the Greek West for nearly five centuries, although no one praises him for his accuracy or his political understanding, and his success is hard to explain unless he captured the imagination of his readers by writing in a way that gave them the same satisfaction as romantic fiction.

It remains to face an entirely different problem which some readers will think should have been cleared up earlier. In each of the preceding chapters, information about Timaeus has been sought from later authors who are known to have read him. If they refer to him on several occasions, it may reasonably be inferred that they also relied on him as a source in places where they do not mention him by name, that they borrowed from him more extensively than they acknowledge. In some instances the proof of extensive borrowing is stronger than in others. There can be no doubt that Diodorus made great use of Timaeus in Books IV, V and XI–XIV, and to a lesser extent in later books, and that Plutarch was heavily indebted to him in his *Dion* and *Timoleon*, to some extent also in his *Nicias*.

The more difficult question to answer is: When Timaeus can be identified as an author's main source, how exclusively does the latter rely on him? Has he consulted other sources also? Did Diodorus in the chapters devoted to the West in Books XI–XIV attempt to combine Timaeus' account with the account of Ephorus or Philistus or Theopompus or some other writer? Did Plutarch, in telling the story of Dion's expedition to Sicily, use another source besides Timaeus? When he mentions Timonides, does this mean that he had read his account, or is he taking a reference from Timaeus' text? and when Diodorus compares some details as given by Ephorus and Timaeus, is he quoting Timaeus (who is known to have

been very free with criticism of his predecessors) or has he himself compared the texts of the two authors?

Different answers to these questions have been offered, and no solution
satisfies everyone. Conclusive proof seems impossible, and argument
about Diodorus' method of work still continues. It seems to me, however,
most unlikely that Diodorus often balanced one source against another or
consulted more than one source when he was writing a chapter of his narrative. There is in fact no real indication that he had read widely. There is
no evidence that he had access to a major library, and I think it is correct
to say that he cites no authority for the history of the West who is later in
date than Timaeus. He cites no author in fact whose work Timaeus himself
could not have read and cited. He uses Ephorus of course for the mainstream of Greek history, and had probably read his entire work. But it is
quite unnecessary to suppose that he made any determined effort to compare or contrast the accounts of western history in Ephorus and Timaeus—
or that he consulted Philistus or any less known historian. The task of comparing the work of two or more authors is possible only with modern
printed books, not with papyrus rolls. An occasional reference from memory of earlier reading is always possible, but there is in fact nothing in his
text that obliges us to think he has the habit of frequent personal comment.[26]

Since, therefore, there is no positive evidence that Diodorus actually
consulted the text of Ephorus at all for western affairs, when he was working with Timaeus as his main source (though he probably used Ephorus in
Book XV), it has seemed a proper procedure to work on the assumption
that a version of Timaeus' account can be recovered from Diodorus, and
also from Plutarch and other authors when they are thought to be familiar
with Timaeus' treatment of the subject that they have in hand. And it has
been assumed that the version recovered in this way will not be misleading,
though it will not necessarily be complete and cannot be regarded as anything like an actual transcription of the original text. An occasional reflec-
tion of Timaeus' language may be suspected, but one cannot often be sure
of having direct evidence of Timaeus' style, except by comparison with
verbatim quotations from Timaeus such as are offered by other writers.

One cannot hope to know exactly how any author treats his source. And
one must always ask if a version of Timaeus recovered in this manner is
consistent with what is otherwise recorded or reported of his work. If this

---

[26] For more detailed discussion see "Ephorus and Timaeus in Diodorus—Laqueur's thesis
rejected," *Historia* 33 (1984) 1–20.

attempt at reconstructing Timaeus' work resulted in something unworthy of him, something that conflicted with the direct evidence of the attested fragments, it would have to be rejected. But when the result is consistent and intelligible and helps to explain both Timaeus' popularity and Polybius' dislike for him, the result must be considered to justify the means used to obtain it.

Egypt has not yet presented papyrologists with even a small fragment that can be identified as part of Timaeus' work. Only when a substantial portion of his text is known from papyri can a reconstruction such as been offered here be finally accepted or rejected.

BIBLIOGRAPHY

COLLECTIONS OF FRAGMENTS

Jacoby, F. *Die Fragmente der griechischen Historiker* (Berlin-Leyden 1923–58).

Peter, H. *Historicorum Romanorum Reliquiae* (2nd edition, Leipzig 1906–14)

Wehrli, F. *Die Schule des Aristoteles* (2nd edition, Basel-Stuttgart 1967–69).

Schmidt, M. *Didymi Chalcenteri Fragmenta* (Leipzig 1854, reprinted Amsterdam 1964).

TEXTS AND COMMENTARIES ESPECIALLY RELEVANT TO TIMAEUS

DIODORUS SICULUS

Diodore de Sicile, *Bibliothèque Historique* (Paris: Budé):
    Livre XII, ed. M. Casewitz (1972).
    Livre XV, ed. C. Vial (1977).
    Livre XIX, ed. F. Bizière (1975).
Diodori Siculi Bibliothecae Liber XVI, ed. M. Sordi (Florence 1969).
Diodorus of Sicily, Books XXI-XXXIII, ed. F. R. Walton (London-Cambridge, Mass.: Loeb Classical Library 1957).

PLUTARCH

Plutarch, *Life of Dion*, ed. W. H. Porter (Dublin 1952).
Plutarque, *Vies* (Paris: Budé), ed. R. Flacelière-E. Chambry:
    Timoléon (vol. iv, 1966), *Pyrrhos* (vol. vi, 1971)
    Nicias (vol. vii, 1972), *Dion* (vol. xiv, 1978).

POLYBIUS

Polybe, *Histoires* (Paris: Budé), Livre XII, ed. P. Pédech (1961).
Walbank, F. W. *A Historical Commentary on Polybius* (Oxford 1957–79).

STRABO

Strabon, *Géographie* (Paris: Budé), Livres V-VI, ed. F. Lasserre (1967).

HISTORY AND ARCHAEOLOGY (SELECTED TITLES)

Bérard, J. *La colonisation grecque de l'Italie méridionale et de la Sicile dans l'antiquité* (Paris 1957).

Bernabò Brea, L. *Sicily before the Greeks* (2nd. edition, New York 1966).

—— "Leggenda e archeologia nella protostoria siciliana," *Kokalos* 10–11 (1964–65) 1–33.

Berve, H. *Die Tyrannis bei den Griechen* (Munich 1967).

—— "Die Herrschaft des Agathokles," *Sitzungsberichte der bayerischen Akademie der Wissenschaften,* Philosophisch-historische Klasse, 1952, 5.

—— "Dion," *Abhandlungen der Akademie der Wissenschaften und der Literatur in Mainz,* Geistes- und sozialwissenschaftliche Klasse, 1956, Nr. 10, 743–881.

Braccesi, L. *Grecità adriatica* (Bologna 1971).

Buchner, G. "Recent work at Pithekoussai (Ischia), 1965–71," Archaeological Reports for 1970–71 (supplement to *Journal of Hellenic Studies* 91 [1971]) 63–67.

Compernolle, R. van. *Étude de chronologie et d'historiographie siciliotes.* Institut historique belge de Rome: *Études de philologie, d'archéologie et d'histoire ancienne* 5 (Brussels-Rome 1960).

—— "Le tradizioni sulla fondazione e sulla storia arcaica di Locri Epizefiri," *Annali della Scuola Normale di Pisa,* Classe di Lettere e Filosofia, Serie III 6,2 (1976) 329–400.

Convegni di Studi sulla Magna Grecia, Atti (Naples 1962–), in particular:
VII. *La città e il suo territorio* (1967).
VIII. *La Magna Grecia e Roma nell' età arcaica* (1968).

Crispo, C. F. *Contributo alla storia della più antica civiltà della Magna Grecia* (Tivoli, 1940).

De Sanctis, G. "Agatocle," *Rivista di Filologia* 23 (1895) 289–331, reprinted in *Per la scienza dell' antichità* (Turin 1909) and in his *Scritti Minori* I (Rome 1966) 205–48.

Ducat, J. "Les thèmes des récits de la fondation de Rhégion," *Mélanges helléniques offerts à Georges Daux* (Paris 1974) 93–114.

Dunbabin, T. J. *The Western Greeks* (Oxford 1948).

Fontenrose, J. *The Delphic Oracle* (Berkeley-Los Angeles 1978).

Franciscis, A. de. *Stato e società in Locri Epizefiri* (Naples 1972).

Frederiksen, M. *Campania* (British School at Rome 1984).

Fritz, K. von. *Pythagorean Politics in Southern Italy* (New York 1940).

Gabba, E.- Vallet, G. (editors). *La Sicilia antica* (Naples 1980).

Galinsky, G. K. *Aeneas, Sicily, and Rome* (Princeton 1969).

Graham, A. J. *Colony and Mother-City in Ancient Greece* (Manchester-New York 1964).

—— "The Western Greeks," *Cambridge Ancient History*, 2nd. edition, III.3 (Cambridge 1982) 94–113, 139–95.

Griffo, P.- Matt, L von. *Gela* (English translation, New York 1968).

Guido, M. *Sicily, an archaeological guide* (London 1967).

Hill, G. F. *Coins of ancient Sicily* (London 1903).

Kirsten, E. *Süditalienkunde* (Heidelberg 1975).

Lacroix, L. "Monnaies et colonisation dans l'occident grec," *Mémoires de l'Académie royale de Belgique*, Classe des lettres, 58.2 (1965).

Lévêque, P. *Pyrrhos* (Paris 1957).

—— "De Timoléon à Pyrrhos," *Kokalos* 14–15 (1968–69) 135–56.

Marconi, P. *Agrigento, Topografia ed Arte* (Florence 1929).

Miller, M. *The Sicilian Colony-Dates* (Albany 1970).

Müllenhoff, K. *Deutsche Altertumskunde* (Berlin 1870).

Pais, E. *Storia dell' Italia antica e della Sicilia per l'età anteriore al dominio romano* (2nd. edition, Turin 1933).

Pareti, L. *La Sicilia antica* (Palermo 1959). Translated into German by L. von Matt and L. Pareti as *Das antike Sizilien* (Würzburg 1972).

Perret, J. *Les origines de la légende troyenne de Rome* (Paris 1942).

Prückner, H. *Die lokrischen Tonreliefs* (Mainz 1968).

Ridgway, D. "The first Western Greeks," in *Greeks, Celts, and Romans*, ed. C. and S. Hawkes (Totowa, New Jersey 1973) 5–38.

Rizzo, F. P. *La repubblica di Siracusa nel momento di Ducezio* (Palermo 1969).

Rizzo, G. E. *Monete greche della Sicilia* (Rome 1946).

Schmidt,G- Griffo, P. *Agrigento antica dalle fotografie aerie* (Florence 1958).

Schubert, R. *Geschichte des Agathokles* (Breslau 1887).

Sordi, M. *Timoleonte. Sikelika* II (Palermo 1961).

Stroheker, K. F. *Dionysios I* (Wiesbaden 1958).

—— "Sizilien und die Magna Graecia zur Zeit der beiden Dionysii," *Kokalos* 14–15 (1968–69) 119–34.

Tillyard, H. J. W. *Agathocles* (Cambridge 1908).

Vallet, G. *Rhégion et Zancle. Bibliothèque des écoles françaises d'Athènes et de Rome* 189 (Paris 1958).

Walbank, F. W. *Polybius. Sather Classical Lectures* 42 (Berkeley-Los Angeles 1972).

Westlake, H. D. *Timoleon and his Relations with Tyrants* (Manchester 1952).

———— *Individuals in Thucydides* (Cambridge 1968).

———— *Essays on the Greek Historians and Greek History* (Manchester-New York 1969).

Wikèn, E. *Die Kunde der Hellenen von dem Lande und den Völkern der Apenninenhalbinsel bis 300 v.Chr.* (Lund 1937).

TIMAEUS AND HIS PREDECESSORS
(Items marked with * have not been accessible to the author)

Alföldi, A. "Timaios' Bericht über die Anfänge der Geldprägung in Rom," *Deutsches Archäologisches Institute, Römische Mitteilungen* 68 (1961) 64–79.

Arnoldt, J. *De Athana rerum Sicularum scriptore* (Programm, Gumbinnen 1846).

——— *De historiis Timaei opinionum ab editore Parisino conceptarum refutatio* (Programm, Gumbinnen 1851).

Bachof, E. *De Dionis Plutarchei fontibus* (Göttingen 1874).

——— "Timaios als Quelle für Diodor XIV 54–78," *Neue Jahrbücher für Philologie und Pädagogik* 119 (1879) 161–73.

Bartoletti, V. "Rileggendo Filisto," *Studi italiani di filologia classica* 24 (1950) 159–60.

Beloch, K. J. "Zu Timaios," *Neue Jahrbücher für Philologie und Pädagogik* 119 (1879) 599–600.

——— "Die Ökonomie der Geschichte des Timaios," *Neue Jahrbücher für Philologie und Pädagogik* 123 (1881) 697–706.

——— "Le fonti di Strabone nella descrizione della Campania," *Memorie dell' Accademia dei Lincei,* Classe di scienze morali, Serie III 10 (1882) 429–48.

*Berteman, W. *De Iamblichi Vitae Pythagoreae fontibus* (Diss. Königsberg 1913).

Bethe, E. *Quaestiones Diodoreae mythographae* (Göttingen 1887).

Biedenweg, W. *Plutarchs Quellen in den Lebensbeschreibungen des Dion und Timoleon* (Leipzig 1884).

Bottin, C. "Les sources de Diodore," *Revue belge de philologie et d'histoire* 7 (1928) 1307–27.

Brown, T. S. *Timaeus of Tauromenium. University of California Publications in History* 55 (Berkeley-Los Angeles 1958).

——— "Timaeus and Diodorus' eleventh book," *American Journal of Philology* 73 (1952) 337–55.

——— "Timaeus and the Aeneid," *Vergilius* 6 (1960) 4–12.

Busolt, G. "Bemerkungen über die Gründungsdaten der griechischen Colonien in Sicilien und Unteritalien," *Rheinisches Museum* 40 (1885) 466–69.

——— "Plutarchs *Nikia*s und Philistos," *Hermes* 34 (1898) 280–97.

Capovilla, C. "Eracle in Sicilia," *Raccolta di Scritti in onore di Giacomo Lumbroso* (Milan 1926) 178–99.

Cavallaro, M. A. "Un 'tendency' industriale e la tradizione storiografica su Agatocle," *Historia* 26 (1977) 33–61.

Christ, W. "Griechische Nachrichten über Italien," *Sitzungsberichte der bayerischen Akademie der Wissenschaften,* Philosophisch-philologische Klasse, 1905, 59–131.

Clasen, C. *Historisch-kritische Untersuchungen über Timaios von Tauromenion* (Kiel 1883).

Columba, G. M. "De Timaei historici vita," *Rivista di Filologia* 15 (1887) 353–63.

——— "Antioco," *Archivio storico siciliano,* Nuova serie 14 (1889) 84–107.

——— "Filisto, storico del IV secolo," Ibid. 17 (1892) 295–311.

Compernolle, R. van. "Ajax et les Dioscures au secours des Locriens sur les rives de la Sagre," *Hommages à Marcel Renard* II. *Collection Latomus* 102 (Brussels 1979) 733–66.

Consolo Langher, S. N. "Quellenfrage o ricostruzione storica," *Scritti in onore di Salvatore Pugliatti* (Milan 1978) V. 349–69.

Coppola, G. "Una pagina del Περὶ Σικελίας di Filisto in un papiro fiorentino," *Rivista di Filologia* 58 (1930) 449–66.

Daebritz, R. *De Artemidoro Strabonis auctore* (Leipzig 1905).

De Sanctis, G. "Una nuova pagina di storia siciliana," *Rivista di Filologia* 33 (1905) 66–73, reprinted in his *Scritti Minori* I (Rome 1966) 113–20.

——— "Ricerche sulla storiografia siceliota," *Sikelika* I (Palermo 1958) 9–16.

Delatte, A. "Un ἱερὸς λόγος pythagoricien," *Revue de Philologie* 34 (1910) 175–98.

Dolce, C. "Diodoro e la storia di Agatocle," *Kokalos* 6 (1960) 124–67.

Dover, K. J. "La colonizzazione della Sicilia in Tucidide," *Maia* 6 (1953) 1–20.

Drews, R. "Diodorus and his sources," *American Journal of Philology* 83 (1962) 383–92.

Ehlers, W. *Die Gründung von Zankle in den* Aitia *des Kallimachos* (Berlin 1933).

——— "Die Gründungsprodigien von Lavinium und Alba Longa," *Museum Helveticum* 6 (1949) 166–75.

Enmann, A. *Untersuchungen über die Quellen des Pompeius Trogus für die griechische und sicilische Geschichte* (Dorpat 1880).

Fontana, M. J. "Fortuna di Timoleonte," *Kokalos* 4 (1958) 3–23.

Gasse, H. *De Lycophrone mythographo* (Leipzig 1920).

Geffcken, J. *Timaios' Geographie des Westens. Philologische Untersuchungen* XIII (Berlin 1892).

Gitti, A. *Studi su Filisto. Le cause dell' esilio* (Bari 1953).

—— "Ricerche sulla vita di Filisto. Adria e il luogo dell' esilio," *Memorie dell' Accademia dei Lincei,* Classe di scienze morali, storiche, e filologiche, Serie VIII 4 (1952) 225–72.

—— "Sulla colonizzazione greca nell' alto e medio Adriatico," *Parola del' Passato* 7 (1952) 161–91.

Guenther, P. *De ea quae inter Timaeum et Lycophronem intercedit ratione* (Leipzig 1889).

*Guercio, V. *Tucidide ed Antioco di Siracusa* (Naples 1921).

Hammond, N. G. L. "The sources of Diodorus XVI. II. The Sicilian narrative," *Classical Quarterly* 32 (1938) 137–51.

Heichelheim, F. H. "The Toronto Epitome of a Sicilian historian," *Symbolae Osloenses* 31 (1955) 88–95.

Hejnic, J. "Das Geschichtswerk des Philistos von Sizilien als Diodors Quelle," *Studia antiqua Antonio Salac septuagenario oblata* (Prague 1955) 31–34.

Hunrath, G. *Ueber die Quellen Strabos im sechsten Buch* (Marburg 1879).

Huxley, G. "Antiochos on Italos," *Φιλίας χάριν.* Miscellanea di studi classici in onore di Eugenio Manni (Rome 1980) 1199–1204.

Immisch, O. "Der erste Platonische Brief," *Philologus* 72 (1913) 1–41.

Koerber, W. *De Philisto rerum Sicularum scriptore* (Breslau 1874).

Kothe, H. *De Timaei Tauromenitani vita et scriptis* (Breslau 1874).

—— "Zu den Fragmenten des Historikers Timaios," *Neue Jahrbücher für Philologie und Pädagogik* 138 (1888) 815–29.

—— "Vergilius und Timaios," Ibid. 139 (1889) 358–60.

—— "Timaios und Ciceros Tusculanen," Ibid. 139 (1889) 637–40.

Lacroix, L. "La légende de Philoctète en Italie méridionale," *Revue belge de philologie et d'histoire* 43 (1965) 5–21.

Laffi, U. "La tradizione storiografica siracusana relativa alla spedizione ateniese in Sicilia (415–413 A.C.)," *Kokalos* 20 (1974) 18–45.

Laqueur, R. "Philistos (3)," Pauly-Wissowa, *Realencyclopädie der classischen Altertumswissenschaft* XIX (1938) 2410–2429.

—— "Timaios (3)" Ibid. VIA (1937) 1076–1203.

Lauritano, R. "Sileno in Diodoro?" *Kokalos* 2 (1956) 206–16.

—— "Ricerche su Filisto," *Kokalos* 3 (1957) 98–122.

Lepore, E. "Timeo in Strabone V.4,3 e le origini Campane," *Mélanges of-*

ferts à Jacques Heurgon. Collection de l'école française de Rome 27 (1976) 573–85.

Levi, M. A. "Timeo in Diodoro," *Raccolta di scritti in onore di Giacomo Lumbroso* (Milan 1926) 152–64.

———— "Studi su Timeo di Tauromenion," *Raccolta di scritti in onore di Felice Ramorino. Pubblicazioni dell' Università di Sacro Cuore* 7 (Milan 1928) 65–87.

———— "La critica di Polibio a Timeo," *Miscellanea di studi Alessandrini in memoria di Augusto Rostagni* (Turin 1963) 195–202.

Manganaro, G. "Una biblioteca storica nel ginnasio di Tauromenion e il P.Oxy. 1241," *Parola del Passato* 29 (1974) 389–409.

Manni, E. "Da Ippi a Diodoro," *Kokalos* 3 (1957) 136–55.

———— "Sicelo e l'origine dei Siculi," Ibid. 156–64.

———— "Timeo e Duride e la storia di Agatocle," *Kokalos* 6 (1960) 167–73.

———— "Licofrone, Callimaco, Timeo," *Kokalos* 7 (1961) 3–14.

———— "La fondazione di Roma secondo Antioco, Alcimo, e Callia," *Kokalos* 9 (1963) 253–68.

———— "Note Siceliote. 1. Un frammento di Antandro," *Kokalos* 12 (1966) 163–71.

———— ""Diodoro e la storia italiota," *Kokalos* 17 (1971) 131–45.

———— "Diocle di Siracusa fra Ermocrate e Dionisio," *Kokalos* 25 (1979) 220–31.

———— "L'oracolo Delfico e la fondazione di Regio," *Perennitas, Studi in onore di Angelo Brelich* (Rome 1980) 311–20.

*Marchesini, A. M. *Filisto e la tirannide siracusana* (Padua 1956).

Mazzarino, S. "Tucidide e Filisto sulla prima spedizione ateniese in Sicilia," *Bollettino storico catanese* 4 (1939) 5–72.

Meister, K. *Die sizilische Geschichte bei Diodor von den Anfängen bis zum Tod des Agathokles* (Munich 1967).

———— *Historische Kritik bei Polybios. Palingenesia* IX (Wiesbaden 1975).

———— "Das Exil des Timaios von Tauromenium," *Kokalos* 16 (1970) 53–59.

———— "Sicilische Dubletten bei Diodor," *Athenaeum* 48 (1970) 84–91.

———— "Die sizilische Expedition der Athener bei Timaios," *Gymnasium* 77 (1970) 508–17.

———— "Absurde Polemik bei Diodor," *Helikon* 13–14 (1973–74) 454–59.

Momigliano, A. "Il nuovo Filisto e Tucidide," *Rivista di Filologia* 58 (1930) 467–70.

———— "The Locrian Maidens and the date of Lycophron's *Alexandra,*" *Classical Quarterly* 39 (1945) 49–53, reprinted in his *Secondo Contributo alla Storia degli studi classici* (Rome 1960) 446–53.

———— "Timeo, Fabio Pittore, e il primo censimento di Servio Tullio," *Miscellanea di Studi Alessandrini in memoria di Augusto Rostagni* (Turin 1963), 180–87, reprinted in his *Terzo Contributo alla Storia degli studi classici* (Rome 1966) 649–56.

———— "Athens in the third century B.C. and the discovery of Rome in the histories of Timaeus," *Essays in Ancient and Modern Historiography* (Oxford-Middletown, Ct. 1977), 37–66, translated from the original Italian version in *Rivista storica italiana* 71 (1959) 529–56, reprinted in *Terzo Contributo* (1966) 23–53.

Moretti, L. "Le origines di Catone, Timeo, ed Eratostene," *Rivista di Filologia* 80 (1952) 289–302.

Munz, R. *Quellenkritische Untersuchungen an Strabos Geographie* (Diss. Basel 1918).

Orlandini, T. "Duride in Diodoro XIX-XXI," *Parola del Passato* 19 (1964) 216–26.

Palm, J. *Ueber Sprache und Stil des Diodoros von Sizilien* (Lund 1965).

Pareti, L. "La cronologia delle prime colonie greche in Sicilia," *Studi siciliani ed italioti. Contributi alla scienza dell' antichità* I (Florence 1914) 310–30.

———— "Basi e sviluppo della 'tradizione' antica sui primi popoli della Sicilia," *Kokalos* 2 (1956) 5–19.

———— "La tradizione greca su Spina," *Studi romani* 5 (1957) 125–35.

———— "L'opera e l'età di Hippys di Regio," *Rivista di cultura classica e medioevale* 1 (1959) 106–12.

Pasquali, G. "La nascita dell' idea di Roma nel mondo greco," *Terze pagine stravaganti* (Florence 1942) 81–94.

Pavan, M. "La teoresi storica di Diodoro," *Rendiconti dell' Accademia dei Lincei,* Classe di scienze morali, storiche, e filologiche, serie VIII 16 (1961) 19–52, 117–51.

Pearson, L. "Myth and *archaeologia* in Italy and Sicily-Timaeus and his predecessors," *Yale Classical Studies* 24 (1975) 171–95.

———— "Some new thoughts about the supposed fragment of Philistus," *Bulletin of the American Society of Papyrologists* 20 (1983) 151–58.

———— "Ephorus and Timaeus in Diodorus. Laqueur's thesis rejected," *Historia* 33 (1984) 1–20.

———— "The speeches in Timaeus' history," *American Journal of Philology* 107 (1986) 350–68.

———— "Some remarks on Graecia mendax," *Studies in honour of T.B.L. Webster* I (Bristol 1986) 190–97.

Pédech, P. "Philistos et l'expédition athénienne en Sicile," *Φιλίας χάριν, Studi in onore di Eugenio Manni* (Rome 1980) 1711–34.

Perrotta, G. "Il papiro fiorentino di Filisto," *Studi italiani di filologia classica* 8 (1930) 311–15.

Philippi, A. *Commentatio de Philisto, Timaeo, Philochoro Plutarchi in vita Niciae auctoribus* (Giessen 1874).

Phillips, E. D. "Odysseus in Italy," *Journal of Hellenic Studies* 73 (1953) 53–67.

Piraino, M. T. "Sulla cronologia delle fondazioni siceliote," *Kokalos* 3 (1957) 123–28.

Radermacher, L. "Studien zur Geschichte der griechischen Rhetorik, I. Timäus und die Ueberlieferung über den Ursprung der Rhetorik," *Rheinisches Museum* 52 (1897) 412–19.

Reuss, F. "Timaios bei Plutarch, Diodor, und Dionys von Halikarnass," *Philologus* 45 (1886) 58–78.

———— "Hellenistische Beiträge: 3. Kleitarchos," *Rheinisches Museum* 63 (1908) 58–78.

Rohde, E. "Die Quellen des Iamblichus in seiner Biographie des Pythagoras," *Rheinisches Museum* 26 (1871) 554–76; 27 (1872) 23–61, reprinted in his *Kleine Schriften* II (Tübingen-Leipzig 1901) 102–72.

Rostagni, A. "Pitagora e i Pitagorici in Timeo," *Atti dell' Accademia delle scienze di Torino*, Classe di scienze morali 49 (1913) 373–95, 554–74, reprinted in his *Scritti Minori* II.1 (Turin 1956) 3–50.

Sanders, L. J. "Diodorus Siculus and Dionysius I of Syracuse," *Historia* 30 (1981) 394–411.

Sartori, F. "Sulla δυναστεία di Dionisio il vecchio nell' opera Diodorea," *Critica storica* 5 (1966) 3–61.

Sbordone, F. "Timeo, Strabone, e il golfo di Napoli," *Studi classici in onore di Q.Cataudella* (Catania 1972) II.409–16.

Schepens, G. "Polybius on Timaeus' account of Phalaris' bull; a case of δεισιδαιμονία," *Ancient Society* 9 (1978) 117–48.

Scherr, A. *Diodors XI Buch: Kompositions- und Quellenstudien* (Tübingen 1933).

Schwartz, E. "Timaios' Geschichtswerk," *Hermes* 34 (1899) 481–93, reprinted in his *Gesammelte Schriften* II (Berlin 1956) 176–89.

Sollima, F. *Le fonti di Strabone nella geografia della Sicilia* (Messina 1897).

Sordi, M. "La leggenda dei Dioscuri nella Battaglia della Sagra e di Lago

Regillo," *Contributi dell' Istituto di Storia Antica. Pubblicazioni dell' Università Cattolica di Sacro Cuore* (Milan 1972) 47–70.

———— "Dionigi e gli Italioti," *Aevum* 52 (1978) 1–16.

———— "I rapporti fra Dionigi e Cartagine fra la pace del 405 e quella del 392–1," *Aevum* 54 (1980) 23–34.

Stein, H. "Zur Quellenkritik des Thukydides," *Rheinisches Museum* 55 (1900) 531–64.

Steinbrück, O. *Die Quellen des Strabo im fünften Buch seiner Erdbeschreibung* (Halle 1909).

Stern, W. *Philistos als Quelle bei Diodor XII 82.3 – XIII 33.2* (Pforzheim 1876).

———— *Beiträge zu den Quellen der griechischen Geschichte. Zur Kritik der Nachrichten des Philistos und Timaios* (Pforzheim 1884).

———— "Zu den Quellen der sicilischen Expedition," *Philologus* 42 (1884) 438–70.

Steup, J. "Thukydides, Antiochos, und die angebliche Biographie des Hermokrates," *Rheinisches Museum* 56 (1901) 443–61.

Stroheker, K. F. "Timaios und Philistos," *Satura. Früchte aus der antiken Welt Otto Weinreich dargebracht* (Baden-Baden 1952) 139–61.

Thiel, J. H. "Rond het Syracusaansche Experiment," *Mededelingen der Nederlandsche Akademie van Wetenschappen*, Afdeeling Letterkunde, Nieuwe Reeks 4.1 (1941) 135–70.

*Toniazzo, G. *Delle fonti per la storia delle colonie elleniche in Sicilia* (Rome 1893).

Unger, G. F. "Diodors Quellen im XI Buch. VII. Die Geschichte von Sizilien und Unteritalien," *Philologus* 41 (1882) 131–38.

Vallet, G. "Note sur la 'maison' des Deinoménides," Φιλίας χάριν. *Studi in onore di Eugenio Manni* (Rome 1980) 2141–56.

Vattuone, R. *Ricerche su Timeo: la 'pueritia' di Agatocle* (Bologna 1983).

———— "Su Timeo F.29 Jacoby," *Rivista di storia dell' antichità* 11 (1981) 139–45.

———— "In margine ad un problema di storiografia ellenistica, Timeo e Pirro," *Historia* 31 (1982) 245–48.

Voit, L. "Zur Dion-Vita," *Historia* 3 (1954) 171–92.

Volquardsen, C. *Untersuchungen über die Quellen der griechischen und sicilischen Geschichte bei Diodor XI-XVI* (Kiel 1868).

Waele, J. A. de. "La popolazione di Akragas antica," Φιλίας χάριν. *Studi in onore di Eugenio Manni* (Rome 1980) 749–60.

Walbank, F. W. "Phalaris' bull in Timaeus," *Classical Review* 59 (1945) 39–42.

——— "Polemic in Polybius," *Journal of Roman Studies* 52 (1962) 1–12.

——— "Three notes on Polybius XII," *Miscellanea di studi Alessandrini in memoria di Augusto Rostagni* (Turin 1963) 203–13.

——— "The historians of Greek Sicily," *Kokalos* 14–15 (1968–69) 476–98.

Westlake, H. D. "The sources of Plutarch's *Timoleon*," *Classical Quarterly* 32 (1938) 65–74.

——— "The Sicilian books of Theopompus' *Hellenica*," *Historia* 2 (1953) 288–307.

Wilamowitz-Moellendorf, U. von. "Hippys von Rhegion," *Hermes* 19 (1884) 442–52.

Wölfflin, E. *Antiochos von Syrakus und Coelius Antipater* (Winterthur 1872).

Zacher, K. "Zu den Heilurkunden von Epidauros," *Hermes* 21 (1886) 467–74.

Zinzow, W. *De Timaei Tauromenitani apud Ovidium vestigiis* (Greifswald 1906).

Zoepffel, R. *Untersuchungen zum Geschichtswerk des Philistos von Syrakus* (Freiburg 1965).

INDEX I.

General Index.

Acestorides 233.

Acragas (Agrigentum),
  description 158–63,
  siege 152, 163–65.
  See also 119–20, 126–28, 131, 139,
  235–38, 244–45.

Acrotatus 237, 254.

Adranum 213–14, 216.

Adria, see Atria.

Aegestes 87.

Aelian, see Index III, and 10, 101–02,
  121.

Aeneas 13, 32, 38, 47, 85–87.

Aeolus 65–66, 253.

Aeschines (orator) 160, 165–66.

Aeschines (Socraticus) 30–31.

Aethalia, see Elba.

Agatharchus 254.

Agathocles 33, 37–38, 140, 225–55,
  narrow escapes 233, 257.

Agyrium 219.

Aitia 80, 98, 152.

Alaenus 74.

Alcibiades 125, 142, 144, 154.

Alcimus 53.

Alexander 40–41, 59, 157, 175, 190,
  246.

Andromachus 37, 196, 210, 213,
  226,264.

Anecdotes, of Dionysii 167, 171–72,
  207–08, 215,
  of Sybaris 108–09.

Antander 32–33, 227–29, 232, 245,
  251, 253.

Antenor 82.

Antigonus of Carystus, see Index III,
  and 9, 54, 62, 96–98.

Antigonus Gonatas 102–03.

Antiochus, see Index II, and 11–18,

34, 55, 78–79, 81, 85, 89, 107,
  135–36, 138, 142.

Apollocrates 203, 205, 210.

Apollodorus *Bibliotheca,* see Index
  III.

Apollonius of Rhodes, see Index III
  and 39, 54, 62, 66, 105–06.

Apollonius of Tyana 115.

Apsias, River 97.

Archagathus 246, 248–51.

Archias 15, 95, 106–07.

Ardea 86.

Arete, wife of Dion 200, 204.

Arethusa 95–96.

Argonauts 62–65, 69, 70, 87, 105.

Argos Hippion (Argyrippa) 74.

Aristaeus 68.

Aristagora 9–10.

Aristocles 76.

Aristodemus 42, 121, 132, 134.

Aristomache 21, 174, 190, 193–94,
  204.

Ariston 98.

Aristophilides 121.

Aristotle, see Index III, and 41, 42,
  99, 101, 103, 106, 119, 121,
  185, 192, 262.

Aristoxenus 114, 118.

Art treasures, sale or looting of 157,
  161.

Artemidorus 18, 76, 78, 80, 93.

Artemon of Pergamum 264.

Asclepius 3, 9–10.

Athanis 23, 31–32, 171.

Athena, her gift of the olive, 59,
  her statue closes its eyes 110.

Athenaeus 98–99, 108–09, 123, 159.

Atria 83.

Auson 65.

INDEX II

INDEX III

8122